PENGUIN BOOKS

THE OLD PATAGONIAN EXPRESS

Paul Theroux was born and educated in the United States. After graduating from university in 1963, he travelled to Italy and then Africa, where he worked as a teacher in Malawi and as a lecturer at Makerere University in Uganda. In 1968 he joined the University of Singapore and taught in the Department of English for three years. Throughout this time he was publishing short stories and journalism, and wrote a number of novels, including *Fong and the Indians*, *Girls at Play* and *Jungle Lovers*. In the early 1970s he moved with his wife and two children to Dorset, where he wrote *Saint Jack*, and went on to live in London. During his seventeen years' residence in Britain he wrote a dozen volumes of highly praised fiction and a number of successful travel books. He has since returned to the United States, but continues to travel widely.

Paul Theroux's many books include *Waldo*; *Saint Jack*; *The Family Arsenal*; *Picture Palace*, winner of the 1978 Whitbread Literary Award; *The Mosquito Coast*, which was the 1981 *Yorkshire Post* Novel of the Year, joint winner of the James Tait Black Memorial Prize, and was also made into a feature film; *My Secret History*; *Millroy the Magician*; *Kowloon Tong*; *The Great Railway Bazaar*; *The Old Patagonian Express*; *Riding the Iron Rooster*, which won the 1988 Thomas Cook Travel Book Award; *The Happy Isles of Oceania*; *Sir Vidia's Shadow*, a memoir of his friendship with Sir Vidia Naipaul; *Fresh-Air Fiend: Travel Writings 1985–2000*; *Hotel Honolulu*; and *Dark Star Safari*. Most of his books are published by Penguin.

Dear Vir,
        Happy Birthday
            & wishing you
        a fabulous 31st year
            Lots of Love always
                Luce
                xx

Paul Theroux

The Old
Patagonian Express

BY TRAIN THROUGH THE AMERICAS

Penguin Books

For my Shanglai Lil, and for Anne,
Marcel, and Louis, with love

PENGUIN BOOKS

Published by the Penguin Group
Penguin Books Ltd, 80 Strand, London WC2R 0RL, England
Penguin Putnam Inc., 375 Hudson Street, New York, New York 10014, USA
Penguin Books Australia Ltd, 250 Camberwell Road, Camberwell, Victoria 3124, Australia
Penguin Books Canada Ltd, 10 Alcorn Avenue, Toronto, Ontario, Canada M4V 3B2
Penguin Books India (P) Ltd, 11 Community Centre, Panchsheel Park, New Delhi – 110 017, India
Penguin Books (NZ) Ltd, Cnr Rosedale and Airborne Roads, Albany, Auckland, New Zealand
Penguin Books (South Africa) (Pty) Ltd, 24 Sturdee Avenue, Rosebank 2196, South Africa

Penguin Books Ltd, Registered Offices: 80 Strand, London WC2R 0RL, England

www.penguin.com

First published in Great Britain by Hamish Hamilton 1979
Published in Penguin Books 1980
21

Printed in England by Clays Ltd, St Ives plc
Set in Monotype Plantin

ISBN-13: 978–0–140–24979–8

Contents

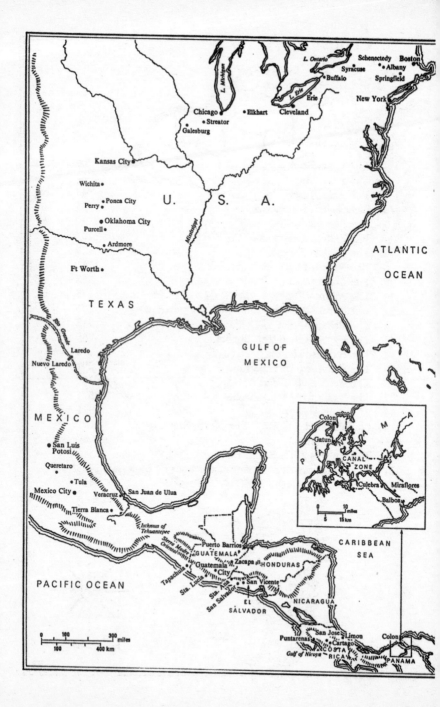

That train was the one piece of life in all the deadly land; it was the one actor, the one spectacle fit to be observed in this paralysis of man and nature. And when I think how the railroad has been pushed through this unwatered wilderness and haunt of savage tribes ... how at each stage of the construction, roaring, impromptu cities, full of gold and lust and death, sprang up and then died away again, and are now but wayside stations in the desert; how in these uncouth places pig-tailed Chinese pirates worked side by side with border ruffians and broken men from Europe, talking together in a mixed dialect, mostly oaths, gambling, drinking, quarrelling and murdering like wolves; how the plumed hereditary lord of all America heard, in this last fastness, the scream of the 'bad medicine waggon' charioting his foes; and then when I go on to remember that all this epical turmoil was conducted by gentlemen in frockcoats, and with a view to nothing more extraordinary than a fortune and a subsequent visit to Paris, it seems to me, I own, as if this railway were the one typical achievement of the age in which we live, as if it brought together into one plot all the ends of the world and all the degrees of social rank, and offered to some great writer the busiest, the most extended, and the most varied subject for an enduring literary work. If it be romance, if it be contrast, if it be heroism that we require, what was Troy town to this?

– Robert Louis Stevenson, *The Amateur Emigrant*

'Romance!' the season-tickets mourn,
  '*He* never ran to catch his train,
'But passed with coach and guard and horn –
  'And left the local – late again!'
Confound Romance ... And all unseen
Romance brought up the nine-fifteen.

– Rudyard Kipling, 'The King'

1 The Lake Shore Limited

One of us on that sliding subway train was clearly not heading for work. You would have known it immediately by the size of his bag. And you can always tell a fugitive by his vagrant expression of smugness; he seems to have a secret in his mouth – he looks as if he is about to blow a bubble. But why be coy? I had woken in my old bedroom, in the house where I had spent the best part of my life. The snow lay deep around the house, and there were frozen footprints across the yard to the garbage can. A blizzard had just visited, another was expected to blow in soon. I had dressed and tied my shoes with more than usual care, and left the stubble on my upper lip for a moustache I planned to grow. Slapping my pockets to make sure my ball-point and passport were safe, I went downstairs, past my mother's hiccupping cuckoo clock, and then to Wellington Circle to catch the train. It was a morning of paralysing frost, the perfect day to leave for South America.

For some, this was the train to Sullivan Square, or Milk Street, or at the very most Orient Heights; for me, it was the train to Patagonia. Two men using a foreign language spoke in low voices; there were others with lunch-boxes and valises and briefcases, and one lady with the sort of wrinkled department store bag that indicated she was going to return or exchange an unwanted item (the original bag lending veracity to the awkward operation). The freezing weather had altered the faces in the multi-racial car: the whites' cheeks looked rubbed with pink chalk, the Chinese were bloodless, the blacks ashen or yellow-grey. At dawn it had been 12° Fahrenheit, by mid-morning it was 9°, and the temperature was still dropping. The cold wind gusted through the car as the doors opened at Haymarket, and it had the effect of silencing the muttering foreigners. They looked Mediterranean; they winced at the draught. Most of the people sat compactly, with their elbows against their sides and their hands in their laps, squinting and conserving their warmth.

They had affairs to attend to in town – work, shopping, banking, the embarrassing moment at the refund desk. Two had hefty textbooks in their laps, and a spine turned towards me read *A General Introduction to Sociology*. A man solemnly scanned the headlines in the *Globe*, another thumb-flicked the papers in his briefcase. A lady told her little girl to stop kicking and sit still. Now they were getting out at the windy platforms – after four stations the car was half-full. They would return that evening, having spent the day speaking of the weather. But they were dressed for it, office clothes under eskimo coats, gloves, mittens, woolly hats; resignation was on their faces and, already, a suggestion of fatigue. Not a trace of excitement; all this was usual and ordinary; the train was their daily chore.

No one looked out of the window. They had seen the harbour, and Bunker Hill, and the billboards before. Nor did they look at each other. Their gazes stopped a few inches from their eyes. Though they paid no attention to them, the signs above their heads spoke to these people. These folks were local, they mattered, the advertising men knew who they were addressing. NEED FEDERAL INCOME TAX FORMS? Beneath it, a youth in a pea-jacket grinned at his newspaper and swallowed. CASH YOUR CHECKS ALL OVER MASSACHUSETTS. A lady with that yellow-grey Hottentot colour hugged her shopping bag. BE A SCHOOL VOLUNTEER IN THE BOSTON PUBLIC SCHOOLS. Not a bad idea for the sick-of-it-all briefcase examiner in the Russian hat. MORTGAGE MONEY? WE HAVE PLENTY. No one glanced up. ROOFS AND GUTTERS. GET A COLLEGE DEGREE IN YOUR SPARE TIME. A restaurant. A radio station. A plea to stop smoking.

The signs did not speak to me. These were local matters, but I was leaving this morning. And when you are leaving, the promises in advertisements are ineffectual. Money, school, house, radio: I was putting them behind me, and in the duration of this short trip from Wellington Circle to State Street, the words of the ads had become merely an imploring jabber, like the nonsense of an unknown language. I could shrug; I was being pulled away from home. Apart from the cold, and the blinding light on the fallen snow, there was nothing of great significance in my going, nothing momentous except the fact that as we drew into South Station I was now a mile nearer to Patagonia.

Travel is a vanishing act, a solitary trip down a pinched line of geography to oblivion.

> What's become of Waring
> Since he gave us all the slip?

But a travel book is the opposite, the loner bouncing back bigger than life to tell the story of his experiment with space. It is the simplest sort of narrative, an explanation which is its own excuse for the gathering up and the going. It is motion given order by its repetition in words. That sort of disappearance is elemental, but few come back silent. And yet the convention is to telescope travel writing, to start – as so many novels do – in the middle of things, to beach the reader in a bizarre place without having first guided him there. 'The white ants had made a meal of my hammock,' the book might begin; or, 'Down there, the Patagonian valley deepened to grey rock, wearing its eons' stripes and split by floods.' Or, to choose actual first sentences at random from three books within arm's reach:

It was towards noon on March 1, 1898, that I first found myself entering the narrow and somewhat dangerous harbour of Mombasa, on the east coast of Africa. (*The Man-Eaters of Tsavo*, by Lt Col J. H. Patterson)

'Welcome!' says the big signboard by the side of the road as the car completes the corkscrew ascent from the heat of the South Indian plains into an almost alarming coolness. (*Ooty Preserved*, by Mollie Panter-Downes)

From the balcony of my room I had a panoramic view over Accra, capital of Ghana. (*Which Tribe Do You Belong To?* by Alberto Moravia)

My usual question, unanswered by these – by most – travel books, is: How did you get there? Even without the suggestion of a motive, a prologue is welcome, since the going is often as fascinating as the arrival. Yet, because curiosity implies delay, and delay is regarded as a luxury (but what's the hurry, anyway?), we have become used to life being a series of arrivals or departures, of triumphs and failures, with nothing noteworthy in between. Summits matter, but what of the lower slopes of Parnassus? We have not lost faith in journeys from home, but the texts are scarce. Departure is described as a moment of panic and ticket-checking in an airport lounge, or a fumbled kiss at a gangway; then silence until, 'From the balcony of my room I had a panoramic view over Accra . . .'

Travel, truly, is otherwise. From the second you wake up you are headed for the foreign place, and each step (now past the cuckoo clock, now down Fulton to the Fellsway) brings you closer. *The Man-Eaters of Tsavo* is about lions devouring Indian railway labourers in Kenya at the turn of the century. But I would bet there was a subtler and just as rivetting book about the sea journey from Southampton to Mombasa. For his own reasons, Colonel Patterson left it unwritten.

The literature of travel has become measly, the standard opening that farcical nose-against-the-porthole view from the plane's tilted fuselage. The joke-opening, that straining for effect, is now so familiar it is nearly impossible to parody. How does it go? 'Below us lay the tropical green, the flooded valley, the patchwork quilt of farms, and as we penetrated the cloud I could see dirt roads threading their way into the hills and cars so small they looked like toys. We circled the airport and, as we came in low for the landing, I saw the stately palms, the harvest, the rooftops of the shabby houses, the square fields stitched together with crude fences, the people like ants, the colourful . . .'

I have never found this sort of guesswork very convincing. When I am landing in a plane my heart is in my mouth; I wonder – doesn't everyone? – if we are going to crash. My life flashes before me, a brief selection of sordid and pathetic trivialities. Then a voice tells me to stay in my seat until the plane comes to a complete stop; and when we land the loud-speakers break into an orchestral version of *Moon River*. I suppose if I had the nerve to look around I might see a travel writer scribbling, 'Below us lay the tropical green –'

Meanwhile, what of the journey itself? Perhaps there is nothing to say. There is not much to say about most aeroplane journeys. Anything remarkable must be disastrous, so you define a good flight by negatives: you didn't get hijacked, you didn't crash, you didn't throw up, you weren't late, you weren't nauseated by the food. So you are grateful. The gratitude brings such relief your mind goes blank, which is appropriate, for the aeroplane passenger is a time-traveller. He crawls into a carpeted tube that is reeking of disinfectant; he is strapped in to go home, or away. Time is truncated, or in any case warped: he leaves in one time-zone and emerges in another. And from the moment he steps into the tube and braces his knees on the seat in front, uncomfortably upright – from the moment he departs, his mind is focused on arrival. That is, if he has any sense at all. If he looked out of the window he would see nothing but the tundra of the cloud layer, and above is empty space. Time is brilliantly blinded: there is nothing to see. This is the reason so many people are apologetic about taking planes. They say, 'What I'd really like to do is forget these plastic jumbos and get a three-masted schooner and just stand there on the poop deck with the wind in my hair.'

But apologies are not necessary. An aeroplane flight may not be travel in any accepted sense, but it certainly is magic. Anyone with the price of a ticket can conjure up the castled crag of Drachenfels or the Lake Isle of Innisfree by simply using the right escalator at, say, Logan Airport in Boston – but it must be said that there is probably more to animate the mind, more of travel, in that one ascent on the escalator, than in the whole plane journey put together. The rest, the foreign country, what constitutes the arrival, is the ramp of an evil-smelling airport. If the passenger conceives of this species of transfer as travel and offers the public his book, the first foreigner the reader meets is either a clothes-grubbing customs man or a moustached demon at the immigration desk. Although it has become the way of the world, we still ought to lament the fact that aeroplanes have made us insensitive to space; we are encumbered, like lovers in suits of armour.

This is obvious. What interests me is the waking in the

morning, the progress from the familiar to the slightly odd, to the rather strange, to the totally foreign, and finally to the outlandish. The journey, not the arrival, matters; the voyage, not the landing. Feeling cheated that way by other travel books, and wondering what exactly it is I have been denied, I decided to experiment by making my way to travel-book country, as far south as the trains run from Medford, Massachusetts; to end my book where travel books begin.

I had nothing better to do. I was at a stage I had grown to recognize in my writing life. I had just finished a novel, two years of indoor activity. Looking for something else to write, I found that instead of hitting nails on the head I was only striking a series of glancing blows. I hated cold weather. I wanted some sunshine. I had no job – what was the problem? I studied maps and there appeared to be a continuous track from my house in Medford to the Great Plateau of Patagonia in southern Argentina. There, in the town of Esquel, one ran out of railways. There was no line to Tierra del Fuego, but between Medford and Esquel rather a lot of them.

In this vagrant mood I boarded that first train, the one people took to work. They got off – their train-trip was already over. I stayed on: mine was just beginning.

And at South Station, my skin crinkling into crêpe from the dull cold, some friends appeared. Vapour billowed from beneath the train; they were like people materializing from mist, their breath trailing in clouds. We drank champagne out of paper cups and hopped to keep warm. My family burst into view, pumping hands. In his excitement, my father forgot my name; but my brothers were calm, one ironical, the other squinting at a trim young man on the platform and saying, 'A dash of lavender, Paul – watch out, he's getting on!' I boarded, too, and waved good-bye to my well-wishers. As the Lake Shore Limited pulled out of Platform 15 I felt as if I was still in a provisional state, as if everyone was going to get off soon, and that only I was riding the train to the end of the line.

It was a nice conceit, but I kept it to myself. If a stranger asked me where I was going, I said Chicago. It was partly superstition – it seemed unlucky, so early in the trip, to give my precise destination. It was also to avoid startling the questioner with a ridiculous place name (Tapachula, Managua, Bogotá), or arousing his curiosity and setting off an interrogation. Anyway, this was still home, still familiar: the bent backs of city brown-stones, the preposterous solemnity of the Boston University spires, and across the frozen Charles River the white steeples of Harvard, each one in its frailty like a failed attempt at an ivory tower. The air was cold and clear, and it carried the cry of the train whistle through Back Bay. American train whistles have a bitter-sweet change in pitch, and the most insignificant train plays this lonesome note perfectly to the dreamers along the tracks. It is what is known in music as a Diminished Third: Hoo-*wee*! Hoo-*wee*!

There was some traffic on the salted roads, but no pedestrians. It was too cold to walk anywhere. The outskirts of Boston looked evacuated: no people, every door and window tightly shut, and the dirt-flecked snow piled beside the empty streets and covering the parked cars. We passed a television station bricked up to look like a country mansion, a solid duck pond, an armoury with grey fake battlements that was about as convincingly military as the kind you see stamped on the back of a cornflakes box to be assembled with scissors and glue. I knew the names of these suburbs, I had been here many times, but because I was headed so far away I saw every point we passed as important. It was as if I was leaving home for the first time, and for good.

Realizing how well I understood these places, I clung to what was familiar and was reluctant to surrender it to the distance. That bridge, that church, that field. There is nothing shocking about leaving home, but rather a slow feeling of gathering sad-ness as each familiar place flashes by the window, and disappears, and becomes part of the past. Time is made visible, and it moves as the landscape moves. I was shown each second passing as the train belted along, ticking off the buildings with a speed that made me melancholy.

Here in Framingham, I had eleven cousins. There were bungalows and tame woods and ice-covered porches on hillsides; cleaner snow than I had seen in Boston. And some humanity.

15

On this winter afternoon, children skidded hunched-over on skates on a frozen rink between derelict buildings. A moment later we crossed a class barrier: big pink, green, yellow and white oblongs of houses, some with swimming pools filled with snow. The Lake Shore Limited stopped traffic on Main Street, where a policeman whose puffy face was chilled the colour of salami, held the cars back with gloves like a bear's paws.

I had not come far. I could have hopped off the train and quite easily found my way back to Medford on a bus. I knew these places well, and yet I saw new things: a different texture in the suburban snow, the pally names on storefronts – 'Wally's', 'Dave's', 'Angie's' – and, repeatedly, American flags, the Stars and Stripes flying over petrol stations and supermarkets and in numerous yards. And a church steeple like a pepperpot. I could not remember having seen it before, but I had never rushed headlong from home like this. The length of the trip I intended allowed me to be attentive to detail. But the flags puzzled me – were these the pious boasts of patriots, or a warning to foreigners, or decorations for a national holiday? And why, in the littered yard of that rundown house, was a pretty little flag flapping loyally from a pole? On the evidence here it seemed an American obsession, a kind of image-worship I associated with the most primitive political minds.

The snow was bronzed by the setting sun and now I saw factories flying the flag, and advertising their products on their tall brick chimneys: SNIDER'S DRESSED BEEF, and on another the single word ENVELOPES. And like the armoury earlier, with its fake battlements, a cathedral with fake buttresses and a bell-less bell-tower, and some houses with columns which offered no support to the roof, purely decorative fakery repeated in a gingerbread villa. There was no pretence that it was not bogus, only an insistence on cuteness so common in American buildings, which have promoted fakery as legitimate in styles of architecture.

And between the small factory towns – now farther and farther apart – the dense woods were darkening, and the trunks of oak trees were black and forbidding, the shape of pulpits. As we neared Springfield night was falling on the bare hills, and in the snowy valleys the phosphorescence of the deep snow slipped towards black brooks, their surfaces roughened by the current. Since leaving Boston, water had been constantly in view: frozen lakes and ponds, half-frozen rivers or streams with conches of ice at their banks and the moving water turned to ink by the twilight. Then the sun sank and the light which had moved down the sky drained into the hole where the sun had gone, and the window specks showing in the woods seemed to brighten. Far down on the road, a man in mittens stood alone by his gas station pumps, watching us pass.

Not long afterward we were in Springfield. I had clear memories of the place, of getting off the train at that very station on a winter night, and crossing the long bridge over the Connecticut River to Route 91, to hitch-hike the rest of the way to Amherst. There were ice-floes on the river tonight, too, and the dark slopes of woods on the far side, and the same knifing wind. Memories of school are always to me like memories of destitution, of inexperience, the joyless impatience I had suffered like poverty. And I had had some sadnesses there. But the movement of travel is merciful: before I could remember much – before this town and river could toss me a particular memory – it whistled and rushed me into the amnesia of night. We travelled west, the rumble of the train muffled by snowbanks, through the forests of Massachusetts. But even in that darkness I recognized it. It was not the opaque night, the uninterrupted dark, of a foreign country's hinterland. It was the darkness that only baffles strangers. It was an average evening for this time of year in this place; and I knew all the ghosts here. It was the darkness of home.

I was still sitting in my compartment. The champagne at South Station had left me groggy, and though I had a copy of William Faulkner's *The Wild Palms* in my lap, I had done no more than read three pages. On the back cover I had scribbled, *policeman's face like salami* and *inky water* and *flags*. And the rest of the time I had spent with my face turned to the window. I had not seen any other passengers – I hadn't looked. I had no idea who was travelling on this train, and in my listless state thought there would be plenty of time for socializing further on – if not tonight, then tomorrow in Chicago, or the day after in

Texas. Or could I leave it all for Spanish America or another climate – just sit here reading until the weather changed, and then go for a stroll? But I found the Faulkner impenetrable; my curiosity overcame my listlessness.

There was a man in the corridor of the sleeping car (it was the only sleeping car on the train; it had a name, 'The Silver Orchid'). His face and forearms were against the window and he was staring, I suppose, at Pittsfield or the Berkshires – a paper-white birch grove smothered by night and snow, a row of fence posts visible because of the drifts in which they lay half-buried, and the shadowy lantern shapes of small cedars, and a frosting of flakes mimicking a contour of wind that streaked the pane of glass in front of his nose.

'This is like the Trans-Siberian,' he said.

'No, it's not,' I said.

He winced and went on staring. I walked to the end of the car, but felt bad for having snapped at him. I looked back and saw him still there, studying the darkness. He was elderly and what he had said to me was a friendly gesture. I pretended to look out of the window myself, and when he stretched and came towards me – he was doing a sort of tango to keep his balance, the way people walk on the decks of ships in storms – I said, 'Actually, there isn't this much snow in Siberia.'

'You don't say.' He kept moving. I could tell from his gruffness that I had lost him.

There would be no food until Albany, when the New York section, with its diner, was hooked to this train. So I went into the Lounge Car and had a beer. I packed my pipe and set it on fire and savoured the trance-like state of lazy reflection that pipe smoke induces in me. I blew myself a cocoon of it, and it hung in clouds around me, so comforting and thick that the girl who entered the car and sat down opposite seemed wraithlike, a child lost in fog. She put three bulging bags on her table, then tucked her legs under her. She folded her hands in her lap and stared stonily down the car. Her intensity made me alert. At the next table a man was engrossed in a Matt Helm story, and near him, two linesmen – they wore their tools – were playing poker. There was a boy with a short-wave radio, but his racket was drowned by the greater racket of the train. A man in a uniform was stirring coffee – a train man: there was an old greasy lantern at his feet. At the train man's table, but not speaking, a fat woman sneaked bites at a candy bar. She did it guiltily, as if she feared that at any moment someone would shout, *Put that thing away*!

'You mind not smoking?'

It was the girl with the bags and the stony gaze.

I looked for a *No Smoking* sign. There was none. I said, 'Is it bothering you?'

She said, 'It kills my eyes.'

I put my pipe down and took a swig of beer.

She said, 'That stuff is poison.'

Instead of looking at her I looked at her bags. I said, 'They say peanuts cause cancer.'

She grinned vengefully at me and said, 'Pumpkin seeds.'

I turned away.

'And these are almonds.'

I considered relighting my pipe.

'And this is cashews.'

Her name was Wendy. Her face was an oval of innocence, devoid of any expression of inquiry. Her prettiness was as remote from my idea of beauty as homeliness, and consequently was not at all interesting. But I could not blame her for that: it is hard for anyone to be interesting at twenty. She was a student, she said, and on her way to Ohio. She wore an Indian skirt, and lumberjack boots, and the weight of her leather jacket made her appear round-shouldered.

'What do you study, Wendy?'

'Eastern philosophy. I'm into Zen.'

Oh, Christ, I thought. But she was still talking. She had been learning about The Hole, or perhaps The Whole – it still made no sense to me. She hadn't read all that much, she said, and her teachers were lousy. But she thought that once she got to Japan or Burma she would find out a lot more. She would be in Ohio for a few more years. The thing about Buddhism, she said, was that it involved your whole life. Like everything you did – it was Buddhism. And everything that happened in the world – that was Buddhism, too.

'Not politics,' I said. 'That's not Buddhism. It's just crooked.'

'That's what everyone says, but they're wrong. I've been reading Marx, Marx is a kind of Buddhist.'

Was she pulling my leg? I said, 'Marx was about as Buddhist as this beer can. But anyway, I thought we were talking about politics. It's the opposite of thought – it's selfish, it's narrow, it's dishonest. It's all half truths and short-cuts. Maybe a few Buddhist politicians would change things but in Burma, where –'

'Take this,' she said, and motioned to her bags of nuts. 'I'm a raw-foodist-non-dairy vegetarian. You're probably right about politics being all wrong. I think people are doing things all wrong – I mean, completely. They eat junk. *They consume junk.* Look at them!' The fat lady was still eating her candy bar, or possibly another candy bar. 'They're just destroying themselves and they don't even know it. They're smoking themselves to death. Look at the smoke in this car.'

I said, 'Some of that is my smoke.'

'It kills my eyes.'

'"Non-dairy",' I said. 'That means you don't drink milk.'

'Right.'

'What about cheese? Cheese is nice. And you've got to have calcium.'

'I get my calcium in cashews,' she said. Was this true? 'Anyway, milk gives me mucus. Milk is the biggest mucus-producer there is.'

'I didn't know that.'

'I used to go through a box of Kleenex a day.'

'A box. That's quite a lot.'

'It was the milk. It made mucus,' she said. 'My nose used to run like you wouldn't believe.'

'Is that why people's noses run? Because of the milk?'

'Yes!' she cried.

I wondered if she had a point. Milk-drinkers' noses ran. Children were milk-drinkers. Therefore, children's noses ran. And children's noses *did* run. But it still struck me as arguable. Everyone's nose ran – except hers, apparently.

'Dairy products give you headaches, too.'

'You mean, they give *you* headaches.'

'Right. Like the other night. My sister knows I'm a vegetarian. So she gives me some eggplant parmyjan. She doesn't know I'm a non-dairy-raw-foodist. I looked at it. As soon as I saw it was cooked and had cheese on it I knew that I was going to feel awful. But she spent all day making it, so what else could I do? The funny thing is that I liked the taste of it. God, was I sick afterwards! And my nose started to run.'

I told her that, in his autobiography, Mahatma Gandhi stated that eating meat made people lustful. And yet at thirteen, an age at which most American children were frolicking with the Little League team or concentrating their minds on making spit-balls, Gandhi had got married – and he was a vegetarian.

'But it wasn't a real marriage,' said Wendy. 'It was a kind of Hindu ceremony.'

'The betrothal took place when he was seven years old. The marriage sealed the bargain. They were both thirteen, and he started shagging her – though I'm not sure one should use that term for describing the Mahatma's love-making.'

Wendy pondered this. I decided to try again. Had she, I asked, noticed a falling-off of her sexual appetite since her conversion to raw vegetables?

'I used to get insomnia,' she began. 'And sick – I mean, really sick. And I admit I lost my temper. I think meat *does* cause people to be hostile.'

'But what about sexual desire? Lechery – cravings – I don't know quite how to put it.'

'You mean sex? It's not supposed to be violent. It should be gentle and beautiful. Kind of a quiet thing.'

Maybe if you're a vegetarian, I thought. She was still droning on in her pedantic college student way.

'I understand my body better now ... I've gotten to know my body a whole lot better ... Hey, I can tell when there's just a little difference in my blood sugar level. I can sense it going up and down, my blood sugar level. When I eat certain things.'

I asked her whether she ever got violently ill. She said absolutely not. Did she ever feel a little bit sick?

Her reply was extraordinary: 'I don't believe in germs.'

Amazing. I said, 'You mean, you don't believe that germs

exist? They're just an optical illusion under the microscope? Dust, little specks – that sort of thing?'

'I don't think germs cause sickness. Germs are living things – small, living things that don't do any harm.'

'Like cockroaches and fleas,' I said. 'Friendly little critters, right?'

'Germs don't make you sick,' she insisted. 'Food does. If you eat bad food it weakens your organs and you get sick. It's your organs that make you sick. Your heart, your bowels.'

'But what makes your organs sick?'

'Bad food. It makes them weak. If you eat good food – like I do,' she said, gesturing at her pumpkin seeds, 'you don't get sick. Like I never get sick. If I get a runny nose and a sore throat I don't call it a cold.'

'You don't?'

'No, it's because I ate something bad. So I eat something good.'

I decided to shelve my inquiry about sickness being merely a question of a runny nose, and not cancer or the bubonic plague. Let's get down to particulars, I thought. What had she had to eat that day?

'This. Pumpkin seeds, cashews, almonds. A banana. An apple. Some raisins. A slice of wholemeal bread – toasted. If you don't toast it you get mucus.'

'You're sort of declaring war on the gourmets, eh?'

'I know I have fairly radical views,' she said.

'I wouldn't call them radical,' I said. 'They're smug views – self-important ones. Egocentric, you might say. The funny thing about being smug and egocentric and thinking about health and purity all the time, is that it can turn you into a fascist. My diet, my bowels, my self – it's the way right-wing people talk. The next thing you know you'll be raving about the purity of the race.'

'Okay,' she conceded in a somersault, 'I admit some of my views are conservative. But so what?'

'Well, for one thing, apart from your bowels there's a big world out there. The Middle East. The Panama Canal. Political prisoners having their toenails pulled out in Iran. Families starving in India.'

22

This rant of mine had little effect, though it did get her on to the subject of families – perhaps it was my mention of starving Indians. She hated families, she said. She couldn't help it – she just hated them.

I said, 'What does a family make you think of?'

'A station wagon, a mother, a father. Four or five kids eating hamburgers. They're really awful, and they're everywhere – they're all over the place, driving around.'

'So you think families are a blot on the landscape?'

She said, 'Well, yes.'

She had been at this college in Ohio for three years. She had never in that time taken a literature course. Even more interesting, this was the first time in her life that she had ever been on a train. She liked the train, she said, but didn't elaborate.

I wondered what her ambitions were.

'I think I'd like to get involved in food. Teach people about food. What they should eat. Tell them why they get sick.' It was the voice of a commissar, and yet a moment later she said dreamily, 'Sometimes I look at a piece of cheese. I know it tastes good, I know I'll like it. But I also know that I'm going to feel awful the next day if I eat it.'

I said, 'That's what I think when I see a magnum of champagne, a rabbit pie and a bowl of cream puffs with hot chocolate sauce.'

At the time, I did not think Wendy was crazy in any important sense. But afterwards, when I remembered our conversation, she seemed to me profoundly loony. And profoundly incurious. I had casually mentioned to her that I had been to Upper Burma and Africa. I had described Leopold Bloom's love of 'the faint tang of urine' in the kidneys he had for breakfast. I had shown a knowledge of Buddhism and the eating habits of Bushmen in the Kalahari and Gandhi's early married life. I was a fairly interesting person, was I not? But not once in the entire conversation had she asked me a single question. She never asked what I did, where I had come from, or where I was going. When it was not interrogation on my part, it was monologue on hers. Uttering rosy generalities in her sweetly tremulous voice, and tugging her legs back into the lotus position when they slipped free, she was an example of total self-absorption and desperate self-advertisement. She had mistaken egotism for Buddhism. I still have a great affection for the candour of American college students, but she reminded me of how many I have known who were unteachable.

The talk of food must have been inspired by the late hour and my hunger. But now we were at Albany. I excused myself and hurried to the dining car which had just been attached to the train. The miles ahead were historic: trains have been running between Albany and Schenectady for 150 years, starting with the Mohawk and Hudson Railway, the oldest in America. Farther on, the route followed is that of the Erie Canal. It was the railway that put the canals and waterways out of business, although the railway's efficiency was bitterly disputed by the rival companies. But the facts were indisputable: in the 1850s it took $14\frac{1}{2}$ days to reach Chicago from New York by water; by rail it was $6\frac{1}{2}$ days.

The Amtrak meal was promptly served by a towel-snapping waiter. The steak sandwich, on which I had poured Tabasco sauce, was my revenge on Wendy and her preference for raw alfalfa. While I ate, a sales manager named Horace Chick (he sold equipment for making photographic driving licenses) sat down and had a hamburger. He was a monologuist, too, but a harmless one. Each time he wished to emphasize a point he whistled through the gap in his front teeth. He munched and yapped.

'All the planes were full. *Pfweet.* So I took the train. Never took this train before. Simple. *Pfweet.* Three A M and we're in Rochester. I'll take a cab home. My wife would go ape-shit if I phoned her from the station at three A M. Next time I'm going to take the kids. Just plop them down. *Pfweet.* Let them run. It's hot in here. I like it cold. Sixty-seven, sixty-eight. My wife hates the cold. I can't sleep. I go over to the window and, *pfweet,* open it up. She screams at me. Just wakes up and, *pfweet,* screams. Most women are like that. They like it four degrees warmer than men. *Pfweet.* I don't know why. Bodies. Different bodies, different thermostat. Is this better than driving? You bet it is! Driving! Eight hours, fourteen cups of coffee. *Pfweet.* This hamburger, though. I taste filler. Hey, waiter!'

24

There was snow and ice outside. Each street-light illuminated its own post and, just in front, a round patch of snow – nothing more. At midnight, watching from my compartment, I saw a white house on a hill. In every window of this house there was a lighted lamp, and these bright windows seemed to enlarge the house and at the same time betray its emptiness.

At two the next morning we passed Syracuse. I was asleep or I would have been assailed by memories. But the city's name on the Amtrak timetable at breakfast brought forth Syracuse's relentless rain, a chance meeting at the Orange Bar with the by then derelict poet Delmore Schwartz, the classroom (it was Peace Corps training, I was learning Chinyanja) in which I heard the news of Kennedy's assassination, and the troubling recollection of a lady anthropologist who, unpersuaded by my ardour, had later – though not as a consequence of this – met a violent death when a tree toppled onto her car in a western state and killed her and her lover, a lady gym teacher with whom she had formed a Sapphic attachment.

Buffalo and Erie were behind us, too, which was not a bad thing. I had no idea where we were. I had woken in my compartment, and it had been so hot my lips were cracked and my fingertips felt flayed. But there were curtains of heavy vapour between the cars, where it was very cold, and frost on the windows of the diner. I rubbed the frost away but could see very little except a blue-grey fog that blurred the landscape with a cloudy fluorescence.

The train stopped in this haze. For several minutes, nothing happened. Then, in the fog, a dim tree stump became apparent. It bled a streak of orange and this widened, a splash, increasing and staining the decayed bark like a wound leaking into a grey bandage. And then the whole stump was alight, and the bunches of grass behind it flaming, and sudden trees. Soon the rubious fire of dawn glittered in the fields, and when the landscape was lit – the stump and the trees and the snow – the train moved on.

'Ohio,' said a lady at the next table.

Her husband, looking uncomfortable in a baggy yellow shirt, said, 'It doesn't look like Ohio.'

I knew what he meant.

The waiter said, 'Yep. That's Ohio all right. Be in Cleveland soon. Cleveland, Ohio.'

Just beyond the tracks there was a forest of frozen branches, poplars made out of frost, like ghostly sails and masts in a sea of snow. The elms and beeches had swelled cleanly into icy manifestations of exploded lace. And flat windswept snow, with hairstrands of brown broken grass buried to their tips. So even Ohio, covered in snow, could be dreamland.

The train was sunlit and emptier. I did not see Mr Chick or hear his *pfweet*; and Wendy, the raw foodist, was gone. It seemed to me here – and I was not very far from home – as if more of the familiar was slipping away. I had not really liked either one of them, but now I missed them. The rest of the people on the train were strangers.

I picked up my book. I had gone to sleep reading it the previous night; it was still *The Wild Palms* and still opaque. What had put me to sleep? Perhaps this sentence, or rather the tail end of a long straggling sentence: '. . . it was the mausoleum of love, it was the stinking catafalque of the dead corpse borne between the olfactoryless walking shapes of the immortal unsentient demanding ancient meat.'

I was not sure what Faulkner was driving at, and yet it seemed a fair description of the sausage I was eating that early morning in Ohio. The remainder of the breakfast was delicious – scrambled eggs, a slab of ham, grapefruit, coffee. Years before, I had noticed how trains accurately represented the culture of a country: the seedy distressed country has seedy distressed railway trains, the proud efficient nation is similarly reflected in its rolling stock, as Japan is. There is hope in India because the trains are considered vastly more important than the monkeywagons some Indians drive. Dining cars, I found, told the whole story (and if there were no dining cars the country was beneath consideration). The noodle stall in the Malaysian train, the borscht and bad manners in the Trans-Siberian, the kippers and fried bread on the Flying Scotsman. And here on Amtrak's Lake Shore Limited I scrutinized the breakfast menu and discovered that it was possible for me to order a Bloody Mary or a Screwdriver: 'a morning pick-me-up', as that injection of vodka into my system was described. There is not another train in the world where one can order a stiff drink at that hour of the morning. Amtrak was trying hard. Near my toast there was an Amtrak brochure which said that for the next 133 miles the track was perfectly straight – not a curve in it anywhere. So I copied down that shin-barking Faulkner sentence without any swerve of the train to jog my pen.

By the middle of the morning, the vapour I had seen between the cars had frozen. Each small passageway smoked like a deep freeze, with complicated crusts of frost covering it, and solid bubbles of ice, and new vapour pouring from cracks in the rubber seal. It was pretty, this snow and ice, and no less pretty outside; but it was also a nuisance. It was now past eleven and we had not yet reached Cleveland. Where was Cleveland? And I was not the only one who was perplexed. Up and down the train, passengers were buttonholing conductors and saying, 'Hey, what happened to Cleveland? You said we were supposed to be there by now. What's the story?' And yet Cleveland might have been right outside the window, buried under all that snow.

My conductor was leaning against a frosted window. I wanted to ask him what happened to Cleveland, but before I could speak he said, 'I'm looking for my switchman.'

'Anything wrong?'

'Oh, no. It's just that every time we go by here, he throws a snowball at me.'

'By the way, where's Cleveland?'

'Way off. Didn't you know we're running four hours late? Frozen switch back in Erie held us up.'

'I have to catch a train at four-thirty in Chicago.'

'You'll never make it.'

'Beautiful,' I said, and started away.

'Don't worry. I'll wire ahead in Elkhart. When we get to Chicago we'll just dump the whole thing in Amtrak's lap. They'll put you up at the Holiday Inn. You'll be in good shape.'

'But I won't be in Texas.'

'You leave this to me, sir.' He touched the visor of his cap. 'Ever see snow like this? God, it's terrible.' He looked out of the window again and sighed. 'Can't imagine what happened to that switchman. Probably got frostbite.'

It was hours before we got to Cleveland and, as with most delays, the slowness of our arrival created a sense of anti-climax: I felt I had already given it all the thought it deserved. Now the snow only bored me, and the houses depressed me – they were tiny bungalows not much bigger than the cars parked beside them. The greatest joke was that Cleveland, which had been smothered by the previous week's snowstorm, which had broadcast news items about survival techniques at home (intelligence – welcome, one would have thought, to Arctic explorers – about sleeping bags, body heat, keeping your condominium warm in an emergency, cooking on Sterno stones and the like) – this city, which was frozen solid under drifts of snow, had to cheer it a long story in the *Cleveland Plain Dealer* about the monstrous inefficiency of the Russians in snow removal. The Russians! Under the headline MOSCOW SNOW DIG-OUT CROWN TARNISHED, with its Moscow dateline, the story began, 'This city's once-renowned snow removal capabilities have been drastically diminished this winter by a combination of bureaucratic blunders and unexpectedly heavy snowfalls.' It continued in the same gloating vein: 'The problem is apparently not a lack of special equipment ... Residents are complaining bitterly this winter about the sad state of the streets ... Still, heavy December snows and inadequate parking regulations seem a poor excuse for streets that are still clogged several weeks later.'

It was Mid-West smugness. In order to boast in Ohio you have to mention the Russians. Even better, a mention of Siberia which, as a matter of fact, Ohio in winter greatly resembles. I read that news item in Cleveland. I read the entire *Plain Dealer* in Cleveland. In Cleveland we were delayed nearly two hours. When I asked the conductor the reason he said it was the snow; and the track had been buckled by ice.

'It's a real bad winter.'

I told him that in Siberia the trains run on time. But it was a cheap crack. I would choose Cleveland over Irkutsk any day, even though – this was obvious – Cleveland was colder.

I went to the Club Car and had a morning pick-me-up and

read *The Wild Palms*. Then I had another pick-me-up, and another. I considered a fourth, ordered it, but decided to nurse it. If I had many more of these pick-me-ups, I'd be under the table.

'What are you reading?'

It was a plump freckled-faced fiftyish lady sipping a can of sugar-free tonic.

I showed her the title.

She said, 'I've heard of it. Any good?'

'It has its moments.' Then I laughed. But it wasn't anything to do with Faulkner. Once, on an Amtrak train not far from here, I had had a book which no one had queried; and yet it had aroused considerable interest. It was the biography of the writer of horror tales, H. P. Lovecraft, and the title *Lovecraft* had led my fellow passengers to believe that throughout a two-day trip I had had my nose in a book about sexual technique.

She was from Flagstaff, she said, and 'Whereabouts you from?'

'Boston.'

'Really?' She was interested. She said, 'Will you say something for me? Say G-o-d.'

'God.'

She clapped her hands delightedly. She was, despite her plumpness, very small, with a broad flat face. Her teeth were crooked, slanting in a uniform way, as if they had been filed. I was baffled by the pleasure I had given her in saying the word.

'Gawd,' she said, mimicking me.

'What do you say?'

'I say gahd.'

'I'm sure He understands.'

'I love to hear you say it. I was on this train a week ago, going east. We were delayed by the snow, but it was fantastic. They put us up at the Holiday Inn!'

'I hope they don't do that to us.'

'Don't *say* that.'

'I've got nothing against the Holiday Inn,' I said. 'It's just that I have a train to catch.'

'Everybody does. I bet I'm going further than you – Flagstaff, remember?' She took another sip of her tonic and said, 'In the end it took us days – *days* – to get from Chicago to New York. There was snow everywhere! There was a boy on the train. He was from Boston. He was on the seat beside me.' She smiled – a kind of demure leer: 'We slept together.'

'That was lucky.'

'I know what you're thinking, but it wasn't like that. He was on his side and I was on my side. But' – she went pious – 'we slept together. What a time that was. I don't drink, but he drank enough for the both of us. Did I tell you he was twenty-seven years old? From Boston. And all through the night he said to me, "Gawd, you're beautiful." and he kissed me I don't know how many times. "Gawd, you're beautiful."'

'This was at the Holiday Inn?'

'On the train. One of the nights,' she said. 'The Chair Car. It was very, very important to me.'

I said it sounded like a very sweet experience and tried to imagine it, the drunken youth pawing this plump freckly woman while the Chair Car (smelling, as it always did at night, of old socks and stale sandwiches) snored.

'Not just sweet. It was very important. I needed it just then. That's why I was going East.'

'To meet this fellow?'

'No, no,' she said peevishly. 'My mother died.'

'I'm sorry.'

'I got word of it in Flagstaff and caught the train. Then we got held up in Chicago, if you call the Holiday Inn being held up! I met Jack round about Toledo – right about here, if this is Toledo.' She looked out the window. '"Gawd, you're beautiful." It really cheered me up. It came between so much.'

'My condolences. It must be very sad to go home for a funeral.'

'*Two* funerals,' she said.

'Pardon?'

'My father died, too.'

'Recently?'

'Tuesday.'

This was Saturday.

'God,' I said.

She smiled. 'I love to hear you say that.'

'I mean, that's terrible about your father.'

'It was a blow. I thought I was going home for my mother's funeral, but it turned out to be both of them. "You should come home more often, honey," Dad said. I said I would. Flagstaff is pretty far, but I've got my own apartment and I'm making good money. Then he died.'

'A sad trip.'

'And I'll have to go back. They couldn't bury them. I have to go back for the interment.'

'I would have thought that would be done by now.'

She looked at me sharply. 'They cain't bury people in New York City.'

I asked her to repeat this strange sentence. She did, in just the same tones.

'God,' I said.

'You sound like Jack.' She smiled: such odd Eskimo-granny teeth.

'Why can't they bury people in New York?'

'The ground's too hard. It's frozen. They cain't dig –'

In the severe winter of '78, I thought, *when the ground was so hard they couldn't bury people, and the mortuaries were stacked to the rafters, I decided to take the train to the sunniest parts of Spanish America.*

The lady from Flagstaff went away, but over the next eight or nine hours, again and again, in the Club Car and the Chair Car and the Diner, I heard her flat, dry corncrake voice repeating slowly, '– because they cain't bury people in New York City.'

Twice, when she saw me, she said *Gawd*! and laughed.

The frozen switch, the buckled track, the snow: we were running very late and my conductor insisted that I did not have a hope of arriving on time or making my connection for Fort Worth. 'You don't have the chance of one of these in Hell,' he said at an Indiana station. He was holding a snowball. And there was a new problem. A wheel was overheating and (I think I have this right) a fuse had blown; there was a frosty stink of gas seeping through the end of the train. To avert an explosion, the speed of the train was brought down to about 15 miles an hour, and we remained at this creeping pace until an opportunity arose to detach the afflicted car from the Lake Shore Limited. At Elkhart we were able to rid ourselves of this damaged car, but the operation took an unconscionably long time.

While we stopped, things were calm in the 'Silver Orchid' sleeping car. Only the conductor fussed. He said the steam was freezing and jamming the brakes. He hurried back and forth importantly with a push-broom and told me that this was much better than his previous job. He had been desk-bound in an electronics firm, 'but I'd rather deal with the public.'

'The trouble with you,' said the ticket collector, who saw the conductor growing anxious, 'is you fret before you stew.'

'Maybe so.' The conductor banged his broom on the ice that had accumulated inside the door.

'Won't be as bad as the last trip, though. That was frozen bananas.'

The conductor said, 'I've got my passengers to think of.'

My passengers. There were three of us in the 'Silver Orchid', the Bunces and me. The first thing Mr Bunce said to me was that his mother's people had been on the *Mayflower*. Mr Bunce wore a cap with earflaps and was zippered into two sweaters. He wanted to talk about his family and Cape Cod. Mrs Bunce said that Ohio was far uglier than the Cape. Mr Bunce also had a Huguenot pedigree. In one sense, old Bunce was an untypical bore. Characteristically, the American boasts about how desperate and poverty-stricken his immigrant ancestors were; Mr Bunce's were a huge success, right from the start. I listened with as much patience as I could muster. It might, I thought, have been Bunce I had offended that first day ('This is like the Trans-Siberian' 'No, it's not'). After that, I avoided the Bunces.

And still at Elkhart a great panic overtook the Lake Shore Limited. Now, everyone knew he would miss his onward connection in Chicago. A large group of single girls were heading for New Orleans and the Mardi Gras. Some elderly couples had to catch a cruise ship in San Francisco: they were very worried. A young man from Kansas said his wife would think he'd left her for good. A black couple whispered, and I heard the black girl say, 'Oh, shoot.' One of the Mardi Gras girls looked at her watch and said, 'We could be partying by now.'

The lady from Flagstaff, whose parents had just died, caused this mood to become festive and, at last, one of celebration. She explained she had been on the train going east just ten days before. The same thing had happened – delays, snow, missed connections. Amtrak had put everyone up at the Holiday Inn in Chicago and given everyone four dollars for taxi fare, and meal vouchers, and one phone call. Amtrak, she said, would do the same thing this time.

The news spread through the train and, as if proof of Amtrak's good intentions, a free meal was announced in the dining car: soup, fried chicken and vanilla ice cream. This vindicated the no longer bereaved lady from Flagstaff, who said, 'And wait till we get to Chicago!'

Elsewhere, passengers were spending the four dollar taxi fare they had not yet been given.

'Okay, Ralph,' said a greasy-haired boy to the bartender, and put a dollar down, 'let's get drunk.'

'We been setting here eight hours,' said the loudest of three youths, 'we already drunk.'

'I'm working overtime,' said Ralph the bartender, but obediently began cramming ice cubes into plastic cups.

There were other voices.

This: 'Never go home in the spring. It's never the same.'

And this: 'Jesus Christ' (a pause) 'was black. Like a Ethiopian. White features and a coloured face.' (pause) 'All them usual descriptions are bullshit.'

And again: '– because they cain't bury people in New York City.'

They were, all of them, frightfully happy. They were glad about the delay, delighted with the snow (it had begun to fall again) and they rejoiced at the promises made by the lady from Flagstaff about a night – or maybe two – at the Holiday Inn. I did not share their joy or feel very kindly towards any of them, and when I discovered that the car to be detached lay between the 'Silver Orchid' and this mob I told the conductor I was going back to bed: 'Wake me up when we get to Chicago.'

33

'We may not be there until nine o'clock.'

'Wonderful,' I said. I fell asleep with *The Wild Palms* over my face.

The conductor woke me at ten to nine. 'Chicago!' I jumped up and grabbed my suitcase. As I hurried down the platform, through the billows of steam from the train's underside, which gave to my arrival that old-movie aura of mystery and glory, ice needles crystalized on the lenses of my glasses and I could hardly see.

The lady from Flagstaff had been dead right. I was given four dollars and a berth in the Holiday Inn and three meal vouchers. Everyone who had missed a connection got exactly the same: the Bunces, the drunken louts from the Club Bar, the young man from Kansas, the Mardi Gras girls, the gaffawing peckerwoods who had slumbered the trip away on cheap seats in the Chair Car, the elderly people on their way to San Francisco, the lady from Flagstaff. We were met by Amtrak staff and sent on our way.

'See you at the hotel!' cried a lady whose luggage was two shopping bags.

She could not believe her luck.

A lout said, 'This is costing Amtrak a fortune!'

The wild snow, the sudden hotel, Chicago – it seemed unreal. But this unreality was amplified by the other guests at the Holiday Inn. They were blacks in outlandish uniforms, bright green bell-bottoms, white peaked caps and gold braid; or red uniforms, or white with medals, or beige with silver braid looped around the epaulettes. Was it a band, I wondered, or a regiment of pop-art policemen? It was neither. These men (their wives were not in uniform) were members of the Loyal Order of Antlers. Their shoulder badges said so, in small print. The men gave Antler salutes and Antler handshakes and paraded very formally around the lobby in white Antler shoes, looking a trifle annoyed at the class of people the storm had just blown in. There was no confrontation. The Amtrak passengers made for the 'Why Not? Discotheque' and the Bounty Lounge, and the Antlers (some of whom wore swords) stood and saluted each other – stood, I suppose, because sitting would have taken the crease out of their trousers.

The swimming pool was floodlit and filled with snow. Green palm trees were painted on the outside wall. These appeared to be rooted in the snowdrifts. The city was frozen. There were cakes of ice in the river. Last week's snow was piled by the roadsides. There was new snow on the streets. And with this newly falling snow was a sleet storm, tiny pelting grains that made driving treacherous. The Gideon Bible in my room was open at *Chronicles* (2, 25). Was there a message here for me? 'The fathers shall not be put to death for the children, or the children be put to death for the fathers; but every man shall die for his own sin.' Amen, I thought. I shut the Bible and unpacked Faulkner.

Coincidentally, Faulkner had a message. 'Now it was winter in Chicago,' I read. '. . . the defunctive days dying in neon upon the fur-framed petal faces of the wives and daughters of cattle and timber millionaires and the paramours of politicians returned from Europe . . . the sons of London brokers and Midland shoe-peg knights . . .' He went on jeering at their status and then described how they all went south and deserted Chicago's snows. They were 'members of that race which without tact for exploration and armed with notebooks and cameras and sponge bags elects to pass the season of Christian holiday in the dark and bitten jungles of savages.'

I was not sure about my tact for exploration, and I had neither a camera nor a sponge bag, but twenty-four hours in the Holiday Inn in wintry Chicago convinced me that the sooner I got to the savage jungle, however dark and bitten, the better.

2 The Lone Star

There seemed to me nothing more perfect in travel than boarding a train just at nightfall and shutting the bedroom door on an icy riotous city and knowing that morning would show me a new latitude. I would leave anything behind, I thought, for a sleeper on a southbound express.

And it was impossible to be on the Lone Star out of Chicago, beginning this crossing of six states, and not hear the melodies of all the songs that celebrate the train. Half of jazz is railway music, and the motion and noise of the train itself has the rhythm of jazz. This is not surprising: the Jazz Age was also the Railway Age. Musicians travelled by train or not at all, and the pumping tempo and the clickety-clack and the lonesome whistle crept into the songs. So did the railway towns on the route: how else could Joplin or Kansas City be justified in a lyric? We rolled out of Union Station towards Joliet and this nice combination of privacy and motion – and the bass notes of the wheels on the tracks – brought me a melody and then words. The wheels were saying, 'It ain't nothing like my daddy's big cigar – no, it ain't –'

I hung up my coat and set out my belongings, poured myself a glass of gin and watched the last pinky sunset flecks disappear from the Joliet snow.

> Keep your money and your liquor and your fancy car –
> It ain't nothing like my daddy's big cigar.
> Don't matter if he's broke,
> 'Cause how that man can smoke . . .
>
> Keep your special table at that downtown bar –
> It ain't nothing like my daddy's big cigar.
> He offers me a puff
> But one just ain't enough . . .

Not a bad start. It seemed to strike the right note, but obviously it needed work. Anyway, here was the ticket-man.

'You've been involuntarily upgraded,' he said, looking at my ticket. He perforated it expertly. 'Anything you need, just holler.'

I said, 'Is there going to be anyone else in this bedroom?'

'Nope. You got the whole place to yourself.'

'What's the weather report like?'

'Terrible,' he said. 'I've been working on this train for fifty years and this is the worst winter I've ever seen. Ten below in Chicago, winds going a hundred miles an hour. It took the signs down in Cleveland. Shee!'

One thing about the cold weather: it brings out the statistician in everyone. The temperatures, the wind speeds, the chill factors were always different, but always bad. And yet, even if they were not the exaggerations they seemed, I would be out of this glaciation in a day or so. I had not seen one green tree or one unfrozen body of water since leaving Boston. But there was hope – I was going south, more southerly than anyone on this southbound express would believe. Somewhere below, the wind was in the palm trees. On the other hand, we were only now in Streator, Illinois.

Streator was dark, and my one glimpse of Galesburg was a rectangle of snow and a sign that said PARKING and a little lighted shed and a half-buried car – a scene with the quaint insignificance of a *New Yorker* cover. This I saw from the dining car, looking up from my halibut and chablis. Propped against the wine bottle was *The Thin Man*, by Dashiell Hammett. I had hurried through the Faulkner and left it in Chicago, in the drawer of the vanity table in the Holiday Inn, with the Gideon Bible.

The criminality in *The Thin Man* was not half so distracting as the drinking. Everyone drank in this book; it was, in the Hammett world, eternally cocktail time. The Faulkner had disturbed me with torrential irrelevance and set my teeth on edge with confederate metaphysics. Hammett's English was more lucid, but the plot was plainly concocted, and the detective-work seemed a poor excuse for boozing sessions.

I turned my attention to the three people at the next table, who were drawling away happily. A middle-aged couple had discovered that the stranger who had seated himself at their table was also a Texan. He was dressed in black and yet looked raffish, like one of those adulterous preachers who occur from time to time in worthy novels set in this neck of the woods – it was nine o'clock, we were in Fort Madison, Iowa, on the west bank of the Mississippi.

'Yep, the mighty Miss,' said the waiter, when I asked him to confirm this. He took my empty plate away and crooned, 'The Mississippi, the Mississippi' to the other diners.

The preacher, like the couple – and this thrilled them – was from San Tone. All three were returning from New York. They took turns telling horror stories – Eastern horror stories of drugs and violence. 'One night we were going back to our hotel and I saw this man –' That sort of story.

And this sort of rejoinder. 'You think that's bad? A friend of mine was over in Central Park –'

Soon they were reminiscing about Texas. Then boasting. Finally, their boasting took an unexpected turn. They talked about all the people they knew in Texas who carried guns. 'My cousin carried a gun his whole life' and 'Ron knew a politician who never went anywhere without his gun' and 'My grand-daddy had a beautiful gun.'

'Everyone had a gun in those days,' said the preacher.

'He gave it to my Daddy,' said the lady.

'My Daddy had two guns,' said the preacher. 'One here and one here.' He spanked two pockets.

The lady said that one day her Daddy had tried to take a gun into a Dallas department store. He was just a stranger in town, from San Tone. Woke up that morning and strapped on his gun, like he always done. Nothing funny about that. Done the same thing every day of his life. Went in the store, packing this old gun. He was a huge man, way over six feet tall. The department store girls figured it was a hold-up as soon as they seen him. They stomped on the alarm. All Hell busted loose, but Daddy didn't mind one bit. He pulled out his gun and when the police came along Daddy said, 'Okay, boy, let's git 'im!'

The lady's husband said that Daddy had been eighty-four years old at the time.

'"Okay, boy, let's git 'im!"'

The preacher had listened to this story with a growing look of defeat. He was silent for a moment, then he spoke up.

He said, 'My Daddy had eight heart attacks.'

The lady squinted at him. Her husband said, 'Wow.'

'Coronary thrombosises,' said the preacher. 'Lived through all eight.'

'He from San Tone, too?' asked the man.

'He surely was,' said the preacher.

'Must have been tough,' said the lady.

'No Easterner could survive that,' said the preacher. 'Only a Westerner could survive eight heart attacks.'

This met with general agreement. I wanted to ask what a Westerner was *doing* with eight heart attacks. But I kept my peace.

'Back East –' the lady began.

It was time to go. I returned to my bedroom, through a succession of deep freezes, the ice chests that lay between the cars. I yanked the covers over my head and said good night to Kansas. I'm staying here, I thought, and if I see snow on the ground tomorrow morning I'm not getting out of bed.

Dawn at Ponca City, Oklahoma, was a wintry shimmer under a sky of grey oatmeal. We were nearly 800 miles south of Chicago and headed towards Perry. The land was flat and barren; but the traces of snow – pelts of it blown into ruts and depressions, like the scattered carcasses of ermine – was not enough to keep me sulking in bed. I did not realize how cold it was out there in Oklahoma until I saw the white ovals of frozen ponds and the narrow ice-paths at the centre of stony riverbeds. The rest was brown; a few bare brown trees; a small herd of brown cattle, lost in all that space, nibbling at brown turves. At the topmost portion of the sky's dome, the mournful oatmeal dissolved and slipped, leaving a curvature of aquamarine. The sun was a crimson slit, a red squint in the mass of cereal, a horizontal inch steadied above the horizon.

For twenty minutes or so, and as many miles, the land remained utterly empty: no houses, no people, very little snow, only that changeless brown. It was the unadorned surface of the earth, old humpless grasslands, every lick of weed combed flat by the wind, and no mooching cow anywhere to give it size.

These are the gardens of the Desert, these
The unshorn fields, boundless and beautiful,
For which the speech of England has no name –
The Prairies.

We came to Perry. Perry's bungalow styles were from Massachusetts and Ohio, and some with tarpaper roofs and air-conditioners rusting on the windows were nearly hidden behind the large sun-faded cars parked in their driveways. The cars were as wide as the roads. But one Perry house was tall and white, with three porches and gables and steeply sloping roofs, and newly painted clapboard. It would not have looked unusual on an acre of green lawn in Cape Cod; but in Perry, surrounded by tramped stones, and towering in the prairie like a beacon, it seemed a puzzle. Yet it was a vivid puzzle, so clear in design it required no solution. The assertive clarity of the thing was distinctly American, and I found it as remarkable in its way as the sudden parking lot (the lighted shed, the sign, the buried car) I had seen the previous night in Galesburg, or the snowy swimming pool with the painted palm trees in Chicago. I could not have found it so beautiful if I had not also found it slightly comic. But it was American humour, unambiguous, newly-minted, half cliché, half genius, and visually memorable, like the minute we spent in Norman, Oklahoma: the Sooner Movie House at the corner of Main and Jones, the Stars and Stripes flying over the store-fronts, the five parked cars, the self-consciously severe row of low buildings, and Main Street a perfectly straight line from here, the train station, to the end of town, that brown smudge of prairie at the end of the street.

'It's cold out there, boy!' the conductor said at Oklahoma City. He advised me to stay in the train. Oklahoma City was really no different from Perry. The sheds, the stores, the warehouses were bigger, but the shapes were the same, and like Perry it had the temporary and unfinished look of a place that had been plunked down in the prairie.

These Western towns had no apparent age. They were settlements of Baptist utility: the citizens worked and prayed, tore down the buildings they ceased to need and put up new square ones and did not bother to decorate them, except with flags. So the towns slipped by, one Main Street scarcely distinguishable from another, church and post office cut to the same pattern, two-storey buildings in the centre of town, one-storey buildings at its edge. It was not until I saw a certain house, or barn, or a side road with a row of blackened fractured sheds, that I remembered how these old places were or received a whiff of their romance.

'Want to hear something awful?' said a man entering the Dining Car for breakfast. 'Forty-five thousand schoolkids just got on the train.'

He grumbled and picked up the menu which served as a place-mat.

I finished my coffee and, heading back to my car, saw what he meant. There were not quite as many as he had said, perhaps two or three hundred, women and children, each wearing a name-tag: *Ricky, Sally, Tracy, Kim, Kathy*. Kathy was gorgeous; she was chatting to Marilyn, who was also a knockout. Both stood near their chubby little girls.

'Daddy's got a real bad cold,' said Kathy, glancing down. 'I had to put him right to bed.'

'Our daddy's at the office as usual,' said Marilyn.

Overhearing them, another woman said in the same TV-mummy voice, 'And where's our daddy, honey? Tell them where our daddy is.' Her small girl sucked a finger and looked at the floor. 'Our daddy's on a trip! And when he comes back, we're going to tell him that *we* took a trip. On a train!'

It was, I was sure, mostly self-parody. Dressed to kill, sprung from their kitchens for a day's outing to Fort Worth, they were lumbered with their kids. It was a taste of freedom, but clearly not enough: tomorrow they would be back home, cursing house-work and hating the mummy–daddy stereotype. They had the wise-cracking good looks of the television commercial house-wives, who sell soap flakes and anti-perspirant. If there had been only a dozen or so, I would not have reflected on their condition. But the hundreds of them, turned into governesses and talking

41

with gentle sarcasm about their daddies, was an impressive example of wasted talent. It seemed unfair, to say the least, that in one of the most socially-advanced countries on earth, here was a group behaving no differently from the wariest folk-society. Apart from me – and I was only passing through – there were no grown men in the three cars they occupied. So there was an atmosphere of purdah in these cars, which was not only grim for a feminist, but rather pitiable for the hard-liners there as well. And since at least half of these bright-looking girls had probably majored in sociology, it could not have escaped their notice how closely they resembled the Dinka womenfolk of the southern Sudan.

I went to my compartment and could not help but brood. Seeing a pump in the prairie I recalled that I had been watching them for the past three hours, the up-and-down motion of a black spindle upraised on a tower, see-sawing all over Oklahoma, sometimes in clusters, but more often a solitary arm-swinging contraption in the middle of nowhere.

After Purcell, 900 miles from Chicago, we emerged from the ice-age. The creeks were soggy, no longer knobbed with frost; and the snow was sparse – hardly snow-like, it lay in scraps in the tight grass like waste paper. Here, a town was two streets of bungalows, a lumberyard, a grocery store, an American flag and, a moment later, prairie. I looked for details and after an hour or so of close scrutiny was glad for the occasional tree or see-sawing well to break the monotony. I wondered what it must be like to be born in a place like this, where only the foreground – the porch, the storefront, the main street – mattered. The rest was emptiness, or did it only seem that way to me because I was a stranger, passing through on a train? I had no wish to stop. The Oklahoma or Texan celebrates his freedom and speaks of the confinement of the New Yorker; but these towns struck me as confining to a suffocating degree. There was a pattern of defensiveness in the way they were laid out, as if they had simply sprung out of a common fear. And the pattern? It was that of a circle of wagons. And the small oblong houses even had the look of wagons – wagons without wheels, which had been parked there for no better reason than that there were others already there. The land was vast, but the houses were in huddles, regarding the neighbours and the narrow street, their backs turned to the immense spaces of the prairie.

Ten miles out of Ardmore, on the Oklahoma–Texas border, an old man at the window said, 'Gene Autry.'

But asking him for an explanation I missed the place, which was not the cowboy but another town and a railway station so small the Lone Star bowled through it without slowing down.

'Maybe he was born there,' said the man. 'Or maybe buried.'

Low dry hills giving on to grey-green plains marked the Texas border. No ice, no snow; the weather looked mild. Followed by blackbirds, a farmer ploughed a field in a tractor, screwing six stripes out of the ground as he went. I was relieved to see that he was not wearing mittens. So the season had changed; it was early spring here in the first week of February, and if I kept to the trains it would be summer for me in a few days. The air traveller can be jetted to any climate at short notice, but the railway passenger on the southbound express has the satisfaction of seeing the weather change hour by hour and watching for its minutest alteration. At Gainesville there was planting, and more ploughing, and some inch-high shoots. There were trees around the houses here and less constriction than I had seen in the Oklahoma settlements. There were homesteads, with wells and wind-vanes and what might have been orchards.

> Here, where the red man swept the leaves away
> To dig for cordial bark or cooling root,
> The wayside apple drops its surly fruit.

The direction of the Lone Star – compare it with any history book map – is the direction of the main cattle drive north, the Chisholm Trail. At first, in the 1860s, the cattle were driven through what was known as the Indian Territory in Oklahoma, to the railhead in Abilene, Kansas. All the great railroad towns – Dodge City, Wichita (which we had passed at 6 A M), Cheyenne – flourished because of the cattle that were penned and graded there before being loaded on the Chicago-bound trains. Some of the cattle on the long drive from the Rio Grande were wild, but all were dealt with Mexican-style – the American cowboys

43

had inherited the lariat and the branding iron and most of the lingo, including the word lingo, from Mexican cattlemen. The Chisholm Trail was only one of the routes; the Sedalia took cattle through Arkansas and Missouri, and the Goodnight-Loving Trail ran along the Pecos River. The railway took over these routes – the water supplies along the way, which had determined the course of the Chisholm Trail, were no less important to the steam locomotives' thirst – and only much later did passengers replace cattle as a source of railway income.

I saw the herds of cattle, and ducks in flight, and large black circling birds that might have been buzzards, but even here – nearly a thousand miles south of Chicago – the trees were bare. I.had not seen one green tree in four days of cross-country travel. I watched for one, but only saw more birds of prey, or windmill pumps, or horses cropping grass. There were houses here, but no towns of any description; what trees I saw were dead but still upright like rather wicked coat-racks along dry creekbeds. Behind the isolated and rusty-roofed farmhouses there was empty space, and nearer the track and usually beside a fence of thorny barbed wire, I saw what I expected to see, the staves of cattle bones, the bleached knuckles and heaps of vertebrae, the cracked and hollow-eyed skulls.

Texas pride, an amiable but tenacious vulgarity, was the grotesquely fat man wearing his ten-gallon hat in the Silver Dollar Saloon in downtown Fort Worth in February. It might have been a gesture of defiance – the day was overcast and chilly, the bar dungeon-dark (its only light the subaqueous flicker from a fish tank bubbling on a shelf of whisky bottles). I had ducked in here to get warm and quietly read *The Fort Worth Star-Telegram*. Once my eyes became accustomed to the dark, I sat near the fish tank to read. I also had a decision to make: I could spend the night in Fort Worth, or leave in a matter of hours for Laredo. But I had left my suitcase at the railway station. I had not liked the look of Fort Worth.

It had been recommended to me as friendlier and more grasp-able than Dallas, and yet that February afternoon it looked merely grey and grit-blown, a Texas town of pompous insignificance, the desert wind whirling gory ketchup-soaked sandwich wrappers at men clutching their ridiculous hats. Every public place displayed the same ominous sign (or rather two signs – I'm not counting *You Don't Have to Be Crazy to Work Here – But It Helps!*). The warning went as follows:

These premises may be occupied by a policeman armed with a shotgun. If ordered to halt – please comply!
                                                        – Fort Worth Police Dept.

It was perhaps a comment on Fort Worth friendliness that the citizens needed to be reminded that a man with a shotgun meant business, and was not the clay-pigeon enthusiast he seemed.

That sign was in all the finance companies, and in the stores selling Western gear – Fort Worth had more than its share of these two enterprises: you could get a mortgage and a gold lamé cowboy suit on every corner. It was also in the Blood Donor Center ($50 a pint, and two scruffy individuals waiting to have their veins opened) and the narrow office of the bail bondsman (*24-Hour Service* said the sign, which also showed a poor devil in handcuffs) and all the chili parlours. It was in the Silver Dollar, too, but by the time I had taken refuge there I had seen it so often it had lost its power to intimidate me.

In the gurgling light of the fish tank I read the newspaper. The headlines were indignant over local issues. I skipped to the sports page; here, the lead story was an exultant blow-by-blow account of the Southwest Exposition at Fat Stock Show Rodeo. No baseball, no football, no hockey – only the American equivalent of bear-baiting. A rodeo – this was sports? The report covered the entire page, and the next page as well ('Bull Riding', 'Calf Roping'). These people were serious.

'Not too awful long ago,' said the fat man in the ten gallon hat, using a construction that was new to me, and making it sound – by saying it slowly – like a complete sentence, 'folks here would have started a revolution if they couldn't read the rodeo scores. Sure, we're glad to have it.'

But rodeo news was little more than a balance sheet listing the winnings of the cowpoke pictured tormenting a bull. I found it

45

a mystifying triumph, and the amassing of two thousand dollars – there was no mention of technique – an ungainly, if not unworthy, victory. Aside from the barbarity of it, this was the first sports page I had ever seen where there were dollar signs beside every score.

Hoping for a little light relief I turned to the Letters to the Editor. After all, if I was going to spend the night here it would help if I had some clue to the city's character. The first letter began, 'It is generally known that the theory of evolution is being taught in the public schools as a fact ...' There followed some rather clumsy sarcasm about science eroding 'moral values', and every indication that a Scopes-like Monkey Trial might follow the Fat Stock Show as Fort Worth's next attraction. Letter Two: Hold on the Panama Canal, for Christ's sake! Letter Three was an extraordinary denunciation of the Texas Democratic Committee for inviting Cesar Chavez to Texas. It implied that Mr Chavez was a troublemaker for wanting to organize farm labourers. This letter ended, 'Unions are doing more to destroy our national economy, promoting unemployment and inflation than any one cause.'

Unions, the Canal, the Bible: they were not getting down to basics in Fort Worth – they had never got away from them in the first place. I really hadn't the strength to grapple with Adam and Eve and the child labour laws, and so I handed my newspaper to Fatty and headed out of the Silver Dollar and past the billboards (*Listen to Redneck Radio!*) to the railroad station.

There was some delay, but waiting I met a very happy man. He was a newcomer to Fort Worth, he said, but six months in the city had convinced him of the limitless opportunities of the place I had no trouble dismissing in an afternoon.

'Tennis, golf, bowling,' he said. 'Swimming.'

I said, 'You can do those things in Cleveland.'

'Here, you can do anythink.'

Anythink?

I said, 'Are you English?'

Yes, indeed, he was a Londoner. He had been a policeman in a wretched precinct of south London, but he had grown sick of the taxes and the general gloom and the British passions for amateurism and failure. He had migrated to Fort Worth: 'More for the kids' sake than anythink else.'

In London, as a bobby in a funny helmet, unarmed except for his truncheon and his whistle, he had been jeered at. He had always wanted to play golf. But policemen in London do not play golf. He liked swimming. But one cannot be a serious swimmer at the Public Baths in Tooting. He had been at the bottom of the pay-scale, on the last rung of the social ladder. Here, as a hotel clerk in the city of bull riders, calf ropers, bail-bondsmen, wholesalers of cowboy suits, Fundamentalist drawlers and – it was their own word – rednecks, his whiffling south London accent marked him out as an aristocrat and gave him a Churchillian authority.

'I'm staying,' he said.

'You could be a policeman here,' I said.

'They do all right here,' he said.

I wished him luck, and then, somewhat reassured, and still sticking to this cattle drive in reverse – the Chisholm Trail which the railway had inherited – made tracks for Laredo.

3 The Aztec Eagle

It was a rainy night in Laredo – not late, and yet the place seemed deserted. A respectable frontier-town, sprawling at the very end of the Amtrak line, it lay on a geometric grid of bright black streets on a dirt bluff that had the clawed and bulldozed look of a recent quarry. Below was the Rio Grande, a silent torrent slipping past Laredo in a cut as deep as a sewer; the south bank was Mexico.

The city lights were on, making the city's emptiness emphatic. In that glare I could see its character as more Mexican than Texan. The lights flashed, suggesting life, as lights do. But where were the people? There were stop-lights on every corner, *Walk* and *Wait* signs winked on and off; the two-storey shop-fronts were floodlit, lamps burned in the windows of one-storey houses; the street-lights made the puddles bright holes in slabs of wet road. The effect of this illumination was eerie, that of a plague city brightened against looters. The stores were heavily padlocked; the churches lit up in cannonades of arc-lamps; there were no bars. All that light, instead of giving an impression of warmth and activity, merely exposed its emptiness in a deadening blaze.

No traffic waited at the red lights, no pedestrians at the crosswalks. And though the city was silent, in the drizzly air was an unmistakable heart-murmur, the *threep-threep* of music being played far away. I walked and walked, from my hotel to the river, from the river to a plaza, and into the maze of streets until I was almost certain I was lost. I saw nothing. And it could be frightening, seeing – four blocks away – a blinking sign I took to be a watering hole, a restaurant, an event, a sign of life, and walking to it and arriving soaked and gasping to discover that it was a shoe store or a funeral parlour, shut for the night. So, walking the streets of Laredo, I heard only my own footsteps, the false courage of their click, their faltering at alleyways, their splashes as I briskly returned to the only landmark I knew – the river.

The river itself made no sound, though it moved powerfully, eddying like a swarm of greasy snakes in the ravine from which every bush and tree had been removed in order to allow the police to patrol it. Three bridges linked the United States to Mexico here. Standing on the bluff I heard the *threep-threep* louder: it was coming from the Mexican side of the river, a just-discernible annoyance, like a neighbour's radio. Now I could see plainly the twisting river, and it struck me that a river is an appropriate frontier. Water is neutral and in its impartial winding makes the national boundary look like an act of God.

Looking south across the river, I realized that I was looking towards another continent, another country, another world. There were sounds there – music, and not only music but the pip and honk of voices and cars. The frontier was actual: people did things differently there, and looking hard I could see trees outlined by the neon beer-signs, a traffic jam, the source of the music. No people, but cars and trucks were evidence of them. Beyond that, past the Mexican city of Nuevo Laredo, was a black slope – the featureless, night-haunted republics of Latin America.

A car drew up behind me. I was alarmed, then reassured when I saw it was a taxi. I gave the driver the name of my hotel and got in, but when I tried to make conversation he responded by grunting. He understood only his own language.

In Spanish I said, 'It is quiet here.'

That was the first time on my trip that I spoke Spanish. After this, nearly every conversation I had was in Spanish. But in the course of this narrative I shall try to avoid affecting Spanish words, and will translate all conversations into English. I have no patience with sentences that go, ' "*Carramba!*" said the *campesino*, eating his *empanada* at the *estancia* . . .'

'Laredo,' said the taxi driver. He shrugged.

'Where are all the people?'

'The other side.'

'Nuevo Laredo?'

49

'Boys' Town,' he said. The English took me by surprise, the phrase tickled me. He said, now in Spanish again, 'There are one thousand prostitutes in the Zone.'

It was a round number, but I was convinced. And that of course explained what had happened to this city. After dark, Laredo slipped into Nuevo Laredo, leaving the lights on. It was why Laredo looked respectable, even genteel, in a rainswept and mildewed way: the clubs, the bars, the brothels, were across the river. The red-light district was ten minutes away, in another country.

But there was more to this moral spelled out in transpontine geography than met the eye. If the Texans had the best of both worlds in decreeing that the fleshpots should remain on the Mexican side of the International Bridge – the river flowing, like the erratic progress of a tricky argument, between vice and virtue – the Mexicans had the sense of tact to keep Boys' Town camouflaged by decrepitude, on the other side of the tracks, another example of the geography of morality. Divisions everywhere: no one likes to live next-door to a whorehouse. And yet both cities existed because of Boys' Town. Without the whoring and racketeering, Nuevo Laredo would not have had enough municipal funds to plant geraniums around the statue of its madly gesturing patriot in the plaza, much less advertise itself as a bazaar of wicker-work and guitar-twanging folklore – not that anyone ever went to Nuevo Laredo to be sold baskets. And Laredo required the viciousness of its sister-city to keep its own churches full. Laredo had the airport and the churches, Nuevo Laredo the brothels and basket-factories. Each nationality had seemed to gravitate to its own special area of competence. This was economically-sound thinking; it followed to the letter the Theory of Comparative Advantage, outlined by the distinguished economist, David Ricardo (1772–1823).

At first glance, this looked like the typical sort of mushroom-and-dunghill relationship that exists at the frontiers of many unequal countries. But the longer I thought about it the more Laredo seemed like all of the United States, and Nuevo Laredo all of Latin America. This frontier was more than an example of cosy hypocrisy; it demonstrated all one needed to know about the morality of the Americas, the relationship between the puritanical efficiency north of the border, and the bumbling and passionate disorder – the anarchy of sex and hunger – south of it. It was not as simple as that, since there was obviously villainy and charity in both, and yet crossing the river (the Mexicans don't call it the Rio Grande; they call it the Rio Bravo de Norte), no more than an idle traveller making his way south with a suitcase of dirty laundry, a sheaf of railway timetables, a map and a pair of leak-proof shoes, I felt as if I was acting out a significant image. Crossing a national boundary and seeing such a difference on the other side had something to do with it: truly, every human feature there had the resonance of metaphor.

It is only two hundred yards, but the smell of Nuevo Laredo rises. It is the smell of lawlessness; it is smokier, scented with chilis and cheap perfume. I had come from the tidy Texas town, and could see, almost as soon as I left it, the crowd of people at the far end of the bridge, the traffic jam, the cat-calling and horn-blowing, some people waiting to enter the United States, but most of them merely gaping across the frontier which is – and they know it – the poverty line.

Mexicans enter the United States because there is work for them there. They do it illegally – it is virtually impossible for a poor Mexican to enter legally, if his intention is to seek work. When they are caught, they are thrown into jail, serve a short sentence and then deported. Within days, they head back for the United States and the farms where they can always find work as low-paid day-labourers. The solution is simple: if we passed a law requiring United States farmers to hire only men with entry visas and work permits, there would be no problem. There is no such law. The farm lobby has made sure of that, for if there were no Mexicans to exploit how would these barrel-assed slavers be able to harvest their crops?

Closer, I could see the chaos particularized. The lounging soldiers and policemen only made it look more lawless, the noise was terrifying and, at once, the national characteristics were evident – the men had no necks, the policemen wore platform shoes and no prostitute was without her natural ally, an old woman or a cripple. It was cold and rainy; there was an atmosphere of impatience in the town; still February – the tourists were not due for months.

Halfway across the bridge, I had passed a rusty mailbox bearing the sign *Contraband*. This was for drugs. The penalties were posted in two languages – five years for soft drugs, fifteen for hard. I tried to peek inside, but unable to see anything I gave it a whack with my fist. It boomed: it must have been empty. I continued to the barrier, five cents in the turnstile slot, and as simply as boarding a bus I was in Mexico. Although I had been growing a moustache to make myself visibly Latin it was clearly not working. I was waved through the customs gate with four other gringos: we looked innocent.

There was no question that I had arrived, for while the neckless men and the swaggering cops and maimed animals had a certain sullen statelessness, the garlic-seller was the personification of Latin America. He was weedy, and wore a torn shirt and a greasy hat; he was very dirty; he screamed the same three words over and over. These attributes alone were unremarkable – he too had a counterpart in Cleveland. What distinguished him was the way he carried his merchandise. He had a garland of garlic cloves around his neck, and another around his waist, and ropes of them on his arms, and he shook them in his fists. He fought his way in and out of the crowd, the clusters of garlic bouncing on his body. Was there any better example of cultural difference than this man? At the Texas end of the bridge he would have been arrested for contravening some law of sanitation; here, he was ignored. What was so strange about wearing bunches of garlic around your neck? Perhaps nothing, except that he would not have done it if he was not a Mexican, and I would not have noticed it if I hadn't been an American.

Boys' Town – the Zone – is aptly named, since so much of it wickedly reflects the sexual nightmare-paradise of forbidden boyhood fantasy. It is fear and desire, a whole suburb of libido in which one can see the dire consequences in every greedy wish. It is the child who numbly craves the thrill of a lover's hug; but no child enjoys this fantasy without knowing the equal and opposite anxiety of being pursued by the same creature. Months of wintry weather and rain and off-season idleness had turned the prostitutes of the Zone into rather woeful examples of demon lovers. They were the howling, sleeve-tugging, arm-grabbing, jostling embodiment of the punitive part of sexual fantasy. I felt like Leopold Bloom steering his timid way through the limitless brothel of nighttown, for here one could not express an interest without risking humiliation. What made it worse for me was that I was merely curious; intending neither to condemn nor encourage, I was mistaken for that most pathetic of emotionally damaged souls, the near-sighted voyeur, a kind of sexual barnacle fastening my attention upon the meat market. *Just looking*, I'd say; but prostitutes have no patience with this attitude.

'Mister!'

'Sorry, I have to catch a train.'

'What time is it leaving?'

'About an hour.'

'That's plenty of time – mister!'

The urchins, the old ladies, the cripples, the sellers of lottery tickets, the frantic dirty youths, the men selling trays of switchblades, the tequila bars and incessant racketing music, the hotels reeking of bedbugs – the frenzy threatened to overwhelm me. I had to admit a certain fascination, and yet I feared that I would have to pay for my curiosity. *If you're not interested in this*, said a pretty girl hiking up her skirt with a casually lazy gesture, *why are you here?*

It was a good question and, as I had no answer, I left. I went to the office of Mexican Railways to buy my train ticket. The town was in great disrepair – no building was without a broken window, no street without a wrecked car, no gutter not choked with garbage; and in this clammy season, without any heat to justify its squalor or give it romance, it was cruelly ugly. But it is our bazaar, not Mexico's. It requires visitors.

Some citizens remain pure. Paying for my sleeper on the Aztec Eagle, I mentioned to the friendly manageress that I had just come from the Zone.

She rolled her eyes and then said, 'Shall I tell you something? I do not know where that place is.'

'It's not far. You just –'

'Don't tell me. I have been here two years. I know my home, I know my office, I know my church. That's all I need.'

She said that my time would be better spent looking at the curios than idling in the Zone. On my way to the station, I took her advice. Inevitably there were baskets and postcards and switchblade knives; but there were also plaster dogs and plaster Christs, carvings of women squatting, religious junk of every description, including rosaries the size of a ship's hawser with beads like baseballs, rained-on ironwork rusting on sidewalk stands, and gloomy plaster saints – martyred rather savagely by the people who had painted them, and each bearing the inscription *Souvenir of Nuevo Laredo*. A curio (the word, practically self-explanatory, is short for 'curiosity') is something that has no purpose other than to prove that you arrived: the coconut carved with an ape's face, the combustible ashtray, the sombrero – they are useless without the Nuevo Laredo inscription, but a good deal more vulgar than anything I saw in the Zone.

Not far from the station there was a man melting tubes of glass and drawing them thin and making model cars. His skill amounted almost to artistry, but the result – always the same car – lacked any imagination. The delicate work, this glass filigree, took hours; he laboured to make what could have been something beautiful, into a ridiculous souvenir. Had he ever made anything else?

'No,' he said. 'Only this car. I saw a picture of it in a magazine.'

I asked him when he had seen the picture.

'No one ever asked me that question before! It was ten years ago. Or more.'

'Where did you learn to do this?'

'In Puebla – not here.' He looked up from his blowtorch. 'Do you think a person could learn anything here in Nuevo Laredo? This is one of the traditional arts of Puebla. I have taught my wife and children to do it. My wife makes little pianos, my son makes animals.'

Over and over again, the same car, piano, animal. It would not have been so disturbing if it was a simple case of mass-producing the objects. But enormous skill and patience went into the making of what was in the end no more than junk. It seemed a great waste, but not very different from the Zone which turned lovely little girls into bad-tempered and rapacious hags.

Earlier that afternoon I had left my suitcase at the station restaurant. I had asked for the baggage department. A Mexican girl at a table on which someone had spewed pushed her tin plate of beans aside and said, 'This is it.' She had given me a scrap of paper and written *PAUL* in lipstick on the suitcase. I had no lively hope of ever seeing it again.

Now, trying to reclaim it, I gave the scrap of paper to a different girl. This one laughed at the paper and called a cross-eyed man over to examine it. He laughed, too.

I said, 'What's so funny?'

'We can't read her writing,' said the cross-eyed man.

'She writes in Chinese,' said the girl. She scratched her stomach and smiled at the paper. 'What does that say – fifty or five?'

'Let's call it five,' I said. 'Or we can ask the girl. Where is she?'

'Chee' – now the cross-eyed man was speaking in English – 'chee go to the veech!'

They thought this was hysterically funny.

'My suitcase,' I said. 'Where is it?'

The girl said, 'Gone', but before I could react, she giggled and dragged it out of the kitchen.

The sleeping car of The Aztec Eagle was a hundred yards down the track, and I was out of breath when I reached it. My English leak-proof shoes, specially bought for this trip, had sprung a leak; my clothes were wet. I had carried the suitcase on my head, coolie-style, but all that served to do was provoke a migraine and funnel rainwater into my collar.

A man in a black uniform stood in the doorway, barring my way. 'You can't get on,' he said. 'You haven't been through Customs.'

This was true, although I wondered how he could possibly have known this.

I said, 'Where is Customs?'

He pointed to the far end of the flooded track, and said disgustedly, 'Over there.'

I heaved the suitcase onto my head again and certain that I could get no wetter splashed back to the station platform. 'Customs?' I asked. A lady peddling bubble-gum and cookies laughed at me. I asked a little boy. He covered his face. I asked a man with a clipboard. He said, 'Wait.'

Rain dribbled through holes in the platform roof and Mexicans carted bales of their belongings and shoved them through the windows of Second Class. And yet, for an express train with a high reputation, there were not many passengers in evidence. The station was dingy and nearly deserted. The bubble-gum seller talked to the fried chicken seller; barefoot children played tag; it continued to rain – and the rain was not a brisk purifying downpour, but a dark tedious drizzle, like flecks of falling soot, which seemed to taint everything it touched.

Then I saw the man in the black uniform who had barred my entry to the sleeping car. He was wet now and looked furious.

'I don't see the Customs,' I said.

He showed me a tube of lipstick and said, 'This is Customs.'

Without inquiring further, he franked my suitcase with a slash of lipstick, then straightened and groaned and said, 'Hurry up, the train is about to leave.'

'Sorry, have I been keeping you waiting?'

The sleeping cars – there were two – were old American ones, from a railway in the States which had gone bankrupt. The compartments had deep armchairs and art-deco angles and three-sided mirrors, and were not only handsome but comfortable and well-carpeted. Everything I had seen in Nuevo Laredo seemed to be in a state of dereliction; nothing maintained, nothing cared-for. Yet this old train with its hand-me-down sleeping cars was in good condition, and in a few years would qualify as an antique in an excellent state of preservation. It had happened by accident: the Mexicans did not have the money to rebuild sleeping cars in chrome and plastic, as Amtrak had done, but by keeping them in trim they had managed to preserve the art-deco originality.

Most of the compartments were empty. Walking through the cars just before the whistle blew, I saw a Mexican family, some children travelling with their mother, a pair of worried-looking American tourists, and a winking middle-aged lady in a fake leopard-skin coat. In the bedroom across the corridor from mine there was an old woman and her pretty companion, a girl of about twenty-five. The old woman was flirtatious with me and sharp with the girl, who I supposed was her daughter. The girl was desperately shy, and her drab clothes (the old woman wore a mink around her neck) and her lovely face with its sallow English sadness, gave her expression a sort of passionate purity. All the way to Mexico City I tried to talk to this girl, but each time the old woman interrupted with cackling questions and never allowed the girl to reply. I decided that the girl's submissiveness was more than daughterly obedience: she was a servant, maintaining an anxious silence. Her eyes were green, and I think that even that aged woman's vanity could not have prevented her from knowing how attractive this girl was, or the true motive for my questions. There was something Russian and old-fashioned and impenetrable about this pair.

I was in my compartment, sipping tequila, and thinking how – so close to the United States (I could see the department stores on eroded bluffs of Laredo from the station) – everything had become so different, such slaphappy Mexican dishevelment. There was a knock at the door.

'Excuse me.' It was the conductor, and as he spoke he bustled into the compartment. He was still bustling, still speaking. 'I'm just going to put this up there.'

He carried a large paper shopping bag in which there were stuffed many smaller bags. He grinned and held it chest-high. He motioned to the luggage rack above the sink.

I said, 'I was going to put my suitcase up there.'

'No problem! You can put your suitcase under the bed. Look, let me do it.'

He got to his knees and pushed the suitcase out of sight, remarking on what a nice fit it was. I had not thought to remind him that this was my compartment.

'What's that?' I asked.

He clutched his bag more tightly and grinned again. 'This?' he said breezily. 'Some things, that's all.' He slid the bag onto the luggage rack – it was too plump to fit under the bed – and said, 'No problem, okay?'

It filled the luggage rack. I said, 'I don't know.'

I tugged at the opening and tried to peek inside the bag. With an insincere laugh, he put his hand on my shoulder and eased me away.

'It's all right!' He was still laughing, now with a kind of shrewd gratitude.

I said, 'Why don't you put it somewhere else?'

'It's much better here,' he said. 'Your suitcase is small. That's a good idea – always travel with a small suitcase. It fits beautifully down there.'

'What *is* this thing?'

He did not reply. And he had not removed his hand from my shoulder. Now he applied gentle pressure and sat me down. He stepped backwards, looked left and right along the corridor, stepped forward and leaned over and in breathy Spanish said, 'It's fine. You're a tourist. No problem.'

'Very well then.' I smiled at him, I smiled at the bag.

He stopped laughing. I think he became alarmed at my willingness to accept the bag. He half-closed the compartment door and said, 'Don't say anything.'

He put a finger to his lips and sucked air.

'Say anything?' I started to get up. 'To whom?'

He motioned me back to my armchair. '*Don't say anything.*'

He shut the door.

I looked at the bag.

A moment later, there was a knock at the door. The same conductor, a new grin: 'Dinner is served!'

He waited, and when I left the compartment he locked the door.

It was in the dining car that I tried to strike up a conversation with the green-eyed girl. The old woman fielded my questions. I had two Bohemian beers and the carcass of a scrawny chicken. I tried again. And I noticed that when the old woman replied she always said, 'I', not 'we' – 'I am going to Mexico City,' 'I have been in Nuevo Laredo.' So the green-eyed girl was almost certainly a servant, part of the old woman's baggage. Concentrating on this problem, I barely noticed that three uniformed men had entered the dining car; I saw them – pistols, moustaches, truncheons, no necks – and then they were gone: Mexico was full of men in ambiguous uniforms – they seemed to be part of the landscape.

'I live in Coyoacan,' said the old woman. Her eating had removed her lipstick; she was putting on more.

'Didn't Trotsky live there?' I said.

A man in a white steward's smock appeared at my elbow.

'Go back to your compartment. They want you.'

'Who wants me?'

'Customs.'

'I've been through Customs.' With an intimation of trouble, I spoke in English.

'You no espick Espanish?'

'No.'

The old woman looked sharply at me but said nothing.

'Da men. Dey wants you,' said the steward.

'I'll just finish this beer.'

He moved my glass out of reach. 'Now.'

The three armed Customs men were waiting for me outside my compartment. The conductor was nowhere in sight, and yet the compartment had been unlocked: obviously he had skipped out and left me to face the music.

'Good evening,' I said – they exchanged grimaces on hearing my English. I took out my passport, rail ticket, health card and waved them to deflect their attention. 'You'll find that I have a Mexican Tourist Card, smallpox vaccination, valid passport – look.' I jerked the concertina of extra pages out of my passport and showed them the Burmese postage stamps glued to my Burma visa, my garish re-entry permit for Laos, the chit that gave me unlimited access to Guatemala.

This distracted them for a moment – they muttered and turned pages – and then the ugliest one of the three stepped into the compartment and whacked his billy club against the luggage rack.

'Is this yours?'

I decided not to understand Spanish. To give a truthful answer would have put the conductor into the soup – probably where he belonged. But earlier in the day I had seen a bullying customs officer tormenting an elderly Mexican with a series of impromptu humiliations. The old man was with a young boy, and their suitcase contained about thirty tennis balls. The customs officer made them empty the suitcase; the tennis balls rolled in all directions, and while the two victims chased them, the customs officer kicked the tennis balls and repeated in Spanish *I am not satisfied with your explanation!* This gave me an unmerciful hatred for all Mexican customs officials that was far greater than my powerful resentment for the conductor who was the cause of my present problem.

Without saying yes or no, I said very rapidly in English, 'That's been there for some time, about two hours.'

Hearing *ours*, he said in Spanish, 'It belongs to you, then.'

'I've never seen it before in my life.'

'It's theirs,' he called out in Spanish. The men in the corridor grunted.

I smiled at the man and said, 'I think there's a great misunderstanding here.' I stooped and pulled my suitcase out from under the seat and said, 'Look, I've been through customs already – there's the lipstick smear on the side. I'd be glad to open it for you. I've got some old clothes, some maps –'

In Spanish, he said, 'Don't you speak Spanish?'

In English, I said, 'I've only been in Mexico one day. We can't expect miracles, can we? I'm a tourist.'

'This one's a tourist,' he yelled to the corridor.

As we talked, the train sped along and lurched, throwing us against each other. When he rocked, the customs officer's hands went to his billy club and his pistol for balance.

His eyes were very tiny and his voice full of threat as he said slowly in Spanish, 'So all this is yours, including that parcel up there?'

In English I said, 'What is it exactly you'd like to see?'

He looked again at the bag. He squeezed it. There was a clinking sound inside. He was very suspicious, but he was also sad because, as a tourist, I was entitled to privacy. That conductor knew the ropes.

The customs officer said, 'Have a good trip.'

'Same to you.'

When they left, I went back to the dining car and finished my beer. The waiters were whispering as they collected the plates from the tables. We came to a station, and when we pulled out I was sure the customs officers had left the train.

I hurried to my compartment, dying to see what the bag contained. I felt, after what had happened, that I had every right to look in. The car was empty, my compartment as I had left it. I locked the door behind me and stood on the toilet to get a better look at the luggage rack. The shopping bag was gone.

We had left Nuevo Laredo at twilight. The few stations we stopped at later in the evening were so poorly lighted I could not make out their names on the signboards. I stayed up late reading *The Thin Man*, which I had put aside in Texas. I had lost the plot entirely, but the drinking still interested me. All the characters drank – they met for cocktails, they conspired in speakeasies, they talked about drinking, and they were often drunk. Nick Charles, Hammett's detective, drank the most. He complained about his hangovers, and then drank to cure his hangover. He drank before breakfast, and all day, and the last thing he did at night was have a drink. One morning he feels especially rotten; he says complainingly, 'I must have gone to bed sober,' and then pours himself a stiff drink. The drinking distracted me from the clues in the way President Banda's facial tic prevented me from ever hearing anything he said. But why so much alcohol in this whodunnit? Because it was set – and written – during Prohibition. Evelyn Waugh once commented that the reason *Brideshead Revisited* had so many sumptuous meals in it was because it was written during a period of war-time rationing, when the talk was of all the wonderful things you could do with soya beans. By midnight, I had finished *The Thin Man* and a bottle of tequila.

Two blankets did not keep me warm in my compartment. I woke three or four times shivering, believing – it is so easy to be deluded on a dark train – that I was back home in Medford. In the morning, I was still cold, the shades were drawn and I was not sure which country I was in. I pushed up the shade and saw the sun rising behind a green tree. It was a solitary tree, and the climbing sun gave it an emblematic quality in the stony land-scape; it was a pale perpendicular, studded with fruit like hand grenades, but as I watched it, it thickened and grew less tree-like and finally stiffened into a cactus.

There were more cactuses, some like burnt-out torches and others the more familiar candelabras. There were no trees. The sun, so early in the morning, was bright and gave a blueness to the hills which twisted off into the distance, and a glitter to the stiletto spikes on the cacti. The long morning shadows lay as still and dark as lakes and patterned the rough ground with straight margins. I wondered whether it was cold outside until I saw a man – the only human in that desert – in a donkey cart, rumbling over a road that might well have been a creek-bed. The man was dressed warmly, his sombrero jammed over his ears, a maroon scarf wrapped around his face, and a wadded jacket of brilliantly coloured rags.

It was still early. As the sun moved higher in the sky, the day became warmer and woke the smells, until that curious Mexican mixture of sparkle and decay, blue sky and bedragglement, asserted itself. In the bright air was the dismal town of Bocas. Here were four green trees, and a church on a steep hill, its whitewash reddened by dust, and cactuses so large cows were tethered to their spiky trunks. But most of the town was mimi-cry: the church was a house, the houses were sheds, most trees were cactuses, and without topsoil the crops – red peppers and corn – were skeletal. Some children in torn clothes skipped over to look at the train, and then, hearing the honk of a horn, ran to the sandy road to see a heavily-laden Coca-Cola truck – up to its axles in sand – straining towards the town's one store.

Mexicans habitually site the town dump along the railway tracks. The detritus of the very poor is unimaginably vile, and though it smoulders it is far too loathsome to catch fire. In the Bocas dump, which was part of Bocas station, two dogs yanked at one heap of garbage, two pigs at another. These animals went on rooting – keeping their distance – and I noticed that both dogs were lame, and one pig's ear was missing. The mutilated animals were appropriate to the mutilated town, the ragged children, the tumbledown sheds. The Coca-Cola truck had parked. Now the children were watching a man dragging a frantic pig across the tracks. The pig's hind legs were roped, and the man yanked the screaming creature backwards.

I do not consider myself to be an animal-lover, but it is a long way from disliking them to maiming and torturing them. And I came to see a resemblance between the condition of domestic animals and the condition of the people who mistreated them. It was the same contempt, and the whipped dog and the woman carrying wood had the same fearful eyes. And it was these beaten people who beat their animals.

'Bocas,' said the conductor 'it min kish.' He smacked his lips and laughed.

In Spanish I said, 'Why didn't you tell me you are a smuggler?'

'I am not a smuggler.'

'What about the contraband you put in my room?'

'It is not contraband. It is just some things.'

'Why did you put it in my room?'

'It is better in your room than mine.'

'Then why did you take it out of my room?'

He was silent. I was going to let up on him, but I remembered again that he might have been the cause of my being in the Nuevo Laredo jail this morning.

I said, 'You put it in the room because it is contraband.'

'No.'

'And you are a smuggler.'

'No.'

'You are afraid of the police.'

'Yes.'

The ragged man outside the train had dragged his pig across the tracks. Now he was dragging the pig backwards to a pick-up truck parked near the station. The pig howled and scattered stones with its scrabbling trotters; it sounded demented because it was intelligent enough to know it was doomed.

'The police bother us,' said the conductor. 'They don't bother you. Look, this is not the United States – these men want money. Understand?' He made a claw of his brown hand and snatched with it. 'That is what they want – money.'

'What was in the bag? Drugs?'

'Drugs!' He spat out the door to show me how ridiculous the question was.

'What then?'

'Kitchen utensils.'

'You smuggle kitchen utensils?'

'I don't smuggle anything. I buy kitchen utensils in Laredo. I take them home.'

'Don't you have kitchen utensils in Mexico?'

'In Mexico we have shit,' he said. He nodded and then said, 'Of course we have kitchen utensils. But they are expensive. In America they are cheap.'

'The customs man asked if they were mine.'

'What did you tell him?'

'You said, "Don't say anything." I did not say anything.'

'See? No problem!'

'They were very angry.'

'Of course. But what can they do? You're a tourist.'

The train whistle sounded, drowning the pig's cries. We started out of Bocas.

The conductor said, 'It is easy for you tourists.'

'It is easy for you smugglers because of us tourists.'

Back in Texas, with a sweep of his hand, taking in Main Street and the new shopping centre and a score of finance companies, the Texan says, 'All this was nothing but desert a few years ago.' The Mexican pursues a different line. He urges you to ignore the squalor of the present and reflect on the glories of the past. As we entered San Luis Potosí towards noon on the day that had started cold and was now cloudless in a parching heat, I noticed the naked children and the lamed dogs and the settlement in the train-yard, which was fifty boxcars. By curtaining the door with faded laundry, and adding a chicken coop and children, and turning up the volume on his radio, the Mexican makes a bungalow of his boxcar and pretends it is home. It is a frightful slum, and stinks of excrement, but the Mexican man standing at the door of the Aztec Eagle with me was smiling. 'Many years ago,' he said, 'this was a silver mine.'

The boxcars, now closer together, became horrific, and even

the geraniums, the women preparing food in the doorways, the roosters crowing from the couplings, did not mask the cruelty of the fact that the boxcars were going nowhere. They were cattle cars, and here in San Luis Potosí they parodied their original function.

The Mexican man was enthusiastic. He was getting off – he lived here. This was a famous place, he said. There were many beautiful churches in San Luis Potosí; very *typical*, very *pretty*, very *ancient*.

'Are there any Catholics?' I asked.

He gave me a nasty little three-beat laugh and an anti-clerical wink. 'Too many!'

'Why are these people living in cattle cars?'

'Over there,' he said, pointing past the tops of the boxcars, 'in the Plaza Hidalgo is a fantastic building. The Government Palace. Benito Juarez was there – you have heard of him. In this very place he ordered the execution of Maximilian.'

He tugged his moustache and smiled with civic pride. But Mexican civic pride, always backward-looking, has its roots in xenophobia. Few countries on earth have greater cause to be xenophobic. And in a sense this hatred of foreigners had its origins here in San Luis Potosí. Like many reformers, Benito Juarez ran into debt: it seems almost to amount to a condition of reforming governments. When he suspended payment on the national debt he was invaded by the combined forces of Spain, Britain and France. Ultimately only France's armies stayed and, seeing that he could not defend Mexico City, Juarez retreated to Potosí. In June 1863, the French army entered Mexico City and made the Archduke Maximilian of Austria the new Emperor of Mexico. Maximilian's rule was muddled and contradictory, a tyranny of good intentions. But he was weak; he needed the French presence to keep him in power and commanded little popular support (though it has been said that the Indians liked him because he was blond, like Quetzalcoatl – Cortez enjoyed the same bizarre notoriety for his resemblance to the Plumed Serpent). Much worse, Maximilian was a foreigner. Mexican xenophobia is far stronger than any tendency towards internal bickering, and it was not long before Maximilian was being denounced from the pulpits of Catholic churches as a syphilitic. His wife, the Empress Carlotta, had not borne him any children: that was the proof. Carlotta made a desperate trip to Europe to rally support for her husband, but her appeal was ignored and she lost her mind and died insane. For much of this time, America was engaged in the Civil War as well as urging the French to withdraw from Mexico. After the Civil War, America – which had never recognized Maximilian – began arming Juarez, and in the guerrilla war that followed in Mexico, Maximilian was captured and shot at Querétaro. This was in 1867; Juarez had retained San Luis Potosí as his capital.

America's help might have endeared us to the cause of Mexican nationalism. After all, Juarez was a Zapotec Indian, ethnically pure, and was one of the few Mexican rulers who died a natural death. But his successor, the devious and greedy Porfirio Diaz, welcomed – for a price – those whom we now think of as philanthropists and trail-blazers, the Hearsts, U.S. Steel, Anaconda Corporation, Standard Oil, and the Guggenheims. Although Ralph Waldo Emerson was writing at the time of Santa Ana's paranoid rule (Santa Ana demanded to be known as 'His Most Serene Highness' – Mexican dictators frequently affected regal titles: the creole butcher Iturbide styled himself 'Agustín I'), his lines are apposite to the Guggenheim adventure:

> But who is he that prates
> Of the culture of mankind,
> Of better arts and life?
> Go, blindworm, go,
> Behold the famous States
> Harrying Mexico
> With rifle and with knife!

Mexico under Diaz had never been so peaceful, so industrialized, or so wretched. Spanish America is cursed with the grandiosity of crooked statesmen; the Indians and peasants remain Indians and peasants. In the bloody revolution that Diaz's dictatorship made inevitable – the peasants' revolt of 1910, described so turgidly in B. Traven's *The Rebellion of the Hanged* and his five other tendentious 'Jungle Novels' – Diaz crept secretly aboard a train he himself had built and fled incognito to Veracruz and his exile in Paris.

'And here' – the Mexican man was talking – 'in Potosí, our national anthem was written.' The train had come to rest beside a long platform. 'And this is one of the most modern railway stations in the country.'

He was speaking of the building itself, a mausoleum of stupefied travellers, which bore on its upper walls frescoes by Fernando Leal. It was very much a Mexican style of interior decoration for public buildings, the preference for mob scenes and battle pieces instead of wall-paper. In this one, a frenzied crowd seemed to be dismantling two locomotives made of rubber. Pandemonium under a thundery sky; muskets, arrows, pickaxes, and symbolic lightning bolts; probably Benito Juarez leading a charge. If Mexican painters used conventional canvases, I never saw the result. 'Diego Rivera's frescoes in the patio of the Ministry of Education are chiefly remarkable for their quantity,' Aldous Huxley wrote in *Beyond the Mexique Bay*. 'There must be five or six acres of them.' From the wall art I saw in Mexico I concluded that the painters had drawn much of their inspiration from Gulley Jimson.

I went into the plaza and bought a Mexican newspaper and four bananas. The rest of the passengers bought comic books. Back on the platform, waiting for the train to leave, I noticed that the sallow-faced girl with green eyes was holding a magazine she had just bought. When I saw it was a comic book most of my ardour died: I find it discouraging to see a pretty woman reading a comic book. But the old woman was carrying nothing. Perhaps the green-eyed girl was holding the old woman's comic book? I became interested in the girl once more, and sidled up to her.

'It was cold last night.'

The girl said nothing.

The old woman said, 'There is no heating on this train.'

I said to the girl, 'At least it is warm now.'

The girl made a tube of the comic book and clutched it.

The old woman said, 'You speak English extremely well. I wish you would teach me some English. I suppose I am too old to learn!' She looked at me slyly from beneath the fringes of her shawl and then boarded the train. The girl obediently followed, lifting the old woman's hem from the dusty steps.

The lady in the leopard-skin coat was also on the platform. She too had a comic book in her hand. She smiled at me and said, 'You're an American. I can tell.'

'Yes, from Massachusetts.'

'Very far!'

'I am going even farther.' At this point I had only been travelling for six days; I grew anxious when I remembered how distant Patagonia was.

'In Mexico?'

'Yes, then Guatemala, Panama, Peru –' I stopped there; it seemed unlucky to speak of destinations.

She said, 'I've never been to Central America.'

'What about South America?'

'Never. But Peru – it is in Central America, no? Near Venezuela?'

'I don't think so.'

She shook her head doubtfully. 'How long is your vacation?'

'Two months, maybe more.'

'Shoo! You will have seen enough!'

The whistle blew. We hurried to the stairs.

'Two months vacation!' she said. 'That's the kind of job I'd like to have. What do you do?'

'I'm a teacher.'

'You're a lucky teacher.'

'That's true.'

In my compartment I unfolded *El Sol de San Luis* and saw, on the front page, a picture of a sinking ship in Boston harbour, and the headline, CHAOS AND DEATH FOLLOW A VIOLENT STORM IN THE US. The story was frightening: two feet of snow in Boston, a number of deaths, and a power-cut that had plunged the city into darkness; one of the worst storms in Boston's history. It made me feel even more like a fugitive, guilty and smug having made a successful escape, as if I had known in advance that I was fleeing chaos and death for this sunny train ride. I put the paper down and looked out the window. In a biscuit-coloured gully in the foreground a large flock of goats champed on tufts of grass, and the herd-boy squatted under a tree. The sun burned in a cloudless sky. Further on, there were the remains of an abandoned silver mine and a wild yellow desert hemmed in by rocky hills, and yucca-like bushes from which tequila is made, and then cactuses in grotesque configurations – great stiff things that looked like swollen trees on which ping-pong paddles are growing, or sword clusters, or bunches of bristling pipe-fittings.

For the next half hour I read about the snow storm, and from time to time – between paragraphs, or turning a page – I would look up to rest my eyes and see a man ploughing dust using two steers and a small plough-blade, or a group of women on their knees, doing their laundry in a shallow stream, or a boy leading a burro loaded with firewood. Then the story: *Cars were left stranded . . . Offices closed . . . Some people suffered heart attacks . . . Ice and snow blocked roads . . .*

I heard a glockenspiel. It was the steward from the dining car, tapping his bundle of chimes. 'Lunch!' he yelled. 'First call for lunch!'

Lunch and the morning paper in the Aztec Eagle: this was perfect. A heat haze lay over the plains which were green with cultivation; and it was now so hot that we were the only thing moving. There was no one in the fields; and at the streams no women doing laundry, though their suds remained in the shallows. We passed Querétaro, where Maximilian was shot, and here dark tough-looking Mexicans sat glowering from doorways of houses. They were quite unlike the gold-toothed buffoons I had seen in Nuevo Laredo, and watching from the shadowy interiors of houses they seemed sinister and disapproving under the brims of their sombreros. Outside those houses there was little shade, and on this afternoon of withering sunlight nothing stirred. We were soon in semi-desert, travelling fast, and through the heat haze I could see the pencilled outline of the Sierra Madre Oriental. In the middle of this great sun-baked plain a small burro was tethered near a tiny tree; a still creature in a puddle of shade.

Lunch had ended. The three waiters and the cook drowsed at

69

a corner table. I had risen and was walking through the dining car when the couplings crashed, and made me stagger. The train came to a sudden jolting halt, knocking the salt and pepper shakers to the floor.

'A fat little bull,' said a waiter, opening one eye. 'But it's too late to worry about him now.'

The Aztec Eagle climbed through the Cerro Rajon, a region of steep scrub-covered hills. It moved slowly enough on these circular climbs for me to pick the wild-flowers along the track, but when it descended it did so with loud racketing speed and a rhumba from the coupling under the vestibule where I stood for the air. The haze had lifted in this cooler altitude, and I could see for fifty miles or more across a blue-green plain. Because the train kept switching back and forth on the hillside, the view continually altered, from this plain to a range of hills and to fertile valleys with tall feathery trees in columns along the banks of frothing rivers, and occasionally a deep gorge of vertical granite slabs. The trees were eucalyptus, as African as the view, which was an enormity of stone and space.

There was no one at the tidy station at Huichapan: no one boarded, no one got off, and only the signalman with his flag ventured out of the train. In this, as in other places, the laundry washed that morning at the river was set out to dry, Mexican-style: it was spiked upon the cactuses and transformed them into crouching figures in clean rags. The train trembling importantly at the platform at Huichapan gave the place a certain grandeur, but when we left, and I looked back, a hot solitude seemed to descend on the little station, as the dust sifted to the ground and the cactuses in their tatters remained in hunched postures, like a mimicry of ghost passengers left behind.

During that long afternoon, I read *The Devil's Dictionary*, by Ambrose Bierce, a grimly humorous book of self-congratulatory cynicism. I had turned first to *Railroad*, which Bierce defines as 'the chief of many mechanical devices enabling us to get away from where we are to where we are no better off'. Two feet of snow in Boston. Chaos and death. Power cuts in sub-freezing weather. And outside my window here, the Mexican sunshine and old hills and pots of crimson geraniums in the window boxes of huts. Bierce goes on, 'For this purpose the railroad is held in highest favour by the optimist, for it permits him to make the transit with great expedition.' Bierce is never brilliant; he is sometimes funny, but more often he misses the mark, forces the point, and ends up sounding strained and pompous. He has been called 'the American Swift', but his fun-poking facetiousness hardly qualifies him for that description. He was not as angry or as crazy or as learned as Swift, and he lived in a time of simpler literary tastes. If America in the nineteenth century had been complicated enough to require a Swift, she would have produced one. Every country has the writers she requires and deserves, which is why Nicaragua, in two hundred years of literacy, has produced one writer – a mediocre poet. I found the jokes by Bierce about women and children conventionally stupid, but it interested me that I was reading this book in a part of Mexico in which he had vanished. Every line sounded like a hastily scribbled epitaph, although his real epitaph was in a letter he wrote in 1913, just before he disappeared. 'To be a Gringo in Mexico,' wrote Bierce – he was seventy-one years old – 'ah, that is euthanasia!'

Towards Tula, a treeless desert of long hills rose into peaks like pyramids. This was the capital of the Toltecs, with pillars and temples and a towering pyramid. The pyramids of Mexico – at Teotihuacan and Uxmal and Chichén-Itzá – are clearly the efforts of people aspiring to make mountains; they match the landscape, and in places mock it. The god-king must demonstrate that he is capable of duplicating divine geography, and the pyramids were the visible proof of this attempt. In the wilderness of Tula, the landscape was in ruins, but the work of the Toltecs would survive into another epoch.

Just before darkness fell, I saw a field of upright swords. It might have been sisal, but more likely was the tequila plant whose fiery juice left me in an hallucinating daze.

The conductor – the smuggler – was all smiles when we arrived at Mexico City. He offered to carry my suitcase, he reminded me not to leave anything behind, he told me how much fun I would have in Mexico City. I did not reward his servility with a tip, and I think he knew as I thanked him coldly that he had overstepped himself in importuning me with his sack of contraband.

The station was huge and cold. I had been here before. Mexico City, with its twelve million people and ingenious beggars (sword-swallowers and fire-eaters perform their tricks on the pavement near bus-stops, to get pesos from people in line) is only in parts an attractive place. And the three-quarters of a million people who live in Netzahualcoyotl near the airport have the dubious distinction of inhabiting what has been called 'the largest slum in the western hemisphere'. I had no strong desire to see Mexico City again. It is, supremely, a place for getting lost in, a smog-plagued metropolis of mammoth proportions, which is perhaps why the two most determined exiles of this century; Leon Trotsky and B. Traven, chose Mexico City as their refuge.

If I am to arrive in a city, I prefer it to be in the early morning, with the whole day ahead of me. So, without a further thought, I went to the ticket counter in the lobby, bought a sleeper ticket to Veracruz and boarded the train. It was cheaper than a hotel room and, anyway, people said that Veracruz, on the Gulf Coast, was much warmer.

4 El Jarocho to Veracruz

Before I boarded the 'Jarocho' – the word means 'a boor; a rude person'; it is what the Veracruzians call themselves – I went to the restaurant in Buenavista Station and bought a box lunch. There wasn't time for me to eat before I left Mexico City, and there was no dining car on the Jarocho. But, even so, the box lunch was an error of judgement. I made a point not to repeat this mistake. The box was gaily decorated, and inside was one of those parody meals that are assembled by people who have a profound dedication of completeness and a total disregard for taste. Two ham sandwiches on stale bread, a semi-liquid egg, an unpeelable orange and a piece of mouldy cake. I made an incision in the orange with my Nuevo Laredo switchblade and used the juice to blunt my tequila. The rest I threw out of the window as soon as we left the station. I suppose that disgusting lunch was one of the penalties of my refusing to stay in Mexico City for longer than an hour. But I was no sightseer; I was glad to be on this sleeper to the coast. Travelling hungry was no fun, but tequila was a great appetite-killer. It also guaranteed solid slumber and lively dreams of fulfilment – its effect on me was more the wild-eyed numbness of a narcotic drug than the giddyness of alcohol – and when I awoke I would be in the middle of Veracruz.

With my feet up and my compartment filled with pipe smoke on that night express to Veracruz, leaving this foggy altitude for the humid heat and palm trees of the coast with two inches of orange-scented tequila in my glass, I felt supremely happy. The whistle shrieked, the sleeping car tipped on a bend and the curtains parted: darkness and a few glaring lights and a faint hint of danger which intensified the romance. I shot my switchblade open and carved a slice from the orange for my drink. I was on a

73

secret mission (now the tequila was starting to take effect), travelling incognito as a simple English teacher to carry out a tricky piece of Mexican reconnaissance. This shiv in my hand was a lethal weapon and I was drunk enough to believe that if anyone was foolish enough to jump me I'd have his guts for garters. The train, the atmosphere, my destination, my mood: it was all fantasy – ridiculous and pleasurable. And when I finished my drink I slipped the knife into the pocket of my black leather jacket and crept into the corridor to sneak a look at the other passengers.

There was a figure lurking near my door: a moustached man with a suspicious-looking box.

He said: 'Want a chocolate cookie?'

And the spell was broken.

'No thanks.'

'Go ahead. I've got plenty.'

To be polite I took one of his chocolate cookies. He was tall and friendly and said his name was Pepe. He was from Veracruz. He said he could tell that I was an American, but quickly added that it was not a reflection on my Spanish but rather the way I looked. It was too bad I was only going to Veracruz now, he said, because the carnival had just ended. I had missed a very wonderful thing. Bands – very loud bands! Dancing – in the streets! Parades – very long ones! Music – drums, horns, marimbas! Costumes – people dressed as princes and clowns and conquistadors! Also church services and eating of wonderful food, and drinking of fantastic tequila, and friendship of all kinds.

His description removed any sense of regret I might have had about missing the Veracruz carnival. I was relieved that I would not have to endure the vulgar spectacle, which I was sure would have depressed and annoyed me, or in any case kept me awake.

But I said, 'What a shame I missed it.'

'You can come back next year.'

'Of course.'

'Want another chocolate cookie?'

'No thanks. I haven't eaten this one yet.' I wanted him to go away. I waited a moment, yawned and said, 'I am very married.'

He looked oddly at me.

'Very married? Interesting.' But the look of puzzlement did not leave his face.

'Aren't you married?'

'I am only eighteen.'

This confused me. I said, 'Married – isn't that what you are when you want to go to bed?'

'You mean *tired*.'

'That's it.' The Spanish words sounded similar to me: *casado*, *cansado*; married, tired.

Yet this double-talk did the trick. He obviously thought I was insane. He said good-night, put his box of cookies under his arm and took himself away. I saw no other people in the sleeping car.

'The journey from Veracruz [to Mexico City] is to my mind the finest in the world from the point of view of spectacular effect,' writes the diabolist Aleister Crowley in his *Confessions*. Go to Veracruz during the day, people told me. See the cane fields and the Orizaba volcano; see the peasants and the gardens. But Latin America is full of volcanoes and cane-fields and peasants; at times, it seems as if there is little else to see. It struck me as a better idea to arrive in Veracruz at dawn; the Jarocho Express was a comfortable train and I had heard that my next connection, to Tapachula and the Guatemala border, was in a sorry state. I would have an extra day in Veracruz to prepare for that. And I *would* be prepared. The Jarocho Express was one of those trains – rarer now than they used to be – which you board feeling exhausted and disembark from feeling like a million dollars. I happened to be drunk in this Mexico City suburb; but the train was moving slowly: I would be sober in the morning in Veracruz.

The compartment was hot and steamy when I awoke; the window was fogged, and when I rubbed it I saw that dawn here was a foamy yellow light and the thin drizzle on the sodden green of a marsh. The clouds were mud-coloured and low and ragged, like dead hanks of Spanish moss. We were approaching the Gulf Coast; there were tall palms on the horizon, silly umbrellas in the rain.

The silence was perfect. Not even the train made a sound. But it was my ears – they hurt badly, and the feeling was that of having landed in a poorly pressurized plane. We had been at a very high altitude and, asleep, I had not been able to compensate by swallowing. Now at sea-level my eardrums, deaf to any chirp this morning, burned with pain.

Anxious to be away from the dirty window and the stuffy compartment, and believing that some deep breathing would be good for my ears, I went to the rear of the sleeping car. The vestibule window was open. I swallowed air and watched the slums go by. My ears cleared: now I could hear the drumroll of the train.

'Look at those people,' said the conductor.

There were shacks by the line, and wet chickens and sombre children. I wondered what the conductor would say next.

'They have the right idea. Look at them – that's the life!'

'What life?' All I saw were shacks and chickens and men whose hat brims were streaming with rain.

'Very tranquil,' he said, nodding in condescension towards the hovels. Truly patronizing people usually adopt a very sage tone when considering their victims. This Mexican squinted wisely and said, 'Very tranquil. Not like Mexico City. It is too rapid there – everyone going this way and that way. They do not know what life is all about. But look how peaceful this is.'

I said, 'How would you like to live in that house?'

It was not a house. It was a shack of cardboard and rusty tin. Holes had been punched in the tin to make windows, and broken bricks held bits of plastic over the leaky roof. A dog sniffed at some garbage near the door, where a fat haggard woman in a torn red sweater watched us pass. We had a glimpse of even greater horror inside.

'Ah!' the conductor said, and looked crushed.

I was not supposed to have asked him that. He had expected me to agree with him – yes, how tranquil! This tiny shack – how idyllic! Most Mexican friendliness seemed to depend on to what extent you agreed with what they said. Disagreement, or simple argument, was taken as a sign of aggression. Was it insecurity, I wondered, or that same mistrust of subtlety that made every painting into a four-acre fresco and every comic book into a violent woman-hating pamphlet. My Spanish was not bad, but I found it hard to hold a conversation with any Mexican that was not pure joshing or else something completely straightforward. One hot afternoon I hailed a taxi just outside of Veracruz, but before I gave him my destination, the driver said, 'Want a whore?'

'I'm tired,' I said. 'I'm also married.'

'I understand,' said the driver.

'Besides, I'll bet they're not pretty.'

'No,' he said, 'not pretty at all. But they're young. That's something.'

I had arrived in Veracruz at seven in the morning, found a hotel in the pretty Plaza Constitucion and gone for a walk. I had absolutely nothing to do: I did not know a soul in Veracruz, and the train to the Guatemalan border was not leaving for two days. Still, this did not seem a bad place. There are few tourist attractions in Veracruz; there is an old fort and, about two miles south, a beach. The guidebooks are circumspect about desscribing this fairly ugly city: one calls it 'exuberant', another 'picturesque'. It is a faded seaport, with slums and tacky modernity crowding the quaintly ruined buildings at its heart. Unlike any other Mexican city, it has pavement cafés, where forlorn children beg and marimba players complete the damage to your eardrums that was started on the descent from the heights of Orizaba. Mexicans treat stray children the way other people treat stray cats (Mexicans treat stray cats like vermin), taking them on their laps and buying them ice cream, all the while shouting to be heard over the noise of the marimbas.

Finding nothing in my plaza to divert me, I walked a mile to the Castle of San Juan de Ulua. Formerly an island – Cortes landed here during Holy Week in 1519 – the harbour has silted up so thoroughly it is now part of the mainland, with a connecting road and the greasy factories, the hovels and graffiti that Mexico appears to require of its urban areas. The Castle contains a permanent exhibit of Veracruz's past, a pictorial record of invasions, punitive missions and local military defeats. It was that most Mexican of enthusiasms – humiliation as history. If the engravings and old photographs showed how cynical and aggressive other countries – but mainly the United States – had been towards Mexico, the prominence of the exhibit in Veracruz invited the Mexican to a morning of wound-licking and self-contempt. Veracruz is known as 'the heroic city'. It is a poignant description: in Mexico a hero is nearly always a corpse.

It had been raining in an inconsequential way all morning, but before I left the castle the clouds lifted and whitened and broke into separate cauliflowers. I found a sunny rampart of the fort and read the paper. The news of the Boston blizzard was still very bad, though here in sight of glittering water and listing palm trees – a fresh sea breeze carrying gulls' cries to me – I found it hard to conjure up a vision of a winter-darkened city or cars buried by snow or the physical pain of the bitter cold. Pain is the hardest feeling to remember: the memory is merciful. Another headline read, BAD END TO THE CARNIVAL and under it *Ten Sex Maniacs Captured*, and under that, *But Another 22 On The Loose*. The story was that a gang of 32 sex maniacs had spent Shrove-tide dragging women ('mothers and their daughters') into bushes and raping them. 'Many women were attacked by the crazies in their hotel rooms.' The gang called themselves 'The Tubes'. The significance of this name escaped me – I wondered whether it had some arch sexual resonance. The ten who had been captured appeared in a colour photograph. They were fairly ordinary-looking youths, sheepishly hunched in baggy sweatshirts and blue-jeans, and might well have been the losing side in a fraternity tug-of-war – a suggestion that was as strong in their glum, smirking faces as in their sweatshirts, which were printed with the names of American colleges, *University of Iowa, Texas State, Amherst College*. They were called 'maniacs' in a dozen places on the page, though none had been convicted. Their full names were given, and after each name – it is customary in Mexican crime reporting – an alias: 'The Chinaman', 'The King', 'The Warbler', 'The Pole', 'The Brave One', 'The Horse', 'The Lion', 'The Magician', and so forth. Stylishness was important to the Mexican male, but a Tube called the Warbler, wearing a college sweatshirt to rape women on a solemn Christian holiday in Veracruz, seemed to me a curious mixture of styles.

Later that day I saw something equally bizarre. I passed a church where there were eight new pick-up trucks being blessed by a priest, with a bucket of holy water, who was attended by four acolytes with candles and crosses. In itself, this was not strange – houses are blessed in Boston, and every year the fishing-fleet is blessed in Gloucester. But what I found odd was that after the priest sprinkled holy water on the doors, the wheels, the rear flap and the hood, the owner unfastened the hood and the priest ducked under it to douse the engine with holy water, as if the Almighty was incapable of penetrating the bodywork of the vehicle. Perhaps they regarded God as just another un-reliable foreigner, and extended their mistrust to Him, as they did to all other gringos. Certainly Jesus was a gringo: the proof was on every pious postcard.

To flatter myself that I had something important to do in Veracruz I made a list of provisions that I intended to buy for my trip to Guatemala. Then I remembered I had no ticket. I went immediately to the railway station.

'I cannot sell you a ticket today,' said the man at the window.

'When can I buy one?'

'When are you leaving?'

'Thursday.'

'Fine. I can sell you one Thursday.'

'Why can't I buy one today?'

'It is not done.'

'What if there are no seats on Thursday?'

He laughed. 'On *that* train there are always seats.'

That was the day I met the taxi driver who said he had a whore for me who was 'not pretty at all'. I said I was not in-terested, but what else was there to do in Veracruz? He said I should go to the Castle. I said I had been to the Castle. Go for a walk around the city, he said: lovely churches, good restaurants, bars full of prostitutes. I shook my head. 'Too bad you were not here a few days ago,' he said. 'The carnival was fantastic.'

'Maybe I'll go swimming,' I said.

'Good idea,' he said. 'We have the best beach in the world.'

It is called Mocambo; I paid it a visit the next morning. The beach itself was clean and uncluttered, the water chromatic with oil-slick. There were about fifty people on the mile of sand, but no one was swimming. This was a caution to me. The beach was flanked by a row of identical restaurants. I had fish soup and was joined by a man whom I took to be a friendly soul until he said that for two dollars he would snap my picture.

I said, 'I'll give you fifty cents.'

He took my picture.

He said, 'You like Veracruz food?'

'This soup has a fish-head in it.'

'We always eat fish-heads.'

'I haven't eaten a fish-head since I was in Africa.'

He frowned, insulted by the comparison, and went to another table.

I rented a beach chair and watched children throwing sand and wished that I was on my way south. It was a fraudulent pleasure, idling on this empty beach. I hated to think that I was killing time, but like the De Vries character I had always admired, I was doing it in self-defence. A bus drew up to the beach and forty people got out. Their faces had a strong Indian cast. The men wore the clothes of farm workers, the women long skirts and shawls. They became two groups: men and boys, women and infants; and they gathered in the shade of two trees. The men stood, the women sat. They watched the surf and whispered. They kept their clothes on, they did not remove their boots. They were unused to the beach and seemed very shy – they had probably come a great distance for this outing. They posed in embarrassment for the photographer, and hours later when I left they were still there, the men standing, the women sitting, staring at the oily waves with curiosity. If they were average rural Mexicans (and they seemed so), they were illiterate, lived in one-room huts, rarely ate meat or eggs, and earned less than $15 a week.

Before the shops closed that afternoon I did my provision-hunting. I bought a basket and filled it with small loaves of bread, a pound of cheese, some sliced ham, and – because a train without a dining car is usually a train on which drinks are unobtainable – bottles of beer, grapefruit juice and soda water. It was like stocking a hamper for a two-day picnic, and it was a sensible precaution. Mexican train travellers do not carry their own food; they urge you to do as they do – buy the local delicacies that are sold by women and children at every railway station. But local delicacies are always carried in a tin wash basin on the seller's head, and because it is out of the seller's sight it is impossible for the hawker yelling, 'Tasty chicken!', to see the flies that have collected on it. Typically, the Mexican food seller is a woman on a railway platform with a basin of flies on her head.

I had planned to get to bed early in order to be up at dawn to buy my ticket to Tapachula. It was when I switched the light off that I heard the music; darkness gave the sounds clarity, and it was too vibrant to be coming from a radio. It was a strong, full-throated brass band:

> Land of Hope and Glory, Mother of the Free,
> How shall we extol thee, who are born of thee?

'Pomp and Circumstance'? In Veracruz? At eleven o'clock at night?

> Wider still and wider shall thy bounds be set;
> God who made thee mighty, make thee mightier yet.

I dressed and went downstairs.

In the centre of the Plaza, near the four fountains, was the Mexican Navy Band, in white uniforms, giving Elgar the full treatment. Lights twinkled in the boughs of the laburnum trees, and there were floodlights, too – pink ones – playing on the balconies and the palms. A sizable crowd had gathered to listen – children played near the fountain, people walked their dogs, lovers held hands. The night was cool and balmy, the crowd good-humoured and attentive. I think it was one of the prettiest sights I have ever seen; the Mexicans had the handsome thoughtful look, the serenity that comes of listening closely to lovely music. It was late, a soft wind moved through the trees, and the tropical harshness that had seemed to me constant in Veracruz was gone; these were gentle people, this was an attractive place.

The song ended. There was clapping. The band began playing 'The Washington Post March', and I strolled around the perimeter of the plaza. There was a slight hazard in this. Because the carnival had just ended, Veracruz was full of idle prostitutes, and as I strolled I realized that most of them had not come here to the plaza to listen to the band – in fact, the greater part of the audience was composed of dark-eyed girls in slit skirts and low-cut dresses who, as I passed them, called out, 'Let's go to my house', or fell into step with me and murmured, 'Fuck?' This struck me as comic and rather pleasant – the military dignity of the march music, the pink light on the lush trees and balconies of the plaza, and the whispered invitations of those willing girls.

Now the band was playing Weber. I decided to sit on a bench and give it my full attention; I took an empty seat next to a couple who appeared to be chatting. They were both speaking at once. The woman was blonde and was telling the man in English to go away; the man was offering her a drink and a good time in Spanish. She was insistent, he was conciliatory – he was also much younger than she. I listened with great interest, stroked my moustache and hoped I was not noticed. The woman was saying, 'My husband – understand? – my husband's meeting me here in five minutes.'

In Spanish the man said, 'I know a beautiful place. It is right near here.'

The woman turned to me. 'Do you speak English?'

I said I did.

'How do you tell these people to go away?'

I turned to the man. Now, facing him, I could see that he was no more than twenty-five. 'The lady wants you to go away.'

He shrugged, and then he leered at me. He did not speak, but his expression said, 'You win.' And he went. Two girls hurried after him.

The lady said, 'I had to hit one over the head this morning with my umbrella. He wouldn't go away.'

She was in her late forties, and was attractive in a brittle meretricious way – she wore heavy make-up, eye shadow, and thick Mexican jewellery of silver and turquoise. Her hair was platinum, with hues of pink and green – perhaps it was the plaza light. Her suit was white, her handbag was white, her shoes were white. One could hardly blame the Mexican for making an attempt on her, since she bore such a close resemblance to the stereotype of the American woman who occurs so frequently in Tennessee Williams' plays and Mexican photo-comics – the vacationer with a tormented libido and a drinking problem and a symbolic name who comes to Mexico in search of a lover.

Her name was Nicky. She had been in Veracruz for nine days, and when I expressed surprise at this she said, 'I may be here a month or – who knows? – maybe for a lot longer.'

'You must like it here,' I said.

'I do.' She peered at me. 'What are you doing here?'

'Growing a moustache.'

She did not laugh. She said, 'I'm looking for a friend.'

I almost stood up and walked away. It was the way she said it.

'He's very sick. He needs help.' Her voice hinted at desperation, her face was fixed. 'Only I can't find him. I put him on the plane at Mazatlan. I gave him money, some new clothes, a ticket. He'd never been on a plane before. I don't know where he is. Do you read the papers?'

'All the time.'

'Have you seen this?'

She showed me the local newspaper. It was folded so that a wide column showed, and under *Personal Notices* there was a black-framed box with the headline in Spanish URGENT TO LOCATE. There was a snapshot with a caption. The snapshot was one of those over-bright pictures that are taken of startled people in nightclubs by pestering men who say 'Peecha, peecha?' In this picture, Nicky in huge sunglasses and an evening gown – radiantly tanned and fuller faced – sat at a table (flowers, wine glasses) with a thin, moustached man. He looked a bit scared and a bit sly, and yet his arm around her suggested bravado.

I read the message: *Señora Nicky – wishes urgently to get in touch with her husband Señor José – , who has been living in Mazatlan. It is believed that he is now in Veracruz. Anyone who recognizes him from this picture should immediately contact –* There followed detailed instructions for getting in touch with Nicky, and three telephone numbers.

I said, 'Has anyone called you up?'

'No,' she said, and put the newspaper back into her handbag.

'Today was the first day it appeared. I'm going to run it all week.'

'It must be pretty expensive.'

'I've got enough money,' she said. 'He's very sick. He's dying of TB. He said he wanted to see his mother. I put him on the plane in Mazatlan and stayed there for a few days – I had given him the number of my hotel. But when he didn't call me I got worried, so I came here. His mother's here – this is where he was headed. But I can't find him.'

'Why not try his mother?'

'I can't find her either. See, he didn't know her address. He only knew that it was right near the bus station. He drew me a picture of the house. Well, I found something that looks like the house, but no one knew him there. He was going to get off the plane at Mexico City and take a bus from there – that way he'd be able to find his mother's house. It's kind of complicated.'

And kind of fishy, too, I thought, but instead of speaking I made a sympathetic noise.

'But it's serious. He's sick. He only weighs about a hundred pounds now, probably less. There's a hospital in Jalapa. They could help him. I'd pay.' She looked towards the bandstand. The band was playing a medley of songs from *My Fair Lady*. Nicky said, 'Actually, today I went to the office of death records to see if he had died. He hasn't died at least.'

'In Veracruz.'

'What do you mean?'

'He might have died in Mexico City.'

'He doesn't know anyone in Mexico City. He wouldn't have stayed there. He would have come straight here.'

But he had boarded the plane and vanished. In nine days of searching, Nicky had not been able to find a trace of him. Perhaps it was the effect of the Dashiell Hammett novel I had just read, but I found myself examining her situation with a detective's scepticism. Nothing could have been more melodramatic, or more like a Bogart film: near midnight in Veracruz, the band playing ironical love songs, the plaza crowded with friendly whores, the woman in the white suit describing the disappearance of her Mexican husband. It is possible that this sort of movie-fantasy, which is available to the solitary traveller, is one of the chief reasons for travel. She had cast herself in the role of leading lady in her search drama, and I gladly played my part. We were far from home: we could be anyone we wished. Travel offers a great occasion to the amateur actor.

And if I had not seen myself in this Bogart role, I would have commiserated with her and said what a shame it was that she could not find the man. Instead, I was detached: I wanted to know everything. I said, 'Does he know you're looking for him?'

'No, he doesn't know I'm here. He thinks I'm back in Denver. The way we left it, he was just going to go home and see his mother. He hasn't been home for eight years. See, that's what's so confusing for him. He's been living in Mazatlan. He's a poor fisherman – he can barely read.'

'Interesting. You live in Denver, he lives in Mazatlan.'

'That's right.'

'And you're married to him?'

'No – what gave you that idea? We're not married. He's a friend.'

'It says in the paper he's your husband.'

'I didn't write that. I don't speak Spanish.'

'That's what it says. In Spanish. He's your husband.'

I was not Bogart any more. I was Montgomery Clift playing the psychiatrist in *Suddenly Last Summer*. Katharine Hepburn hands him the death certificate of Sebastian Venable; Sebastian has been eaten alive by small boys, and the mutilation is described on the certificate. *It's in Spanish*, she says, believing the horrible secret is safe. Montgomery Clift replies coldly, *I read Spanish*.

'That's a mistake,' said Nicky. 'He's not my husband. He's just a beautiful human being.'

She let this sink in. The band was playing a waltz.

She said, 'I met him a year ago when I was in Mazatlan. I was on the verge of a nervous breakdown – my husband had left me. I didn't know which way to turn. I started walking along the beach. José saw me and got out of his boat. He put his hand out and touched me. He was smiling . . .' Her voice trailed off. She began again, 'He was very kind. It was what I needed. I was in a breakdown situation. He saved me.'

'What kind of boat?'

'A little boat – he's a poor fisherman,' she said. She squinted. 'He just put out his hand and touched me. Then I got to know him better. We went out to eat – to a restaurant. He had never had anything – he wasn't married – he didn't have a cent to his name. He had never had any good clothes, never eaten in a good restaurant, didn't know what to do. It was all new to him. He couldn't understand why I was giving so much to him. "You saved me," I said. He just smiled. I gave him money and for the next few weeks we had a wonderful time. Then he told me he had TB.'

'But he didn't speak English, right?'

'He could say a few words.'

'You believed him when he said he had TB?'

'He wasn't lying, if that's what you think. I saw his doctor. The doctor told me he needed treatment. So I swore I would help him, and that's why I went to Mazatlan a month ago. To help him. He was much thinner – he couldn't go fishing. I was really worried. I asked him what he wanted. He said he wanted to see his mother. I gave him money and things and put him on the plane, and when I didn't hear from him I came here myself.'

'It seems very generous of you. You could be out having a good time. Instead, you're searching Veracruz for this lost soul.'

'It's what God wants me to do,' she whispered.

'Yes?'

'And I'll find him, if God wants me to.'

'You're going to stick at it, eh?'

'We Sagittarians are awful determined – real adventurous types! What sign are you?'

'Aries.'

'Ambitious.'

'That's me.'

She said, 'Actually, I think God's testing me.'

'In what way?'

'This José business is nothing. I've just been through a very heavy divorce. And there's some other things.'

86

'About José. If he's illiterate, then his mother's probably illiterate. In that case, she won't see your ad in the paper. So why not have a poster made – a picture, some details – and you can put it up near the bus station and where his mother's house is supposed to be.'

'I think I'll try that.'

I gave her more suggestions: hire a private detective, broadcast messages on the radio. Then it occurred to me that José might have gone back to Mazatlan. If he had been sick or worried he would have done that, and if he had been trying to swindle her – as I suspected he had – he would certainly have done that eventually, when he ran out of money.

She agreed that he might have gone back, but not for the reasons I said. 'I'm staying here until I find him. But even if I find him tomorrow I'll stay a month. I like it here. This is a real nice town. Were you here for the carnival? No? It was a trip, I can tell you that. Everyone was down here in the plaza –'

Now the band was playing Rossini, the overture to *The Barber of Seville*.

' – drinking, dancing. Everyone was so friendly. I met so many people. I was partying every night. That's why I don't mind staying here and looking for José. And, um, I met a man.'

'Local feller?'

'Mexican. He gave me good vibrations, like you're giving me. You're positive – get posters made, radio broadcasts – that's what I need.'

'This new man you met – he might complicate things.'

She shook her head. 'He's good for me.'

'What if he finds out that you're looking for José? He might get annoyed.'

'He knows all about it. We discussed it. Besides,' she added added after a moment, 'José is dying.'

The concert had ended. It was so late I had become ravenously hungry. I said that I was going to a restaurant, and Nicky said, 'Mind if I join you?' We had red snapper and she told me about her divorces. Her first husband had been violent, her second had been a bum. It was her word.

'A real bum?'

'A real one,' she said. 'He was so lazy – why, he worked for me, you know? While we were married. But he was so lazy I had to fire him.'

'When you divorced him?

'No, long before that. I fired him, but I stayed married to him. That was about five years ago. After that, he just hung around the house. When I couldn't take any more of it I divorced him. Then, guess what? He goes to his lawyer and tries to get me to pay him maintenance money. *I'm* supposed to pay *him*!'

'What sort of business are you in?'

'I own slums,' she said. 'Fifty-seven of them – I mean, fifty-seven units. I used to own a hundred and twenty-eight units. But these fifty-seven are in eighteen different locations. God, it's a problem – people always want paint, things fixed, a new roof.'

I ceased to see her as a troubled libido languishing in Mexico. She owned property; she was here living on her slum rents. She said she didn't pay any taxes because of her 'depreciations' and that on paper she looked 'real good'. She said, 'God's been good to me.'

'Are you going to sell these slums of yours?'

'Probably. I'd like to live here. I'm a real Mexico freak.'

'And you'll make a profit when you sell them.'

'That's what it's all about.'

'Then why don't you let these people live rent-free? They're doing you a favour by keeping them in repair. God would love you for that. And you'll still make a profit.'

She said, 'That's silly.'

The bill came.

'I'll pay for myself,' she said.

'Save your money,' I said. 'José might turn up.'

She smiled at me. 'You're kind of an interesting guy.'

I had not said a single word about myself; she did not even know my name. Perhaps this reticence was interesting? But it wasn't reticence: she hadn't asked.

I said, 'Maybe I'll see you tomorrow.'

'I'm at the Diligencia.'

I was at the Diligencia, too. I decided not to tell her this. I said, 'I hope you find what you're looking for.'

The next day I rose early and hurried to the station to buy my ticket for Tapachula. It was a simple operation, and there was still time to return to the hotel for breakfast. As I was eating I saw Nicky pass through the lobby. She bought a newspaper. She looked around. I hid behind a pillar. When the coast was clear I made my way to the station. The sun was above the plaza. It was going to be a very hot day.

5 The Passenger Train to Tapachula

I had been on the train for twelve hours. There was something wrong with this train; a whole day of travelling and we had gone only a hundred miles or so, mostly through swamps. The heat had made me nauseous, and the noise of the banging doors, the anvil clang of the coupling, had given me a headache. Now it was night, still noisy, but very cold. The coach was open – most of the eighty seats were occupied, nearly all the windows were broken, or jammed open. The bulbs on the ceiling were too dim to read by, too bright to allow me to sleep. The rest of the passengers slept, and one across the aisle was snoring loudly. The man behind me who, all day, had sighed and cursed and kicked the back of my seat in exasperation, had made a pillow of his fist and gone to sleep. The spiders and ants I had noticed during the day crawling in and out of the horsehair of the burst cushions had begun biting me. Or was it mosquitoes? My ankles itched and stung. It was just after nine o'clock. I held a copy of *Pudd'n-head Wilson*. I had given up trying to read it.

I turned to the flyleaf and wrote: *Two classes: both uncomfortable and dirty. No privacy, no relief. Constant stopping and starting, broken engine, howling passengers. On days like this I wonder why I bother: leaving order and friends for disorder and strangers. I'm homesick and feel punished for my selfishness in leaving. Precisely what Crusoe says on his island. Impossible to get comfortable in this seat. A jail atmosphere: the brown walls and dim light of the condemned cell. Noise, too: a factory din – our pile-driving sound hammered back at us through open windows from the close walls of jungle beside the track.*

I stopped. Writing can make you very lonely.

I saw one thing today: a thin white heron standing in a swamp.
There was a half-inch left on the page.

These people are going home. They complain about the journey, but they will be home tomorrow. I am travelling to another train. I would rather . . .

Then I was asleep. The difference between sleep and waking on this train was that, awake, I swatted the mosquitoes. Asleep, though I was aware of being stung, I was helpless; I did not have the will to stop them.

The heron: I had seen it in the marshland near Piedras Negras; it had been tall and watchful, such a slender creature, so finely formed and so strange in that marshy salad. An hour later there was no moisture anywhere in sight: dusty trees rooted in dry ground, withered grass, limp burned leaves, and mud huts thatched with palm fronds, like those you see in the poorest parts of Africa. The train continued to stop, usually next to a cane field; there was seldom a station nearby, and I suspected that there was a fault in the engine. I could see groups of men prodding the locomotive and adjusting their straw hats. Then we would start again and move slowly for a few miles and stop.

At one stop – a station, not a breakdown – a boy got on and stood at the front of the coach. He sang in a very sweet voice. At first the passengers were embarrassed, but with the second and third songs, they applauded. The boy was encouraged. He sang a fourth. The whistle blew. He walked to the back of the coach, collecting money from the people. What impressed me as much as his voice was his age – he was about twenty, old enough to be a cane-cutter or a farm labourer (but farm labourers in Mexico work on average only 135 days a year). This singing seemed an unlikely occupation, but perhaps he only performed when the train passed through his village.

We came to Tierra Blanca. The descriptive name did not describe the place. Spanish names were apt only as ironies or simplifications; they seldom fit. The argument is usually stated differently, to demonstrate how dull, how literal-minded and unimaginative the Spanish explorer or cartographer was. Seeing a dark river, the witness quickly assigned a name: Rio Negro. It is a common name throughout Latin America; yet it never matched the colour of the water. And the four Rio Colorados I saw bore not the slightest hint of red. Piedra Negras was marshland, not black stones; I saw no stags at Venado Tuerto, no lizards at Lagartos. None of the Laguna Verdes was green; my one La Dorada looked leaden, and Progreso in Guatemala was backward, La Libertad in El Salvador a stronghold of repression in a country where salvation seemed in short supply. La Paz was not peaceful, nor was La Democracia democratic. This was not literalness – it was whimsy. Place names called attention to beauty, freedom, piety, or strong colours; but the places themselves, so prettily named, were something else. Was it wilful inaccuracy, or a lack of subtlety that made the map so glorious with fine attributes and praises? Latins found it hard to live with dull facts; the enchanting name, while not exactly making their town magical, at least took the curse off it. And there was always a chance that an evocative name might evoke something to make the plain town bearable.

I looked hard at Tierra Blanca. It was poor and brown. There were chickens strutting on the station platform, and men heaving bales, and children pointing at passengers gaping from the windows of the train. And food sellers (it was lunchtime) shrieking the name of the item they carried: pancakes, beans, fritters, corn on the cob, cupcakes, cheese sandwiches, fried chicken, bananas, oranges, pineapples, watermelons. I had my own food. I slit one of the small loaves and filled it with ham and cheese. Across the aisle, a large family travelling to Guatemala, eating the flyblown chicken they had just bought, stared at me.

'That is a big sandwich,' said the mother.

'We call this a submarine sandwich,' I said.

They continued to stare.

'Because of the shape,' I said. I held it up. 'Like a submarine.'

They squinted. They had never seen a submarine.

The mother said, 'Of course.'

In the next few hours the train stopped eight more times. It did not stop at stations. It slowed near cane fields or on marshland or in hot woods, and then the trumpeting engine went silent and it jerked to a halt; the passengers groaned and looked out the windows, and seeing no station they said, 'Nowhere' or 'I don't know'. And though they might have been talking happily while the train was moving, when it stopped they became laconic, and grunted and sighed. Usually, this hot silence was broken by a cry from outside the window: 'Bananas?'

No matter where we stopped, in a swamp or in apparently empty woods, a food-seller would materialize – a small girl in a torn dress – and yell, 'Bananas?' I had no fear, on this train to Tapachula, of ever going hungry.

Passing some cane fields at about two that afternoon, and marvelling how densely packed they were – practically impenetrable green stalks, like a wall of bamboo – I felt the train slowing down. I looked out of the window: more cane fields. The train stopped. The passengers grunted. I picked up *Pudd'nhead Wilson* and read it. An hour went by – a slow humid mid-afternoon hour, with a radio twanging in the next car. The banana-seller had come and gone. I made myself a sandwich, I drank a bottle of soda water. And I became aware that I might eat all my food and finish my book before we started moving again. This food, this book: it was all I had to keep me going.

The train started; I put my feet up and breathed a sigh of relief. The train went a hundred yards and stopped. Someone in the next car cried, 'Mother of God!'

We were on a long red bridge of steel girders, and beneath us was a river. I dug out my map and traced the railway line from Veracruz. I found Tierra Blanca, the swamps, a river: so this was the Rio Papaloapan. The handbook said that the river basin drained by the Papaloapan was 'twice the size of the Netherlands' but that the nearby town contained 'little of note'. We remained on the bridge for another hour – an irritating hour, because we could not get out and walk around: there was no walkway on the bridge, and the river itself had a treacherous-looking current. I considered eating, but thought better of it. At this rate of speed we would not be in Tapachula for days. The passengers, trapped in the train which was itself trapped on the bridge, grew restive, and now the Guatemalan children in the large family hung out of the window and yelled, 'Let's go! Let's go!' They continued to yell this until sundown.

I wondered if I should continue reading. It was all that kept me sane during periods like this of utter boredom. But if I finished *Pudd'nhead Wilson* – a book I was enjoying – I would have nothing else to read. I paced up and down the long train and already it seemed as if I had been on it for more than a day. Soon, it moved, about two hundred yards, no more, then it stopped.

We were in the village of Papaloapan. 'Little of note' was a wild overstatement. There were two shops, some huts, some pigs, some pawpaw trees. The sun had dropped to the level of the windows and burned through the train.

There had been a Mexican sitting on a broken bench some distance from the tracks when the train drew in. The tree he had chosen to sit under was rather small, and I watched him closely to see what he would do when the sunlight reached him. For half an hour he did not stir, although two hogs tied to the tree were whining and snuffling at the ends of their tethers. He appeared not to see the hogs, he did not look at the train, he paid no attention to the sun. The sun slipped from the lower branches to his hat. The man remained motionless. The hogs squawked. The sun moved down, lighting the man's nose. The man did not move immediately – he shuffled his feet and winced, but very slowly, as if he were entering a new phase of slumber; and then with one finger he tilted his hat and put his nose in shadow. He was reposeful once again. But the sun was moving: the light found his face (and found the hogs – they tried to yank themselves out of it), the man poked his hat again with his finger. He had not regarded the train, he ignored the hogs, he was neither asleep nor awake, and the only significant change was that yellow disc of hat, now like the watchful face of a wilting sunflower following the sun, jammed vertically against his head.

While I studied this man, who was as good as a sundial, a dwarf climbed into the train. His eyes were level with mine, though I was sitting, and I could see how they protruded, how their sour grey colour was not penetrated by any pupil: he was blind. But he was chirping, pleading in a bantering way for money. His clothes were ripped and he was tied with twine like a bundle of rags – there were knots and loops of fraying string tightened all over his body. The passengers spoke to him as he collected coins; he limped through the car, chuckling and replying.

'Let's get this train moving,' they said.

The blind man said, 'I'm doing the best I can.'

'Where are we?' they said.

'Papaloapan,' said the blind dwarf. 'It's a nice town. Why don't you stay?'

'We don't want to stay here!' the passengers said.

The blind dwarf laughed and tapped his stick into the next car. I heard him say, 'Good evening –'

There were more people who boarded to beg – an old woman with an infant in her arms, two skinny children; and food-sellers – children with jugs of coffee, basins of fritters, women with bread and bony fish. Other children from Papaloapan ran in and out of the train, and men sauntered over from the shop nearby to chat with the passengers.

In the space of a few hours (now it was late afternoon, and men coming back from cutting in the cane fields stopped beside the train to see what was up), the stalled train ceased to be seen as something that roared through the riverbank village of Papaloapan. Villagers, who presumably had always watched at a distance, boarded and used the toilets and waved to their friends from the windows; and the chickens pecked and gabbled under the cars, as confidently as the passengers had drifted to the shop where they roosted swigging soft drinks. Now the train had become part of the town.

No one was sure what was wrong with our train. A wreck up ahead, one man said; another man told me our engine was broken. There was no panic. The ninety-degree heat all day had taken the starch out of everyone. Few people inquired; there was no panic – most had begun to feel at home here in Papaloapan. We were not due at Tapachula until the next day, and no one was quite sure how far we had come. (To kill time, I asked people how far we were from Veracruz; no one gave me the right answer: 100 miles.) In a country where delays are chronic, a delay like this was to be expected; and anyway, the village was friendly, the weather was warm, and each pair of seats had been turned into a nest of food wrappings and pillows and dozing children. The man behind me had stopped kicking my seat. He was completely calm. He said, 'I think we will have to spend the night here.'

The Guatemalan lady said to her children, 'I think he is right. Oh, well.'

Nothing seems longer than the unexpected delay. Nothing is harder to describe or more boring to read. 'An hour passed,' one writes, and there is no tedium in the phrase, no smell, no heat, no noise, none of the flies swarming unsteadily from the toilet door which, warped and without a handle, refused to shut. 'Another hour passed' – how hard to suggest the two radios, the whining hogs, the shrieks of children, the lumpy seat with the spiders hunching out of its horsehair. Heat itself seems to slow time. If the village had been any larger I think I would have packed my belongings and checked into the nearest hotel. But the village was small, and there would not be another train to Tapachula for three days.

I realized that I had only fifty pages more to read of *Pudd'n-head Wilson*. I decided to save it, to keep the best part for later, when my nerves might be stretched and I would need it. I resisted the impulse to go on with the story, and instead read the Introduction. This was a very disturbing experience, the serious phraseology of the essay contrasting with the approaching twilight, the noise and smells of this ramshackle Mexican village, the crowded train. *One way to see how he establishes this as an irony is to compare him with Jane Austen in whose novels the social life is approved, and provides the basis for her own exacting moral values –*

Yaaaaaaaa! A child across the aisle screamed. Her brother smiled and pinched her again. The Mexican in the shade scratched his head without moving his hat. The hogs grunted. The radio in the shop yelled and crackled. Two men by the door laughed out loud. 'Cold beer!' shouted a hawker. 'Bananas!' 'Ice-cream!' 'He pinched me!'

– In her work social values are not moral values as such; but her irony works to show how they can be, how a certain kind of full and tested –

A giggle and 'I did not!' and two pretty girls in green school uniforms strolled by the train, hugging their books. They had black hair and bright eyes and they were laughing.

– full and tested social awareness is also, finally, a realized moral awareness –

I shut the book. A quarrel had started at the end of the car –

nothing serious: shouting, mulishness, arm-swinging. The toilet smell had grown much worse. We had been stationary for hours, but people had continued to shit down the tin pipe and there was a disgusting heap on the tracks under the car. It excited the flies: they were loud and fat and they swarmed in a cloud and tumbled through the windows which would not close. The beer-seller came back, put his crate down and sat on it. He was hoarse from shouting. He asked me in a whisper if I wanted one. Although I had two of my own, I bought two more: it was, after all, Happy Hour, and it was going to be a long night.

There was an empty row of seats at the far end of the train. I stretched out to have my sundowner, puffed my pipe and allowed myself another chapter of *Pudd'nhead Wilson*. Night was falling on Papaloapan. Dogs barked, the village voices had become murmurs, the radios still played, and in the train people talked more quietly in the darkness. There were crickets, as rapid as castanets – I had not heard crickets for ages; the sound was soothing. And the novel cheered me: what a superb book this was! I thought I had known the story, but all I had remembered was the fingerprinting business and the identical children and the crime. I had missed the ironies: it was a story about freedom and slavery, identity and disguise, and the tinctures of race were made into attributes. It was a savage masterpiece, with a cruelly grim jollity, more ingenious and pessimistic than anything I had ever read by Twain. It was patterned on a folktale: the switched infants, the slave child becoming master, the master's son a slave. But the implications of race made it a nightmare of masked injustices. It had begun as a farce about a pair of Siamese twins. Twain saw this as a defect, 'two stories in one, a farce and a tragedy.' He decided to revamp the story: 'I pulled out the farce and left the tragedy.' But the tragedy is so bitter, this seldom-read novel – one of the gloomiest comedies in American literature – is treated as the story of a country lawyer, a funny-looking figure who wins a case using fingerprints. His victory does not quite overshadow the fact that everyone else in the novel, even the worthiest character, is defeated. It gave me a lecture topic: How, by careful selection, we make our writers simple; American literature is an anthology of what is bearable.

Meanwhile, it had grown darker in Papaloapan. I looked up

and saw a solitary engine approaching from the bridge. It passed by, and five minutes later there was a bump, a lurch, and a renewed activity on the tracks. Then a shrill whistle and the Guatemalan children crying, 'Let's go!' The lights had come on in the village, but they were unshaded and dazzling; soon, they were moving past the train and the villagers were watching us go, and some were waving tentatively as if they half-expected us to stop again. But we did not stop. A breeze purified the cars and out of the trees a dazzle of the village we had a glimpse of sky, of a sunset which, five hundred years ago, had been seen in this very place by an Aztec poet:

> Our father, the Sun
> Dressed in rich feathers, thrusts himself
> Down into a vase of gems,
> Decked with a turquoise necklace
> Among many-coloured flowers
> Which fall in perpetual rain.

The glimmer remained for some minutes, then the green jungle and swamp became a mass of shadows, and the darkness was complete. Four small lightbulbs – the rest were dead or missing – were not enough for me to read by. I put my book away and drank and looked out of the window.

There were few stops – some villages, some settlements that were less than villages. I saw doorways flickering in candlelight and hut interiors whitened by lanterns. At one doorway the highly erotic sight of a girl or woman, leaning against the jamb, canted forward, her legs apart, her arms upraised, and the light behind her showing the slimness of the body beneath her gauzy dress – this lovely shape in a lighted rectangle surrounded by the featureless Mexican night. It left me flustered and a bit anxious.

At one town, a boy leaned out of the train and called to a girl selling corn. He said, 'Where are we?'

The girl took the tray of corn from her head and stared at him. It was a difficult question.

The boy said, 'She doesn't know where we are!'

The girl looked at the laughing boy on the train. She knew where she was. But the boy had not asked that.

The boy roused his father, his brother, and he wagged his head at me. 'She doesn't know where we are!'

Loud enough for the girl with the tray to hear, I said, 'I know where we are.'

'Where?' asked the boy.

'On a train.'

They thought this was extremely funny. The boy repeated it and they laughed harder. In fact, we were at the town of Suelta, a congested place, the name of which meant 'loose'.

After this, unable to read or sleep, I scribbled some notes on the flyleaf of my book: *Two classes: both uncomfortable and dirty* . . . I was homesick. Was there any point in this trip aside from the fact that I had been too restless to stay at my desk and endure another winter? I had left in fine spirits, but I was no explorer: this was supposed to be enjoyment, not a test of stamina or patience. I did not take any pleasure in suffering the torments of travel merely so that I could dine out on them. I had been curious about the process of rising in the morning at home, and catching the local train and staying on it as the commuters got off to go to work, and changing trains at the end of the line, and repeating this until there were no more trains and I was in Patagonia. More melancholy than the thought of *Homesick: A Travel Book* was the memory of something I had read about Jack Kerouac. At the age of fifty, with *On the Road* well behind him, he decided to hitch-hike across America again. He was fatter now, and felt defeated, but he was convinced he could repeat his cross-country epic. So he left New York, seeking California. His menacing features were ineradicable, and times had changed. The lugubrious man reached New Jersey; there he stood for hours in the rain, trying to thumb a ride until, at last, he gave up and took a bus home.

Without realizing that I had been asleep, I woke from the mosquitoes and the cold. I tucked my trousers into my socks (but these mosquitoes could sting through socks) and put on the heavy sweater and leather jacket I had plucked for the altitudes of the Andes. And curling up once more I slept like a log until dawn. I had not thought I was capable of such adjustment, and overcoming the misery of a dreadful night on the torn seat of a cold and stinking train gave me the lucid optimism and good humour that always accompanies such excursions. I felt virtuous and even knew that my virtue was laughable.

At six that morning, I blinked at my watch. The lights in the car had fused: it was pitch dark. Moments later, it was dawn. No bulb of sun, but a seepage of light that dissolved the darkness and rose on all sides bringing a bluer ozone-scented softness to a sky which became gigantic. With it was a warm buoyancy of air, and scale was restored to the landscape, and the car was sweetened with the odour of desert dew. I had never seen dawn break so swiftly, but I had never slept that way. The windows were open, there were no shades: it was like sleeping on a park bench.

Yonder were mountains: the sunlight revealed their tiny heads and wide shoulders as craggy and purple, with small black trees on their slopes as delicate as eyelashes. It was a mountain range erupting jaggedly eastward; to the south were sparse dusty woods. The train stopped. This was emptiness. A girl appeared at the window: 'Coffee!' She poured me some in a paper cup and I sipped it as we resumed our journey along the lowland periphery of the escarpment.

This was the Pacific side of the Isthmus of Tehuantepec, the narrowest point in Mexico – so narrow, it was for a long time considered an ideal place to dig a coast-to-coast canal. And more convenient than Panama because it was so much nearer the United States. Tehuantepec – a hot, dismal-looking place – had had an interesting history. It had always been populated, and often dominated, by Indians. These Indians – the Zapotecs – were a matrilineal people – the women owned land, fished, traded, farmed, and ran the local government; the men, with that look of silliness that comes of being bone-idle, lounged around. The stations that morning showed this tradition to be unchanged: enterprising women, empty-handed men. But one could easily underestimate their capacity for outrage: patience so often looks like defeat, or silence like conversion. One of the earliest Indian uprisings in Mexico took place here in 1680; these people rebelled and for the next eight years controlled most of the Isthmus. And when in later years great projects were conceived to make the Isthmus important the Indians did not cooperate – they simply stood aside and watched the projects fail.

In his joyously energetic travel book, *The West Indies and the Spanish Main*, Anthony Trollope wrote that this part of Mexico was 'the passage selected by Cortez, and pressed by him on the Spanish government ... the line would be from the Gulf of Campechay, up the river Coatzacoalcox, to Tehuantepec and the Pacific'. Trollope, who believed more southerly routes through Panama and Costa Rica (he travelled through both places) would be expensive and impractical, was writing in 1860. Ten years later, President Ulysses S. Grant (yes, of all people) sent the Tehuantepec Expedition here and charged them with exploring the possibilities of digging a canal. Altogether there were seven expeditions but, though no canal was built, the Isthmus was crossed by tens of thousands of travellers, first on mule back and stage coaches, and then by train. It was one of the better ways of reaching California from the eastern seaboard of the United States, and the Gold Rush of 1849 had vastly increased the traffic. With so many people tumbling back and forth across Tehuantepec (under, one assumes, the baleful or jeering eyes of the Indians), the profit in annexing the strip was obvious, and several times the American government urged the Mexicans to hand it over. Mexican tenacity could not match American rapaciousness and the Mexicans eventually conceded all of what are now regarded as Western states, but against the odds they refused to surrender Tehuantepec. In 1894, the railway was built across the Isthmus and did a roaring trade. One of the busiest railways the world has ever known, at the height of its operation there were sixty trains a day. It is an astonishing fact, because so little of that bustle and efficiency remains, such a tiny portion of the builders' and speculators' handiwork. There is less left of the great Tehuantepec National Railway than of the Mayan ruins of Uxmal or Palenque, and no sign in the shrivelled riverbeds or the dusty tracks that link the poor towns that this was once a great crossroads of the world. Yet some of the railway still stands. In 1913, the line was extended to join the so-called Pan American Railway at the Guatemalan frontier. But this was a hopeless effort. The next year the Panama Canal opened and bankrupted every railway, mule track, ferry crossing and stagecoach route in Central America. From that year, Tehuantepec began to die and not even the discovery of oil (long

101

before, the Aztecs had found it in sticky lumps which had squeezed from the ground – they burned this magic stuff at religious ceremonies) managed to work a cure on the Isthmus or to bring it any degree of prosperity. Today it looks pathetic; it is rough country, and hot and infertile; the Indians, living an ordinary existence in a hand-to-mouth way, look embattled; the towns and villages are less than they were in the Aztec times. But Mexicans have learned how to derive comfort from the past – from actual events or the reassuring simplicity of myths and even among the cactus-covered hills and bumpy desert of Tehuantepec the backward-looking Mexican was greatly encouraged by the thought that it had once known glorious days.

The mountain range – now like a fortress, now like a cathedral (it was yet another protectively maternal strip of the Sierra Madre) – stayed with us the whole day. But we never climbed it. We moved south along the hot lowland, and the more southerly we penetrated the more primitive and tiny became the Indian villages, the more emblematic the people: naked child, woman with basket, man on horseback, posed in the shattering sunlight before a poor mud hut. As the morning wore on the people withdrew and by eleven o'clock we were watched from the windows of huts which had grown much smaller. Shade was scarce: skinny village dogs slept under the bellies of cows which were themselves transfixed by hanks of course grass.

There was water to the south-west – a blue-green haze, a shimmering emptiness, the flat land receding to a sparkle and brown bizarrely suspended boats. This was the Dead Sea, a lozenge of lake on the shore of the Pacific. Nearer the train, horses were tied to the verandah posts of village bars, and men sat at tables near the windows; women and girls hawked prawns and pink-scaled fish which they carried in pails. My eyes were moist from the heat, and through this blur I saw dark pigs and coconut groves and banana trees and, behind them, bouldery mountains.

We crossed into the state of Chiapas. In Chiapas the mountains looked higher, the surrounding land hotter, and these two contrasting landscapes were so inhospitable and unmarked by any human effort, the people seemed like pioneers, hardy new arrivals who had yet to make any dent in the place. That was between stations, but the stations seemed like outposts, too. At the town of Arriaga I asked the conductor when we could expect to arrive in Tapachula. He counted on his fingers, then he laughed because we were more than ten hours late.

'Maybe tonight,' he said. 'Don't worry.'

'I'm not worried.'

Not worried, but rather sick of this hot crowded train. A slow train, which this was, could be a joy, if the seats were not broken and the toilet worked and the dust was mopped off the floor. The passengers, prostrate in the heat, lay collapsed on the seats, their mouths open, as if they had all been gunned down or gassed.

'I'll come back,' said the conductor. 'I'll tell you when we are near Tapachula. Right?'

'Thank you.'

But to arrive in Tapachula was to accomplish very little. Tapachula was nowhere. It was, simply, where this train stopped for good.

I had finished most of my food by the time we reached Pijijiapan; and what remained – some discoloured slices of ham, some sweating cheese that had softened to putty in the heat – I threw out of the window. I had also finished *Pudd'nhead Wilson*. Pijijiapan was a market town, a mob scene which the arrival of the train only maddened further – the train stayed in the middle of town for half an hour and none of the shoppers or hawkers or battered cars could cross the road. Nor would the conductor allow anyone to pass through the train. So they stood in the hot sun with their baskets, and the fish they carried grew more rancid-smelling as they waited. They carried chickens and turkeys, too, and corn and beans. They were Indians, short, square-featured people who glowered at this intrusion.

If one wonders who precisely they are, one needs only to listen to Jacques Soustelle on the Aztecs. Before treating the artistic and cultural achievements of the nobles, he directs our attention in a kind of whispered prologue, to another group. 'On the fringe of the rich and brilliant cities,' he writes, 'the peasant – Nahuatl. Otomí, Zapotec, etc. – continued to lead his patient and laborious life in obscurity. We know almost nothing about him ... He was of no interest to the native or the Spanish chronicler, with his hut, his maize field, his turkeys, his little monogamous family and his narrow horizon, and they mention him only in passing . . . But it is important to speak of him at this point, if only to make his silent presence felt, in the shadows beyond the brilliance of the urban civilization; and the moreso, because after the disaster of 1521 [the Spanish conquest] and the collapse of all authority, all concepts, the whole frame of society and all religion, he alone survived, and he alone still lives.'

He – or rather she – sold me some fritters and rice at Pijijiapan; I drank the last of my soda water (I had used the other half of the bottle for brushing my teeth) and we set off again. It was frustrating to be so tired in such a beautiful landscape, like dozing at a concert. The train picked up speed and shot along this savannah, skirting the majestic mountains, but the heat and the dirt and my fatigue, and now the noise of the speeding train, prevented me from being able to concentrate or steady my gaze on the bright rocks or the trees whipping past. It was punishing to feel so battered and incapable, but also a further punishment to know how the best of Chiapas was eluding me. Struggling to stay awake to see it, the effort exhausted me; the bright air and yellow land overwhelmed me, and I slept.

I woke perspiring whenever the train stopped, at little towns, like Mapastepec and Margaritas, where the foreground swam with colour: jacaranda, bougainvillea, hibiscus – electric contending hues in what was otherwise a desert of frail trees and barren soil, broken by fields of corn and tobacco. We were in the deep hinterland now, and later I was to recognize the remote place, the combination of Indian villages and bad roads and the one railway line producing – but it was not so unusual: they had come with the railway and they had stayed – the Chinese, who advertised themselves on shop signs: *Casa Wong* or *Chen Hermanos*. I had thought it had been hot in the morning; the afternoon was almost unbearable and at Soconocusco I felt nauseated by the heat.

Walking the length of the train to find some bottled water to have with my fruit salts I came upon a man I at first took to be an American. I had not met an English speaker since leaving Veracruz, so I greeted him – glad to have someone who might understand my feeling of discomfort. He winced at me. He wore a jacket; the lenses of his glasses were coated with dust; he had a small map; he sat alone in Second Class. He was of course German.

And he spoke neither English nor Spanish. Where, I asked him in faulty German, had he boarded the train? In Veracruz, he said. But I had not seen him in Veracruz, or Papaloapan, or anywhere else. Well, he said, he had not left his seat. What had he eaten?

'A sandwich. Cheese.'

In two days?

'Yes,' he said. 'I do not like the toilets. I don't eat, so I don't use the toilets. I had a Pepsi-Cola. But I will eat in Guatemala.'

'We may not be in Guatemala until tomorrow.'

'Then I will eat tomorrow. It is good to be hungry for a few days. People eat too much – especially these people. You see them? Using the toilet?'

'Where are you going in Guatemala?'

'Maybe to the ruins. I don't know – I have to go back to work next week.'

'Back to –?'

'Germany.'

'Ah.' He was riding in Second Class. Second Class had torn black plastic seats. First Class had torn red plastic seats. Some of First's had arm-rests. But Second was slightly more crowded. How did he like it?

He gave me a smile – it was the first time he had smiled, and it was one of triumph and real pleasure. He said. 'Three dollars.'

Neither an explorer nor a hitch-hiker; no rucksack, no compass. Just a tidy little suitcase and small gold-rimmed glasses covered with dust, an empty Pepsi bottle and a sandwich wrapper, sitting with Teutonic uprightness through the tumbling hinterland of Chiapas. His map was small, he had no other book, he did not drink beer. In a word, a skinflint.

Another train, with seat numbers and compartments, might have thrown us together, and I would have suffered his leaden company for two days. If there was a virtue in the disorder of this carelessly-run Mexican train it was that it allowed a passenger the freedom of its shabby cars. There were no rules; or, if there were, no one followed them. So it was easy for me to reject the companionship of this fellow – not that he offered any: tightfisted people are as mean with friendship as they are with cash; suspicious, unbelieving and incurious. In a way, I admired his aloofness, though his aloofness was inspired by nothing more admirable than his egoism and his craving for the cheap. And yet, by refusing to take any risk he was taking the greatest risk of all: being solitary in a place so hot and anarchic one really needed friends.

'Have a good trip,' I said.

He nodded, he did not smile. And that was all. A chance meeting – nothing more. We merely brushed past each other at that far side of the world.

Another Chinese store, more tobacco fields, and the afternoon grew cloudy but no less hot. I lay on the seat and went to sleep again and did not wake until I heard one of the Guatemalan children yelling – as he had done since Veracruz – 'Let's go!' But this time he was yelling at me. I woke in darkness; the train had stopped, and now the Guatemalan mother was bending over me.

'If you are going to the frontier – you said you were – we could share a taxi and save some money. I have only three suitcases and these four children. We can fit in the back seat and you can sit in front with the driver. What do you say?'

It had been an awful trip and listening to her I saw my chance of leaving Mexico and this train and this town – just stepping across the border. Later, I decided that I would have been better off in a hotel in Tapachula, but at the time I was very eager to leave it. So I said yes and half an hour later, in darkness, I was walking across the bridge over the Suchiate River. Behind me were the rolling hills and banana groves of Mexico; ahead, a black brow of rock and on its cliffs and outcrops dim blue jungle and white lianas and vines, picked out in moonlight; and when the river ceased to thunder I could hear the screech of bats.

6 The 7:30 to Guatemala City

Guatemala had begun suddenly: a river-frontier and on the far bank jungly cliffs and hanging vines. Storm clouds were passing in front of the moon, which gave them druids' hooded shapes and grey rags. The border town of Tecún Umán was so small it made Tapachula seem a metropolis, and a Tapachula billboard I had seen advertising a hotel (*Good Food, Comfortable Rooms, Low Prices*), stayed in my memory as I ate a vile meal of beans in an ill-lit room of a much meaner hotel in Tecún Umán. This was called the Pearl. A hundred years ago, a British traveller in Guatemala wrote, 'A stranger, arriving without introductions, can only go to a very low public house ... intended for the accommodation of mule drivers, cattle herds and petty retail dealers.' But I was alone – not a mule driver in sight; I would have welcomed his company. There was a dog by the door, chewing at the fleas on his hindquarters. I gave him a lump of gristle from my plate and, watching his wild eyes as he champed it, I thought how lucky I was that there was a train out of this place in the morning. 'Very early,' the hotel-keeper had said. I had replied, 'The earlier the better.'

Tecún Umán was a tiny railhead – no more. But once, from here to Panama – then a neglected province of Colombia – it was all regarded as the Kingdom of Guatemala. It was an unstable and quarrelsome kingdom and, when a series of revolts resulted in a constitutional regime and a kind of futile independence, it became even more unstable. It was also menaced by Mexico – by the absurd Iturbide who had had himself crowned in a self-flattering ceremony: 'emperor by the grace of God and of bayonets,' was Bolivar's jeer. Guatemalan independence had meant the setting up of town councils, and in 1822 these councils voted to annex Guatemala to Mexico, reasoning that it was better to join the Mexicans than be humiliated in battle by them. But Mexican instability was apparent from the first, Iturbide was recognized as a tyrant, and a year later Guatemala withdrew and her National Assembly declared the independence of the five provinces: Guatemala, Costa Rica, Honduras, Nicaragua and El Salvador.

This was nominally a confederation, the United Provinces of Central America, though for the next eighty years the foreign traveller continued to call them 'Guatemala' and to treat his adventuring in the jungles of Costa Rica and Nicaragua and his canoe trips across El Salvador's Lake Ilopango as travel in Guatemala. If Guatemala was merely a misnomer for this jumble of countries, 'United Provinces' was the kind of fatuous violation of language that in our day terms the grotesque dictatorship a 'People's Republic'. Civil war was almost immediate in the five countries: it was woodsman against townie, conservative against liberal, Indian against Spaniard, tenant farmer against landlord; the provinces battled, and unity disintegrated in sabre charges and cannon fire. Within fifteen years the area was political and social bedlam – or, as one historian has written, 'quintuple confusion'. American and British travellers grumbled heartily about the difficulties of cutting their way from village to village, and remarked on how little was known of this attenuated tissue of geography on which South America swung from North America.

It is hard to keep the names straight. Guatemala is the anvil-shaped one next to Mexico; El Salvador is the tiny one being squashed by the blob of Honduras to the shape of a rectangular raft and proving unseaworthy on its launch into the Pacific; Nicaragua is a wedge, Costa Rica the cuff on Panama's extended sleeve. There are no railways in Belize. Considering their history – not only the riots, civil wars and revolutions, but also the uproarious earthquakes and incessant vulcanism – it is a wonder they exist at all and have not furiously vanished beneath the sea. These countries lie on one of our planet's worst fault-lines, a volcanic fissure which, each year, threatens to shift in the tremendous way it has been promising, and swallow them and their wranglings. Oddly, the proudest boast of these countries is their volcanoes: they are on every national emblem, on most of the money, and figure prominently in their superstitions.

All this lay ahead of me, but I intended to stick to my route and deal with one country at a time. I had got some puzzled looks from the hotel-keeper when I told him I was going to catch the train.

'The bus is quicker,' he said.

'I'm not in a hurry,' I said.

'The train is very old.'

'The Mexican train to Tapachula was old.'

'But this one is dirty as well.'

'I'll have a bath when I get to Guatemala City.'

'All the other tourists take buses. Or taxis.'

'I'm not a tourist.'

'Yes,' he said, seeing that my mind was made up, 'the train is very interesting. But for some reason no one ever takes it.'

He was mistaken about that, for one thing. There was a crowd of people at the station early the following morning. They were undersized – farmers in slouch hats and straw sombreros, Indian women with papooses and pigtails, barefoot children. Each person had a large bundle, a basket tied with vines or a home-made suitcase. I concluded that this was the reason they had chosen to take the train – their belongings would have been unwelcome on a bus. The train also took a different route from any of the buses, and the train-fare from Tecún Umán to Guatemala City was less than two dollars. Until ten minutes before the train was to leave, a policeman kept us away from the platform barrier, and we stood clutching our tickets – strips of paper with all the intermediate stations listed: one's ticket was guillotined at the station where one was to disembark.

The difference between Mexican trains and Guatemalan trains was obvious as soon as we were permitted to board. The cars – four of them – were very small wooden contraptions with large windows. There was no glass in the windows, no paint on the wood. It was narrow gauge and had the look of a train you might see in a decayed amusement park, too tiny and decrepit to take seriously. The seats were also tiny and they were filled within five minutes of our departure. I sat knee to knee with an Indian woman who, as soon as we left, put her chin against the red blanket on her shoulder and went to sleep. Her thin restless child, a small girl in a torn dress, stared at me. No one in the train spoke except to haggle with the hawkers boosting fruit on us, at the stations along the way.

Although I had the satisfaction of knowing that the train was a continuation of the one I had taken that frosty morning two weeks before in Boston, this passenger train to Guatemala City held no promise of comfort or companionship, and on this day obscured with smoke and mist I had no real expectation of anything but a fairly rough ride through damp and shrouded jungle. The jungle, where it was not an overhang of dark trees, gave the impression of dumped litter – wrappings, string, broken boxes, bits of rag; these I saw were not junk, but dead leaves and vines and flowers. The jungle itself was grey this cloudy morning, and the train rocking on the track and showing its scars (the scorched ceiling, the splintered seats), and stopping and starting with great uncertainty, seemed to me highly unreliable, if not downright dangerous. On the map it seemed a simple transit: Veracruz–Tapachula–Tecún Umán–Guatemala City – two days at most. But the map was misleading, and this train – which emitted groans on curves and slight ascents – did not really seem capable to me of completing the trip. The passengers' faces were set in frowns, as if they shared my conviction. The track had been cleared, but ten feet away the jungle dripped and was so dense no light showed through it.

A Bostonian had come this way in 1886, and charmed by the wildness of the place had regarded the arrival of the railway with a kind of horror. His was in a sense a typical curmudgeonly snobbery about travel, a bragging about the glory of travelling through trackless woods with a pack of Indians and muleskinners (Evelyn Waugh fills the Introduction to *When The Going Was Good* – the curmudgeon's catch-phrase – with the same grumpy boasts). 'Old travellers know how soon the individuality of a country is lost when once the tide of foreign travel is turned through its towns or its by-ways,' writes William T. Brigham in his *Guatemala*. (I think he is the same William Brigham who nearly electrocuted himself in Hawaii when he touched a wooden stick which a native magician had loaded with some high voltage mumbo-jumbo.) Brigham soon makes his fears particular: 'When the Northern Railroad extends through Guatemala, when the Transcontinental Railway traverses the plains of Honduras, and the Nicaraguan Canal unites the Atlantic and the Pacific, the charm will be broken, the mulepath and the *mozo de cargo* (carrier of bundles) will be supplanted, and a journey across Central America become almost as dull as a journey from Chicago to Cheyenne.'

How wrong he was.

Chiapas had been arid – a stony exposed landscape that looked as if it had yet to be possessed by man. This part of Guatemala was heavily forested at the border – the national frontier was abruptly apparent in the rising land and the vine-covered trees – and as we descended to Coatepeque and Retalhuleu the scenery became tropical in its disorder – the jungle sprawled, the huts were poor and small and badly-made – and the only symmetries were the stretches of cane fields. In Mexico I had seen the cut cane in railway freight cars; here it was loaded on wagons and old tottering trucks, and sheaves of it dragged on the road and dropped, so that most of the roads were strewn and looked as if a fierce storm had just blown through and knocked these bare branches down.

The cane cutting had given Guatemala a sickly sweet odour. The sugary smell was released by the men with machetes, but as the day grew hotter the smell weighted the air. It was a noxious sweetness, like syrup made into smoke, with a whiff of vegetables and an abrasive chemical aftertaste. And there was in it, too, a sharper stink, the nauseating gust you would get by burning sugar over a fire and reducing it to black junk. This was the height of the cane harvest and the smells and the stacked trucks and the worker gangs made Guatemala seem a place of considerable enterprise, but of an old-fashioned plantation sort.

We travelled parallel to a road, and crossed it occasionally, but for most of the time we were not near to places that were very densely inhabited. The towns were small and tumbledown and in this busriding country most of the people lived on the main roads. After a few stops I could see that this was regarded as a

111

local train – no one was going any great distance. Passengers who had got on at Tecún Umán were going to the market at Coatepeque, which was on a road, or to Retalhuleu to get to the coast, about twenty-five miles away. By noon we were at La Democracia. At the time I had concluded that this was an ironical name, but perhaps it was a fitting name for a place with a sweet-sour smell, and huts made out of sticks and cardboard and hammered-out tins, and howling radios and clamouring people – some boarding buses, some selling fruit, but the majority merely standing wrapped in blankets and looking darkly at the train. And tired children were hunkered down in the mud. Here was a fancy car among the jalopies, and there a pretty house among the huts. Democracy is a messy system of government, and there was a helter-skelter appropriateness in the name of this disordered town. But how much democracy was there here?

There were election posters pasted on the pillars of the shop verandahs. There would be an election in a few months. On the way to Guatemala City I tried to engage passengers in political talk, but I quickly discovered that Guatemalans had none of the candour I had found in Mexicans. 'Echeverria was a bandit and a hypocrite,' one man told me; 'Lopez Portillo is just the same – give him time.' Guatemalans were more circumspect: they shrugged, they spat, they rolled their eyes; they did not utter their political preferences. But who could blame them? For twelve years the country had been governed by a party of fanatical anti-communists – a party greatly fancied by America's Central Intelligence Agency, which has yet to perceive that fanatical anti-communists are almost invariably fanatical anti-democrats. In the late 1960s and early 1970s there was a wave of guerrilla activity – kidnappings, murders and bombings; but the army proved ineffectual against the guerrillas and in Guatemala due process of law had always been notoriously slow. The answer was simple. Using the advice of the United States Embassy's military attaché (later found murdered), a number of vigilante groups were set up. A vigilante assassination-squad is answerable to no one, and the 'White Hand', Guatemala's version of a volunteer Gestapo unit, has been responsible for thousands of murders and torturings. It seems strange that such a small country could produce such an appalling haemorrhage, that a system of terror and counter-terror could be responsible for so many deaths. And you might ask: What is the point? Seventy-five percent of Guatemalans are peasants of a classical sort: subsistence farmers and part-time cane-cutters, coffee-pluckers and cotton-pickers. The government, while insisting that it is democratic and does not imprison people, rigs elections and allows the 'White Hand' and a score of other vigilante groups to terrorize a justifiably sullen population. (There are plenty of freelance gunmen in Guatemala; in 1975, the vice-president claimed that he had enough armed men in his party alone to invade Belize, if the army proved gutless or unwilling.) Given the circumstances, it did not seem to me unusual that La Democracia was a mess or that my fellow passengers on the train were gloomy.

I had a political reverie on that train. It was this: the government held elections, encouraged people to vote and appeared to be democratic. The army appeared to be impartial, the news-papers disinterested. And it remained a peasant society, basically underfed and unfree. It must perplex any peasant to be told he is living in a free country, when the facts of his life contradict this. It might be that this does not perplex him; he has every reason to believe, in accordance with the evidence, that democracy is feudal, a bureaucracy run by crooks and trigger-happy vigilantes. When one sees a government of the Guatemalan sort professing such high-mindedness in its social aims and producing such mediocre results, one cannot be surprised if the peasant con-cludes that communism might be an improvement. It was a Latin American sickness: inferior government gave democracy an evil name and left people no option but to seek an alternative. The cynic might say – I met many who did – that these people are better off with an authoritarian government. I happen to think this is nonsense. From Guatemala to Argentina, the majority of the countries are run by self-serving tyrannies which are only making the merciless vengeance of anarchy inevitable. The shabby deceits were as apparent from this train as a row of Burma-Shave signs.

The stinging sweetness of the sugar cane, the putrefaction in every dismal village, the sorry children, the very frail huts and the sombre faces of the passengers in the train – it all made my mood reflective. And, having taken the train, I had the illusion that I was not terribly far from Boston – I had left the American border just a week ago. The train had given me a sense of continuity which, unlike the dislocation and disconnection one experiences after a plane journey, had made Guatemala seem incongruous and puzzling. On this branch-line from Boston I had found barefoot Indians and starving children and rather ominous-looking peasants with two-foot knives resting on their knees.

The atmosphere in the train was grim. This was the bottom of the social scale, mainly people going to the next village, a ten-cent ride to sell a dollar's worth of bananas. The children chattered; no one else did. The adults seemed incurious, even surly, and those whose eyes I caught watching me appeared guiltily suspicious and turned away. In conversation they were off-hand. They aked no questions at all; their replies were brief.

At Coatepeque I said to a man on the platform, 'It's cold here. Is it always this cold?'

'Sometimes,' he said. He walked away.

At Santa Lucia I asked a man how far he had come. He said Mazatenango.

'Do you live at Mazatenango?'

'No.' He said nothing more. When the train moved on he changed his seat.

At La Democracia I told a man I was headed for Zacapa. He said nothing. I said I was taking the train to Zacapa. He said nothing. I wondered if he was deaf. I said, 'Is it hard to get to Zacapa?'

'Yes,' he said, and lapsed into silence once again.

He was smoking a cigarette. Most of the passengers had cigarettes in their mouths. It seemed to be a country of chain-smokers. A British traveller remarked, 'There are fashions in Guatemala which it would require more than common charity to speak of with respect; and among these stands foremost the immoderate use of tobacco, by both sexes.' That was in 1828. The traveller – his name was Henry Dunn – estimated that men

114

smoked twenty cigars a day and women fifty cigarettes. No one on my train smoked a cigar, but as I have said the passengers represented the poorest class in the country.

It helps to take the train if one wishes to understand. Understanding was like a guarantee of depression, but it was an approach to the truth. For most tourists, Guatemala is a four-day affair with quaintness and ruins: veneration at the capital's churches, a day sniffing nosegays at Antigua, another at the colourful Indian market at Chichicastenango, a picnic at the Mayan temples of Tikal. I think I would have found this itinerary more depressing, and less rewarding, than my own meandering from the Mexican border through the coastal departments. The train creaked and whimpered but, incredibly, it kept to its schedule: at 3:20 we were at Santa Maria – as promised in *Cook's International Timetable* – and, eating my fifth banana of the day, I studied our progress on our climb to Escuintla and the greater heights of Guatemala City.

Now there were volcanoes all around us, or volcanic hills with footstool shapes that the Mexicans call 'little ovens'. It was cooler, and as the sun grew pinker and a ridge of hills rose to meet it where it hovered drawn to the shape of a chalice near the Pacific, the gathering darkness threw half-tones across the hills; those fragments of white were the hats and shirts of cane-cutters marching home. But it was not an ordinary jungle twilight, the mould of shadow under wide gleaming leaves, flickering hut fires and the jostlings of mottled pigs and goats. The sky was in flames far-off, and when we came closer the fire was revealed as enormous: bonfires of waste cane burned in sloping fields and sent up cloud tides that were purple and orange and crimson; they floated and lost their colour, becoming white until the night absorbed them. Then this smoke fogged the tracks and it was as if we were travelling on some antique steam locomotive in a mountain pass in Asia, through fog that smelled of stale candy. In the words of Hart Crane, we 'roared by and left / three men, still hungry on the tracks, ploddingly / watching the tail lights wizen and converge, slip- / ping gimleted and neatly out of sight.'

The last landscape I had seen in daylight had been a row of volcanoes, shaped like a child's drawing of mountain peaks, with stiff steep sides and narrow summits. As we drew near to Guatemala City there was no landscape to speak of. There were the cane fires, and I could see the headlamps of cars on roads, but the rest was black with a scattering of lanterns, and now and then an illuminated church steeple at a mountain village. It was chilly as we passed through the highlands to enter the city on the plateau: huts, houses, street-lights, buildings. We crossed a bridge over the main street. The passengers who had come from the coast looked down at the glare and the crowds with what seemed like alarm.

Guatemala City, an extremely horizontal place, is like a city on its back. Its ugliness, which is a threatened look (the low morose houses have earthquake cracks in their façades; the buildings wince at you with fright lines), is ugliest on those streets where, just past the last toppling house, a blue volcano's cone bulges. I could see the volcanoes from the window of my hotel room. I was on the third floor, which was also the top floor. They were tall volcanoes and looked capable of spewing lava. Their beauty was undeniable; but it was the beauty of witches. The rumbles from their fires had heaved this city down.

The first capital had been destroyed by torrents of water. So the capital was moved three miles away to Antigua in the middle of the sixteenth century. In 1773, Antigua was flattened by an earthquake, and a more stable site – at least it was farther from the slopes of the great volcanoes – was found here, in the Valley of the Hermitage, formerly an Indian village. Churches were built – a dozen, of Spanish loveliness, with slender steeples and finely finished porches and domes. The earth shook – not much, but enough to split them. Tremors left cracks between windows, and separated, in the stained-glass of those windows, the shepherd from his brittle flock, the saint from his gold staff, the martyr from his persecutors. Christs were parted from their crosses and the anatomy of chapel Virgins violated, as their enamelling, the porcelain white of faces and fingers, shattered, sometimes with a report that startled the faithful in their prayers. The windows, the statues, the masonry were mended; and gold leaf was applied thickly to the splintered altars. It seemed the churches had been made whole again. But the motion of earthquakes had never really ceased. In Guatemala they were inescapable. And in 1917 the whole city was thrown into its streets – every church and house and brothel. Thousands died; that unprecedented earthquake was seen as a judgement; and more fled to the Caribbean coast, where there were only savages to contend with.

The Guatemalans, sullen at the best of times, display a scolded resignation – bordering at times on guiltiness – when the subject of earthquakes is raised. Charles Darwin is wonderful in the sense of dislocation and spiritual panic that earthquakes produce in people. He himself experienced an earthquake, when the *Beagle* was anchored off the Chilean coast. 'A bad earthquake,' he writes, 'at once destroys our oldest associations: the earth, the very emblem of solidity, has moved beneath our feet like a thin crust over a fluid; – one second of time has created in the mind a strange idea of insecurity, which hours of reflection would not have produced.'

And, speaking of his own frequent earthquakes, the Guatemalan seems to imply in his undemonstrative way that the punishment is deserved. It *is* a judgement, and it was foretold in *Revelation* ('what must soon take place'), in Chapter Six, the opening of the sixth seal: 'I looked, and behold, there was a great earthquake; and the sun became black as sackcloth, the full moon became like blood, and the stars of the sky fell to the earth as the fig tree sheds its winter fruit when shaken by a gale; the sky vanished like a scroll that is rolled up, and every mountain and island was removed from its place. Then the kings of the earth and the great men and the generals and the rich and the strong, and every one, slave and free, hid in the caves and among the rocks of the mountains . . .'

Guatemalan earthquakes are no worse than this doomsday spectacle.

The city has been rebuilt. There is no other place to shift it. Succeeding earthquakes have left their marks on Guatemala City, but these wrinkles – part of the look of Guatemala – are less of a disfigurement than the styles of building that supplanted the Spanish architecture. Terraces of huts, the spattered stucco of mock-colonial houses, two-storey blocks and now the taller American-style hotels (how long, one wonders, will these monstrosities last?) constitute the city today. Some of the churches have been put back together, their refinements blunted in the rebuilding.

I found the churches gloomy, but after a few days churchgoing was my single recreation. 'The inhabitants of Guatemala appear to have little of the desire for public amusements seen in most cities,' wrote Robert Dunlop in 1847. It was hard to knock holes in any of these old assessments. 'Almost the only recreation of the natives being the religious processions, at which the figures of saints are paraded ... of these, there are two or three every month.' For historical, religious and seismic reasons I chose the church of La Merced. It was the feast day of Our Lady of Mercy, to whom the church is consecrated. The church showed earthquake damage, though not so much as the Cathedral which, with its cracked arches and pillars and part of its ceiling missing, ought to be condemned as unsafe. La Merced also was damaged, but it had been recommended by the Chevalier Arthur Morelet (described by his translator as 'a French gentleman of leisure and extensive scientific acquirements'), who in his *Travels in Central America* (1871) called it, 'a pretty church with a fine site. From an artistic point of view, its massive towers are open to criticism, notwithstanding that they give to the edifice a great part of its originality.'

There were several hundred people in front of La Merced, waiting to go in – so many, that I had to enter by a side door. Inside, there were three activities in progress: a very large crowd in the centre aisle were pushing to get near a robed priest who held a tall candle in a silver candlestick – the object was about the size of a shotgun; another group was more scattered – these were families having their pictures taken by men with Polaroid cameras; the last large group had congregated around a table set up near a brutal crucifixion and they were signing a clipboard of papers and handing coins to a man – this, I discovered, was a lottery. And at the small chapels and minor altars people were praying, lighting candles, carrying tapers or chatting amiably. At a side chapel was the Virgin of Chiquiniquira, a black madonna with an ebony face. Black Guatemalans (there are many; a settlement of blacks at Livingstone on the Caribbean coast is English-speaking) had prostrated themselves before the nigrescent virgin who 'loaded down with sumptuous toys,' remarks Morelet, 'receives exclusively the homage of the faithful of the African race.'

Travellers less sympathetic than Morelet – one supposes them to be unyielding Protestants – have seen Guatemalan Catholicism as barbarous. Dunlop regarded saints' days in Guatemala as no more than occasions for the combustion of 'great quantities of fireworks' and disgusted by the statues Dunn wrote, 'most of the images of the saints . . . are very common pieces of sculpture, and disfigured by absurd and vulgar dresses.' Aldous Huxley, who affected a kind of comic, stuporous Buddhism (his senile transcendentalism he gave fictional form in his silly novel *Island*) jeered at Guatemalan penitents until his package tour called him to Antigua, where his jeers were resumed.

Anyone who finds a frenzied secularity at a church service in Guatemala – and thinks it should be stamped out – ought to go to the North End of Boston on the feast day of Saint Anthony and consider the probability of redemption in the scuffles of ten thousand Italians frantically pinning dollar bills to the cassock of their patron saint, who is borne on a litter past pizza parlours and mafia hangouts in a procession headed by a wailing priest and six smirking acolytes. Compared to that, the goings-on at La Merced were solemn. The priest with the silver candle appeared to be fighting his way through the crowd of women – there were only women in that part of the church. Actually, what he was doing was allowing the women to get a grip on the candle. A woman waited, lunged, gripped the candle in both hands and yelled an ejaculation; the priest yanked the candle from her hands and another woman made a dive for it. The priest continued to move in a circle; his perspiration had turned his white surplice grey.

The Polaroid cameramen were slightly better organized. They had touts who were rushing up to family groups and, for two dollars, posing them near especially punished-looking saints in order to have their pictures taken. There was heavy competition. I counted fourteen photographers and as many touts. They had deployed themselves from the sacristy door to the baptismal font, and in every niche and near every altar – there were two photographers near St Sebastian: that martyring was particularly prized – flashbulbs popped and credulous Indians gasped as they saw their startled faces sharpening in full colour on snapshot squares. It was in a way the miracle they had hoped for, though the price was high – two dollars was a week's pay.

The lottery was much cheaper. At that table near the crucifixion the crowd was so large I had to stand for fifteen minutes before I could get a glimpse at the clipboard or the fee or, for that matter, the prize. This was not a literate country – that much was clear. Only a handful of the people were able to sign their names; the rest told their names to a lady in a black shawl. She slowly copied the name down, with the person's address; the person handed over ten cents and received a slip of paper with a number on it. Most of the people were Indian women, carrying babies on slings on their backs like slumping rucksacks or papooses. I waited until a man signed the paper and followed him as he walked away smiling at his coupon.

'Excuse me,' I said. 'But what are you hoping to win?'

'You did not see the statue?'

'No.'

'It is on the table – come.' He took me around the back of the crowd and pointed. The lady in the black shawl, seeing that I was a foreigner who craved a look at the statue, lifted it up for me to admire.

'It is beautiful, no?'

'Very beautiful,' I said.

'I think it is very expensive.'

'Of course.'

Some Indian women heard. They nodded; they grinned – they had no teeth; they said it was very lovely, and they went on speaking their names, or signing, and paying their money.

The prize in the lottery – it was more than a statue – was extraordinary. It was an image of Jesus, about two feet high, with his back turned. He wore a crown of gold and a bright red cape with gold fringes, and with his right hand he was knocking on the door of a cottage. It was almost certainly a copy of an

English country cottage – a plastic cottage wall of stone, and plastic beams at the eaves; a mullioned window with plastic panes; and an oaken plastic door surrounded by rambling plastic roses, some blue and some yellow. They were not morning glories – they had plastic thorns. A Catholic education had introduced me to Jesus on the cross, in a boat, being flogged, working in a carpentry shop, praying, denouncing the moneychangers and standing in a river to be baptized. I had never seen Jesus knocking at the door of an English country cottage, though I had a dim memory of a painting depicting something similar (five months later, walking through St Paul's Cathedral in London I saw Holman Hunt's 'The Light of the World' and was able to link it to that Guatemalan set-piece).

'What is Jesus doing?' I asked the Guatemalan man.

'As you see,' he said. 'Knocking on the door.' *Knocking* is a violent word in Spanish – more like hammering or throttling. Jesus was not doing that.

'Why is he doing that?'

The man laughed. 'He wants to go in. I *think* he wants to go in.'

The lady in the black shawl put it down. She said, 'It is heavy.'

'That house,' I said, gesturing. 'Is it in Guatemala?'

'Yes,' said the man. He stood on tiptoe and looked again. 'I cannot say.'

'Does the house represent anything?'

'The little house? It represents a house.'

We were getting nowhere. The man excused himself. He said he wanted to have his picture taken.

There was a priest nearby.

'I have a question, Father.'

He nodded benignly.

'I have been admiring the statue of Jesus in the lottery.'

'A beautiful statue.' he said.

'Yes, but what does it represent?'

'It represents Jesus, who is visiting a house. The house is represented. You are an American, no? Many Americans come here.'

'I have never seen anything like it before.'

'This is a very special lottery. Our feast day.' He bowed. He wanted to get away from me.

'Is that in the Bible? Jesus at the little house?'

'Oh, yes. Jesus goes to the little house. He visits the people, he preaches and so forth.'

He sounded as if he was making this up. I said, 'Where exactly in the Bible –'

'You will excuse me?' he said. He gathered his skirts. 'Welcome to Guatemala.'

Perhaps he thought I was mocking – I wasn't; I was only seeking information. If my hotel had been something other than a flophouse, run by a bad-tempered hag, I might have found a Gideon Bible in a table in my room. But there was no table, no Bible. 'I have a room with a bath,' the hag had said; the bath was a rusty shower pipe suspended from the ceiling on a loop of wire. Two days in this hotel and I was ready to board any train – even a Guatemalan one.

Some time later, I found the Biblical text from which that lottery prize had been derived. It was in *Revelation*, not far from the earthquake reference ('behold there was an earthquake, and the sun became black ...'). In Chapter Three, Christ says, 'Those whom I love, I reprove and chasten; so be zealous and repent. Behold, I stand at the door and knock; if any one hears my voice and opens the door, I will come in and eat with him, and he with me.'

I used my time in Guatemala City to recuperate from the strenuous train-ride I had had from Veracruz. I needed long walks and a couple of good nights' sleep; I made a phone call to London (my wife missed me, I told her I loved her; my children said they had made a snowman; this telephone call cost me $114), and then a tour of the bars where, hoping to meet Guatemalans with lively stories, I was surrounded by disappointed tourists. I walked from one end of the city to the other, from zone to zone, through the curio market (embroidered shirts, baskets, pottery – the clumsy work of defeated-looking Indians) and the food market (skinned pigs' heads, black sausages and the medieval sight of small children binding up bouquets of flowers with bleeding fingers and being shouted at by cruel old men). It was a large city, but not a hospitable one. It had a reputation for thievery; and yet it did not strike me as dangerous, only commonplace and sombre. I suggested to the hag at the hotel that the city seemed to me sadly lacking in entertainment.

'You should go to the market at Chichicastenango,' she said. 'That's what everyone does.'

And that's why I don't want to do it, I thought. I said, 'I am planning to go to Zacapa.'

She laughed. I had not seen her laugh before. It was quite horrible.

'You came here to go to Zacapa!'

'That's right.'

'Do you know how hot it is in Zacapa?'

'I have never been there.'

'Listen,' she said. 'There is nothing in Zacapa. Nothing, nothing.'

'There is a train to Zacapa,' I said. 'And a train out of it, to San Salvador.'

She hooted again. 'Have you seen that train!'

This was starting to annoy me. I wanted to tell her what I thought of her hotel.

She said, 'When I was a small girl my father had a farm in Mazatenango. I used to ride the train all the time. It took a full day! I liked it, because I was a small girl. But I am not a small girl anymore' – this was incontestable – 'and I have not taken the train since. You should take the bus. Forget Zacapa – go to Tikal, see Antigua, buy some things at the market – but don't go to Zacapa.'

I went to the railway station. There was a sign over the two ticket windows. It said, *It Is Much Cheaper To Go By Train!* Over one window was lettered, *To The Pacific*, over the other, *To The Atlantic*. I paid a dollar and bought a ticket to Zacapa, which was halfway down the Atlantic line.

The train was not leaving until seven the next morning, so I went for my last long walk. This took me to Zone Four and a church I had not really expected to find in Guatemala, or this hemisphere. To say the Capilla de Yurrita is mock-Russian orthodox in style is to say nothing, though it has onion domes and ikons. It is a crazy castle. Pink rectangles are painted on its concrete walls to resemble brickwork, and on its main steeple are four gigantic ice-cream cones; beneath the steeple are fourteen pillars, decorated like barber-poles. It has balconies and porches, and rows of cement buds on its castellated roof, four clocks showing the wrong time, gargoyles and a twice-life-sized dog clinging to one of the cones. On the façade are the four Evangelists, and peeping out of windows the twelve Apostles, and three Christs and a twoheaded eagle. It is red and black, rusty metal and tiles. The oak door panels are carved, the left shows Guatemalan ruins, the right Guatemalan tombs, and over the door, in Spanish, a scroll reads 'The Chapel of Our Lady of Anguish' with a dedication to Don Pedro de Alvarado y Mesia. On Don Pedro's shield a conquistador is shown driving an army into retreat and beneath it are three volcanoes, one in eruption.

Inside, there were three old ladies in the front pew singing a hymn to Mary. *Mah-ree-ah*; they sang with passion but off-key; *Mah-ree-ah*. At the back of the church was a lady with a little dog, and five Indians. These pious people were overwhelmed – as who would not be? – by the moorish-style choir loft, the ornate Spanish altar-piece, the vast supine Christ covered with a lace-curtain and attended by a dark-robed Mary with seven silver daggers in her breast. All the statues were clothed and many of the bouquets in the heavy gilt vases were real. The walls were covered with murky gloating frescoes and stone carvings – trees, candles, sunbeams, flames; near the pulpit was a bas-relief of the Sermon on the Mount. Even the small dog was silent. Somehow this maniacally opulent church had survived a hundred years of earthquakes.

But the Polytechnic School further down the Avenida Reforma also was unscathed. It seemed only the most bizarre buildings had withstood the tremors. The Polytechnic was a fake fortress two city blocks wide, with fake watchtowers and sentry posts and what looked like slits for gun emplacements. It was painted grey and on the central tower was the motto 'Virtue – Science – Strength'. The wide shady avenue on which the Polytechnic stood was lined with statuary: a great bronze bull (its penis daubed with red paint), a panther, a stag, another bull – this one charging, a lion killing a crocodile, two large wild boars fighting – one biting the other's belly; at the junction of this avenue and a main street there was a statue – lions, wreaths, maidens and a succession of plinths surmounted by a patriot. Nearby was an open manhole, as deep as a well and twice as wide.

The street was empty; there were no other strollers. I walked and it seemed to me that the way the joke church, the fake palace and the savage statues had endured the worst earthquakes in the world had the makings of a maxim; they had remained intact, as fools survive scorn. I kept walking and, just after nightfall, found a vegetarian restaurant in a darkened suburb. The dining room held only three people, one of whom – in a turban and long beard and the silver bracelet required by the Sikh religion – was a young Californian. He told me that he was on the point of rejecting Sikhism, but had not got around to shaving, and the turban gave him confidence. These three were architects, designing houses for the people who had been made homeless in the earthquake of 1976, two years before.

'Are you just designing the houses?' I asked. 'Or are you building them, too?'

'Designing, making concrete blocks, planning villages, building the houses – the whole bit,' said the man in the turban.

I put it to him that this sort of idealism could be carried too far. Surely it was the government's job to see that people were housed. If they needed money they could sell some of those bronze statues as scrap metal.

'We're working under the government,' said one of the others.

Wouldn't it be better, I said, to teach people how to make houses and let them get on with the job?

'What we do,' said the man in the turban, 'is put up three walls. If someone wants the house he has to finish it – put up the fourth wall and the roof.'

I approved of this effort. It seemed to strike the right balance, the trust in idealism tempered by a measure of caution. I said that, so far, I had found the Guatemalans a pretty gloomy bunch. Was this their experience?

'You answer,' said one to the man in the turban. 'You've been here for a year.'

'They're heavy,' said the man in the turban, stroking his beard sagely. 'But they've got a lot to be heavy about.'

7 The 7:00 to Zacapa

It was a brutal city, but at six in the morning a froth of fog endowed it with a secrecy and gave it the simplicity of a mountain-top. Before the sun rose to burn it away, the fog dissolved the dull straight lines of its streets, and whitened its low houses and made its sombre people ghostly as they appeared for moments before being lifted away, like revengers glimpsed in their hauntings. Then Guatemala City, such a grim thing, became a tracing, a sketch without substance, and the poor Indians and peasants – who had no power – looked blue and bold and watchful. They possessed it at this hour. There was no wind; the fog hung in fine grey clouds, a foot from the ground. Even the railway station, no more than a brick shed, took on the character of a great terminus: there was no way of verifying that it did not rise up for five stories in a clock tower crowned by pigeons and iron-work, so well hidden was its small tin roof by the fog the volcanoes had trapped. There were about twenty people standing near the ticket window of the station – in rags; but their rags seemed just another deception of the fog.

They carried baskets, cardboard boxes, bananas and machetes. They were Indians and weatherbeaten farmers, standing in silence in the dampness. One distinguished-looking man in a spotless sombrero and white moustache and frock coat smoked a cheroot. From the waist up he could have been the mayor, but his trousers were ragged and he wore no shoes – as the shoe-shine boys lingering near by were quick to point out. They too were barefoot.

A bell was rung. The gate was opened. We went through to the platform. The cars – in much worse shape than the ones that had taken me from Tecún Umán – had the further disadvantage of having been soaked by the fog. The padded seats were torn –

springs and stuffing protruded; the wooden seats were shaky; all the seats were wet. The car itself, a relic from the 1920s, was neither quaint nor comfortable, but merely a small uncared-for box, with bare wires hanging from the ceiling, and stinking of dirt. It was shaped, as all Central American railways cars were shaped, like a trolley car – wooden, with a curved roof and a verandah platform at either end. Zacapa was not on the tourist route; if it was, there would have been a well-sprung bus serving the Zacapa Department. The Guatemala Tourist Board was attentive to the needs of the visitors. But only barefoot peasants lived in Zacapa and their train matched them in looking woebegone.

We sat in the wet car listening to the jabber on a girl's green radio. The girl held it in the crook of her arm; in her other arm was an infant.

A man with a monkey-wrench walked through the car.

The man sitting next to me said, 'This car is broken.'

'That is true,' I said.

There was a shout, followed by a general stampede, as the passengers from this car ran into the next one. I watched Indians dragging baskets, and women pushing children, and men with machetes. Most people merely put their heads down and butted their way into the next car. I was alone in the car a few minutes later. 'Get out,' said the man with the monkey-wrench, so I followed the others – two cars' passengers jammed into one – and considered myself lucky to find a seat.

'Good morning,' I said to the Indians, trying to ingratiate myself with people who would share this all-day journey to the eastern province. 'How are you?'

A sniggering man to my left, dandling a large skinny boy on his leg, said, 'They do not speak Spanish. They know a few words – that is all.'

'That is all I know,' I said.

'No – you are doing extremely well.'

'On the other hand, my English is a little better.'

The man laughed – much too loud. I could see he was drunk, though how he had managed this so early in the morning I could not tell.

127

Our train was shunted back and forth, and the broken car – no more broken-looking than the one we were in – was removed. I had expected a delay; I had the morning paper and a novel to read, but on the dot of seven the train's harsh horn blew, and we began racing through the fog at the edge of a muddy road.

At the first level crossing, there was great confusion outside the train, and inside a woman stood up and began to laugh and shout. The train had slowed down for the crossing, and now I could see a boy running alongside with a bundle. The woman yelled to the boy, telling him to hurry, but at that moment a soldier by the door (there were two soldiers in each of the train's three cars) put down his automatic rifle and leaned out and caught the bundle. The soldier handed it to the woman.

'It is my food,' said the woman.

The passengers continued to stare at her.

'I forgot it this morning,' she said. 'That was my son.'

'He is a fast runner!' said the drunken man next to me. 'That soldier is pretty quick, too. Hyah!'

The soldier had tucked his rifle under his arm. He took up his position by the door and glowered at the man. You might have thought, from the way the soldiers scanned the huts by the track side and kept their rifles ready, that they expected to come under heavy fire. But nothing more lethal than a banana peel was aimed at the train.

These huts, and some in a horrific slum outside San Salvador, were the worst I saw in Latin America. Rural poverty is bad, but there is hope in a pumpkin field, or the sight of chickens, or a field of cattle which, even if they are not owned by the people in the huts, offer opportunities to the hungry cattle rustler. But this slum outside Guatemala City, a derangement of feeble huts made out of paper and tin, was as hopeless as any I had ever seen in my life. The people who lived here, I found out, were those who had been made homeless in the last earthquake – refugees who had been here for two years and would probably stay until they died, or until the government dispersed them, and set fire to the shacks, so that tourists would not be upset by this dismal sight. The huts were made out of waste lumber and tree branches, cardboard and bits of plastic, rags, car doors and palm fronds, metal signboards that had been abstracted from poles, and grass woven into chicken-wire. And the slum, which remained in view for twenty minutes – miles of it – smouldered; near each house was a small cooking fire, with a blackened tin can simmering on it. Children rise early in the tropics; this seemed to be an entire slum of children, very dirty ones, with their noses running, waving at the train from curtains of yellow fog.

The train passengers on their way to Zacapa did not take much interest in this slum, but one could hardly blame them. They were as ragged as the people in the huts.

And then there was nothing. No shacks, no trees, no people, no smoke, no barking dogs. The ground gave way and there was emptiness; the sound of birds and insects was eclipsed, and in that silence was a thin echo of crows. It was a startling experience of space. We were on a bridge and crossing a deep gorge. I looked out of the window; the sight took my breath away – my legs went numb and a buzz began in my ears. Hundreds of feet down, at the rusty struts of a bridge, a gash of rock lay beneath us. We were leaving Guatemala City's plateau and making our way across this rickety bridge – but a long one: I could not see the far side – to the mountains on the north-east of the city. It seemed a particularly dangerous traverse for this train, not only because it was so old and trembled on the bridge, but also because all the windows were open.

Steeling myself for the shock, I leaned out and took another look at the gorge. There was no water in it. There were pinnacles of rock which had snagged scraps of fog, as country hedges and thorns snag bunches of fleece; and through this streaming whiteness a pair of crows flew and steadied themselves. I looked down upon the crows' backs, and this sight, with the white behind it, was like a glimpse of sky – the birds' silhouette in the clouds – as if the train had turned upside down. There was nothing but fog above the train, but below it were broken clouds, and birds, and a glint of sun. This topsy-turvy sight made my head swim. I shut the window.

'Open the window!' A boy of about eight or nine hit me on the knee.

'No,' I said.

'I want to look out!'

'It is dangerous,' I said.

'I want to see!' he yelled, and tried to get past me.

'Sit down,' I said. People were staring at me. 'It is very dangerous.'

The boy spoke to his father – the drunken man. 'I want to look out of the window. He will not let me!'

I smiled at the old man. 'He will fall into the valley.'

'You,' said the old man, pushing the child aside, 'you will fall into the valley!' The boy sulked. The old man said to me, 'He is always causing trouble. One day, something terrible will happen to him.'

I could see that the old drunken man was angry. Trying to calm him I said, 'Your son is a good boy, but this train is very dangerous – so –'

'This train is not very dangerous,' said the man. 'It is an old useless train. It is worth nothing.'

'Right,' I said. The Indians nodded. It gladdened me to know that these people recognized that the train was a piece of junk. I had thought, from their silence, that they had not noticed.

There were more bridges, more gorges filled with cloud and fog, but none was so frightening as that first one. And yet this part of the trip reminded me of the route through the Khyber Pass taken by the battered train to Peshawar. It was more than the view from a similarly beat-up car of rocky mountainsides; it was the sight of a dozen sections of track – ahead, across the valley, and one beneath that, and one over there, and another lying parallel, and more above and below all the way to the valley floor. Not a dozen railways, but pieces of the one we were on, sections that would lead this wheezing engine around four mountains to a descent, another bridge, another climb to the winding sections that ringed those far-off cliffs. Round and round we went; sometimes the engine was silenced by its distance from us on the far side of a ridge, while at other times the curves were so tight it roared past us on a hairpin and seemed like a different train altogether, going in the opposite direction.

The valley floors were stony; the fog had lifted here. The sun revealed the landscape as dead and brown, and the plants which appeared as pale green woods from on high were thorn bushes and bunches of cactus, so thin they cast no shadows. I had thought Guatemala was green – the whole of it like the jungly part around Tecún Umán – but passing from west to east and then pushing north-east to Zacapa, the country had become barer and poorer and stonier. Now in the Motagua Valley – shown on the map as hilly, with a river running though it – we were in a waterless desert: no sign of the river in this parched wasteland. The mountains were stone, the riverbeds rocky; no people. And it looked even worse up ahead as the empty land stretched dustily into the sun.

Every ten or fifteen minutes, the train halted. The soldiers jumped out and positioned themselves in a crouch on the ground, a firing posture. Then a few people would hop to the ground and, without looking back at the train, begin walking into the desert – gone, lost behind the boulders, before the train started again. Most of these stations were not listed on the ticket; they were signboards, a clump of cactus, nothing more than that. Aguas Calientes was one of these: a sign, some cactus, a heap of rocks at the foot of a dry mountain. We started, and I saw a dry riverbed that mimicked a road, but near the riverbed an odd sight – great spurts of white steam from the hot springs that gave this place its name, bubbling from beneath that mountain which was a volcano. There were hot pools around the shooting steam, and women were doing their washing in them. Not even a cactus could live among these geysers – the boiling water foamed in the bare rock and drained through the cracks; and the only live things visible in that dead corner of desert were the bent-over women scrubbing their laundry.

The first large station was not a station at all, but a row of shops, a school, and some tall dead trees. People watched from the porches of the shops and children ran into the schoolyard to look at the train (there were only two trains a week). Here, a number of people got off the train, but no one got on. And the train was so infrequent and undependable that not even food-sellers bothered to show up at this station. A boy with a case of tonic hollered to ask whether anyone wanted a drink – that was all. But one Indian in the opposite seat from mine had got off, so now I could stretch out my legs.

The heat had put most of the passengers to sleep. They were small people, they fit these seats and could be recumbent in them. I hunched forward and forced myself to take notes on the blank pages of the book I was too tired to read, Poe's *Narrative of Arthur Gordon Pym*. From time to time I smoked my pipe. I did not talk to anyone. No one talked to anyone. There was no conversation on this train.

It struck me that since leaving Veracruz the trains I had taken had not been noticeably congenial. I was continually reminded that I was travelling alone. I had not expected the people to be so dour or the trains to be in such a state of decay. I had assumed there would be the usual free-for-all – planters and tenant-farmers, Indians, hippies, ranch-hands, coastal blacks, Americans with rucksacks and road-maps, a few tourists. But the train held only the very poor – everyone else had taken the bus. And these were not just poor people, but defeated people, who wore hats but no shoes, and regarded not only strangers but each other with suspicion. They were hardly the stuff of boon companions, and though I liked the rattle of the train and congratulated myself on having found a little-known route through Central America, this made for rather lonely travel.

The penalty for this sense of discovery – who would have guessed Guatemala to be such desert? – this sustaining experience of making my way among marvels of erupted landscape, was that I was a stranger travelling with strangers. They were either oblivious to, or mystified by my presence. They stole glances at my pipe, but when addressed by me in their own language displayed (in shrugs and grunts) a marked reluctance to chat.

Across the aisle an old woman was hawking and spitting. She would clear her throat and then spit – *pah*! – on the floor at her feet. This annoyed me (and the passengers walking through the mess nauseated me), but there was worse to follow. A woman selling coffee out of a large clay jar entered the train at a tiny station. I had had no breakfast, and more, thought that a hot coffee would be just the thing to bring on a sweat that would cool me. In the hottest areas of Burma, the wise Burmese drink cups of steaming tea and stay cool that way. The coffee-seller dipped a tin cup into her jar and decanted this into a cup she pulled out of her pocket, and handed this to a buyer. When the person finished the coffee, the woman took the cup back and repeated the process. So everyone used the same cup. If I had not known, or if I had been able to persuade myself that I was in no danger, I might have bought a coffee. But, before it was my turn, the spitting woman called the coffee-seller over.

'How much?' she said.

The coffee-seller told her the price: two cents.

The woman spat, drank, wiped her mouth and handed the cup back.

It was my turn next.

I said, 'Do you have another cup?'

'Sorry,' she said and moved away.

Further on, a small girl boarded with some watermelon. Most of it had been sliced. I said, 'Those pieces are too big for me,' and took out my switchblade. As I cut my own piece ('This is about the right size, eh?') – my cutting was a guarantee against cholera – I noticed that what I had taken for seeds on the cut pieces were glossy black flies.

The mountains receded into the distance. We had circled around their slopes and descended to a blighted area, a straight line of track. For the next few hours I looked for the Motagua River, but it was nowhere in view. This was Death Valley. The earth here was finer and duller than sand; it was powder, light brown, that was stirred by the movement of the little train. There was a dusting of it on all the cactuses, which gave them the look of stumps. There is no more hopeless object than a dead cactus; it does not collapse, but rather turns grey and hard and seems to petrify. The rest was scrub or single stones, and once, not far from the track, the ribs and skull of a cow, much whiter than the one I had seen in Texas. The only odour was the dust of this pulverized plain. The chief characteristic of a desert, apart from the absence of water, was this absence of smell.

I kept thinking of what the lady in the hotel had said to me: *Don't go to Zacapa!*

But if I had not come here I would not have known the extent of this desolation. The heat was intense, but it was still tolerable, and hadn't I complained of the cold just a short time ago in Chicago? I had asked for this. And this was the route the muleteers had taken into El Salvador; it was also – though hardly used these days – the principal way of travelling to Puerto Barrios and the so-called Atlantic coast. It was bad, but if it got no worse than this – it was hard to imagine anything worse – it would be bearable.

I did have one fear: that the train would stop, just like that, no warning, no station; that the engine would seize up in the heat and that we would be stuck here. It had happened on what was regarded as a fine railway a hundred miles out of Veracruz, and the Mexicans had no explanation. This railway was clearly much older, the engine more of a gasper. And suppose it does, I thought, suppose it just stops here and can't start? It was ten in the morning, the open cars were full of people, the train carried no water, there was no road for miles, nor was there any shade. How long did it take to die? I guessed it would not take long in this boundless desert.

It was no reassurance, half an hour later, to arrive at the town of Progreso. Aldous Huxley had come this way in 1933: 'As we steamed out of the station, I noticed that the place was called Progreso. The fact annoyed me; I can detect an irony without having it underlined for me.' Progreso was huts of unbaked mud-bricks, with palm-frond roofs (odd: there were no palms nearby, no trees of any sort). And Rancho, some miles further on, was no better: no progress in Progreso, no ranches in Rancho. This was the hottest, dustiest, most derelict place I had seen outside the boondocks of northern Uganda.

But there was one great difference. The graveyard near Rancho was large and easily identifiable as a graveyard. The tombs were nearly as big as Rancho's mud huts; they were solid and looked newly whitewashed, cottage-shaped with pillars and slanting roofs. They were much stronger than the huts. But I could see the logic in this. A man spent a life-time in a mud-hut, but these tombs had to house his remains for all eternity. The mud huts were not built to withstand earthquakes – the tombs were.

In this scorching heat, I was very thirsty. My mouth was so dry I felt as if I had eaten a handful of moths. An hour later I bought a bottle of soda water and drank it warm. But the heat did not let up, nor did the landscape change. From halt to halt, the cactus and the pulverized soil were all there was to see. People scrambled onto the train, people scrambled off; people slept; the old woman spat. Every so often I thought: *What if the engine dies on us – what then?* And saw a skinny man, like the Angel of Death, watching us from the rag of a cactus's shade.

I had passed the point of expecting to see anything different, when a long trough of black water appeared beside the train – an irrigation ditch. It became a narrow canal and poured from spouts into fields – corn at Malena, tobacco at Jicaro. The green was dazzling and I had got so used to the desert tones, this colour seemed miraculous. But it was, after all, no more than a small patch in an immense desert.

Jicaro appeared to be in earthquake country. There were not many huts here, but those I saw all had a crack or a collapsed roof or wall. They were still lived in, however; the people had accommodated themselves to missing walls or gaps. There were houses being built here, too – without a doubt the houses planned by those American architects I had met in Guatemala City. But I could not say that the government-assisted project was a success. There were many three-walled houses, without roofs, which demonstrated the lack of inclination of anyone to finish them off and take up residence. The town of Jicaro was wrecked: the catastrophe showed, and very little of it had been rebuilt.

We came to Cabañas. Here were coconut trees. A woman with a pile of coconuts sliced them open with a machete and passed them into the train – five cents. The passengers drank the coconut water and threw the rest away. Pigs tried to stick their snouts into the coconuts and eat the flesh. But the woman had swiped deftly at the coconuts – three cuts and it became a drinking vessel: the pigs could not get their snouts inside. They whined and chomped the husks.

We were a long time at Cabañas. It was a wooden station, and I supposed that the village was somewhere on the other side of the sand-dune. In Central America, the train station always seemed to be at the edge of town, not in the centre. The temperature in the train rose, and it seemed like an oven now. The rubbish-pile of coconuts had brought out the flies; people snored. I saw some workmen fussing beside the engine and tried to get out.

'Is this your station?' It was a soldier, one of our armed guards.

'No,' I said.

'Get back then.' He pushed his rifle at me.

I hurried to my seat.

It might be here, I thought. *Perhaps this is the end of the line.*

An old man began to shout. He was mocking the place. I think the heat had got to him.

'Cabañas! That is a laugh! Know what cabañas are? They are little huts – you find them near hotels and refreshment stands. Sometimes near the beach.'

The passengers were silent, but the man needed no encouragement.

'Cabañas are pretty and pleasant. You sit there and have nice cool drinks. That is what they call them – cabañas. *And they call this filthy place Cabañas!*'

Hearing this shout, the Indian woman in the next seat opened one eye, but seeing no more than a red-faced man wiping sweat out of his sombrero with a hanky she shut her eye.

'This is not Cabañas – it should have another name.'

The alarm had passed. He was out of breath and gasping.

'I have seen the real cabañas. They are not like this at all.'

No one cared, really. But I thought it was interesting that even these toothless farmers and slumbering Indians found this place laughable. The desolation was obvious to them, and they knew the train was junk. After this, I did not indulge in any charitable self-censorship of my thoughts. Another thing, and more curious, was the fact that people who were not disposed to conversation had no inhibitions about standing up and shouting mad speeches. The man was quiet when the train started again.

The hamlet of Anton Bram was so small its name was not shown on the ticket.

'Anton Bram!' It was the man behind me – hooting.

'What a silly name!' It was his wife.

The passengers smiled. But why hadn't they laughed at Progreso?

We entered another dead valley, and like the first, all the colour had been burned away by the sun. It was flatter than the previous one, and seemed to me much hotter. The vegetation was weird. Here, cactuses grew as tall as elms and were the same shape. The smaller real trees had died and with their bark missing had the paleness of human skin. There were spurges, plants of the genus euphorbia, which were used by some people for medicinal purposes; and other cactuses, with cylindrical limbs, the size of apple trees. The cactus is tenacious. After the shrubs with less complicated root-systems and more munchable leaves have died or been grazed into extinction, the cactus remains, its spines keeping animals away, its fine white hairs shading its tough hide and preventing evaporation. And, under the sky of clearest blue, even more fantastic plants – dog tails sprouting in clusters – hairy brown tubes, prickly pear cactuses, and sprawling nets of weed.

The train was going at ten miles an hour, so it was possible to botanize here on the back pages of my Poe novel, and make some sense of the creeping confusion on the cracked nests of mud-wasps. This business absorbed me until, two hours later, I saw a tractor, a shed, some wrecked houses and then a four-storey structure of grey planks, with a porch on each floor: *Railway Hotel*.

We were in Zacapa.

It was a dusty station at the end of a dusty road and now, in the middle of the afternoon, suffocatingly hot. A group of people at the station barrier yelled at the train. I passed through and, approaching the hotel – it was a ghostly, comfortless place – heard the racket of a generator and saw some men digging near the hotel. The ground was hardened clay: they needed a pneumatic drill to penetrate it. There would be no rest in that hotel. What I could see of the town did not persuade me to linger: cracked huts, a yellow church steeple, more cactuses. So this was Zacapa. The woman in Guatemala City had not exaggerated. It seemed a terrible place, as hot as any of the miserable villages on the railway line, if a bit larger.

I found the Station Manager's office. He had a fan, a calendar, a wooden filing cabinet, a spike of papers. The noise of the generator was loud even here, so I had to raise my voice.

'Excuse me,' I said. 'What time does the train leave for the border?'

'Which border are you crossing?'

It was not an idle question: we were nearer Honduras than El Salvador.

'I'm trying to get to Metapan, in El Salvador.'

'Yes, there is a train to Metapan in two days – on Wednesday. At six-thirty in the morning. Do you want a ticket?'

Two days here! I said, 'No, thank you.'

The train had pulled out of Zacapa and was now on its way north to Puerto Barrios. The station platform was empty, the dust still settling. I studied my Cook's Timetable and saw that if I crossed the border to Metapan or Santa Ana I could get a connection to San Salvador the next day. I decided to do this – the border was not very far, perhaps thirty miles.

A man was watching me. I went over to him and asked him whether there was a bus station in Zacapa.

'Where are you going?'

'El Salvador.'

'Too bad. All the buses to El Salvador leave in the early morning.'

But he was smiling.

I said, 'I would like to go to Santa Ana.'

'I have a car,' he said. 'But petrol is very expensive.'

'I will give you five dollars.'

'For ten I will take you to Anguiatu. That is the border.'

'Is it far?'

'Not very.'

As soon as we left Zacapa we were out of the desert. I could see green hills, rounder ones, with a river running through them. I talked to the man. His name was Sebastiano; he had no job – no one had a job in Guatemala, he said. He was from Zacapa. He hated Zacapa, but he had been to Guatemala City and he thought that was a lot worse.

'There is one thing I think I should tell you,' he said some time later, slowing down at a bend in the road. He drew over to the side and stopped, and smiled sheepishly. 'I have no driving license, and this car – it is not registered. No insurance either – if you do not have a registration what is the point of insurance?'

'Interesting,' I said. 'But why did you stop the car?'

'I cannot take you any further. If I do, the policemen at the border will ask to see my licence and so forth. As I do not have one, they will arrest me and probably treat me badly. I cannot give them a bribe – I do not have any money.'

'You have ten dollars,' I said.

He laughed. 'That will pay for the petrol!'

'So what am I supposed to do?'

He reached across and opened the door. 'Walk,' he said.

'Is it far?'

'Not very.'

He drove away. I stood for a moment on this road at the edge of Guatemala, and then started walking. Not very far, he had said. It was a mile. There was no traffic. There were green trees here and singing birds. My suitcase was not heavy, so I found the hike rather pleasant.

The border was a shed. A boy in a sports shirt stamped my passport and demanded money. He asked me if I was carrying any drugs. I said no. What do I do now? I asked him. You go up the road, he said. There you will find another house. That is El Salvador.

It was a shady road, circling around a hill, past a meadow and a glugging stream. What a transformation in landscapes. Earlier in the day I had thought I was going to wither and die in the wastes of the Motagua Valley, and here I was ambling through green humpy hills to the sound of birdsong. It was sunny late-afternoon as I walked from Guatemala into El Salvador, as fresh and breezy as a summer day in Massachusetts. That border-crossing was as happy a hike as I have ever made and reminded me pleasantly of strolling down the Amherst road into Shutesbury.

A car was parked near a hut, the frontier post. A soldier got out and examined my suitcase. 'What is this?'

'A book. In English, *The Narrative of Arthur Gordon Pym.*'

'Over there,' he said, 'Show your passport.'

'Where are you going?' asked the Immigration Officer.

'Santa Ana.'

A car had arrived at the shed, and a man had got out and was now behind me. He said, 'I am going through Santa Ana. Want a ride?'

'How much?'

'Free!'

So I went to Santa Ana, which was not far away. We passed Lake Guija and more volcanoes and fields of coffee and tobacco.

'Why don't you come with me to San Salvador?' said the man, when we arrived at Santa Ana. 'I am leaving tonight.'

'I think I will stay here.'

'I would advise you not to. This place is full of thieves, pick-pockets and murderers. I am not joking.'

But it was nightfall. I decided to stay in Santa Ana.

8 The Railcar to San Salvador

The town only looked Godforsaken; in fact, it was comfortable. It was a nice combination of attributes. In every respect, Santa Ana, the most Central American of Central American towns, was a perfect place – perfect in its pious attitudes and pretty girls, perfect in its slumber, its coffee-scented heat, its jungly plaza, and in the dusty elegance of its old buildings whose whitewash at nightfall gave them a vivid phosphorescence. Even its volcano was in working order. My hotel, the Florida, was a labyrinthine one-storey affair, with potted palms and wicker chairs and good food – fresh fish, from nearby Lake Guija, was followed by the crushed velvet of Santa Ana coffee, and Santa Ana dessert, a delicate cake of mashed beans and banana served in cream. This pleasing hotel cost four dollars a night. It was a block from the plaza. All Santa Ana's buildings of distinction – there were three – were in the plaza: the Cathedral was neo-gothic, the town hall had the colonnaded opulence of a ducal palace, and the Santa Ana theatre had once been an opera house.

In another climate, I don't think the theatre would have seemed so special, but in this sleepy tropical town in the western highlands of El Salvador – and there was nothing here for the luxury-minded or ruin-hunting tourist – the theatre was magnificent and strange. Its style was banana republic Graeco-Roman; it was newly whitewashed, and classical in an agreeably vulgar way, with cherubs on its façade, and trumpeting angels, and masks of comedy and tragedy, a partial sorority of Muses – a pudgy Melpomene, a pouncing Thalia, Calliope with a lyre in her lap, and – her muscles showing through her tunic as fully developed as a gym teacher's – Terpsichore. There were columns, too, and a Romanesque portico, and on a shield a fuming volcano as nicely proportioned as Izalco, the one just outside town, which was probably the model for this emblem. It was a beautiful turn of the century theatre and not entirely neglected; once, it had provided Santa Ana with concerts and operas, but culturally Santa Ana had contracted and catering to this shrunken condition the theatre had been reduced to showing movies. That week, the offering was *New York, New York*.

I liked Santa Ana immediately; its climate was mild, its people alert and responsive, and it was small enough so that a short walk took me to its outskirts, where the hills were deep green and glossy with coffee bushes. The hard-pressed Guatemalans I had found a divided people – and the Indians in the hinterland seemed hopelessly lost; but El Salvador, on the evidence in Santa Ana, was a country of half-breeds, energetic and full of talk, practising a kind of Catholicism based on tactile liturgy. In the Cathedral, pious Salvadoreans pinched the feet of saints and rubbed at relics, and women with infants – always remembering to insert a coin in the slot and light a candle first – seized the loose end of Christ's cincture and mopped the child's head with its tassel.

But no citizen of this town had any clear idea of where the railway station was. I had arrived from the frontier by car, and after two nights in Santa Ana thought I should be moving on to the capital. There was a train twice a day, so my time-table said, and various people, without hesitation, had directed me to the railway station. But I had searched the town, and the railway station was not where they had said it was. In this way, I became familiar with the narrow streets of Santa Ana; the station continued to elude me. And when I found it on the morning of my third day, a mile from the hotel in a part of the town that had begun to tumble into ploughed fields and cash crops, behind a high fence and deserted apart from one man at an empty desk – the station master – I understood why no one knew where it was. No one used the train. There was a major road from Santa Ana to San Salvador. *We take the bus*: it seemed to be a Central American motto in reply to all the railway advertising which said, *Take the Train – It is Cheaper*! It was a matter of speed: the bus took two hours, the train took all afternoon.

The station was like none I had ever seen before. In design it looked like the sort of tobacco-curing shed you see in the Connecticut Valley, a green wooden building with slatted sides and a breeze humming through its splinters. All the rolling stock was in front – four wooden cars and a diesel. The cars were labelled alternately *First* and *Second*, but they were equally filthy. On a siding was a battered steam locomotive with a conical smoke stack, its boiler-plate bearing the inscription *Baldwin Locomotive Works, Philadelphia, Pa – 110* – it could have been a hundred years old, but the station master assured me that it ran perfectly. Nearer the station was a silver-painted wooden railcar, the shape of a cable car. This contraption had its own engine, and it was this, the station master said, that made the run from here to San Salvador.

'Where have you come from?' asked the stationmaster.

'Boston.'

'Plane?'

'Train.'

He shook my hand and said, 'Now that is something I would like to do!' He had been to Zacapa, he said, but he hadn't liked it much – the Guatemalans were a confused people. The Hondurans were worse. But what about my route from Boston? He questioned me closely: how many hours from Chicago to Fort Worth? What sort of trains? And the Mexican railways – were they as good as people said they were? Which trains had dining cars and pullmans? And had I seen anything like his steam locomotive? 'People tell me it is now worth a lot of money – I think they are right.' Where was I going from here? When I told him Argentina, he said, 'Wonderful! But be careful in Nicaragua – there is a rebellion there at the moment. That cruel man, Somoza.'

We were standing near the railcar. The station master shook his head at it. 'It is rather old,' he said, 'but it goes.'

It was leaving for San Salvador after lunch. I checked out of the Florida and, at the station, bought my ticket – a bargain at thirty-five cents for thirty-five miles. I had planned to sit near the front of the railcar, but the engine was noisy and as soon as we were on our way I had found two Salvadoreans in the back to talk to. They were both salesmen, in their mid-twenties. Alfredo was stocky and dark and looked athletic in a squat muscular way; he sold plastic basins and household fixtures. Mario was thin and had a mirthless chattering laugh. He sold toothpaste, oil, soap and butter. They had been sent by their companies to Santa Ana and their territory was in and around Santa Ana, nearly the whole of western El Salvador. It seemed a big area, I said. They reminded me that it was a very small country: they had to visit twenty or thirty shops a day to make a profit.

We were speaking in Spanish. Did they speak English?

'Enough,' said Mario, in Spanish, and chattered out his laugh.

'I know enough,' said Alfredo, in Spanish. 'I was in Arrisboorg for two months – studying English.'

'Pennsylvania?'

'Meeseepee.'

'Say something in English.'

Alfredo leered at me. 'Titty,' he said. Then he uttered several obscenities which, in his terrible pronunciation, did not sound at all offensive.

'Spanish is better than English,' said Mario.

'I think that is true,' said Alfredo.

'Nonsense,' I said. 'How can one language be better than another? It depends on what you are trying to say.'

'For all things,' said Mario. 'Spanish is a more amplified language. English is short and practical.'

'Shakespeare is short and practical?'

'We have Shakespeare in Spanish,' said Alfredo.

Mario stuck to his point. He said, 'We have more words in Spanish.'

'More words than English?'

'Lots more,' he said.

The railcar had halted to take on passengers. Now we started and not far from the track was a hairy mottled pig ploughing grass with its snout. Mario gestured at the pig.

He said, 'For example, take "pig" – we have five words for pig. How many do you have?'

Hog, sow, piglet, swine. I said, 'Four.'

'Listen,' he said, and counted on his fingers. '*Cuche, tunco, marano, cochino, serdo.* What do you think of that?'

'And two words for "dog",' said Alfredo. '*Chucho* and *can.*'

'We have about seven words for children, or child,' said Mario. 'In Honduras they have eight!'

Alfredo said, 'How many have you got for dog?'

Puppy, mutt, mongrel, cur. 'Four,' I said. 'That is more than you have.'

'Well, we have four for bull,' said Mario.

My God, I thought, what a ridiculous conversation.

Mario listed the words for bull: *novillo, buey, torrete, guiriche.*

'You win,' I said. The railcar stopped again, and while Alfredo and Mario went out to buy Cokes I dug my Spanish dictionary out of my suitcase and checked some of the words. When the railcar resumed its jangling progress I said, '*Buey* does not mean bull. It means "ox".'

'It is the same animal,' said Mario.

We argued about this until Alfredo conceded, 'Yes, in the United States the ox is different from ours. I have seen them in Arrisboorg.'

We were passing through lovely mountains, very steep and volcanic. On many of the lower slopes were coffee bushes. We were not very far from Guatemala even now, and it struck me as amazing that landscape could change so quickly from country to country. This was not only greener and steeper than what I had seen just over the border in the Motagua Valley, but had a cared-for look, a rustic neatness and a charm that made it quite attractive. I did not know then that El Salvador imported most of its vegetables from Guatemala, and yet El Salvador was clearly the busier-looking of the two, the better integrated. Its real burden was its size: what claim could such a small place make? I had heard that it was run by fourteen families, a melancholy statistic suggesting ludicrous snobberies and social jostling as well as an infuriated opposition to them, Marxist students sweating with indignation. Mario and Alfredo confirmed that this was true.

'I do not like to talk about politics,' said Alfredo. 'But in this country the police are cruel and the government is military. What do you think, Mario?'

Mario shook his head. It was obvious that he preferred to talk about something else.

At about three-thirty we came to the town of Quetzaltepeque. Seeing a church, Mario and Alfredo made the sign of the cross. The women in the railcar did the same. Some men removed their hats as well.

'You are not a Catholic?' said Alfredo.

I rapidly made the sign of the cross, so as not to disappoint him.

Alfredo said, 'In English, what is the meaning of *huacha*?'

What was this, some Nahautl word? Alfredo giggled – no, he said, there were no Indian languages spoken in El Salvador. *Huacha* was English, he insisted, but what did it mean? I said I was not familiar with it – could he use it in a sentence? He cleared his throat and hunched and said in English, 'Huacha gonna do when da well rons dry?'

'English,' said Mario, with a derisory snort.

Although they were both travelling salesmen, they hoped to rise in their firms and, one of these days, be promoted to a desk job in San Salvador. Mario worked on a straight commission, Alfredo's profit was based on a credit system which I could not understand – he had a salesman's knack for long opaque explanations, exhausting the listener into submission without allowing comprehension to occur. I said that they both seemed very ambitious. Oh, yes, said Alfredo, Salvadoreans were much cleverer than other Central Americans.

'We are like Israelis,' said Alfredo.

'Are you going to invade anyone?'

'We could have taken Honduras a few years ago.'

'I have an ambition,' said Mario. He said the salesman in his company who sold the most boxes of Rinso that year was going to win a free trip to San Andres Island. He thought he had a good chance of winning – he had sold thousands of boxes.

The valleys were deepening, the mountains growing shadowy in the setting sun. The railcar was small, but at no time was it full, and I guessed that it would not be long before it was removed and the railway service suspended except for shipments of coffee. Towards late afternoon we passed through dense forest. Alfredo said there was a swimming pool nearby, fed by a waterfall; it was a wonderful place for picking up girls. He would be glad to take me there. I said I had to be moving along, to Cutuco and Nicaragua. He said he would not go to Nicaragua for anything in the world. Neither Alfredo nor Mario had ever been to Honduras or Nicaragua, which were next-door.

San Salvador remained hidden. It lies in a bowl, surrounded by mountains which trap the air and keep it smoggy. To our right was a highway – the Pan-American Highway. Alfredo said it was a fast road, but had its dangers. Chief among these was the fact that, ten miles out of San Salvador, the Pan-American Highway is sometimes used as an emergency landing strip for planes. I said that I would rather be in this railcar pottering gently through the coffee plantations than in a bus careering towards a taxiing plane.

What were these two going to do in the capital? Business, they said, see the manager, file orders. Then Mario said a bit hesitantly that he was also going to see his girl-friend – he did not yet have a girl-friend in Santa Ana and was being driven to distraction by the provincial morality of the place. Alfredo had two or three girl-friends. His main reason for this trip to San Salvador ('please do not tell my manager!') was to see the football game that night. It promised to be one of the best games of the year – El Salvador was playing Mexico at the National Stadium and, as Mexico was scheduled to play in the World Cup in Argentina, it was El Salvador's chance to prove itself.

I had read about Latin American soccer – the chaos, the riots, the passionately partisan crowds, the way political frustrations were ventilated at the stadiums. I knew for a fact that if one wished to understand the British it helped to see a soccer game; then, the British did not seem so tight-lipped and proper. Indeed, a British soccer game was an occasion for a form of gang-warfare for the younger spectators. The muscular ritual of sport was always a clear demonstration of the wilder impulses in national character. The Olympic Games are interesting largely because they are a kind of world war in pantomime.

'Would you mind if I went to the game with you?'

Alfredo looked worried. 'It will be very crowded,' he said. 'There may be trouble. It is better to go to the swimming pool tomorrow – for the girls.'

'Do you think I came to El Salvador to pick up girls at a public swimming pool?'

'Did you come to El Salvador to see the football game?'

'Yes,' I said.

The San Salvador railway station was at the end of a torn-up section of road in a grim precinct of the city. My ticket was collected by a man in a pork-pie hat and sports shirt, who wore an old-fashioned revolver on his hip. The station was no more than a series of cargo sheds, where very poor people were camped, waiting for the morning train to Cutuco: the elderly and the very young – it seemed to be the pattern of victims in Central American poverty. Alfredo had given me the name of a hotel and said he would meet me there an hour before kick-off, which was nine o'clock. The games were played late, he said, because by then it wasn't so hot. But it was now after dark and the humid heat was choking me. I began to wish that I had not left Santa Ana. San Salvador, prone to earthquakes, was not a pretty place; it sprawled, it was noisy, its buildings were charmless, and in the glare of headlights were buoyant particles of dust. Why would anyone come here? 'Don't knock it,' an American in San Salvador told me. 'You haven't seen Nicaragua yet!'

Alfredo was late. He blamed the traffic. 'There will be a million people at the stadium.' He had brought along some friends, two boys who, he boasted, were studying English.

'How are you doing?' I asked them in English.

'Please?' said one. The other laughed. The first one said in Spanish, 'We are only on the second lesson.'

Because of the traffic, and the risk of car-thieves at the stadium, Alfredo parked half a mile away, at a friend's house. This house was worth some study; it was a number of cubicles nailed to trees, with the leafy branches descending into the rooms. Cloth was hung from sticks to provide walls, and a strong fence surrounded it. I asked the friend how long he had lived there. He

148

said his family had lived in the house for many years. I did not ask what happened when it rained.

But poverty in a poor country had subtle gradations. We walked down a long hill towards the stadium, and crossing a bridge I looked into a gorge expecting to see a river and saw lean-tos and cooking fires and lanterns. Who lived there? I asked Alfredo.

'Poor people,' he said.

Others were walking to the stadium, too. We joined a large procession of quick-marching fans, and as we drew closer to the stadium they began yelling and shoving in anticipation. The procession swarmed over the foothills below the stadium, crashing through people's gardens and thumping the fenders of stalled cars. Here the dust was deep and the trampling feet of the fans made it rise until it became a brown fog, like a sepia print of a mob scene, with the cones of headlights bobbing in it. The mob was running now, and Alfredo and his friends were obscured by the dust cloud. Every ten feet, boys rushed forward and shook tickets at me, screaming, 'Suns! Suns! Suns!'

These were the touts. They bought the cheapest tickets and sold them at a profit to people who had neither the time nor the courage to stand in a long rowdy line at a ticket window. The seat-designations were those usual at a bullfight: *Suns* were the cheapest, bleacher seats; *Shades* were more expensive ones under the canopy.

I fought my way through the touts and, having lost Alfredo, made my way uphill to the kettle-shaped stadium. It was an unearthly sight, the crowd of people emerging from darkness into luminous brown fog, the yells, the dust rising, the mountainside smouldering under a sky which, because of the dust, was starless. At that point, I considered turning back; but the mob was propelling me forward towards the stadium where the roar of the spectators inside made a sound like flames howling in a chimney.

The mob took up this cry and surged past me, stirring up the dust. There were women frying bananas and meat-cakes over fires on the walkway that ran around the outside perimeter of the stadium. The smoke from these fires and the dust made each searchlight seem to burn with a smoky flame. The touts re-appeared nearer the stadium. They were hysterical now. The game was about to start; they had not sold their tickets. They grabbed my arms, they pushed tickets in my face, they shouted.

One look at the lines of people near the ticket window told me that I would have no chance at all of buying a ticket legally. I was pondering this question when, through the smoke and dust, Alfredo appeared.

'Take your watch off,' he said. 'And your ring. Put them in your pocket. Be very careful. Most of these people are thieves. They will rob you.'

I did as I was told. 'What about the tickets? Shall we buy some Suns from these boys?'

'No, I will buy Shades.'

'Are they expensive?'

'Of course, but this will be a great game. I could never see such a game in Santa Ana. Anyway, the Shades will be quieter.' Alfredo looked around. 'Hide over there by the wall. I will get the tickets.'

Alfredo vanished into the conga line at a ticket window. He appeared again at the middle of the line, jumped the queue, elbowed forward and in a very short time had fought his way to the window. Even his friends marvelled at his speed. He came towards us smiling, waving the tickets in triumph.

We were frisked at the entrance; we passed through a tunnel and emerged at the end of the stadium. From the outside it had looked like a kettle; inside, its shape was more of a salver, a tureen filled with brown screeching faces. In the centre was a pristine rectangle of green grass.

It was, those 45,000 people, a model of Salvadorean society. Not only the half of the stadium where the Suns sat (and it was jammed: not an empty seat was visible); or the better-dressed and almost as crowded half of the Shades (at night, in the dry season, there was no difference in the quality of the seats: we sat on concrete steps, but ours, being more expensive than the Suns, were less crowded); there was a section that Alfredo had not mentioned: the Balconies. Above us, in five tiers of a gallery that ran around our half of the stadium, were the Balcony people.

Balcony people had season tickets. Balcony people had small rooms, cupboard-sized, about as large as the average Salvadoreans hut; I could see the wine bottles, the glasses, the plates of food. Balcony people had folding chairs and a good view of the field. There were not many Balcony people – two or three hundred – but at $2,000 for a season ticket in a country where the per capita income was $373 one could understand why. The Balcony people faced the screaming Suns and, beyond the stadium, a plateau. What I took to be lumpish multi-coloured vegetation covering the plateau was, I realized, a heap of Salvadoreans standing on top or clinging to the sides. There were thousands of them in this mass, and it was a sight more terrifying than the Suns. They were lighted by the stadium glare; there was a just-perceptible crawling movement among the bodies; it was an ant-hill.

National anthems were played, amplified songs from scratched records, and then the game began. It was apparent from the outset who would win. Mexico was bigger, faster, and seemed to follow a definite strategy; El Salvador had two ball-hoggers, and the team was tiny and erratic. The crowd hissed the Mexicans and cheered El Salvador. One of the Salvadorean ball-hoggers went jinking down the field, shot and missed. The ball went to the Mexicans, who tormented the Salvadoreans by passing it from man to man and then, fifteen minutes into the game, the Mexicans scored. The stadium was silent as the Mexican players kissed one another.

Some minutes later the ball was kicked into the Shades section. It was thrown back into the field and the game was resumed. Then it was kicked into the Suns section. The Suns fought for it; one man gained possession, but he was pounced upon and the ball shot up and ten Suns went tumbling after it. A Sun tried to run down the steps with it. He was caught and the ball wrestled from him. A fight began, and now there were scores of Suns punching their way to the ball. The Suns higher up in the section threw bottles and cans and wadded paper on the Suns who were fighting, and the shower of objects – meat pies, bananas, hankies – continued to fall. The Shades, the Balconies, the Ant-hill watched this struggle.

151

And the players watched, too. The game had stopped. The Mexican players kicked the turf, the Salvadorean team shouted at the Suns.

Please return the ball. It was the announcer. He was hoarse. *If the ball is not returned, the game will not continue.*

This brought a greater shower of objects from the upper seats – cups, cushions, more bottles. The bottles broke with a splashing sound on the concrete seats. The Suns lower down began throwing things back at their persecutors, and it was impossible to say where the ball had gone.

The ball was not returned. The announcer repeated his threat.

The players sat down on the field and did limbering-up exercises until, ten minutes after the ball had disappeared from the field, a new ball was thrown in. The spectators cheered but, just as quickly, fell silent. Mexico had scored another goal.

Soon, a bad kick landed the ball into the Shades. This ball was fought for and not thrown back, and one could see the ball progressing through the section. The ball was seldom visible, but one could tell from the free-for-alls – now here, now there – where it was. The Balconies poured water on the Shades, but the ball was not surrendered. And now it was the Suns' turn to see the slightly better-off Salvadoreans in the Shades section behaving like a swine. The announcer made his threat: the game would not resume until the ball was thrown back. The threat was ignored, and after a long time the ref walked onto the field with a new ball.

In all, five balls were lost this way. The fourth landed not far from where I sat, and I could see that real punches were being thrown, real blood spurting from Salvadorean noses, and the broken bottles and the struggle for the ball made it a contest all its own, more savage than the one on the field, played out with the kind of mindless ferocity you read about in books on gory medieval sports. The announcer's warning was merely ritual threat; the police did not intervene – they stayed on the field and let the spectators settle their own scores. The players grew bored: they ran in place, they did push-ups. When play resumed and Mexico gained possession of the ball it deftly moved down the field and invariably made a goal. But this play, these goals – they were no more than interludes in a much bloodier sport which, towards midnight (and the game was still not over!), was varied by Suns throwing firecrackers at each other and onto the field.

The last time play was abandoned and fights broke out among the Suns – the ball bobbing from one ragged Sun to another – balloons were released from the upper seats. But they were not balloons. They were white, blimpy and had a nipple on the end; first one, then dozens. This caused great laughter, and they were batted from section to section. They were of course contraceptives, and they caused Alfredo no end of embarrassment. 'That is very bad,' he said, gasping in shame. He had apologized for the interruptions; for the fights; the delayed play. Now this – dozens of airborne rubbers. The game was a shambles; it ended in confusion, fights, litter. But it shed light on the recreations of Salvadoreans, and as for the other thing – the inflated contraceptives – I later discovered that the Agency for International Development's largest Central American family planning programme is in El Salvador. I doubt whether the birth-rate has been affected, but children's birthday parties in rural El Salvador must be a great deal of fun, what with the free balloons.

Mexico won the game, six to one. Alfredo said that El Salvador's goal was the best one of the game, a header from thirty yards. So he managed to rescue a shred of pride. But people had been leaving all through the second half, and the rest hardly seemed to notice or to care that the game had ended. Just before we left the stadium I looked up at the ant-hill. It was a hill once again; there were no people on it, and depopulated, it seemed very small.

Outside, on the stadium slopes, the scene was like one of those lurid murals of Hell you see in Latin American churches. The colour was infernal, yellow dust sifted and whirled among crater-like pits, small cars with demonic headlights moved slowly from hole to hole like mechanical devils. And where, on the mural, you see the sins printed and dramatized, the gold lettering saying *Lust, Anger, Avarice, Drunkenness, Gluttony, Theft, Pride, Jealousy, Usury, Gambling*, and so on, here after midnight were groups of boys lewdly snatching at girls, and knots of people fighting, counting the money they had won, staggering and swigging from bottles, shrieking obscenities against Mexico, thumping the hoods of cars or duelling with the branches they had yanked from trees and the radio aerials they had twisted from cars. They trampled the dust and howled. The car horns were like harsh moos of pain – and one car was being overturned by a gang of shirtless, sweating youths. Many people were running to get free of the mob, holding handkerchiefs over their faces. But there were tens of thousands of people here, and animals, too, maimed dogs snarling and cowering as in a classic vision of Hell. And it was hot: dark grimy air that was hard to breathe, and freighted with the stinks of sweat; it was so thick it muted the light. It tasted of stale fire and ashes. The mob did not disperse; it was too angry to go home, too insulted by defeat to ignore its hurt. It was loud and it moved as if thwarted and pushed; it danced madly in what seemed a deep hole.

Alfredo knew a short cut to the road. He led the way through the parking lot and a ravaged grove of trees behind some huts. I saw people lying on the ground, but whether they were wounded or sleeping or dead I could not tell.

I asked him about the mob.

'What did I tell you?' he said. 'You are sorry you came, right?'

'No,' I said, and I meant it. Now I was satisfied. Travel is pointless without certain risks. I had spent the whole evening scrutinizing what I saw, trying to memorize details, and I knew I would never go to another soccer game in Latin America.

That soccer game was not the only event in San Salvador that evening. At the Cathedral, as the fans were rioting in the National Stadium, the Archbishop of El Salvador was receiving an honorary doctorate from the President of Georgetown University. The Archbishop had deliberately made it into a public ceremony, to challenge the government and give a Jesuitical oration. There were 10,000 people at the Cathedral and I was told that this crowd was equally frightening in its discontent.

And ten years before, there had been 'The Football War' – also known as 'The 100 Hour War'. This was between El Salvador and Honduras – first the soccer teams and the rioting specta-

154

tors, then the national armies. It had grown out of El Salvador's chronic shortage of land. Salvadoreans slipped over the border into Honduras to farm, to squat, to work on the banana plantations. They worked hard, but when the Hondurans got wind of it they tried to restrict entry on the Salvadorean border; they persecuted squatters, then repatriated them. And, as in all such squabbles, there were atrocity stories: rapes, murders, torturings. But there were no large-scale hostilities until the crucial soccer matches were played in preparation for the 1970 World Cup. In June 1969, there was violence after the El Salvador–Honduras match in Tegucigalpa, and this was repeated a week later in San Salvador. Within days, the El Salvador army began its armed attack on Honduras – its cue had come from the soccer match: the fans' belligerence was to be taken seriously. Although the war lasted only a little more than four days, at the end of it 2,000 soldiers and civilians – mainly Hondurans – lay dead.

A year ago, an election was held in El Salvador. The election was rigged. There was violence, and there were mob scenes of the sort I had seen at the soccer game, but this time enacted on the streets of the capital. Students were shot and people imprisoned. And so El Salvador found itself with yet another military dictatorship. This was a particularly brutal one. Politics is a hideous subject, but I will say this: people tell you that dictatorships are sometimes necessary to good order, and that this sort of highly-centralized government is stable and dependable. But this is seldom so. It is nearly always bureaucratic and crooked, unstable, fickle and barbarous; and it excites those same qualities in those it governs.

Back at my hotel, which was not a good hotel, I wrote about the soccer game. The writing made me wakeful, and there were noises in the room – occasional scratchings from the ceiling. I opened Poe's *Narrative of Arthur Gordon Pym* and began to read. It was, from the first chapter, a terrifying story: Pym is a stowaway; he becomes trapped between decks and, without food or water, he suffers the pitching of the ship. His dog is with him. The dog becomes maddened and goes for him. Pym nearly dies, and is released from this prison only to find that there has been a mutiny on board, and there is another storm. All this

155

time, in my own narrow room, I had been hearing the sinister scratchings. I switched out the light, went to sleep and had a nightmare: a storm, darkness, wind and rats scrabbling in a cupboard. The nightmare woke me. I groped for the light-switch. And in this lamp's glare I could see that there was a hole in the ceiling, directly overhead, the size of a quarter. It had not been there before. I watched it for some minutes, and then a pair of yellow teeth appeared at its chewed edge.

I did not sleep that night.

9 The Local to Cutuco

Even Salvadoreans, with their little-country loyalty and their violent nationalism, regard Cutuco as a hole. And you know, as you see Nicaragua just across the border, that the end of the line cannot be far away. This is an observable fact. The train from Boston comes to a complete stop in Cutuco. After that, there is a ferry ride of anywhere from eight to eleven hours (it depends on the tide) across the Gulf of Fonseca to Nicaragua. If there is no Indian uprising, or peasant revolt, or civil war, it ought to be possible to make your way by road through Nicaragua, if only to judge how much reckless exaggeration there is in the commonly held view that Nicaragua is the worst eyesore in the world: the hottest, the poorest, the most savagely governed, with a murderous landscape and medieval laws and disgusting food. I had hoped to verify this. The inhospitable country, like the horrible train ride, has a way of bringing a heroic note to the traveller's tale. And though I had had a few set-backs on the trip from South Station to San Salvador Central it had, for the most part, been fairly clear sailing. But Nicaragua was something of a problem.

I had been thinking hard about Nicaragua ever since I had read, months before leaving Boston, that the guerrilla war (which was in part an Indian uprising) had spread from Managua to smaller villages. And why was it, I wondered, that all these villages seemed to be on my proposed route through the country? My method for making an itinerary usually did not include newspapers. I got the best maps I could and, with guidebooks and what railway timetables I could lay my hands on, tried to determine how I might join one railway with another. I never gave any thought to hotels; if a town was important enough to be lettered on a map I assumed it was worth visiting (some surprises were inevitable: Zacapa was on most maps, Santa Ana was not; but that kind of discovery sustains and emboldens the traveller). I had heard that Nicaragua was Central America's answer to Afghanistan, but apart from this cloudy image and the historical fact that from 1855 to 1857 Nicaragua had been governed by a five-foot Tennessean named William Walker (he changed the national language to English, instituted slavery and had plans for annexing Nicaragua to the American South; this midget was shot in 1860), I knew little about the country. It had been ruled barbarously by the Somoza family for nearly forty years – that was common knowledge. But this guerrilla war? The newspaper reports, which I now depended on, differed in assessing its seriousness.

Through Mexico, Guatemala and El Salvador I bought the local papers and tried to discover what was happening in Nicaragua. The news was always bad and it appeared to grow worse. GUERRILLAS ATTACK POLICE STATION one day was followed the next day by SOMOZA IMPOSES CURFEW. Then it was GUERRILLAS ROB BANK – I made careful translations of the headlines – and SOMOZA LAYS A FIRM HAND. In Santa Ana I read GUERRILLAS KILL TEN, in San Salvador the headline was SOMOZA ARRESTS 200 and INDIANS TAKE UP ARMS. Latterly I had read UNEASY CALM PREVAILS IN NICARAGUA, but just before leaving San Salvador there was a news item in *La Prensa* headlined GUERRILLAS BUY $5 MILLION OF ARMS FROM UNITED STATES. President Carter had remained prudently neutral on the Nicaragua issue; it was apparently hoped in the United States that Somoza would be overthrown. This was a pious hope, and it was no help to me. By the end of February the revolution had yet to occur; there was still sporadic fighting and reports of massacres and Somoza was in power. It looked as if he would remain in office for another forty years, or at the very most pass the machinery of government – in Nicaragua's case these are instruments of torture – on to his son. I began to worry about crossing Nicaragua. I decided to go to the frontier. I would talk to the people there. If the news was still bad I would take a detour around it. I went by train to Cutuco, to examine Nicaragua. It was like going to the dentist and hoping that the office was shut, the dentist laid up with a bad case of lumbago. This had never happened to me at the dentist's, but on the frontier of Nicaragua my reprieve came in just that way.

'You cannot go into Nicaragua,' said the Salvadorean at his border post by the ferry landing. Was there a muddier sight in all the world, a gloomier prospect, than the Gulf of Fonseca? 'The border is closed. The soldiers will send you back.'

This was better than a stay of execution. I was absolved of any responsibility to travel through Nicaragua. I returned to San Salvador. I had changed my hotel room to one in which I was sure there were no rats. But I had nothing more to do in San Salvador. I had given a lecture on the topic that had occurred to me on the train to Tapachula: Little-known Books by Famous American Authors – *Pudd'nhead Wilson, The Devil's Dictionary, The Wild Palms*. I had looked at the university (and no one could explain why there was a mural, in the university of this right-wing dictatorship, of Marx, Engels and Lenin). I had a day in hand, so I decided to take the Cutuco train again, but this time to stop along the way.

I knew from my previous trip that long before San Miguel, which was three-quarters of the way to Cutuco, the journey ceased to be interesting. As before, there were two passenger cars and not more than twenty-five people travelling. While we were waiting for the train to be shunted to the platform I asked some of them where they were going. They said San Vicente. It was market day in San Vicente. Was San Vicente pretty? Oh, very, they said. So I decided to get off the train at San Vicente.

No two trains are alike. Salvadorean trains are just as broken down as Guatemalan ones, but there are differences. They might have been given life by the same fruit company, but they have evolved differently. This is true of the world's railways – I have never seen two even remotely similar. 'El Jarocho' is as distinct from 'The Golden Blowpipe' as its name. It is more than national differences; trains take on the character of their routes. On the Local to Cutuco the uniqueness is obvious as soon as you board. Here, at the gate, was the same sad dark little man who had greeted me from the Railcar. He wore his sports shirt and carried his old revolver in a holster and some bullets in an ammo belt. I hoped he would not be provoked to fire it, because I was sure it would explode in his face if he did and I would be killed, not by the bullet, but by shrapnel. He punched my ticket, the train creaked to the platform, and I boarded. All the seats were torn. They were stuffed with horse-hair: it was agony to lean back.

'These seats are really in bad condition.' The Salvadorean man across the aisle was apologizing. He kicked the seat in front and went on, 'But they are strong – look, the seats themselves are fine. But they are ripped and dirty. They should fix them.'

I said, 'Why don't they fix them?'

'Because everyone takes the bus.'

'If they fixed them, everyone would take the train.'

'True,' he said. 'But then the train would be crowded with all the world.'

I agreed with him, not because I believed what he said but because I was sick of lecturing people on disorder. Central America was haywire; it was as if New England had gone completely to ruin and places like Rhode Island and Connecticut were run by maniacal generals and thuggish policemen; as if they had evolved into motiveless tyrannies and become forcing-houses of nationalism. It was no wonder that, seeing them as degenerate states, tycoons like Vanderbilt and imperial-minded companies like the United Fruit Company took them over and tried to run them. It should have been easy enough. But tycoons and big companies did not have the morality or the compassion or the sense of legality to make these places work; they acted out of contempt and self-interest; they were less than colonial – they were racketeers, and they spawned racketeers. Lawless, the countries became bizarre with inequality, and hideously violent. El Salvador deserves to be serene, but it is not. Football, the simplest sport in the world, in this place had become a free-for-all of punchy frustration in which the spectators made themselves the centre of attention. Why shouldn't we have some fun, they might reply: we live like dogs. Football wasn't football, the Church was not the Church, and this train was unlike any I had ever ridden on. By the time it had got to this condition, any sensible railway company would have collected the insurance money for the damage and started all over again, the way they do in India.

But this was El Salvador, not India – indeed, this heap of junk would have been laughed out of West Bengal, which is saying something.

But, truly, the worst trains take one across the best landscapes. The crack express trains – the bullet trains in Japan, 'The Blue Train' from Paris to Cannes, 'The Flying Scotsman' – these are joyrides, nothing more; the rapidity diminishes the pleasure of the journey. But the Local to Cutuco is a plod through the spectacular. If one is not put to flight by the pistol-toting ticket-puncher, or the filthy cars or painful seats, one is rewarded by the grandest scenery south of Massachusetts. And the train is so geriatrically slow, one gets the impression that El Salvador is as big as Texas. It is the effect of the feeble engine and all the stops: three and a half hours to go the forty miles to San Vicente.

The spectacle takes a while to begin.

El Salvador had seemed to me to be tidy, fertile and prosperous. And it is, in the west. But east of the capital, on the other side of the tracks – here, desolation lies. It starts where the station precincts end, at a quarry on the edge of town. For a full hour as the train moves there is nothing but the stone-age horror of little huts: mud and bamboo, cardboard and sticks, tin and mud, and on the roofs every sort of refuse to hold the things down, since one can't drive nails into mud or cardboard. The roofs are amazing collections of broken things. Look at this one: an old rusted sewing machine, an iron stove in pieces, six tyres, bricks, tins, boulders; and on that one splintered lumber and a tree branch and some stones. The huts lean against each other and are propped against the steep sides of the quarry, pressed against the track, with no decoration but a picture of Jesus or a saint, and no colour but the rags hanging out to dry on a tripod of timbers. It is a coffee-growing country. The price of coffee is very high. But these people really do live like dogs, and the dogs themselves seem to have evolved downward into cowering creatures which never bark, but only limp and skulk and forage in dusty bushes with their snouts. The dogs have been turned into a species of scavenging burrower, like a particularly mangy sort of aardvark. Now the train was moving so slowly, and was so empty and neglected, that children from the slum climbed shrieking into it and ran down the aisles, jumping from seat to seat. They hopped off at the continuation of the slum, on the next curve.

If the slum children had lingered another ten minutes on the train they would have seen open country, trees and wild flowers and singing birds. But the children do not stray into the country-side. Perhaps it is forbidden, or perhaps they are obeying the slum-dweller's instinct, which is to seek the protection of the slum and not to go beyond its boundaries. They are vulnerable in the outer world to policemen, landowners, tax inspectors; and in their rags they are easy to identify and humiliate. So, in the daylight hours, the slum is full and active and in Central America it nearly always has as its frontier a creek or stream or a railway track. And just past that natural frontier the slum ends and jungle or pasture land begins. Here, the slum gave on to coffee planta-tions, and it was reasonable to assume that those destitute people I had seen earlier were coffee-pickers. From what I found out later, their wages bore no relation to the price of coffee.

We climbed some low hills and then passed along the ridge of a higher one. I looked across the valley and saw a lake – Lake Ilopango – and a volcano – Chinchontepec. From these heights to San Vicente, where the vistas are shortened by the train's sinking into the eastern lowlands, the lake and the volcano grow huger and alter in colour as the sun shifts behind them. The first glimpse is impressive, but the lake swells and the volcano rises and for miles and miles they grow to almost unbelievable loveli-ness. The lake waters are blue, then grey, then black as the train mounts its own volcanic range and travels along the spine, pass-ing the north side of this lake. There is an island in the lake. It appeared in 1880, when the water level suddenly fell, and is still there, like a dismasted flagship in this darkly chromatic sea. Between the lake and the train are low hills of green vegetation and a long sweep of tree-tops which, closer to the train, are banana and orange groves and tall clusters of yellow swaying bamboos. The foliage nearby is faded and dusty, but at a distance it is emerald green and looks dense and lush.

Now the lake is silver, with an enamelling of blue discs; now black, with furrows of frothy whiteness; now it is suffused with pinkness and at its shores takes the colour from the greenest trees. It was, to the lakeside Indians, much more than a body of water in which they washed and fished and quenched their thirst. The guidebooks merely repeat falsifications of its importance for credulous tourists. One guidebook says that before the Spanish conquest the Indians 'used to propitiate the harvest gods by drowning four virgins here every year'. Well, this might have been true, and it provides a cue for the joke that the ritual was abandoned for lack of suitable victims. But human sacrifice continued well into the last century at this lake, and it had nothing to do with the harvest gods. It was a complicated procedure, and purposeful.

There was a witness. His name was Don Camillo Galvar. He was Visitador-General in San Salvador in the 1860s. In 1880 he described what he had found out about the supposedly bloodthirsty practices of the Indians who lived near Lake Ilopango. 'The people of the pueblos around the lake,' he wrote, 'Cojutepeque, Texacuangos, and Tepezontes, say that when the earthquakes came from the lake, which they knew by the disappearance of the fish, it was a sign that the monster lord of these regions who dwelt in the depths of the lake was eating the fish.'

Not a harvest god, but a monster; and the Indians' fear was that unless this monster was 'provided with a more delicate and juicy diet worthy of his power and voracity' he would eat all the fish and there would be none for the fishermen to catch. The Indians said that the monster only ate fish 'as men eat fruit, to refresh and allay hunger.' The lake and the volcano rumbled and the fish began to disappear; the Indians 'deeply afflicted by the fish famine . . . collected at the command of their chiefs.' Sorcerers came forth in their ceremonial robes and headdresses and outlined what the Indians were to do: they were to throw flowers and fruits into the lake. Sometimes, this worked: the tremors ceased. But if they continued, the Indians assembled again and were told to throw in animals, preferably gophers, racoons and armadilloes and ones they called taltusas. The animals had to be caught alive and thrown into the water still kicking. Any Indian found throwing a dead animal into the water faced the severe penalty of being hanged with a zinak vine, because the monster lord would be enraged by having to feed on dead flesh.

Days were given to the study of the water level, the numbers of fish, the evidence of tremors. If the signs were still bad the 'wizards' acted. They took a girl of from six to nine years old, decked her with flowers and 'at midnight the wizards took her to the middle of the lake and cast her in, bound hand and foot, with a stone fast to her neck. The next day, if the child appeared upon the surface and the tremors continued, another victim was cast into the lake with the same ceremonies.

'In the years 1861 and 1862,' Don Camillo goes on, 'when I visited these towns they told me that they kept to this barbarous custom to prevent the failure of the fish.' So there was a reason; and the Indians did not gloat about it. Indeed, Don Camillo adds that they spoke to him 'with much reserve'.

The lake had assumed a more ominous blueness, chased by ghost-grey mists, and still the train was rising. Below was not one valley, but fifty of them, and a landscape of green peaks. It was hard to believe that the hills so far down could be high, but the train was crossing the ridge at such a great altitude, and it was a lesson in scale to compare the hills with the volcano Chinchontepec. We were nowhere near it, and it continued to increase in size; now it seemed mammoth and black and unclimbable.

But it remained in the distance, in that other lush climate. The train crossed a hotter mountain range. The dust flew into the cars. I got up and walked from car to car to stretch my legs, and when I went back I recognized my seat by its colour: it had a thinner layer of dust than the others, which were covered by the brown powder. There were no doors on the cars, no glass in the windows – they were completely open, and whirling with such a dust storm the porters and conductors, and all the train staff, rode on the roofs of the cars where the dust could not reach them. They sat, gripping the pipes and wheels on the roof, or else stood straddling the centre of the car. The train to Zacapa had been dusty, but there was no wind in the Motagua Valley. Here, we were high and the movement of the train and the stiff mountain winds combined to create gusts of considerable velocity which drew a brown veil over the train and made it impossible for long periods to see anything. The passengers crouched and put their heads down, holding their shirts against their faces. The train's noise was a loud hammering and clattering; it was hard to draw a breath and, more than anything, it was as if we were roaring through a small dirt tunnel fleeing a cave-in.

Outside the village of Michapa, the train coursed through a trough of steep sandbanks. A young girl, perhaps eight years old, had pressed herself against the bank, and the dust churned around her. She held a tiny goat in her arms to prevent him from scampering in fright onto the tracks, and she looked persecuted by the dust and noise, her face fixed in a pained suffocated expression.

When the dust storm passed and the sky turned blue and large, the train's racket was swallowed by the empty air, and we seemed to be in a low-flying plane, gliding at tree-top height towards the valleys below. It was a trick of the landscape, the way the train balanced on its narrow ridge and gave a view of everything but its tracks. And though the train had been slow before, on this downhill run it had gathered speed: but the clatter was not so obvious. This old engine and its cars had taken to the air like a railway lifted and travelling down the sky. It is not often that one gets a view like this in a train and it was so beautiful that I could forget the heat and dust, the broken seats, and was uplifted by the sight of the hills way down and the nearer hills of coffee and bamboo. For the next half-hour of this descent, it was an aerial railway diving across hills of purest green.

The landscape changed; the villages remained the same. You think: *I've been here before.* The village is small and has a saint's name. The station is a shed, open on three sides, and near it are piles of orange peels and blown-open coconut husks with fibrous hair, and waste paper and bottles. That grey trickle of waste water gathering in a green-yellow pool; that woman with a basket on her head, and bananas in the basket, and flies on the bananas; that heap of black railway ties and the stack of oily barrels, the Coca-Cola sign faded to pink, the ten filthy children and the small girl with the naked infant on her back, the boy with a twanging radio the size of a shoe-box, the banana trees, the four huts, the limping dog, the whining pig, the dozing man with his

165

head resting on his left shoulder and his hat-brim crushed. You were here, you saw the trampled path and the smoke, the sun at just that scorching angle above the trees, the wrecked car resting on its rims, the chickens pecking pebbles out of the shade, the face behind the rag of curtain in the hut window, the station-master in his shirt sleeves and dark trousers standing at attention in the sun holding his log-book, the leaves of the village trees so thick with dust that they appear to be dead. It seems so familiar you begin to wonder if you have been travelling in a small circle, leaving in the morning and every day arriving in the heat of the afternoon at this same village with its pig and its people and its withered trees, the vision of decrepitude repeating like the dream that demands that you return again and again to the same scene; the sameness of it has a curiously mocking quality. Can it be true that after weeks of train travel you have gone no farther that this and only been returned once again to this squalid place? No; though you have seen hundreds like it since crossing the Rio Grande, you have never been here before.

And when the train whistle squawks and you pull out, because you have seen so many departures like this, the village leaves no impression. The dust from the accelerating train rises and the huts vanish beneath it. But somewhere in the memory these poor places accumulate, until you pray for something different, a little hope to give them hope. To see a country's poverty is not to see into its heart, but it is very hard to look beyond such pitiable things.

We ascended another range of hills and the gorge to the south distracted me. Tall crooked trees, looped with the entrails of slender vines, grew on the slopes and cliffs of the gorge, like the beginnings of jungle. The land was too precipitous for crops, too steep even for huts or paths. It was wild and uninhabited; birds flew along the sides of the gorge, but seemed too timid to risk flying across it. They whistled at the train. I looked for more, leaned out of the window and just then everything went black.

We had entered a tunnel. The passengers began to scream. Central Americans always scream in tunnels, but whether they screamed with enthusiasm or terror I could not tell. The train had no lights in its cars, and with the darkness was a rush of dust which thickened as the train blundered on. I could feel the dust blowing into my face and could feel it on my hair as if I was in a hole and the dust was being shovelled onto me. I did what I had seen the passengers do earlier: I buried my face in my shirt and breathed through the cloth. We were in the tunnel for five minutes, which is a long time to be blindly choking and hearing people scream. But not everyone had screamed. In front of me was an old lady who had told me she was going to San Vicente to sell her crate of oranges. She had gone to sleep an hour before. She was sleeping when we entered the tunnel; she was sleeping when we left it. Her head was thrown back and her mouth was open; she had not shifted her position.

The train plunged out of the tunnel and lost its racket in the sunlight and clear air. We teetered on a mountainside, and the subdued chug of the engine – muffled by the tide of air – was like a hushed reverence for the ten fertile miles of the Jiboa Valley, which began at the tunnel entrance and descended as evenly as a ski slope before rising at the foot of the volcano. The volcano was a darker green than the landscape it sprang out of, and it had leonine contours of light and shade, some like shoulders and forepaws, some muscled like flanks and hindquarters. But it had a carved considered look to it and seemed, as I sped towards it on the train, like a headless sphinx, green and monumental, as if its head had rolled away leaving its lion's body intact. It was easy to understand how the Indians hereabouts had come to believe that their lands were inhabited by monster lords. Not only did the mountains have a monstrous aspect, the animal shapes and clumsy claws of giants and demons, but they growled and rumbled and trembled and hollered, and shook down the flimsy huts of the Indians; they burned the Indians alive and buried them in ashes and made their fish disappear and ate their children. And these oddities of landscape were still a source of fear.

For the next forty minutes we rolled down the mountain valley towards the shadows of the volcano. And yet, so slowly were we moving, it seemed as if we were stuck fast at the rim of the valley and the volcano was rising and turning, revealing the lion's svelte back and lengthening, perhaps stretching to pounce in eruption, until finally, and just as I expected it to rise and roar, it disappeared – everything but those two ridges which were tensed like front legs. We were at San Vicente, its nearest town, and deep between its forepaws.

Most of the passengers got out here and stumbled across the tracks. There was no one collecting tickets. The officials watched from the coolness of a grove of trees. The whistle blew; the train lurched towards Cutuco. Then the dust settled and with it the mournful stillness of the country town on a hot afternoon.

I asked the way to the market. A boy gave me simple directions: follow this road. He seemed surprised that anyone should need directions in this tiny place. But the railway station was not in the centre of town; it was half a mile, along the town's main street, from the station to the plaza. Most of San Vicente's houses are on that street; the street begins as dust, turns bouldery, then cobbled, and nearer the plaza is concrete. The market, which I had been told was interesting, was like an oriental bazaar – tent-shelters pitched along several small lanes. Each tent enclosure was piled with fruit or vegetables, or dead animals hung on makeshift gallows, or boxes of pencils or pocket combs. All the people in a particular section were selling the same thing: a section of fruit, one of vegetables, one of meat or household items; and further away was a section reeking of decayed fish. I bought a bottle of soda water and noticed that no one was hawking anything. The hawkers had gathered into groups – men here, women there – and were talking companionably.

At the end of the market precinct was the plaza, and fronting onto the plaza San Vicente's church. It is one of the oldest churches in Central America, and called El Pilar. Built by the Spanish in this remote town, it has not been restored: no restoration has been necessary. It was made to withstand the sieges of pagans and the ravages of earthquakes. It has survived them all; apart from a few broken windows it shows few signs of age or ruin. Its walls are three feet thick; its columns, twelve feet in circumference, are low plump pillars the thickness of a cathedral's. But El Pilar is little more than a chapel; it is the shape of the mausoleums I had seen in rural Guatemala, white and rounded, with the mosque-like domes and squat arabesques that the Spanish gave their country churches. But its whitewash did not disguise its look of belligerence, nor did its stained-glass windows or crosses prevent it from looking like what it perhaps always has been – a fortress.

In the early nineteenth century there were a number of Indian wars in this part of Central America. By force of numbers and in their ferocity the Indians were able to overwhelm the Spanish in certain areas and create Indian strongholds, little kingdoms within the Spanish colony. From these places they made forays into Spanish towns and occasionally terrorized the inhabitants. Throughout the 1830s there were battles, and the largest number of Indians was led by a chief, Agostino Aquinas – he was a Christian – whose bravado brought him here to El Pilar in San Vicente. As a taunt to the Spanish, Aquinas rushed into El Pilar and snatched the crown from the statue of Saint Joseph. This he crammed onto his own head, declaring war on the Spanish. He then made for the mountains and, controlling a sizable district with his Indians, fought a guerrilla war.

The church could not have looked much different when Aquinas whooped in and desecrated it. The arches are heavy, the tiles immovable, the carved wooden altarpiece merely darker, and there is a narrow tomb-like quality to the interior. It may be the holiest building in town; it is certainly the strongest. It has, without any doubt, known service as a fortification.

Eleven old ladies were kneeling in the front pews and praying. The church was cool, so I took a pew at the rear and tried to spot the statue of Saint Joseph. From the eleven black-shawled heads came the steady murmur of prayer; it was a simmer of incantation, low voices like thick Salvadorean soup mumbling in a pot, the same bubbling rhythm of formula prayers. They were like spectres, the row of crones draped in black, uttering muffled prayers in the shadowy church; the sunbeams breaking through the holes in the stained-glass windows made logs of light that seemed to prop up the walls; there was a smell of burned wax, and the candle flames fluttered in a continuous tremble, like the voices of those old ladies. Inside El Pilar the year might have been 1831, and these the wives and mothers of Spanish soldiers praying for deliverance from the onslaught of frantic Indians.

A tinkling bell rang from the sacristy. I sat primly and piously,

169

straightening my back, in an instinctive reflex. It was habitual: I could not enter a church without genuflecting and dipping my fingers in the holy water font. A priest scuffed to the altar rail, flanked by two acolytes. The priest raised his arms and, in that gesture – but perhaps it was his good looks, the well-combed curate rather stuck on his clerical smoothness – a stagey flourish of a nightclub master of ceremonies. He was praying, but his prayers were mannered, Spanish, not Latin, and then he extended one arm towards a corner of the church that was hidden from me. He performed a little wrist-play, a wave of his hand, and the music began.

It was not solemn music. It was two electric guitars, a clarinet, maracas and a full set of drums – as soon as it had started to blurt I shifted my seat for a look at the musicians. It was the harsh wail of tuneless pop music that I had been avoiding for weeks, the squawk and crash that I had first heard issuing from Mexico as I stood on the high riverbank at Laredo. I had, since then, only rarely been out of earshot of it. How to describe it? With the guitar whine was an irregular beat, and each beat like a set of crockery dropped on the floor; a girl and boy shook maracas and sang – this was a cat's yowl attempt at harmonizing, but off-key it did not even have the melodiousness of a set of madly scraping locusts.

They were of course singing a hymn. In a place where Jesus Christ was depicted as a muscular tough, a blue-eyed Latin with slicked-down hair, a deeply handsome young fellow, religion was a kind of love affair. In some Catholicism, and frequently in Spanish America, prayer has become a romancing with Jesus. He is not a terrible God, not a destroyer, not a cold and vindictive ascetic; he is princely and with it the ultimate macho figure. The hymn was a love song, but very much a Spanish American one, crowing with lugubrious passion, the word *heart* repeated in every verse. And it was extremely loud. This was worship, but there was no substantial difference between what was going on here in this old church and what one could hear in the juke-box down the street in El Bar Americano. The church had been brought to the people; it had not made the people more pious – they had merely used this as an opportunity to entertain themselves and take the boredom out of the service. A mass or these evening prayers was an occasion to concentrate the mind in prayer; this music turned it into a distraction.

Music of this special deafening kind seemed important in Spanish America, because it prevented any thought whatsoever. The goon with the transistor in the train, the village boys gathered around their yakketing box, the man in Santa Ana who brought his cassette machine to breakfast and stared at its groaning amplifier, all the knee-jerks and finger-snapping and tooth-sucking seemed to have one purpose – a self-induced stupor for people who lived in a place where alcohol was expensive and drugs illegal. It was deafness and amnesia; it celebrated nothing but lost beauty and broken hearts; it had no memorable melody; it was splinters of glass ceaselessly flushed down a toilet, the thud of drums and the grunts of singers. People I met on my trip were constantly telling me they loved music. Not pop music from the United States, but this music. I knew what they meant.

Meanwhile, the priest had sat down beside the altar, looking pleased with himself. Well he might: the music had its effect. As soon as it had started, people had begun to pour into the church: schoolchildren with satchels and wearing uniforms, young children – barefoot urchins, kids with twisted nitty hair who had been frolicking in the plaza; mumbling old men with machetes, and two farm-boys clutching straw hats to their chests, and a lady with a tin wash basin and a gang of boys, and a bewildered dog. The dog sat in the centre aisle and beat its stub of tail against the tiles. The music was loud enough to have reached the market up the street, for here were three ladies in full skirts carrying empty baskets and leather purses. Some sat, some waited at the back of the church. They watched the band, not the tabernacle, and they were smiling. Oh, yes, this is what religion is all about – rejoice, smile, be happy, the Lord is with you; snap your fingers, He has redeemed the world. There were two shattering clashes of cymbals.

The music stopped. The priest stood up. The prayers began.

And the people who had come into the church during the song pushed to the rear door. The eleven old ladies in the front pews did not move, and only they remained to say the Confiteor. The priest paced back and forth at the altar rail. He gave a short sermon: God loves you, he said; you must learn how to love Him. It was not easy in the modern world to find time for God; there were temptations, and the evidence of sin was everywhere. It was necessary to work hard and dedicate each labour to the glory of God. Amen.

Again, a wave of the hand, and the music started. This time it was much louder, and it attracted a greater number of people from the plaza to hear it. It was a similar song: yowl, thump, *heart, heart,* yowl, crash, dooby-doo, thump, crash, crash. There was no hesitation among the on-lookers when it ended. At the final crash, they fled. But not for long. Ten minutes later (two prayers, a minute of meditation, some business with an incense burner, another pep-talk) the band again began to play and the people returned. This routine continued for a full hour, and it was still going on when I took myself away – during a song, not a sermon or prayer; I had a train to catch.

The sky was purple and pink, the volcano black; lurid chutes of orange dust filled the valleys, and the lake was fiery, like a pool of molten lava.

10 The Atlantic Railway: The 12:00 to Limón

I was a bit surprised to find a Chinese man in a bar in San José, Costa Rica. The Chinese are not, typically, bar-flies. Once a year, if the occasion is special and they are in the company of some other men, they might, on a dare, drink a whole bottle of brandy. Then they turn red, say silly or abusive things very loudly, throw up and have to be carried home. Drinking is their mad fling at gaiety; but it is perverse – they take no pleasure in it. So what was this Chinese man doing here? We talked circumspectly at first, as strangers do, reaching agreement on trivialities before risking anything personal. And then he told me. Well, he said, he happened to own this bar. He also owned a restaurant and a hotel. He was a Costa Rican citizen. It had been a deliberate choice. He disliked every other country he had seen.

'Which ones?' I asked. We spoke in Spanish. He said his English was shaky; I told him my Cantonese was far from perfect.

'All the countries,' he said. 'I left China in 1954. I was a young man and I liked to travel. I looked at Mexico – I went all over. But I didn't like it. I went to Guatemala and all around – Nicaragua – that was very bad. Panama – I didn't like it. Even Honduras and El Salvador – those countries.'

'What about the United States?'

'I went all around it. Maybe it is a good country, but I didn't think so. I could not live there. I was still travelling, and I thought to myself, "What is the best country?" It was Costa Rica – I liked it here very much. So I stayed here.'

I had so far only seen San José, but I took his point. It seemed an exceptional city. If San Salvador and Guatemala City were hosed down, all the shacks cleared and the people rehoused in tidy bungalows, the buildings painted, the stray dogs collared

173

and fed, the children given shoes, the refuse picked up in the
parks, the soldiers pensioned off – there is no army in Costa
Rica – and all the political prisoners released, those cities would,
I think, begin to look a little like San José. In El Salvador I had
chewed the end of my pipestem to pieces in frustration. In
San José I was able to have a new pipestem fitted (and I bought
a spare for Panama) – it was that sort of place. The weather
was fine, the service efficient, the city orderly. And they had just
had an election. In the rest of Central America an election could
be a harrowing piece of criminality; in Costa Rica the election
had been fair and something of a fiesta. 'You should have been
here for the election,' a woman told me in San José, as if I had
missed a party. Costa Ricans were proud of their decent government, their high literacy rate, their courtly manners. The only
characteristic Costa Rica shares with her Central American
neighbours is a common antipathy. You don't hear a good word
about Guatemala or El Salvador; and Nicaragua and Panama –
the countries Costa Rica is wedged between – are frankly
loathed. Costa Rica is as smug as any of them, but has more
reason to be so. 'They hate gringos in those places,' a shop-
keeper said to me. He was really saying two things: that gringos
are not hated in Costa Rica, and that Costa Ricans are honorary
gringos. It is with reluctance that foreigners tell you why they
think Costa Rica works so well. 'It's a white country,' they say
with hesitation. 'I mean, it's all white people, isn't it?'

This – you only have to take the train to Limón to find out –
is a falsehood. But I was enjoying myself in San José, so I
delayed my train-trip to Limón.

The Costa Ricans I discovered were courteous and helpful.
The foreigners were otherwise. You go to a stinking place like
Cutuco and you think how exactly it matches the fly-blown
setting of a Bogart movie; it has the heat and the seedy cinematic
romance, the end-of-tether squalor and rather vicious-looking
bars that you associate with whiskery gringos on dangerous
missions. But there are no gringos in Cutuco and the danger is
all in the drinking water. It is not the malarial jerk-town that
the foreigner seeks, but the hospitable tropical city where, for
all its boredom, it is possible to have a good meal, frequent a

safe brothel, start a business or make a killing. Costa Rica is enjoying a boom; the prosperity is obvious in San José. San José is hardly a romantic place but, next to Panama, it has the highest concentration of foreigners in Central America. Some are small-time crooks and hustlers, others are grand-scale con-men. Robert Vesco claims he lives in the suburbs of San José because he likes the climate; but he is also alleged to have embezzled almost half a billion dollars from an investment company. (Vesco's house, with its high fence and burglar-proof TV cameras in the shrubbery, is one of San José's sights; it is pointed out to tourists on their way to the Irazu volcano.) Not all San José's foreigners are crooks. There are timber merchants and booksellers, pharmacists and ice-cream tycoons. And there are retired people from all over the United States who have bought condominium apartments and plots of land and who sit in the shade and thank God they are not in Saint Pete. The difference is that, unlike Florida, there aren't so many geriatrics in Costa Rica to remind them that they have come down to die.

'I think they'd be better off in Florida,' said Captain Ruggles. 'For one thing, they'd have a better standard of medical care. God knows what kind of cattywampus you'd have to start here to get a doctor to look at you.'

Andy Ruggles – the 'captain' was honorific: he was an airline pilot – was from Florida himself; he kept asking out loud what in the name of God he was doing in San José. We were in the bar of the Royal Dutch Hotel and Andy was resolutely making himself drunk. He could not drink on duty, he said. He could not drink at all if he was scheduled to fly. A good vacation for him, he said, was a binge in the company of a really stunning prostitute. 'But we have beer like this in Florida, and the girls are much better looking. Paul,' he said, 'I think I made a real bad mistake coming here. But I got a discount on the air-fare.'

We talked about religion: Andy was a Baptist. We talked about politics: in Andy's view, Nixon had been framed. We talked about race. In this respect, Andy was enlightened. He said there were five races in the world. A more narrow-minded man would have said two. The Indians in Central America were of course Mongolians. 'They came down through the Bering Straits, when there was land there. Take our Indians – they're Mongolian to the core.'

Conversations about race make me uneasy; the general direction of such talk is towards Auschwitz. I was glad when he said, 'How do you pronounce the capital of Kentucky? Louieville or Lewisville?'

'Louieville,' I said.

'Wrong. It's Frankfort.' He guffawed. 'That's an old one!'

I asked him to give me the capital of Upper Volta. Andy did not know that Ouagadougou is the capital of Upper Volta. He countered with Nevada. I did not know that Carson City was its capital, and I missed Illinois too. Andy knew more capital cities that anyone I had ever met, and I prided myself on my knowledge of capitals. He missed New Hampshire (Concord) and Sri Lanka (Colombo), but that was all, apart from Upper Volta. He bought me three beers. I ended up buying six.

Andy was an even-tempered drunkard and he said that as he had been in San José for three days he wanted to show me around. But a man on his right had been listening to our conversation, and as Andy rose to leave, the man said in a strong Spanish accent, 'I think your airline is the worst one in the world. That's what I think. I'm on my way to Miami, but I'm not going to fly on your airline. It's the worst.'

Andy grinned at me. 'You always get one dissatisfied customer, don't you?'

The man said, 'It stinks. Really stinks.'

I thought Andy was going to hit him. But his smile returned to his reddened face and he said, 'Guess you had a bad flight. Little turbulence?' Andy fluttered his hand. 'Plane sort of going up and down, huh?'

'I have flown many times.'

'Correction,' said Andy. 'Two bad flights.'

'I would never fly with your airline again.'

'I'll mention that to the president next time I see him.'

'You can tell him something else for me –'

'Hold on a minute, sir,' said Andy very calmly. 'What I want to know is what's a Scotchman like you doing here?'

The Spaniard looked puzzled.

Andy turned his back on him and clawed his cuff from his wristwatch. 'Time to eat.'

'I'm going to show you around town, boy. You're new in this here town. Gonna introduce you to the main features. If we meet any of my pals you just keep your mouth shut. I'm gonna say you're an Englishman, just in from London. Don't you say a word – they won't know the difference.'

We went to a bar called 'Our Club'. It was noisy and dark and in the shadows I could see furtive men canoodling with prostitutes.

'Set them up,' said Andy. 'This gentleman and I will have some beer. Any kind will do.' The girl behind the bar wore a low-cut dress. She wiped the bar with a rag. 'You look like an intelligent girl,' said Andy. 'Know who' – the girl walked away – 'aw, she ain't listening. Paul, know who's the greatest poet in the world? No, not Shakespeare. Can't guess? Rudyard Kipling.'

The girl brought us two bottles of beer.

Andy said, 'I've taken my fun where I've found it. Give the girl two dollars, Paul – you still owe me for Oregon. Salem, remember? And I've rogued and I've ranged in my time.'

He settled into his recitation of 'The Ladies'. He did not seem to see that four feet down the bar was a grossly fat man who, drinking alone and scooping peanuts from a bowl, had been watching us. The man rattled the peanuts in his hand, a crap-shooter's motion, before tossing them into his mouth; then his other hand went to his drink. He sipped and reached for more peanuts. He put his drink down, shook the peanuts and shot them into his mouth. His movements were ceaselessly gluttonous, but his eyes remained fixed on us.

Andy's voice was hoarse, almost gruff, but touched with melancholy.

> 'Doll in a teacup she were –
> But we lived on the square, like a true-married pair,
> An' I learned about women from 'er.'

'This used to be a great country,' said the fat man, munching peanuts.

I looked over at him. He was chuckling ruefully. His left hand found the peanut bowl. He had not looked down.

Andy was saying,

> 'An' I took with a shiny she-devil,
> The wife of a nigger at Mhow;
> 'Taught me the gypsy folks' *bolee*
> Kind of volcano she were . . .'

'Hookers everywhere,' said the fat man. I estimated that he weighed three hundred pounds. His hair was pushed back. He had huge lard-white arms. 'You could hardly move for the hookers.'

Andy said,

> 'For she knifed me one night 'cause I wished she was white
> And I learned about women from 'er.'

'Americans come down. They buy little businesses – taxi-companies, soft drinks, gas stations. Then they sit on their asses and count their money. The government wanted them, so they cleaned the place up, sent the hookers to Panama. Because of these people who come down. Practically all of them are from New York. Mostly sheenies.'

Andy had not stopped reciting, but he finished quickly, saying, 'The colonel's lady and Judy O'Grady are sisters under the skin. Did you say something, sir?'

'Sheenies,' said the fat man; his chewing was like a challenge.

'Hear that, Paul?' said Andy. He turned to the fat man. 'But you're here, ain't you?'

'I'm just passing through,' said the fat man. Drink, peanuts, drink, peanuts; he didn't stop.

'Sure,' said Andy, 'you bring your money down here. But someone else does it and you criticize.' So he had heard the fat man's complaint! He had been reciting 'The Ladies', but he had heard. Andy's tone was judicious. He said, 'Well, sir, you're entitled to your opinion. I am not going to dispute what you say. But I'm entitled to my opinion, too, and I say Robert W. Service is the second greatest.'

178

Andy began to recite 'The Cremation of Sam McGee'. He faltered, cursed, then recovered and recited in its entirety a Robert Service poem called 'My Madonna'.

> 'I haled me a woman from the street,
> Shameless, but, oh, so fair!'

For several minutes, the fat man was silenced, but when Andy finished he piped up again.

'Not only sheenies,' he said. 'Anyone with a few bucks. They've ruined the place. I'll tell you one thing – Carazo just got elected, and he's going to kick them all out. They'll all be back in New York, where they belong. The trouble is, the hookers won't come back.' His hand went to the bowl and scrabbled. Now he looked down. The bowl was empty. He said again, 'The hookers won't come back.'

Andy said, 'Where are you from, sir?'

'Texas.'

'I knew it. Know how I knew it? Cause I could tell you were interested in poetry, Tex. Yes, I did. Now, listen, I know you're not a red-neck –'

'That's the beer talking,' said the fat man. His hand, without peanuts, foraged on the bar, a large greedy lump of fingers looking for food.

'—but I wonder if you could do me a favour?'

'Yeah?'

'Just an application,' said Andy. He was perched on his bar-stool. His voice was matter-of-fact, but he sipped between phrases and broke up his sentences. 'I wonder if you could get me, um,' he sipped his beer, 'an application to, um,' he sipped again, 'join the, um,' now he sipped and smacked his lips, 'Ku Klux Klan.'

The fat man hoicked phlegm and spat on the floor.

Andy said, 'Could you do that little thing for me?'

'You can wash the sheets,' snarled the fat man.

'I knew he had a sense of humour,' said Andy. 'That Tex is a real fun guy, and I tell you, I'd like to sit here all night just swapping jokes with him. But, Paul, I think I've had enough beer.'

Andy climbed off his bar-stool and trying to stand started to topple. He balanced himself against the bar, blew out his cheeks and said, 'Yep, if you can't stand up you've had enough. Now tell me, what's the name of that hotel I'm in?'

After Andy had gone, the fat man said, 'He's lucky I'm in a good mood. I could snap his arms off.'

The fat man's name was Dibbs. He had been a policeman in Texas, but he had quit, and he hinted that his reason for quitting was that policemen were not allowed to be violent enough. Dibbs? Well, two or three times he had wanted to blow people's brains out; but you weren't supposed to do that sort of thing. He could have done it easily and called it resisting arrest. And he had been taunted by punks he was not allowed to shoot. He became a construction worker, operating a bulldozer, and then he had quit because everybody else was collecting social security money, so why not him? Now he was a personal bodyguard ('to a sheeny') and a courier.

'What exactly does a courier do?' I asked him.

'They carry things. Me, I carry money.'

In the past few weeks he had been to Mexico, Panama and Honduras. He had carried fifty thousand dollars' worth of pesos to Montreal, and eighty thousand Canadian dollars to Honduras and Panama. He worked for a certain man, he said. When I asked why these large amounts of currency were being shunted back and forth across national frontiers, he laughed. But he did say how the money was carried – in a suitcase.

'A big suitcase.'

He said, 'You'd be surprised how much money you can get into a little suitcase. It's easy. No country checks your baggage when you leave. And customs people in the States and Canada don't care if they open a suitcase and find it filled with pesos. Sometimes they don't even open it. But when they do, they shit. They've never seen so much money in their life.'

It was clear to me why Dibbs had been hired for this job. He was strong; he was as big as a house; he was fairly stupid and completely loyal. He would not go into detail about his employer or the reason for transporting the money, and he said at one point, 'Maybe my name's Dibbs and maybe it ain't.' He had a fantasy of self-importance; carrying these sums of money fed his fantasy. He was proud of the fact that no one had ever succeeded in mugging him. 'Guess why?'

I said I couldn't guess.

'Because I'm an alcoholic,' he said. He picked up his glass. 'See that? It's a Coke. If I drink anything stronger, I'm finished. So I don't drink. Can't drink. Drunks get mugged. You – you'll probably get mugged. You've been drinking beer all night. I could carry fifty grand through the worst part of Panama City and nothing would happen to me.'

'You'd be sober.'

'Guess why else?'

'Can't guess.'

'Because I know karate. I could snap your arms off.' Dibbs leaned forward. He looked as though he wanted to snap my arms off. He said, 'Also, I'm not stupid. People who get mugged ask for it. They're stupid. They go to the wrong places. They get drunk. They don't know karate.'

Also, I thought, they weigh less than three hundred pounds.

Dibbs struck me as being a very sinister character, and without Andy Ruggles around to distract Dibbs's attention I felt rather defenceless. Dibbs had one passion: hookers. He liked to take them two or three at a time. 'I just lie there – they do all the work.' He boasted that he never paid them. They liked him; he walked into a brothel and they were all over him, clamouring, fighting to go to bed with this mountain of meat. He didn't know why this was so. 'Maybe it's because I'm so handsome!'

He wanted to take me to what he said was the only good brothel in San José. It was too late, I said, nearly midnight. He said midnight was the best time – the hookers were just waking up. 'How about tomorrow?' I said, knowing that tomorrow I would be in Limón. 'You're a chicken,' he said, and I could hear him laughing as I descended the stairs to the street.

There are two railways in Costa Rica, each with its own terminal in San José. Their routes dramatize Costa Rica's indifference to her neighbours: they go to the coasts, not to any frontier. The Pacific Railway travels down to Puntarenas on the Gulf of Nicoya; The Atlantic up to Puerto Limón. The Atlantic station is the older of the two, and part of its line has been in operation for almost a hundred years. Outside that station there is a steam locomotive mounted on blocks for travellers to admire. In El Salvador such an engine would be puffing and blowing up the track to Santa Ana; in Guatemala it would have been melted down and made into anti-personnel bombs for the White Hand.

A Limón train leaves the Atlantic station every day at noon. It is not a great train, but by Central American standards it is the Brighton Belle. There are five passenger coaches, two classes, no freight cars. I had been eager to take this train, for the route has the reputation of being one of the most beautiful in the world, from the temperate capital in the mountains, through the deep valleys on the north-east, to the tropical coast which, because of its richly lush jungle, Columbus named Costa Rica when he touched there on his fourth voyage in 1502. He believed that he had arrived at the green splendour of Asia. (Columbus tacked up and down the coast and was ill for four months in Panama; cruelly, no one told him that there was another vast ocean on the other side of the mountains – the local Indians were deaf to his appeal for this information.)

The most scenic of Central American routes; but I had another good reason for wanting to take this train out of San José. Since arriving in Costa Rica I had spent much of my time in the company of hard-drinking American refugees – Andy Ruggles and the diabolical Dibbs were but two. I was glad of their company; El Salvador hadn't been much fun. But now I was ready to set off alone. Travel is at its best a solitary enterprise: to see, to examine, to assess, you have to be alone and unencumbered. Other people can mislead you; they crowd your meandering impressions with their own; if they are companionable they obstruct your view, and if they are boring they corrupt the silence with non-sequiturs, shattering your concentration with *Oh, look, it's raining* and *You see a lot of trees here.* Travelling on your own can be terribly lonely (and it is not understood by Japanese who, coming across you smiling wistfully at an acre of

Mexican buttercups, tend to say things like *Where is the rest of your team?*). I think of evening in the hotel room in the strange city; my diary has been brought up to date; I hanker for company: what do I do? I don't know anyone here, so I go out and walk and discover the three streets of the town and rather envy the strolling couples and the people with children. The museums and churches are closed, and towards midnight the streets are empty. *Don't carry anything valuable*, I was warned; *it'll just get stolen.* If I am mugged I will have to apologize in my politest Spanish: *I am sorry, sir, but I have nothing valuable on my person.* Is there a surer way of enraging a thief and driving him to violence? Walking these dark streets is dangerous, but the bars are open. Ruggles and Dibbs await. They take the curse off my boredom, but I have a nagging suspicion that if I had stayed home and lingered in downtown Boston until midnight I would have met Ruggles and Dibbs in the Two O'Clock Lounge ('*20 Completely Nude College Girls!!!*'). I did not have to take the train to Costa Rica for that.

It is hard to see clearly or to think straight in the company of other people. Not only do I feel self-conscious, but the perceptions that are necessary to writing are difficult to manage when someone close by is thinking out loud. I am diverted, but it is discovery not diversion that I seek. What is required is the lucidity of loneliness to capture that vision which, however banal, seems in my private mood to be special and worthy of interest. There is something in feeling abject that quickens my mind and makes it intensely receptive to fugitive impressions. Later, these impressions might be refuted or deleted, but they might also be verified and refined; and in any case I had the satisfaction of finishing the business alone. Travel is not a vacation, and it is often the opposite of a rest. *Have a nice time*, people said to me at my send-off at South Station. It was not precisely what I had hoped for. I craved a little risk, some danger, an untoward event, a vivid discomfort, an experience of my own company, and in a modest way the romance of solitude. This I thought might be mine on that train to Limón.

I found a corner seat by a window and watched the houses get smaller as we approached the outskirts of San José. They got smaller but, unlike the houses in the rest of the suburbs in Central America, they did not get dingier and more tumbledown on the periphery of the city. The campaign flags were still flying, and election slogans and posters were stuck to the walls of some of them. They were ranch houses, bungalows, square tin-roofed houses; houses of clapboard and concrete. They were pink and green and lemon-yellow in the small settlements, and in the smart outer suburbs they were red-brick and white and had rolling lawns. And then, without passing a dump or a slum, or the dirty river with its grey froth of soapsuds that was the boundary of every other town I had seen so far, we sped into the countryside, past banana groves and fields of coffee. These were shady plantations, with wooded green hills surrounding them. It was sunny and cool on this day in late February, and there by the tracks was a Costa Rican bee-keeper, like Sherlock Holmes in retirement, just as hawk-nosed and skinny; he looked up from his swarming hives and grinned at the train.

Even the poorest, the smallest house was neatly painted, the stairs swept, and starched curtains flapped through windows. In the yards were the piles of firewood, the vegetable garden, the borders of flowers. They were proud little houses, and the pride gave them dignity. There was a completeness to this, a certain formality, and it was reflected in the way the train passengers were dressed, the girls in sunhats, the ladies in shawls, the men in fedoras.

More than half the passengers on the train were black. I found this odd: I could not remember having seen any blacks in San José. Their baskets and shopping bags marked them out as Costa Ricans, not tourists, and for the early part of the trip they chatted with the whites on the train. They spoke in Spanish, getting acquainted, laughing and joking. *I hope I've got enough food*, said a black lady in a sunbonnet. *My children are always eating*.

Then I heard, 'Take yo haid out de winda!'

It was the same woman, now yelling in English. One of her small sons, in a blue jersey, was hanging out of the window. But his head was so far out he could not hear her.

'Tree gonna lop it off!'

Now he heard. He turned his head to her, but did not withdraw it.

'You kyant do dat!' She punched his shoulder. The boy sat back in his seat and giggled at his sister.

'I have to watch them all the time,' said the black woman in Spanish. Her English was sing-song, her Spanish a stutter.

We passed through blobs of sunlight in a pretty, shady wood. It was unusual to travel in the shade, through woods which overhung the track. Normally there was heat on either side of the track and sun beating through the windows. But here the sunlight speckled the glass and flashed in the train, and the trees were so dense it was impossible to see beyond the pickets of slender trunks and the cracks of light. We were among mountains. A space between the trees opened like a gate and, far-off, pine groves grew darkly on the hills and below them in a ditch of shade there was a dairy and a saw-mill and a village of timber houses and a wood-lot. A river ran through it, sparkling just before it tumbled into the shady valley, and the place looked to me like a town in Vermont I had seen as a child, perhaps Bellows Falls or White River Junction. The illusion of Vermontness persisted even though in this village I saw a row of royal palms.

We came to Cartago. This was a market town. Here, in 1886, the railway line was begun by an American speculator, Minor Keith. The silver commemorative shovel, with an appropriate inscription, is on display in the National Museum in San José, along with pre-Columbian pottery and masks and gold jewellery and portraits of moustached Costa Rican patriots and presidents (their walking sticks, each one as individual as their moustaches, are also on display). In that museum is a painting of Cartago depicting the result of the great earthquake of 1910. It is an interesting picture, for right through the middle of town, in the foreground of the painting, are the railway tracks, a whole section of them covered by masonry which had fallen from a convent wall. That earthquake flattened Cartago, but the line was repaired; nothing else of old Cartago remains.

The seat next to me had been empty. Just as we left Cartago a young man took it and asked me how far I was going. He said he was going to Siquirres. Limón, he said, was interesting, but I might find it crowded. It would be hours before we'd reach Siquirres; he hoped I would teach him some English. He had tried to learn it, but found it very difficult. His name was Luis Alvarado, he said. I asked him if we could skip the English lesson.

'It is just that you look like a teacher. I think you could help me,' he said in Spanish. 'How do you like Costa Rica?'

I told him that I thought it was a beautiful country.

'Why do you think so?'

The mountains, I said.

'They are not so beautiful as those in Oregon. Or so high.'

The river, I said. That was a lovely river in the valley.

'The rivers in Oregon are much more beautiful.'

I told him I thought the people in Costa Rica were extremely pleasant.

'The people in Oregon always smile. They are more friendly than Costa Ricans.'

It was a green country, I said.

'Have you been to Oregon?'

'No,' I said. 'Have you?'

He had. It was his single visit outside Costa Rica, a summer in Oregon, trying to learn English. It was a wonderful visit, but the English lessons were a failure. He had not been to Nicaragua or Panama: they were loathsome places. He said that instead of my going on to Panama I should return to the States and visit Oregon.

The river was beneath us; the landscape had opened and become simple and terrifying, two parallel mountain ranges and between them, so deep it made me anxious, a gorge. There were fountains of mist in the gorge, the flung spray of the foaming river. This was the Rio Reventazón. It is a swift river and its strength has pulled down the sides of these mountains and made a canyon, filled with the rubble of its destruction, and this – the fallen walls of boulders, the river heaving over rocks, the turbulent suds of rapids – lay four hundred feet below the train. The low coffee bushes could not obscure the view. I saw how the gorge had been levelled by the rushing whiteness on the valley floor. The valley of the Reventazón is forty miles long. The mountains are in places so precipitous the train has to descend through tunnels (screams, exalted yells in the car, and the odour of damp walls) to a cliffside that brings it so near the river the spray hits the windows. Then up again, along a cut to switchbacks and bridges.

The bridges were always approached at an angle, so that they were seen whole, from the side; they appeared as a framework of slender girders, or sometimes wooden beams, tensed across two cliffs. It seemed as if this was the view of a bridge on another track, as if we were going to bypass it. But always the train turned sharply, and became noisy as it started onto it; and the torrent beneath it looked peculiarly menacing – a staircase of cataracts frothing into the greater torrent yonder. I wondered how it was that Costa Rica could be so cool and piney, and it was not just that it was so different from its near neighbours, but that it was cool and piney like Vermont, and freshly watered – here a sawmill and there a dairy, the cows cropping grass on the hillsides; and horses, oblivious to the train, tethered to fences. Later, I was to meet an American horse-dealer in Costa Rica. He said, 'My horses would bolt and hang themselves if I tied them that near the tracks.'

It is, for the first third of the trip, a mountain railway, the train travelling along a narrow shelf that has been notched into the mountainside. How narrow? Well, at one point a cow had strayed onto the line. To the left was the sheer mountain wall, to the right the drop into the river; the cow was baffled and for almost a mile she lolloped ahead of the engine, which had slowed so as not to kill her. At times she stopped, put her nose against the mountainside, sniffed at the precipice, then started away again, rocking back and forth, stifflegged, the way cows run. The track was too narrow to give her space to allow us to pass, so she ran ahead rocking, her tail swinging, for amost a mile on this high shelf.

Nearer the river the coffee bushes were thick, and there was cocoa, too, the wide leaves, the plump, bobbin-like pods. It was easier to make notes here, as the train moved slowly on the flat tracks by the riverbed. But my notes were not extensive. *Boulders,* I wrote, *Valley – River – Spray – Frail bridge – Trapped cow – Cocoa.*

'You Americans like to travel alone.' It was Luis.

I said, 'I hate to travel alone. It is depressing. I miss my wife and children. But if I am alone I see more clearly.'

'You never talk to each other, you Americans.'

'You mean in Oregon?'

'Here, when you travel.'

'We talk all the time! Who says Americans don't talk to each other?'

'There is an American,' said Luis. 'You see him? Why don't you talk to him?'

The man wore a blue cap, a Barney Oldfield cap with a peak; his shirt was bright green, his trousers cut like a sailor's. Although he was seated, the strap of his bag was over his shoulder and he clutched the bag tightly, as if it had something valuable in it. He was sunburned and I guessed he was in his sixties – the hair on his arms was white. He was seated near the blacks, who were talking in Spanish and English; but he did not speak to anyone.

I said, 'I did not know he was an American.'

Luis found this funny.

'You did not know *he* was an American?'

I suppose it was his cap, which Luis took to be foolishly youthful. Costa Ricans wore felt hats and fedoras. This man's cap was tilted at a rakish angle, and it did not quite go with his craggy face.

'Talk to him,' said Luis.

'No, thank you.'

Talk to this old man, just because Luis wanted to hear us speak English? I had met enough Americans in San José. It was the reason I had left the city, to seek out and assess the reputedly uninhabited Atlantic coast, perhaps wind up swapping stories with a grizzled black in a Limón bar, tales of mule-skinning and piracy on the Mosquito Coast.

'Go ahead.'

'You talk to him,' I said. 'He might teach you some English.'

It was, mainly, my other fear: the distortion of companion-ship. I did not want to see things with anyone else's eyes. I knew this experience. If they point out something you have seen already you realize that your own perception was rather obvious; if they indicate something you missed you feel cheated, and it is a greater cheat to offer it later as your own. In both cases, it is annoying. *Oh, look, it's raining* is as bad as *Costa Ricans have their own unit of length – the vara.*

I wanted to concentrate my whole attention on what was outside the window; I wanted to remember this valley, this river, these mountains, the breeze freshening the train, the fragrance of the wildflowers that grew next to the track. *Pretty flowers*, I wrote.

Smiling nervously, Luis got up. He went up the aisle and mumbled to the old man. The old man did not understand. Luis tried again. You bastard, I thought. Now the old man turned and smiled at me. He rose. Luis took the old man's seat. The old man came towards me and took Luis's seat. He said, 'Boy, am I glad to see you!'

He had missed his tour. It would have been all-inclusive, the train to Limón, a boat-trip up the coast, a chef travelling with the party, some wonderful meals. He would have seen monkeys and parrots. Back to Limón: some swimming, a four-star hotel, then a bus to the airport and a plane to San José. That was the tour. But (the river was dashing an old canoe to pieces, and those little boys – surely they were fishing?) the hotel manager had gotten the time wrong and the tour had left at six, not nine, so on the spur of the moment, and with nothing else to do in San José, the old man asked about the train and hopped on, just like that, and you never knew, maybe he'd catch up with the rest of them; after all, he had paid his three hundred dollars and here was his receipt and his booklet of coupons.

Six hours lay ahead of us, before we would reach Limón.

'Did you know the train was going to take so long?'

I said, 'I would not mind if this train took four days.'

That took care of him for a while, but as soon as the splendour of the valley returned he began chattering. His name was Thornberry, he lived in New Hampshire, and he was a painter –

of pictures. He had not always been a painter. Until recently he had had to make his living as a commercial artist and designer. It had been a real grind, worrying about how he was going to buy groceries; but a few years ago he had come into some money – quite a lot of money – and he had set about seeing the world. He had been to Hawaii, Italy, France, the West Indies, Colombia, Alaska, California, Ireland, Mexico and Guatemala. His impressions of Guatemala were different from mine. He loved Guatemala. He liked the flowers. He had been two weeks in Antigua with a charming fellow who gave parties every night. On Mr Thornberry's report, the fellow was an alcoholic. Mr Thornberry had not gone to Zacapa.

'This scenery,' said Mr Thornberry, 'it blows my mind.' Mr Thornberry had a curious way of speaking, he squinted until his eyes were not more than slits; his face tightened into a grimace and his mouth went square, mimicking a grin, and then without moving his lips he spoke through his teeth. It was the way people talked when they were heaving ash barrels, sort of screwing their faces up and groaning their words.

Lots of things blew Mr Thornberry's mind: the way the river thundered, the grandeur of the valley, the little huts, the big boulders, and the climate blew his mind most of all – he had figured on something more tropical. It was an odd phrase from a man of his age, but after all Mr Thornberry was a painter. I wondered why he had not brought his sketchbook. He repeated that he had left the hotel on the spur of the moment. He was, he said, travelling light. 'Where's your bag?'

I pointed to my suitcase on the luggage rack.

'It's pretty big.'

'That's everything I have. I might meet a beautiful woman in Limón and decide to spend the rest of my life there.'

'I did that once.'

'I was joking,' I said.

But Mr Thornberry was still grimacing. 'It was a disaster in my case.'

Out of the corner of my eye I saw that the river was seething, and men were standing in the shallows – I could not make out what they were doing – and pink and blue flowers grew beside the track.

'That fellow in Antigua had a beautiful house,' said Mr Thornberry. 'A wall all around it, with morning glories just like those.'

'So those are morning glories, eh?' I said. 'I was wondering.'

Mr Thornberry told me about his painting. You couldn't be a painter during the Depression; couldn't make a living at it. He had worked in Detroit and New York City. He had had a miserable time of it. Three children, but his wife had died when the third was still an infant – tuberculosis, and he had not been able to afford a good doctor. So she died and he had to raise the kids himself. They had grown up and married and he had gone to New Hampshire to take up painting, what he had always wanted to do. It was a nice place, northern New Hampshire; in fact, he said, it looked a hell of a lot like this part of Costa Rica.

'I thought it looked like Vermont. Bellow Falls.'

'Not really.'

There were logs in the water, huge dark ones tumbling against each other and jamming on the rocks. Why logs? I did not want to ask Mr Thornberry why they were here. He had not been in Costa Rica longer than me. How could he know why this river, on which there were now no houses, carried logs in its current as long as telegraph poles and twice as thick? I would concentrate on what I saw: I would discover the answer. I concentrated. I discovered nothing.

'Sawmill,' said Mr Thornberry. 'See those dark things in the water?' He squinted; his mouth went square. 'Logs.'

Damn, I thought, and saw the sawmill. So that's why the logs were there. They had been cut up-river. They must have –

'They must have floated those logs down to be cut into lumber,' said Mr Thornberry.

'They do that back home,' I said.

'They do that back home,' said Mr Thornberry.

He was silent for some minutes. He brought a camera out of his shoulder bag and snapped pictures out the window. It was not easy for him to shoot past me, but I was damned if I would yield my corner seat. We were in another cool valley, with rock columns all around us. I saw a pool of water.

'Pool of water,' said Mr Thornberry.

'Very nice,' I said. Was that what I was supposed to say?

Mr Thornberry said, 'What?'

'Very nice pool of water.'

Mr Thornberry hitched forward. He said, 'Cocoa.'

'I saw some back there.'

'But there's much more of it here. Mature trees.'

Did he think I was blind?

'Anyway,' I said, 'there's some coffee mixed in with it.'

'Berries,' said Mr Thornberry, squinting. He heaved himself across my lap and snapped a picture. No, I would not give him my seat.

I had not seen the coffee berries; how had he? I did not want to see them.

'The red ones are ripe. We'll probably see some people picking them soon. God, I hate this train.' He fixed that straining expression on his face. 'Blows my mind.'

Surely a serious artist would have brought a sketchpad and a few pencils and be doodling in a concentrated way, with his mouth shut. All Mr Thornberry did was fool with his camera and talk; he named the things he saw, no more than that. I wanted to believe that he had lied to me about being a painter. No painter would gab so aimlessly.

'Am I glad I met you!' said Mr Thornberry. 'I was going crazy in that seat over there.'

I said nothing. I looked out the window.

'Kind of a pipeline,' said Mr Thornberry.

There was a rusty tube near the track, running parallel in the swamp that had displaced the river. I had not seen the river go. There were palm trees and that rusty tube: kind of a pipeline, as he had said. Some rocky cliffs rose behind the palms; we ascended the cliffs and beneath us were streams –

'Streams,' said Mr Thornberry.

– and now some huts, rather interesting ones, like share-croppers' cottages, made of wood, but quite solidly built, upraised on poles above the soggy land. We stopped at the village of Swampmouth: more of those huts.

'Poverty,' said Mr Thornberry.

192

'Don't be silly,' I said. These were good timber houses, with wide corrugated tin roofs and healthy faces in the windows and well-dressed children standing on the big porches. They were not wealthy people, but neither were they poor. It seemed to me amazing that so far from San José – so far from Limón – in what was the borderland of thick viney jungle and dense savannah, people lived in dry well-made bungalows. Most of the people were black, and now most of the passengers on the train were black. I walked to the rear of the car to get away from Mr Thornberry, and talked to an old black man. The blacks he said had been brought over from Jamaica to build the railway. 'We didn't get the diseases,' he said in English. 'The British people got all the diseases.' His father had been a Costa Rican, his mother Jamaican; English had been his first language, which allowed me a glimpse of the sociology of the family – he had been raised by his mother. He was critical of the black boys hooting and laughing in the corridor of the train. 'Their grandparents were willing to work, but they ain't.'

The houses in style were perhaps West Indian, too. They were certainly the sort I had seen in the rural south, in the farming villages of Mississippi and Alabama; but they were trimmer and better-maintained. There was a banana grove in each mushy yard and in each village a general store, nearly always with a Chinese name on the store sign; and most of the stores were connected to another building, which served as a bar and a pool room. There was an air of friendliness about these villages, and though many of the households were pure black, there were mixed ones as well; Mr Thornberry pointed this out as soon as I returned to my seat.

'Black boy, white girl,' he said. 'They seem to get along fine. Pipeline again.'

Thereafter, each time the pipeline appeared – and it did about twenty times from here to the coast – Mr Thornberry obligingly indicated it for me.

We were deep in the tropics. The heat was heavy with the odour of moist vegetation and swamp water and the cloying scent of jungle flowers. The birds had long beaks and stick-like legs and they nose-dived and spread their wings, becoming kite-shaped to break their fall. Some cows stood knee-deep in swamp, mooing. The palms were like fountains, or bunches of ragged feathers, thirty feet high – no trunks that I could see, but only these feathery leaves springing straight out of the swamp.

Mr Thornberry said, 'I was just looking at those palm trees.'

'They're like giant feathers,' I said.

'Funny green fountains,' he said. 'Look, more houses.'

Another village.

Mr Thornberry said, 'Flower gardens – look at those bougain-villeas. They blow my mind. Mama in the kitchen, kids on the porch. That one's just been painted. Look at all the vegetables!'

It was as he said. The village passed by and we were again in swampy jungle. It was humid and now overcast. My eyelids were heavy. Note-taking would have woken me up, but there wasn't room for me to write, with Mr Thornberry darting to the window to take a picture every five minutes. And he would have asked why I was writing. His talking made me want to be secretive. In the damp greenish light the woodsmoke of the cooking fires clouded the air further. Some of the people cooked under the houses, in that open space under the upraised floor.

'Like you say, they're industrious,' said Mr Thornberry. When had I said that? 'Every damn one of those houses back there was selling something.'

No, I thought, this couldn't be true. I hadn't seen anyone selling anything.

'Bananas,' said Mr Thornberry. 'It makes me mad when I think that they sell them for twenty-five cents a pound. They used to sell them by the hand.'

'In Costa Rica?'

'New Hampshire.'

He was silent a moment, then he said, 'Buffalo.'

He was reading a station sign. Not a station – a shed.

'But it doesn't remind me of New York.' Some miles earlier we had come to the village of Bataan. Mr Thornberry reminded me that there was a place in the Philippines called Bataan. The March of Bataan. Funny, the two places having the same name, especially a name like Bataan. We came to the village of Liverpool. I braced myself.

'Liverpool,' said Mr Thornberry. 'Funny.'

It was stream-of-consciousness, Mr Thornberry a less allusive Leopold Bloom, I a reluctant Stephen Dedalus. Mr Thornberry wás seventy-one. He lived alone, he said; he did his own cooking. He painted. Perhaps this explained everything. Such a solitary existence encouraged the habit of talking to himself: he spoke his thoughts. And he had been alone for years. His wife had died at the age of twenty-five. But hadn't he mentioned a marital disaster? Surely it was not the tragic death of his wife.

I asked him about this, to take his attention from the passing villages which, he repeated, were blowing his mind. I said, 'So you never remarried?'

'I got sick,' he said. 'There was this nurse in the hospital, about fifty or so, a bit fat, but very nice. At least, I thought so. But you don't know people unless you live with them. She had never been married. There's our pipeline. I wanted to go to bed with her right away – I suppose it was me being sick and her being my nurse. It happens a lot. But she said, "Not till we're married." ' He winced and continued. 'It was a quiet ceremony. Afterwards, we went to Hawaii. Not Honolulu, but one of the little islands. It was beautiful – jungle, beaches, flowers. She hated it. "It's too quiet," she said. Born and raised in a little town in New Hampshire, a one-horse town – you've seen them – and she goes to Hawaii and says it's too quiet. She wanted to go to night-clubs. There weren't any night-clubs. She had enormous breasts, but she wouldn't let me touch them. "You make them hurt." I was going crazy. And she had a thing about cleanliness. Every day of our honeymoon we went down to the launderette and I sat outside and read the paper while she did the wash. She washed the sheets every day. Maybe they do that in hospitals, but in everyday life that's not normal. I guess I was kind of disappointed.' His voice trailed off. He said, 'Telegraph poles . . . pig . . . pipeline again,' and then, 'It was a real disaster. When we got back from the honeymoon I said, "Looks like it's not going to work." She agreed with me and that day she moved out of the house. Well, she had never really moved in. Next thing I know she's suing me for divorce. She wants alimony, maintenance, the whole thing. She's going to take me to court.'

'Let me get this straight,' I said. 'All you did was go on a honeymoon, right?'

'Ten days,' said Mr Thornberry. 'It was supposed to be two weeks, but she couldn't take the silence. Too quiet for her.'

'And then she wanted alimony?'

'She knew my sister had left me a lot of money. So she went ahead and sued me.'

'What did you do?'

Mr Thornberry grinned. It was the first real smile I had seen on his face the whole afternoon. He said, 'What did I do? I counter-sued her. For fraud. See, she had a friend – a man. He had called her up when we were in Hawaii. She told me it was her brother. Sure.'

He was still looking out the window, but his thoughts were elsewhere. He was chuckling. 'I didn't have to do a thing after that. She gets on the witness-stand. The judge asks her, "Why did you marry this man?" She says, "He told me he had a lot of money." He told me he had a lot of money! Incriminated herself, see? She was laughed out of court. I gave her five grand and was glad to get rid of her.' Almost without pausing he said, 'Palm trees,' then, 'Pig,' 'Fence,' 'Lumber,' 'More morning glories – Capri's full of them.' 'Black as the ace of spades,' 'American car.'

The hours passed; Mr Thornberry spoke without let-up. 'Pool table,' 'Must be on welfare,' 'Bicycle,' 'Pretty girl,' 'Lanterns.'

I had wanted to push him off the train, but after what he had told me I pitied him. Maybe the nurse had sat beside him like this; maybe she had thought *If he says that one more time I'll scream.*

I said, 'When was this abortive honeymoon?'

'Last year.'

I saw a three-storey house, with a verandah on each storey. It was grey and wooden and toppling, and it reminded me of the Railway Hotel I had seen in Zacapa. But this one looked haunted. Every window was broken and an old steam locomotive was rusting in the weedy front yard. It might have been the house of a plantation owner – there were masses of banana trees near by. The house was rotting and uninhabited, but from the remainder of the broken fence and the yard, the verandahs and the barn, which could have been a coach-house, it was possible to see that long ago it had been a great place, the sort of dwelling lived in by tyrannical banana tycoons in the novels of Asturias. In the darkening jungle and the heat, the decayed house looked fantastic, like an old ragged spider's web, with some of its symmetry still apparent.

Mr Thornberry said, 'That house. Costa Rican gothic.'

I thought: I saw it first.

'Brahma bull,' said Mr Thornberry. 'Ducks.' 'Creek.' 'Kids playing.' Finally, 'Breakers.'

We were at the shore and travelling alongside a palmy beach. This was the Mosquito Coast, which extends from Puerto Barrios in Guatemala to Colón in Panama. It is wild and looks the perfect setting for a story of castaways. What few villages and ports lie along it are derelict; they declined when shipping did, and returned to jungle. Massive waves were rolling towards us, the white foam vivid in the twilight; they broke just below the coconut palms near the track. At this time of day, nightfall, the sea is the last thing to darken: it seems to hold the light that is slipping from the sky; and the trees are black. So in the light of this luminous sea, and the pale still-blue eastern sky, and to the splashings of the breakers, the train racketed on towards Limón. Mr Thornberry was still talking. He said, 'I think I'm going to like this place,' then reported that he had spotted a house, an animal, a sudden fire, until at last we were travelling in darkness and his voice ceased. The surf was gone, the heat oppressive. I saw through the trees a combustion of awful flaring light, and Mr Thornberry croaked, 'Limón.'

Limón looked like a dreadful place. It had just rained, and the town stank. The station was on a muddy road near the harbour, and puddles reflected the decayed buildings and over-bright lights. The smell was dead barnacles and damp sand, flooded

197

sewers, brine, oil, cockroaches and tropical vegetation which, when soaked, gives off the hot mouldy vapour you associate with compost heaps in summer, the stench of mulch and mildew. It was a noisy town, as well: clanging music, shouts, car horns. That last sight of the palmy coast and the breakers had been misleading. And even Mr Thornberry, who had been hopeful, was appalled. I could see his face; he was grimacing in disbelief. 'God,' he groaned. 'It's a piss-hole in the snow.' We walked through the puddles, the other passengers splashing us as they hurried past. Mr Thornberry said, 'It blows my mind.'

That does it, I thought. I said, 'I'd better go look for a hotel.'

'Why not stay at mine?'

Oh, look it's raining. It blows my mind. Kind of a pipeline.

I said, 'I'll just sniff around town. I'm like a rat in a maze when I get to a new place.'

'We could have dinner. That might be fun. You never know – maybe the food's good here.' He squinted up the street. 'This place was recommended to me.'

'It wasn't recommended to me,' I said. 'It looks pretty strange.'

'Maybe I'll find that tour I was supposed to be on,' he said. He no longer sounded hopeful.

'Where are you staying?'

He told me. It was the most expensive hotel in Limón. I used that as my reason for looking elsewhere. A small, feeble-minded man approached and asked sweetly if he could carry my suitcase. It dragged on the street when he held it in his hand. He put it on his head and marched bandy-legged like a worker-elf to the market square. Here, Mr Thornberry and I parted.

'I hope you find your tour,' I said. He said he was glad we had met on the train: it had been kind of fun after all. And he walked away. I felt a boundless sense of relief, as if I had just been sprung from a long confinement. This was liberation. I tipped the elf and walked quickly in the opposite direction from Mr Thornberry.

I walked to savour my freedom and stretch my legs. After three blocks the town didn't look any better, and wasn't that a rat nibbling near the tipped-over barrel of scraps? *It's a white coun-*

try, a man had told me in San José. But this was a black town, a beach-head of steaming trees and sea-stinks. I tried several hotels. They were wormy staircases with sweating people minding tables on the second-floor landings. No, they said, they had no rooms. And I was glad, because they looked so disgustingly dirty and the people were so rude; so I walked a few more blocks. I'd find a better hotel. But they were smaller and smellier, and they too were full. At one, as I stood panting – the staircase had left me breathless – a pair of cockroaches scuttled down the wall and hurried unimpeded across the floor. *Cockroaches*, I said. The man said, *What do you want here?* He too was full. I had been stopping at every second hotel. Now I stopped at each one. They were not hotels. They were nests of foul bedclothes, a few rooms and a portion of verandah. I should have known they were full: I met harassed families making their way down the stairs, the women and children carrying suitcases, the father sucking his teeth in dismay and muttering, 'We'll have to look somewhere else.' It was necessary for me to back down the narrow stairs to let these families pass.

In one place (I recognized it as a hotel by its tottering stairs, its unshaded bulbs, its moth-eaten furniture, its fusty smell), a woman in an apron said, 'Them – they're doublin' up.' She indicated a passageway of people – grandmothers, young women, sighing men, glassy-eyed children, black, fatigued, pushing old valises into a cubicle and several changing their clothes as they stood there in the passageway.

I had no idea of the time. It seemed late; the people in Limón who were not room-hunting were strolling the wet streets. They had that settled look of smugness which the stranger interprets as mockery or at least indifference. Saturday nights in strange cities can alienate the calmest of travellers.

Further on, a man said to me, 'Don't waste your time looking. There are no hotel rooms in Limón. Try tomorrow.'

'What do I do tonight?'

'There is only one thing you can do,' he said. 'See that bar over there?' It was a peeling storefront with a string of lights over the door; insides, shapes – human heads – and smoke; and broken-crockery music. 'Go in and pick up a girl. Spend the night with her. That is your only hope.'

I considered this. But I did not see any girls. At the door were a gang of boys, jeering at men who were entering. I tried another hotel. The black owner saw that his reply to my question distressed me. He said, 'If you really get stuck and got no other place, come back here. You can sit out here on that chair.' It was a straight-backed chair on his verandah. There was a bar across the street: music, another mob of gawping boys. I slapped at the mosquitoes. Motorbikes went by; they sounded like outboard motors. This sound, and the boys, and the music made a scream. But I left my suitcase with this man and searched more streets. There were no hotels – no bars, no boarding houses; even the music was muffled. I decided to turn back, but I had gone too far: now I was lost.

I came to a precinct of Limón known as 'Jamaicatown'. In this white, Spanish-speaking country, a black, English-speaking area; a slum. These were the worst streets I had seen in Costa Rica, and each street corner held a dozen people, talking, laughing; their speech had a cackle in it. I was watched, but not threatened; and yet I had never felt so lost; it was as if I had burst through the bottom of my plans and was falling through darkness. I would continue to fall: there was absolutely nothing to do until dawn. My feet hurt; I was tired, dirty, sweating; I had not eaten all day. This was not the time or the place to reflect on the futility of the trip, and yet Costa Rica had seemed to promise better than this dark dead-end.

At one corner I asked some loitering men the way to the market. I asked in Spanish; they replied in English: they knew I was a stranger. Their directions were clear: they said I couldn't miss it.

I saw the row of hotels and boarding houses I had entered earlier in the evening. I had been disgusted by them then, but now they didn't seem so bad to me. I kept walking, and near the market square, skipping feebly across the street, one shoulder lower than the other because of the bag he carried, funny blue cap, bright green shirt, sailor pants, shuffling deck shoes: Thornberry.

'I've been looking all over for you.'

I needed his company: I was glad – someone to talk to. I said, 'I can't find a room anywhere. There aren't any in Limón. I'm screwed.'

He took my arm and winced. 'There are three beds in my room,' he said. 'You stay with me.'

'You mean it?'

'Sure – come on.'

My relief was inexpressible.

I got my suitcase from the hotel where the man had said that I could spend the night on his verandah chair. Mr Thornberry called the place a piss-hole (and over the next few days, whenever we passed it, he said, 'There's your verandah!'). I went to his room and washed my face, then we had a beer and grumbled about Limón. In gratitude I took him out to eat; we had broiled fish and hearts of palm and a bottle of wine, and Mr Thornberry told me sad stories about his life in New Hampshire, about his loneliness. Maybe he'd rent a house in Puntarenas for the winter. He couldn't take another cold winter. He had made a mess of his life, he said. It was the money – the IBM stock his sister had bequeathed to him. 'The things I want money can't buy. Money's just bullshit. If you have it. If you don't have it, it's important. I didn't always have it.'

I said, 'You saved my life.'

'I couldn't let you walk around all night. It's dangerous. I hate this place.' He shook his head. 'I thought I was going to like it. It looked okay from the train – those palm trees. That travel agency was lying to me. They said there were parrots and monkeys here.'

'Maybe you can get on a tour tomorrow.'

'I'm sick of thinking about it.' He looked at his watch. 'Nine o'clock. I'm bushed. Shall we call it a day?'

I said, 'I don't normally go to bed at nine o'clock.'

Mr Thornberry said, 'I always do.'

So we did. There was only one room-key. We were like an elderly couple, fussing silently at bed-time, yawning, chastely putting on our pyjamas. Mr Thornberry pulled his covers up and sighed. I read for a while, then switched off the light. It was

still early, still noisy. Mr Thornberry said, 'Motorbike.'
'Music.' 'Listen to them yakking.' 'Car.' 'Train whistle.'
'Those must be waves.' Then he fell asleep.

In spite of the ill-will I had felt towards him on the train, I
considered Mr Thornberry my rescuer. To return the favour,
I found a tour for him – a boat trip northwards up the coastal
canal to the Laguna Matina, and an afternoon on the long
lava beach at the mouth of the Rio Matina. Mr Thornberry
insisted that I accompany him and ('Money's just bullshit')
bought me a ticket. The boat was small, the canal was choked
with hyacinths, so the going was slow. But orchids grew in
clusters on the tropical trees, and there were herons and egrets
soaring past us, and further on brown pelicans which flew in
formation like geese.

'I don't see any parrots,' said Mr Thornberry. 'I don't see
any monkeys.'

I went to the bow of the boat and sat there in the sun watching
the jungle pass.

'Butterflies,' said Mr Thornberry, who had stayed under the
canopy astern.

They were electric blue, and squarish, the size of pot-holders,
mimicking the orchids they fluttered among.

'More herons,' said Mr Thornberry. 'Where are the parrots?'

Rising in me was an urge to push him off the boat. But I was
ashamed of my irritation: he had saved me.

'Look how green everything is,' said Mr Thornberry.

We reached the lagoon at one-thirty, and moored the boat
there because the black pilot feared that the tides at the estuary
might drag us into the sea. We walked to the beach of grey
lava. I swam. The black pilot screamed in Spanish for me to
leave the water. There were sharks in the water, he said – the
hungriest, the fiercest of sharks. I asked him whether he had
seen any sharks. No, he said, but he knew they were there. I
plunged back into the water.

'Sharks!' the black pilot yelled.

'Where?' I said. I was waist-deep in surf.

'There! Get out! Get out!'

202

Backing out of the water I saw the black dorsal fin of a shark slitting the water's surface. But the creature itself looked no more than a yard long. I had seen bigger sharks in East Sandwich on Cape Cod, and told the black pilot this. He insisted that I was crazy to swim, so I indulged him in his fears and went for a walk instead.

Mr Thornberry met me on the beach. We walked along the shoreline. 'Driftwood,' he said. 'It's all lava, you know. That's why the sand's so black.'

The boat's engine broke a shear-pin on the return journey. The pilot hailed a passing canoe and disappeared for an hour or more searching the canal huts for a new shear-pin.

'The other tour boat had a special chef,' said Mr Thornberry. 'This one doesn't even have an engine.'

'We might be stranded here for days,' I said. But this was malice; already I could see the black pilot making towards us in a canoe.

Back in Limón I found my own hotel. The weekend visitors had gone home: I had my pick of places. It was not a bad hotel, though the bed was damp with the sea-dampness of the air, and I was tormented by mosquitoes, and the noisy slosh of surf kept me awake for half the night. And yet, in solitude, I could think straight; I tried to work out the Thornberry paradox.

The next day I gave to roaming Limón, but on closer inspection Limón did not look any better than it had that first night, a steaming stinking town of mud puddles and buildings discoloured by dampness. The stucco fronts had turned the colour and consistency of stale cake, and crumbs of concrete littered the pavements. In the park there were three-toed sloths creeping in tree branches, and in the market and on the parapets of the crumbling buildings there were mangy vultures. Other vultures circled the plaza. Was there a dingier backwater in all the world? Columbus had come here with his son, Ferdinand. Ferdinand, fourteen at the time, had written an account of that fourth voyage, and he had described Limón as 'lofty, full of rivers, and abounding in very tall trees, as also on the islet [Uva Island, the Indians called it Quirivi] where they grew thick as basil, and full of very lofty groves of trees ... For this reason the Admiral

[Columbus] called it La Huerta [The Garden].' It might have been so; but the accounts of this voyage are contradictory. Ferdinand sometimes saw things differently from his father. In Limón, Ferdinand wrote, to calm the fears of the sailors, the Indians sent out an old man with 'two little girls, the one about 8, the other about 14 years of age . . . the girls showed great fortitude, for despite the Christians being complete strangers to them in appearance, manners and race, they gave no signs of grief or fear, but always looked cheerful and modest. So the Admiral showed them good usage . . .' In his *Lettera Rarissima* to the Sovereigns, Columbus gave a different version of this. 'In Cariai [Limón] and the neighbouring lands,' he wrote, 'there are sorcerers. They would have given the world for me not to stay there an hour. As soon as I got there they sent right out two girls, all dressed up; the elder was hardly 11, and other 7, both behaving with such lack of modesty as to be no better than whores. They had magic powder concealed about them. As soon as they arrived, I gave orders that they be presented with some of our trading truck and sent them directly ashore . . .'

My desire to leave Limón was sharpened one morning while, with nothing better to do, I was standing in the plaza watching the vultures: were they vultures, or buzzards, or another bird of prey? I heard a sharp voice and saw an enormous black man coming towards me. He was carrying something silver; he wore a wool cap; he was barefoot. His eyes glinted with lunacy. He had a twitching gait.

'I am the Son of God,' he said.

He shook the silver object, then held it in blessing like a pyx. It was a ballpoint pen.

'I am the Son of God.'

People smiled. They let him pass. Perhaps they did not speak English.

'I am the Son of God.'

I stood aside.

Mr Thornberry was seated in the small lobby of his hotel. He looked deeply worried. He was studying a travel brochure. He jumped to his feet when he saw me.

'Let's get out of here,' I said.

'I tried,' he said. 'The plane's full. The bus doesn't leave until tonight.'

The train had left, too, at five that morning. I said, 'We can take a taxi.'

'A *taxi*? To San José?'

We went to the taxi rank in the plaza. I approached the driver of the least-dented car I could see and asked him: how much to San José? He thought for a moment, then uttered a ridiculously high figure. I translated this for Mr Thornberry, who said, 'Tell him we'll take it.'

On principle I beat him down ten dollars and insisted that he had to get us to San José in time for lunch. He agreed and smiled. 'I've never done this before,' he said.

'This was a terrific idea,' said Mr Thornberry. 'I thought I'd never get out of that place.' He looked out of the window and squinted. 'Hut,' he said. 'Pig.' 'Cow.' 'Bananas.' Towards San José he became excited. 'Look,' he said, 'there's our pipeline!'

11 The Pacific Railway: The 10:00 to Puntarenas

Walking down the main street of San José one morning after the Limón episode, I saw Captain Ruggles with a suitcase in each hand, hurrying away from his hotel. He wasn't leaving town, he said, he was only changing hotels. The previous night, and for the first time since arriving in San José, he had tried to hustle a girl up to his room. In the event, the manager had not allowed her past the lobby. What riled Andy was that the manager had said he had 'standards to maintain'. So Andy checked out.

'I'm going down the road,' he said. 'It's real fine. Where I'm going you can take anyone you want to up to your room.'

'You've got your standards to maintain, too.'

'You bet. I make it a practice not to stay in any hotel where you can't take a two-headed nigger.'

I accompanied him to the hotel. It was a ramshackle building in the red-light district, catering to Panamanian sailors. The lobby was stacked with duffle bags, but that great stuffed thing near the check-in desk only *looked* like a duffle bag. It was Dibbs, eating a banana. What a small world this was.

'This is more like it,' said Andy.

Dibbs had seen us enter. 'Chicken-shit,' he said, and went back to his banana.

As the days wore on, Andy became dispirited. Each time I saw him he had the same complaint. 'I hate this place. I don't know what it is, but I can't fight it. I change hotels so I can take a hooker in, and I ask for a quiet room. They put me in the front. Sort of louvred windows, permanently open, like the front of a Ventura. The horns, the motorcyles, the exhaust fumes – they're driving me batty. I can't close the windows, I can't sleep – I haven't even brought a girl up. I wouldn't bring

206

a girl in there. Listen, I don't even think these girls are pretty, do you?'

But it was also the red-necks. They depressed Andy more than the Panamanian sailors. He introduced me to a sixty-seven-year-old Texan. 'This is my forty-first trip to San José,' the man boasted. 'These girls cost money, but they're worth every cent.' His friend had been here twelve times, but his friend was younger. Andy's hotel was full of red-necks who had come down for the beer-drinking and the whore-hopping. They wore cowboy hats and boots, baseball caps and tee-shirts printed with slogans. They said you could have a fine time in San José. To his credit, Andy said, 'I don't want to end up like these jokers.' On his last evening, at my urging, he recited again Robert Service's poem, 'My Madonna'.

San José was not really vicious, but only superficially so. And yet I felt excluded from the serious, peaceable life of the city; it made my stay here seem odder than what I had experienced in Limón. It was odd in any case to be a traveller in a place where people were busily occupied: going to the dentist, buying curtains, searching for motor spares, taking their children to school, leading their lives in dedicated and innocent ways. The Costa Rican with his satchel of groceries and his young son, entering the government office to pay his electric light bill: he was everything that I was not. The red-necks were simply a fragment of the foreground. As a traveller in this settled society I was an intruder, a stranger watching people go through familiar motions that I could not affect or enter into. I had no business here, but it was worse when I noticed how closely their lives resembled the one I had left at home. What about my family? My car? My light bill? My teeth? In San José, the orderliness was a reproach; I had a sense of having deserted my responsibilities. I saw a young couple picking out a vacuum cleaner, and I felt guilty and homesick. Nothing was more unconsoling to me in all of Central America than the sight of this couple proudly carrying their new vacuum cleaner out of the San José store. I think I began to understand then why I was always happier in a backwater, why the strangeness of Santa Ana had charmed me, and why I had sought the outlandish parts of Guatemala or the wastes of Mexico. Perhaps this explained my need to seek out the inscrutable magnetisms of the exotic: in the wildest place everyone looked so marginal, so temporary, so uncomfortable, so hungry and tired, it was possible as a traveller to be anonymous or even, paradoxically, to fit in, in the same temporary way.

The map shows a railway that runs east of Limón and over the border into Panama; but this banana line is defunct. Even if it had been running it would have got me nowhere except to a place called Bocas de Toro where I would have had to charter a plane to fly to Panama City. This left me only one choice, the slow train to Puntarenas on the Pacific coast, and then by road or air to Panama.

But my chief reason for taking the Puntarenas train had nothing to do with travel. More than anything, I wanted to read a book. And I had a good book. Twice in San Salvador and once in Limón I had opened Poe's *Narrative of Arthur Gordon Pym*; each time it had been night and, while I had read the novel with fascination, on turning off the light the horrors of the story returned to me and made me wakeful. It was, without any doubt, the most terrifying story I had ever read: claustrophobia, shipwreck, thirst, mutiny, cannibalism, vertigo, murder, storm – it was a nightmare journey, and it produced nightmares in me. At home it might not have seemed so bad, but in three Central American hotel rooms – hot, stifling, narrow; the bulb-blistered lamp shade, the strange bed, the rat gnawing the ceiling – the book was an experience of pure terror. I put it away, and I vowed that I would not open it again until I was in a sunny railway compartment. It did not matter where the train was going; what mattered to me was that I should read it under ideal conditions, on a train, with my feet up, my pipe drawing nicely. This book was my reason for going to Puntarenas on that train.

The Pacific Station looked promising. One man was mopping the floor of the lobby, another washing the windows: such attentions are a good indicator that the trains run on time. And there was an eight-foot statue of Jesus Christ across from the ticket window: Godliness and cleanliness. The railway itself is much newer than the Atlantic line; it is electrified, it is swift and smoothly-running, and, apart from its quacking horn, it is silent; the seats inside the blue carriages are not broken, and because there are eight trains a day it is seldom crowded: perfect for reading.

Nor is the landscape remarkable enough to intrude. Costa Rica's south-west is very different from the north-east. The land seems to slope away to the Pacific coast, from the coffee bushes in the high suburbs, to areas of light industry, the cement factories and timber yards that supply material for the country's growth. By the time we left these industrial suburbs it was not yet noon; but it was lunch-time, not only for the factory hands, but for office workers and managers too. Costa Rica has a large middle-class, but they go to bed early and rise at dawn; everyone – student, labourer, businessman, estate manager, politician – keeps farmer's hours.

On this passenger train most of the people were off to the beach. The mood was festive, the luggage baskets of swim-fins, towels, sunhats, hampers of food. For most, this was a holiday. There were only a few blacks on the train (their homeland lies on the opposite coast) and the way the passengers had seated themselves – girls on these seats, boys over there, mothers minding children, older men and husbands sitting together at a safe distance from their womenfolk – reminded me of outings I had seen on holiday weekends in Boston, from the Italian neighbourhoods near North Station on the trains to City Point. The faces of these Costa Ricans had a Neapolitan cast, and their luggage was redolent of meatballs. They had radios, they sang, they shouted and ate ice creams.

Between chapters of *Pym* I looked out of the window. There were brilliant orange flowers on the branches of tall trees, and in fields near these trees rows of ripe tomatoes, peppers and beans. The day grew hotter, the land flatter; here, most of the tomatoes had been picked, the vines had started to wither, and some of the fields were yellow-dry. It could have been a different season from the one I had seen in the north-east, where – before the train had passed into the tropical lowlands – we had spent hours in altitudes that had the new green gardens of early spring. The look was autumnal for much of the way to Puntarenas: dry broken cornstalks drooped in the fields, the trees were bare or else held a few boughs of fluttering brown leaves, the grass was burned, and even the fence posts which had conveniently sprouted into saplings and become a thicket of trees were losing their leaves to the dry air. In Ojo de Agua and Cirvelas the farmers were haymaking.

But there was no consistency in this country's agriculture. Latitude was no help in reading the crops: Costa Rica was mountainous as well as swampy and tropical, and it was flanked by two oceans. No sooner had I decided that autumn had come to this province than we entered shady villages and orange groves. And just before the village of Atena we climbed to the edge of a deep ravine of grey and brown rock. The ravine continued to the west and was a cut on the horizon, but a dust cloud hung in it and though I guessed it was deep I could not see to its bottom. The villages at its rim were dusty, too, six-barn hamlets and fruit farms, and the children at station platforms selling bunches of purple balls, a kind of fruit I had never seen before.

... the brig came on slowly, and now more steadily than before, and – I cannot speak calmly of this event – our hearts leaped up wildly within us, and we poured out our whole souls in shouts and thanksgiving to God for the complete, unexpected, and glorious deliverance that was so palpably at hand. Of a sudden, and all at once, there came wafted over the ocean from the strange vessel (which was now close upon us) a smell, a stench, such as the whole world has no name for ...

The heat had quieted the passengers. They had stopped singing, and the train had become a sleepy local clicking in and out through the woodland slopes.

... we had a full view of her decks. Shall I ever forget the triple horror of that spectacle? Twenty-five or thirty human bodies, among whom were several females, lay scattered about between the counter and the galley in the last and most loathsome state of putrefaction. We plainly saw that not a soul lived in that fated vessel. Yet we could not help shouting to the dead for help!

210

Even the locusts were louder than this engine, and the passengers hardly noticed the fruit sellers who appeared on the short platforms of the village stations.

As our first loud yell of terror broke forth, it was replied to by something, from near the bowsprit of the stranger, so closely resembling the scream of a human voice that the nicest ear might have been startled and deceived . . .

There was a family just in front of me. The mother was seated across the aisle from her two daughters, who were pretty – one about sixteen, the other a year or two older. The father was standing some distance away, swigging from a beer bottle. There was an empty seat between the two girls; on this seat was a basket. I had shut my book to rest my eyes, and then I saw a boy lingering by the rear door. At first I thought he was watching me. He came closer. He was watching the two girls, the empty seat. He crept towards them and summoning his courage said, 'Is that seat occupied?'

The girls giggled and moved the basket. The boy sat down. After an awkward interval the boy began to talk: Where were they going? What were they doing? He said he was a student. Wasn't it lucky that they all seemed to be going to Puntarenas? He had a radio with him, he said. Would they care for a bit of music?

Please, I thought, *not that*.

The girls only smiled. The boy had not understood that they were travelling with their parents. The father went on drinking, but the mother on the other side of the aisle was staring at the boy. She had a fat face, and it was darkening with indignation. Her fingers were knotted and she was hunched in fury. Now the boy was describing the dance halls in Puntarenas. You could have a wonderful time, he said; he knew all the good places. He began naming the night-spots.

This was too much for the mother. She stood up and began screaming abuse at the boy. And she spoke so rapidly, at such a pitch, I caught only shrill phrases of it; but I did hear her accusing him of trying to pick up her daughters, talking to them as if he had no respect. *You have no right*, she said. *Who do you think you are?* She stopped screaming. The boy grinned in shame. He did not reply, and he could not leave. He was standing his ground, according to the code of the Latin male; but he was sheepish. The girls, who had said very little to the boy, said nothing at all now.

The mother began again. She called him a pig and an intruder. She threatened to report him to the conductor. With each accusation she inched towards the boy, putting her fat furious face very near to his. Then she brought up her arm and, feinting with her fist, jabbed her elbow against his jaw. The boy was knocked sideways by the blow, and his hand went to his mouth. He looked at his fingers: blood. Now he started to protest, but he did so timidly, expecting to be hit again.

There was more. A young girl, about eleven – perhaps another daughter – rushed forward with a bottle of Coke. She shook the bottle and sprayed foam into the boy's face. Still, the two girls said nothing. The boy pulled a hanky out of his pocket and, wiping his face, made a pleading explanation: 'They said the seat was not occupied . . . they said I could sit down . . . ask them, go ahead, they'll tell you . . .'

The father swallowed beer. He looked around helplessly as his wife yelled herself hoarse. I rather admired the boy for not bolting, but at last under the woman's onslaught he took himself away and hid between the cars, nursing his wound. I made a point of seeking him out. I asked him about the mother. Was she a typical Costa Rican mother?

'Most of them are like that. She is angry. She does not want me to talk to her daughters. They said the seat was not occupied! Look what she did to my mouth.'

He yanked his lower lip down and showed me his bloody gum.

'But the father – that man drinking beer – he apologized to me. He came up to me a little while ago and said, "I am very sorry about this, but what can I do?" That woman is a pig.'

. . . on his back, from which a portion of the shirt had been torn, leaving it bare, there sat a huge sea-gull, busily gorging itself with the horrible flesh, its bill and talons deep buried, and its white plumage spattered all over with blood. As the brig moved further round so as to bring us close in view, the bird, with much apparent difficulty, drew out its crimsoned head, and, after eyeing us for a

moment as if stupefied, arose lazily from the body upon which it had been feasting, and, flying directly above our deck, hovered there awhile with a portion of clotted and liverlike substance in its beak. The horrid morsel dropped at length with a sullen splash immediately at the feet of Parker . . .

There was a hand on my knee. Earlier, a woman had sat next to me. Now she gave my knee a squeeze. She said, 'I will be right back. Do not let anyone steal my suitcase!' Another squeeze; and she smiled. She was about thirty-five and had two gold teeth. She walked to the rear of the car, and as she passed the ticket-collector, pinched his bottom. This excited the ticket-collector, and when the woman returned to her seat the man wandered over to flirt with her. But, uncertain of the nature of the relationship between the woman and me, he withdrew. The woman squeezed my leg again. 'You like to read that book!'

. . . I sprang forward quickly, and, with a deep shudder, threw the frightful thing into the sea . . .

'What is it about?'

'Ships,' I said.

'You will have plenty of ships at Puntarenas.'

We were passing a church. In El Salvador or Guatemala, the passengers would have blessed themselves, made a slow sign of the cross; and the men would have removed their hats. Here, the church was not an object of much interest – and it was an imposing church, with two Spanish towers like plump thermos jugs, and scrollwork, and stained glass, and a pair of belfries. It aroused no reverential gestures among the train passengers. It might as well have been a barn, though a barn that size would certainly have had the train passengers crowing with approval.

Costa Rica is considered unique in Central America; prosperity has made it dull, but this is surely preferable to the excitements and urgencies of poverty. What is remarkable is its secularity. I was not prepared for this; I had never seen this commented upon; and I naturally expected, after my church-going in Guatemala and El Salvador, to see a similarly priest-ridden society, genuflections, the poor wearing rosaries as necklaces, and *Never mind those huts – look at the cathedral!*

213

Mexico struck me as both pious and anti-clerical: priestly authority does not suit the Mexican temper. Costa Rica was neither. It seemed indifferent towards religion. I guessed that it had something to do with political pluralism – if that is the right phrase to describe the enlightened certainty that an election was rather more than a piece of fakery or an occasion to riot. The Costa Rican election had coincided with Shrove Tuesday; indeed, from what I had been told, it had supplanted it. It had been a fiesta – literally, a feast-day – full of self-congratulation and not distinguished by a high level of debate. The new president had not yet been sworn in: the holiday was still on. But a free election was like man's answer to the bossy authoritarianism of a religion that demanded humility and repentance; it seemed to prove that competition was possible without violence or acrimony. The Costa Rican's dislike of dictators had made him intolerant of priests. Luck and ingenuity had made the country properous, and it was small and self-contained enough to remain so.

The unambiguous wish in, say, geriatric parts of Florida (which Costa Rica much resembles) is to have comfort and the good life now, on earth. Only the poor peasant believes that he will become bourgeois in Heaven. A rising class wants its comforts on earth and has neither the time nor the inclination to be religious: this was obvious in Costa Rica. In time of crisis – sickness, collapse, the mortal wound – the Costa Rican would turn to the Church and demand a miracle, but middle-class people generally haven't the time to believe in miracles, and so, without consciously rejecting the Church, they seek answers in politics or business. It has made them fair, but boring. The greatest church in Costa Rica is in Cartago, the Basilica of Our Lady of the Angels, the Patroness of Costa Rica. But the Cartago brochures merely point out that the Inter-American Highway passes through town; that there is a San José bus every five minutes; that it is cool there and 'Also, famous Irazú Volcano close by'. No brochure I saw mentioned churches. The Basilica is hardly an example of fine architecture, but that is not the point. The Costa Ricans are prouder of their modernity, their absence of militarism, their climate, their factories and their volcano than their churches. 'Fine medical and hospital facilities,' says the note on San José in a tourist leaflet, which sounds less a boast than an assurance to prospective immigrants. Seismically-cracked cathedrals and bloody statuary tottering on plinths have not prevented other Latin American countries from advertising their churches; but of course they have very little else to brag about. And, what is more important, they have kept the faith. The secularism of Costa Rica means that the church is something of an embarrassment, or at least a superfluity – history's legacy as a dusty artefact rather than a programme for the soul. For this reason, the Costa Ricans are probably the most predictable people in Latin America and, lacking religious enthusiasm, the most avowedly political.

The town, the church was now far behind. There were more stations, and the landscape changed at each one: now open and flat, now a ravine, now full of deforested hills, now an unlikely village of deflected light – green huts, blue trees and a whole hill of red grass, pastels glowing through a prism of dust.

... and now I was consumed with the irrepressible desire of looking below. I could not, I would not, confine my glances to the cliff; and with a wild indefinable emotion, half of horror, half of relieved oppression, I threw my vision far down into the abyss. For one moment my fingers clutched convulsively upon their hold, while, with the movement, the faintest possible idea of ultimate escape wandered, like a shadow, through my mind – in the next my whole soul was pervaded by a longing to fall ...

After fifty miles or so – and it was blazing hot – the line straightened, and some food-sellers (they were dark-eyed, almost middle-eastern looking girls and women, in shawls and long skirts) got on the train. They carried baskets of oranges, tangerines, mangoes and paper cones filled with peanuts and burned cashews. Ahead, past miles of parched farmland, was a blue lake. The train climbed a hillside: the lake was immense and the sun had whitened a portion of it, bleached the blueness out of it.

The knee-squeezer was still next to me.

'Is that a lake?'

'That is the ocean,' she said.

The Pacific; I looked around with a wild surmise, and then

resumed my reading. When I glanced up again we were travelling along a narrow peninsula towards Puntarenas.

There were very few trees on this spit of land. There was the railway line, and a road, and a row of houses; there wasn't room for anything more. On the Pacific side freighters were anchored, on the protected side, sailing-boats and dinghies. For no apparent reason, halfway down the peninsula, the train stopped, and here we remained for twenty minutes. Hot stiff breezes blew through the open windows of the train and rattled the shutters; sluggish brown waves pushed at the rocky jetties beneath the train. The sun was low; it slanted through the car and heated it. The passengers were tired, and so silent. The only sounds were the wind and the sea. On the left side of the train there was no land, but only limitless ocean. The train could not have been stiller or more full of light.

. . . we rushed into the embraces of the cataract, where a chasm threw itself open to receive us. But there arose in our pathway a shrouded human figure, very far larger in its proportions than any dweller among men. And the hue of the skin of the figure was of the perfect whiteness of the snow.

I shut my book. At length, the train started and continued the last half-mile into Puntarenas. Puntarenas was very hot, and even in the breeze very humid. I walked the streets. There were boarding houses and cheap hotels, bars, restaurants, curio stalls, people selling plastic water-wings and back-scratchers and sunhats. It was a run-down but busy resort. There was not much to do here but swim, and I did not care for the water which was littered with seaport detritus, frayed rope and old bottles, oil-slick and seaweed which had become like greasy rags. I had a glass of lemonade; I wondered if I should stay here, on the Gulf of Nicoya.

'You should go over to the other side,' said the stallholder who had sold me the lemonade. 'That is where all the Americans live. Is is very beautiful.'

I saw some of them, shuffling through the streets of Puntarenas, the people who had come down here to die in this sunny youthful place. I was almost tempted to board a bus and look at their houses, but I had a feeling I knew what I would find. A suburb in the tropics might be worth seeing, but I doubted that it was worth examining in much detail; and I did not relish that sense of exclusion that I would feel, faced by people mowing the lawn and pushing vacuum cleaners. Nor, after all my travelling, did I wish to find myself describing Sarasota, down to its last funeral parlour and miniature golf course. Travellers do not belong in the suburbs, and the most civilized places tire the eye quickest; in such places, the traveller is an intruder, as he is in Sarasota. I wanted something altogether wilder, the clumsier romance of strangeness; these friendly Americans only made me homesick.

12 The Balboa Bullet to Colón

It was 'Save Our Canal Day'. Two United States congressmen had brought the news to the Canal Zone that New Hampshire was solidly behind them in their struggle to keep the Zone in American hands (reminding me of the self-mocking West Indian joke, 'Go ahead, England, Barbados is behind you!'). The New Hampshire governor had declared a holiday in his state, to signify his support. One congressman, speaking at a noisy rally of Americans in Balboa, reported that 75 per cent of the United States was against the Canal Treaty. But all this was academic; and the noise – there was a demonstration, too – little more than the ventilation of jingoistic yawps. Within very few months the treaty would be ratified. I told this to a Zonian lady. She said she didn't care. She had enjoyed the rally: 'We've been feeling left out, as if everyone was against us.'

The Zonians, 3,000 workers for the Panama Canal Company, and their families, saw the treaty as a sell-out; why should the Canal be turned over to these undeserving Panamanian louts in twenty years? Why not, they argued simply, continue to run it as it had been for the past sixty-three years? At a certain point in every conversation I had with these doomed residents of Panama, the Zonian would bat the air with his arms and yell, *It's our canal!*

'Want to know the trouble with these people?' said an American political officer at the embassy. 'They can't decide whether the Canal is a government department, or a company, or an independent state.'

Whatever it was, it was certainly a lost cause; but it was not the less interesting for that. Few places in the world can match the Canal Zone in its complex origins, its unique geographical status or in the cloudiness of its future. The Canal itself is a marvel: into its making went all the energies of America, all her genius and all her deceits. The Zone, too, is a paradox: it is a wonderful place, but a racket. The Panamanians hardly figure in the canal debate – they want the Canal for nationalistic reasons; but Panama scarcely existed before the Canal was dug. If justice were to be done the whole isthmus should be handed back to the Colombians, from whom it was squeezed in 1903. The debate is between the Ratifiers and the Zonians, and though they sound (and behave) like people whom Gulliver might have encountered in Glubbdubdrib, they are both Americans: they sail under the same flag. The Zonians, however – when they become especially frenzied – often burn their Stars and Stripes and their children cut classes at Balboa High School to trample on its ashes. The Ratifiers, loud in their denunciation of Zonians when they are among friends, shrink from declaring themselves when they are in the Zone. A Ratifier from the embassy, who accompanied me to a lecture I was to give at Balboa High, flatly refused to introduce me to the Zonian students for fear that if he revealed himself they would riot and overturn his car. Two nights previously, vengeful Zonians had driven nails into the locks of the school gates in order to shut the place down. What a pestilential little squabble, I thought; and felt more than ever like Lemuel Gulliver.

It is, by common consent, a Company town. There is little in the way of personal freedom in the Zone. I am not talking about the liberal guarantees of freedom of speech or assembly, which are soothing abstractions but seldom used; I mean, the Zonian has to ask permission before he may paint his house another colour, or even shellac the baseboard in his bathroom. If he wishes to asphalt his driveway he must apply in writing to the Company; but he will be turned down: only pebbles are permitted. The Zonian is living in a Company house; he drives on Company roads, sends his children to Company schools, banks at the Company bank, borrows money from the Company Credit Union, shops at the Company store, (where the low prices are pegged to those in New Orleans), sails at the Company club, sees movies at the Company theatre, and if he eats out will take his family to the Company cafeteria in the middle of Balboa and

219

eat Company steaks and Company ice-cream. If a plumber or an electrician is needed the Company will supply one. The system is maddening, but if the Zonian is driven crazy there is a Company psychiatrist. The community is entirely self-contained. Children are born in the Company hospital; people are married in Company churches – there are many denominations, but Baptists predominate; and when the Zonian dies he is embalmed in the Company mortuary – a free casket and burial are part of every Company contract.

Society is haunted by two contending ghosts, that of Lenin and that of General Bullmoose. There are no Company signs, no billboards or advertising at all; only a military starkness in the appearance of the Company buildings. The Zone seems like an enormous army base – the tawny houses, all right-angles and tiled roofs, the severe landscaping, the stencilled warnings on chain-link fences, the sentry posts, the dispirited wives and stern fattish men. There are military bases in the Zone, but these are indistinguishable from the suburbs. This surprised me. Much of the Canal hysteria in the States was whipped up by the news that the Zonians were living the life of Riley, with servants and princely salaries and subsidized pleasures. It would have been more accurate if the Zonian was depicted as an army man, soldiering obediently in the tropics. His restrictions and rules have killed his imagination and deafened him to any subtleties of political speech; he is a Christian; he is proud of the Canal and has a dim unphrased distrust of the Company; his salary is about the same as that of his counterpart in the United States – after all, the fellow is a mechanic or welder: why shouldn't he get sixteen dollars an hour? He knows welders who get much more in Oklahoma. And yet the majority of the Zonians live modestly: the bungalow, the single car, the outings to the cafeteria and cinema. The high Company officials live like viceroys, but they are the exception. There is a pecking order, as in all colonies; it is in miniature like the East India Company and even reflects the social organization of that colonial enterprise: the Zonian suffers a notoriously out-dated lack of social mobility. He is known by his salary, his club and the nature of his job. The Company mechanic does not rub shoulders with the Company administrators who work in what is known all over the Zone as The Building – the seat of power in Balboa Heights. The Company is uncompromising in its notion of class; consequently, the Zonian – in spite of his pride in the Canal – often feels burdened by the degree of regimentation.

'Now I know what socialism is,' said a Zonian to me at Miraflores.

I tried to explain that this was not socialism but rather the highest stage of capitalism, the imperial company; profit and idealism; high-minded exploitation. It was colonialism in its purest form. And by its nature colonialism is selective. Where are the victims, then, the poor, the exploited? The Zone is immaculate, but it only appears to be a haven of peace. About four years ago the schools in the Zone were reclassified – it meant they did not have to be integrated. Blacks, who had been brought years ago to work in the Zone, were regarded as Panamanians. So the integration issue was simplified: the blacks were encouraged to move out of the Zone. They did not move far – they couldn't, they still had jobs in the Zone. The fringes of the Zone are occupied by these rejects, and the far side of the Fourth of July Highway is a slum. They cross the highway to go to work, and in the evening they return to their hovels. And what is interesting is that the Zonian, when particularly worked up about the civilization he has brought to the Isthmus, points to the dividing line and says, 'Look at the contrast!' But it was the Zonian who decreed that those people should live there and that all Panama should stand aside and let him get on with the job.

It is hard to exaggerate the tenacious attitude of the Zonians. Their mirror-images are less the time-servers in Suez than the toilers in India during the last years of the British Raj. The Zonian is not noted for his command of Spanish, but on his own turf he is efficient and hardworking. A week before I arrived, the Zonian workers tried to organize a strike, to prove they had some bargaining power. But they failed, as strikers in Poland and Czechoslovakia always fail, and perhaps for the same reason: they were sat on and, when it came to it, the shutdown could not last – they did not have the heart to close down the Canal. In sympathy their children cut classes at Balboa High

School, played hooky for their parents' sake – and for their own reasons. Zonians are aware that the world they inhabit is special, and they know it is threatened with extinction. But, because they keep to themselves, the menacing world is closer than the demon countries they whisper about – Russia, China, Cuba, 'the Arabs', 'the Communists'. The big stupid clumsy world of squinting cannibals begins where the Zone ends – it is right there, across the Fourth of July Highway, the predatory world of hungry unwashed people gibbering in Spanish. Even the sweetest Zonians haven't got a clue. A testimonial dinner was given for a librarian in the Zone. She was retiring after forty years in the Company library – forty years of residence in the Zone, supervising the local staff, ordering books, hovering in the stacks, attending functions, initialling memos, issuing directives, coping with the Dewey Decimal System. Everyone she had known came to her testimonial, and most – to her credit – were Panamanians. Speeches were made; there was praise, and a presentation. At the end of it, the librarian got to her feet and attempted to thank them in Spanish. She faltered and finally fell silent. In forty years she had not learned enough Spanish to utter a complete sentence of gratitude to the Spanish workers who organized the dinner.

'I don't care what you say,' the Zonian at Miraflores was saying to me, 'but it sure *feels* like socialism.'

We were watching the Chilean freighter *Palma* pass through the lock. There were no pumps in the Canal. The freighter enters the lock; the gates shut; and within a few minutes the huge ship is dropping to the level of the Pacific on this last liquid stair in its descent. The upper gates are closed, too, and 50,000 gallons of water flow from Lake Madden to replace the water the *Palma* used for its journey through the Canal. The freighter is towed by small engines on canal-side tracks – this is the single improvement that has been necessary in sixty years. Once, the ships were drawn by mules; the engines are still called 'mules'. One cannot fail to be impressed by the running of the Canal; there are few works of man on earth that can compare with it.

'Who are those people?' I asked.

There were five men in clean white Panama-style shirts,

vaulting coils of cable and occasionally tripping as they made their way towards the steel front of the lock which was the shape of a battleship's bow. They were hurrying, puffing and blowing in the ninety-degree heat; their fancy shoes were not made for these slippery surfaces. I had asked whether I could roam around the lock, but I was told it was forbidden.

'Them are congressmen,' said the guide. 'That's all we get around here these days. Congressmen.'

The guide was black, a Panamanian, from Chiriqui Province. He had written his thesis at the University of Panama on the history of the Canal. He was completely bi-lingual. I wondered whether he was in favour of the Canal being handed over.

He said, 'If this Canal Treaty is ratified that's going to be the end of this place.'

'You want to see the Americans run it forever?'

He said, 'I sure do.'

It was not a Panamanian view, but he was untypical. After that, every Panamanian I met said the Canal belonged to them; though the terms on which it should be given back varied from person to person. And yet the Zonians are probably right when they say that the Canal will be mismanaged when it is in Panamanian hands. It does not take much to upset its balance sheet; in fact, some years it loses money, and to show a profit the Panama Canal Company must tow an average of thirty-five or forty ships a day through the three locks, repeating this complicated procedure every day of the year. Was it outmoded? No, said the guide; apart from a few super-tankers it could handle all the ships in the world. Wouldn't a sea-level canal be simpler? No, said the guide; the Atlantic tides were different from the Pacific ones, and did I know that there was a poisonous variety of sea-snake in the Pacific? A sea-level canal would allow this creature into the Caribbean, 'and God knows what would happen then.'

'I'm glad you're on our side,' said the Zonian to the guide.

'Send anyone you want down here,' said the guide. 'I'll tell them the truth.'

I suggested to him that the truth of it was that, like the arguments for the British staying in India or the U.S. Marines patrolling Veracruz or Colonel Vanderbilt in Nicaragua, the adventure could not last. For better or worse ('Worse!' he said quickly), the Canal would have to become the property of the Republic of Panama. Surely, it was plain to him that the Treaty would be ratified and that this would happen.

'Maybe it will happen and maybe it won't,' he said. 'I can't say. But it if *does* happen it's going to be bad.'

'Good for you!' said the Zonian, then turned to me. 'We're going to give the Canal away, just like we gave Vietnam away. It's terrible. We should stay. We should have kept Taiwan –'

'*Taiwan?*' I said.

'We gave it to the Chinese. That's why we have to keep this Canal. This is our last chance. Look at what happened to Vietnam after we gave it away.'

I said, 'We didn't give Vietnam away.'

'Yes, we did.'

'Madam,' I said, 'we lost the war.'

'We should have won it,' she said. 'Now you're talking like the reporters. They come here and say all the Zonians are red-necks, living in beautiful homes. Goodness, we're ordinary people!'

'That I can vouch for,' I said.

But when people said *We* in Panama I had to think hard to know who they meant. The Zonian lady's *we* referred to all Zonians, Ambassador Jorden said *we* and he meant the United States of America, the Ratifier's *we* ignored the Zonian: there was always exclusion in the pronoun. The American soldiers in the Zone were officially neutral, but when a military man said *we* he implied that he was against the treaty. The third or fourth generation West Indians, mainly from Barbados, said *we* in English and feared for their jobs, other Panamanians said *we* in Spanish and spoke of their long tradition and subtle culture; of the three tribes of Indians, the Cuñas, the Guaymíes and the Chocóes, only 3 per cent speak Spanish, and their *we* – spoken in their own tongues – is in opposition to the treaty. Alluding to the Canal (and in Panama people alluded to nothing else) no one I heard ever said *I*. People held the identity and opinions of their particular group, and they did not venture far from their tribal areas. Like Gulliver, I was in transit; I went from group to group, noting down complaints in handwriting which grew ever more bewildered and uncertain.

Not everyone complained. A girl I met in Panama City said, 'In most places you go, people say, "You should have been here last year." They said that to me when I went to Brazil, then Peru, then Colombia. But no one says it in Panama. This is the time to be here.'

The Canal, and the Miraflores Locks, had been my first stop. But I wanted to know a bit more about the place. I spent an evening at the casino in the Holiday Inn, watching people lose money by the armful. Winning made them grimmer, since the gambler's felt wish is to lose. They were pale, unsmiling, actually throwing their money down – and, say, those men at the blackjack table, hunched over diminishing towers of chips and gloomily flicking at playing cards: the congressmen! There were men in cowboy boots and ladies pulling hundred-dollar bills out of their cleavage and uproarious Americans being reprimanded by squinting croupiers in dainty suits because the Americans were spitting on the dice ('Do me a favour!' screamed one crap-shooter, and threw a pair of dice at the croupier). Gambling looked such a joyless addiction, and I had to leave – another minute would have turned me into a Marxist. The next day I took a closer look at the black tenements of Panama City; although their condition was dismal – broken windows, slumping balconies, blistered peeling paint on the wooden walls – they dated from the French occupation of Panama and retained some of the elegance of the original design. But it was not enough to hold my interest and the conversations I had with the aggrieved tenants told me only that this was yet another tribal area at odds with its neighbours.

One morning I gave a lecture at Canal Zone College. The subject was travel, and how strange it was to speak of the world and the romance of distance to people who could not conquer their timidity long enough to endure the short drive to Panama City, and who regarded the town of Colón just up the road as more savage and dangerous than a whole jungle of Amazonian head-hunters.

After the lecture I fell into conversation with a Zonian lady who said, 'I don't know what you expected to find here in the Zone, but I can tell you we live a very quiet life.'

That *we* again; and yet it was not the mob pronoun I had been hearing, but a more intimate word, spoken with a kind of marital tenderness and defiance. She was talking about her family. They had come down from Pennsylvania, initially for two years, but they had liked the Zone and decided to stay. After eleven years the place still had an attraction, though the Company was often oppressive in the way it managed their lives.

'And what do you do?' I asked.

'It's not me – it's my husband. He's the head of the Gorgas Mortuary. Don't laugh.'

'I'm not laughing,' I said. 'That's interesting.'

'You think it's interesting?' She had started to laugh. I could not contain my curiosity, my enthusiasm for visiting the mortuary; and when I thought I had convinced her that I really did want a tour, and as we were driving to the old grey building, she kept saying, 'Are you sure you want to do this?'

John Reiss was a tall stout mortician with a pink complexion and a friendly manner. His wife had said, 'He's wonderful with bereaved relatives – he just calms them down, I don't know how he does it.' He was soft-spoken and precise, interested in his work – interested particularly in embalming – and proud of the fact that corpses were sent to him from all over Central and South America. Like many other Zonians he was a member of the Elks' Club, the V.F.W., the Rotary, but his mortician's interest perhaps made him more of a joiner than most: a mortician is a public figure in America, like a mayor or a fire chief, and the Zone was a version of America. But Mr Reiss was also a member of the local barber shop quartet, and there was in his voice a kind of melodious croon, a singer's modulation, a mortician's concerned coo.

'To start off with,' said Mr Reiss in the Coffin Room, an instructional whisper in his voice, 'here we have the coffins themselves. If you were a local employee you got this coffin.'

It was a plain silvery steel coffin, with unornamented handles, a buffed metal box the length of a man and the depth of a horse trough. It was shut, the lid fastened. It was difficult for me to see this closed coffin and not to feel a distinct uneasiness about what it might contain.

'And if you were an American you got this one.'

This one was bigger and a bit fancier. There were rosettes on the side and simulated carving on the corners of the lid, some romanesque scrollwork, leaf clusters and the sort of handles you see on doors in Louisburg Square in Boston. Apart from the foliage, and the size, I wondered whether there was any other difference between this coffin and the silver one.

'This is much more expensive,' said Mr Reiss. 'It's hermetically sealed, and look at the difference in the colours.'

Of course, this one was goldy bronze, the other was silver. They matched the status of the deceased. It was a racial distinction. From about the turn of the century until very recently, race was expressed by the Panama Canal Company not in terms of black and white but by the designations gold and silver. The euphemism was derived from the way workers were paid: the unskilled workers, most of them black, were paid in silver; the skilled workers, nearly all white Americans, were paid in gold. The terms applied to all spheres of life in the Zone; there were gold schools, and silver schools, gold houses and silver houses, and so on, to gold coffins and silver coffins, the former hermetically sealed, the latter – like the silver house – leaky. So, even in his casket, the canal employee could be identified, and long after he had turned to dust, the evidence of his race lost in decay, his remains could be disinterred and you would know from the hue of that box whether the grit in that winding sheet had once been a white man or a black man. It must have been some satisfaction for the Company to know that, however evenly the grass covered these graves, the colour line that had been the rule in schools and housing (and even water fountains and toilets, the post office and cafeterias), was still observed beneath the ground.

'Nowadays,' said Mr Reiss, 'everyone gets this good coffin. That's why the mortuary loses money. These things cost an awful lot.'

Upstairs was the Receiving Room. There were refrigerators here, and on the wall of the bare flint-grey room the large steel drawers that most people know from the morgue scenes in movies, the floor-to-ceiling arrangement that resembles nothing so much as stacks of over-sized filing cabinets.

Mr Reiss's hand went to one drawer. He balanced himself by gripping the handle; underneath it was a label: a name, a date.

'I have a man in here,' he said, tugging as he spoke. 'Died a month ago. We don't know what to do with him. From California. No family, no friends.'

'I'd rather you didn't open that drawer,' I said.

He pushed it gently and released it. 'No one wants to claim him.'

It was cold in the room; I shivered and noticed my skin was prickling with gooseflesh. This was the coldest I had been since leaving the sleet storm in Chicago.

'Shall we move on?' I said.

But Mr Reiss was reading a new label. 'Yes,' he said, tapping another drawer. 'This is a little boy. Only six years old.' His fingers were under the handle. 'He's been there since last June – anything wrong?'

'I feel chilly.'

'We've got to keep the temperature down in here. What was I saying? Oh, yes.' he said, glancing at his hand, at the label, 'he's going to be here until next June. But he'll be all right.'

'All right? In what sense?'

Mr Reiss smiled gently; it was professional pride. 'I embalmed him myself – he's all ready to go. Well,' he went on – and now he was speaking to the drawer, 'just to make sure, I look at him about once a month. I open him up. Check him over.'

'What do you see?'

'Dehydration.'

On our way to the Cremation Room, I said, 'For a minute, I thought you were going to open one of those drawers back there.'

'I was,' said Mr Reiss. 'But you didn't want me to.'

'I think I would have keeled over.'

'That's what everyone says. But it's something you should see.

A dead person is just a dead person. It happens to everybody. Death is one of the things you have to accept. It's nothing to be frightened of.' This was obviously the tone he adopted with the bereaved; and he was convincing. I felt ignorant and superstitious. But what if it had frightened me? How to erase the image of a death-shrunken six-year-old from my mind? I was afraid that, seeing it, I would be scared for the rest of my life.

The Cremation Room was hot: the air was stale and dusty and I could feel the heat across the room from the furnaces, which were larger versions of the old coal burners of my childhood. The heat had reddened the iron doors and they were coated with fine powder. Shafts of sunlight at the windows lighted tiny particles of dust which the hot air kept in turbulent motion.

'The reason it's so hot in here,' said Mr Reiss, 'is because we had a cremation just this morning.' He went to the side of one of the furnaces and jerked open the iron door. 'Local fellow,' he said, peering in. He pushed at some white smouldering flakes with a poker. 'Just ashes and a little bone.'

There were two aluminium barrels near the furnaces. Mr Reiss lifted the lid of one – an ash barrel. He reached in, groping in the ashes and took out a fragment of bone. It was a dry chalky hunk of splinters, bleached to sea-shell whiteness by the heat and dusted with grey biscuit-flakes of ash; and it had a knob on the end, like a prehistoric half of a ball-peen hammer.

'These are just odds and ends mostly.'

'That looks like a femur.'

'Good for you,' said Mr Reiss. 'That's what it is. How'd you know that?'

'I'm a failed medical student.'

'You shouldn't have failed – you certainly know your bones!' Mr Reiss closed his hand on the bone and squashed it like a cookie, reducing it to crumbs: *I will show you fear in a handful of dust.* 'We get a lot of amputations. This was a whole leg.'

He dropped the dust back into the barrel and clapped crumbs from his hands. I looked into the barrel and saw scorched safety pins and scraps of mummified cloth.

'There's a teaching hospital next door. They send us things to cremate. After the lessons are over. They're in terrible shape –

brains removed, all cut open and dissected. Hardly recognize some of them.'

There were no other people in these mortuary rooms, no live ones. The emptiness, the absence of voices and furniture, made it seem like a mausoleum, and I had the feeling I had been locked in, sealed up with this soft-spoken guide who treated coffins and dehydrating corpses and friable thigh bones with an ordinariness that chastened me and made me wonder if perhaps in his casual way he was successfully concealing some horror from me. But Mr Reiss was saying, 'We're losing money hand over fist – because of the pay-grades. The hardware and coffins are so expensive we can't even cover our costs. The local workers are getting those real nice – ah, here we are,' he said, interrupting himself at the threshold of another empty room, 'the Embalming Room.'

There were four sloping sinks in the centre of the room, and beneath them rubber hoses draining into the floor. There were grey marble slabs as well, arranged as tables, and two ceiling fans and a strong odour of disinfectant.

'We've been asking for air-conditioning for years,' said Mr Reiss.

'I can't imagine why,' I said. 'It's quite cool in here.'

He laughed. 'It's about eighty degrees!'

Strange: I was shivering again.

'But they won't give it to us,' he said. 'Those fans aren't enough. It can get pretty smelly in here when we're working.'

'I've been meaning to ask you what you call the corpses,' I said. 'Do you ever refer to it as "the loved one"? Or the body, the victim, the corpse, or what?'

' "The loved one" is what they say in books,' said Mr Reiss. 'But they're just exaggerating. People have a lot of funny ideas about morticians. Jessica Mitford – that book. She didn't go many places. We're not really like that. "The remains" – that's what we usually call it.'

He stepped to one of the deep sinks and went on, 'We put the remains on the table here and slide it into the sink. Then we raise an artery. The carotid's a good one – I like the carotid myself. Drain it completely. Blood goes all down there, through the pipe' – he was speaking to the sink and using his hand to indicate the flow of the blood – 'into the floor. Then – see that hose? – we fill it with embalming fluid. It takes time and you have to be careful. It's harder than it looks.'

I was mumbling, making notes with frozen fingers. I said I thought it was interesting. Mr Reiss seized on this.

'It *is* interesting! We get every type in here. Why, just recently,' he said, beating his palm on the embalming sink in emphatic excitement, 'a bus went off the bridge – you know the big bridge across the Canal? Thirty-eight people died and we had them all, right in here. Boy, that was something. Planes, car crashes, drownings, murders on ships, people who get mugged in Colón. Take a murder on a ship passing through the Canal – that's real tricky, but we handle it. And Indians? They drink and then they try to paddle their canoes and they drown. We get every type you can mention. Interesting is the word for it.'

I had gone silent. But Mr Reiss remained by the sink.

'I've been down here in the Zone for eleven years,' he said, 'a mortician the whole time.' Now he spoke slowly and wonderingly, 'And you know what? I've had something different every single day. Want to see the Autopsy Room?'

I looked at my watch.

'Golly,' he said, looking at his own. 'It's past one o'clock. I don't know about you, but I'm real hungry.'

The Elks kitchen was shut. We went to the Veterans of Foreign Wars Post 2537 and, ordering chop suey and iced tea, Mr Reiss said, 'But there's no comparison with the States service-wise. You don't get the attention here that they offer there. In the States you get a real nice service and big cars and a little ceremony. Here, all we give you is a hearse.'

'And an embalming.' I said.

'I've always been interested in embalming,' he said.

The chop suey came, a large helping of wet vegetables, a dish of noodles. There were very few other diners in the V.F.W. cafeteria, but, clean and dark and air-conditioned, it was like any post in America. I asked Mr Reiss how he had become a mortician.

231

'Usually, it's a family-type business. Your father's a mortician, so you become one, too. So I'm very unusual in a way – my family wasn't in the business.'

'Then you just decided, like that, to be a mortician?'

Mr Reiss swallowed a mouthful of chop suey and patting his lips with his napkin said, 'I *always* wanted to be a funeral director – as far back as I can remember. Know something? It's the earliest memory I have. I must have been about six years old when my old granny died. They put me upstairs and gave me a candy to keep me quiet. They were liquorice things in the shape of hats – derby hats and Stetsons. Well, I was upstairs – this was in Pennsylvania – and I started yelling and I said, "I want to see Granny!" "No," they said, "keep him upstairs, give him some more candy." But I kept yelling and they finally gave in and let me come down. My cousin took me by the hand and we went over to Granny in her casket. See, they had the funerals in houses then. When I saw her I asked all sorts of questions, like "How to they do it?" and "Who did this?" and so forth. I was real interested. And I decided then what I wanted to be – a funeral director. When I was nine or so I was sure that's what I wanted to be.'

I could not help imagining a classroom in Pennsylvania, and a curious teacher leaning over a quiet pink-faced boy, and asking, 'Tell me, Johnny, what do you want to be when you grow up?'

Inevitably, our talk turned to the Canal Treaty. I asked what would happen to him and the Gorgas Mortuary if the Treaty was ratified.

'I think we'll be all right, whatever happens. I don't know what's going to happen about the Treaty, but if they take us over I hope they keep us on. Most of us love this Canal, and we do a good job at the mortuary. I think they'll just rehire us. Everyone's worried, but why? They can't run the Canal without us. And I'm real interested in staying here.'

That night I was invited to a dinner. 'You're going to have to sing for your supper,' the host said. I asked him what I should talk about. He said it didn't matter very much – perhaps something about writing? 'No matter what you say,' he said, 'the only thing they're really interested in is what you think about the treaty.' I said it was my favourite subject.

I talked to the assembly of Panamanian writers and artists about *The Narrative of Arthur Gordon Pym*. No one had read it and so it was like speaking about a book which had just appeared, a candidate for the best-seller list, as fresh and full of news as a spring morning in Boston. They listened with rapt attention to the plot, the sequence of atrocities, the muffled music of the thrilling ending; and they looked at me with the near-sighted commiserating expressions I had seen on the faces of my students in faraway lecture halls, as I attempted to explain how, with such clever knots and loops, Poe had made of such stray pieces of string such a convincing hangman's noose.

'I am interested to know,' said a fellow afterwards, at question-time, 'what your position is with regard to the Panama Canal Treaty. Would you mind telling us?'

'Not at all,' I said. I said they were welcome to their opinion of the Zonians, but that they could easily underestimate the sentiment Zonians had for the Canal. It was not an age when people were very attached to their jobs, but the Zonians were proud of the work they had done and were dedicated to the running of the Canal. No amount of Panamanian nationalism or flag waving could compare with the technical skill it took to get forty ships a day through the Canal safely. I admitted that Zonians were fairly ignorant of Panama, but that Panamanians had little idea of the complexities of life in the Zone and the sort of fervour Zonians had.

This view brought smiles of disagreement from the audience, but, as no one challenged me, I went on to say that in essence the Canal Zone was colonial territory, and that one could not really understand any colony unless he had read *Frankenstein* and *Prometheus Bound*.

Over dinner, I talked with an elderly architect. He also wrote stories, he said, and most of his stories were satires about the Chief of Government and Commander of the National Guard, General Omar Torrijos. What did Torrijos think of his stories? He had wanted to ban them, said the architect, but this was impossible because the stories had won a literary prize.

I said, 'There are people who think that Torrijos is a mystic.'

'He is a demagogue, not a mystic,' said the architect. 'A showman – very astute, but full of tricks.'

'So you think the Americans should keep the Canal?'

'No. I will tell you. The Canal is every Panamanian's dream. Just as you have your American dream, this is ours. But it is all we have. The real tragedy is that it will come to us while Torrijos is in power. He will take credit for it, you see. He will say, "Look what I have done! I have gotten our Canal back!"'

That was probably true. The American government, through an aid programme, had built a number of apartment houses just outside Panama City. It was public housing, a sop to the thousands of homeless Panamanians. Officially, the apartments were known as 'Torrijos Houses'. It would have been far more just to give them the name of their real benefactor, the American tax-payer. I explained this to the architect and said I had more right than Torrijos to have my name on the apartment houses, since I paid American taxes and the General did not.

'But you put him in power.'

'I did not put General Torrijos in power,' I said.

'I mean, the United States government put him in power. They wanted him there so that they could negotiate with him. They would have had a much harder time dealing with a democratically elected government. It is well-known that Torrijos has made concessions that a democratically elected leader would never have made.'

'Didn't Torrijos hold a referendum on the treaty?'

'That was a bluff. No one knew what it was about. It proved nothing. The people have had no say whatsoever in this treaty. And, look, the United States is giving Torrijos fifty million dollars for his army alone! Why? Because he demanded it. They have given much less to Somoza in Nicaragua and he has stayed in power.'

'So you're stuck with Torrijos?'

'No,' said the architect. 'I think that when the United States gets what it wants from him they will throw him away – like trash.'

The architect was becoming quite heated. He had forgotten his food; he was gesturing with one hand and mopping his face with the handkerchief in his other hand.

'Do you want to know what Torrijos is really like?' he said. 'He is like a boy who has crashed his first car. That car is our republic. Now he is waiting for a second car to crash. The second car is the treaty. What I say to Torrijos is, "Forget about the car – learn how to drive!"'

'You should eat something,' I said.

'We are not used to him,' he said, glancing at his plate. 'This dictatorship is strange to us. Since we got our independence in 1903 he is the first dictator we've had. I have never known anyone like him before. Mr Theroux, we are not used to dictators.'

I was so interested in what the architect had said that I made a point, a few days later, of speaking with a Panamanian lawyer who had helped to draft the legal aspects of the treaty. I concealed the architect's name: the lawyer was a close friend of Torrijos and I did not want the man thrown into jail for uttering seditious opinions. The lawyer listened to the arguments and then said in Spanish, 'Rubbish!'

He continued in English, saying, 'Omar wasn't put there by the gringos.'

I found his phraseology objectionable. But the American Ambassador was present. I could not say, 'Don't call me a gringo and I won't call you a spic,' to this swarthy citizen of Panama.

'In 1967 none of the elected people could agree on a draft treaty,' said the lawyer.

'Is that why General Torrijos overthrew the government in 1968?' I said, averting my eyes from the Ambassador.

The lawyer was snorting. 'Some people,' he said slowly, 'think the attempted coup against Torrijos in 1969 was instigated by the CIA. What would your friend say to this?'

I said, 'If the coup was unsuccessful the CIA was probably not behind it. Ha-ha.'

'We make mistakes occasionally,' said the Ambassador, but I was not very sure what he meant by that.

'Torrijos showed great courage in signing the treaty,' said the lawyer.

'What courage?' I said. 'He signs and he gets the Canal. That's not courage, it's opportunism.'

'Now you're talking like your friend,' said the lawyer. 'He is obviously of the extreme Left.'

'As a matter of fact, he's rather conservative.'

'Same thing,' said the lawyer, and walked away.

My last task, before I took the train to Colón, was to give a lecture at Balboa High School. Mr Dachi, the Public Affairs Officer at the American Embassy, thought this might be a good idea: the Embassy had never sent a speaker to Balboa High. But I was not an official visitor; the State Department wasn't paying my way, and there was no reason why the traditional hostility the Zonians felt for the Embassy should be directed towards me. Out of friendship for Mr Dachi (whom I had met in Budapest) I agreed to give the lecture. The American Embassy man who accompanied me said that he preferred to remain anonymous: it was a rowdy place.

Everyone who went to an American high school in the 1950s has been to Balboa High. With its atmosphere of simmering anarchy – the sort of anarchy that takes the form of debagging first-year students in the john or running a Mickey Mouse pennant up the flagpole – and a devotion to spit-balls, sneakers, crew-cuts, horsing around in the gym, questing after intellectual mediocrity in the pages of literary anthologies ('Thornton Wilder has been called the American Shakespeare') and yet distrusting excellence because anything unusual must be a flaw (if you wear glasses you're a brain and known throughout the school as 'Einstein'), taking 'science' because that is what the Russians do and using it as an opportunity for leering at ana-tomical drawings in the biology book, regarding education as mainly social, coming to terms with sweaty palms and pimples, praising the quarterback, mocking the water-boy – yes, Balboa High was familiar to me. The current craze for rock-and-roll made it seem even more of a throw-back: *Elvis* read the motto on one tee-shirt, and on another *Buddy Holly*.

To confirm my impression I went into *Boys* and looked around. It was empty but the air was whiffy with illicit cigarette smoke, and on the walls: *Balboa is Number One, America's Great* and, repeatedly, *Panama Sucks*.

I had not been inside an American high school for twenty years; how strange it was that the monkey house from which I had graduated had been reassembled, down to its last brick and home-room bell and swatch of ivy, here in Central America. And I knew in my bones what my reaction would have been at Medford High if it had been announced that, instead of Latin at ten o'clock, there would be an assembly: a chance to fart around!

It was probably good-natured unruliness, the buzz, the yakking, the laughing, the poking and paper-rattling. Half the student body of 1,285 was there in the memorial auditorium. The microphone – of course! – gave off a locust-like whine and now and then cut out entirely, making my voice a whisper. I watched the mob of tubby and skinny students and saw a teacher hurry across an aisle, shove her way along a row of seats and, rolling the magazine she held into a truncheon, smack a giggling boy on the head.

The principal introduced me. He was booed the moment he approached the lectern. I took my place and was applauded, but as the applause died away the booing increased. My subject was travel. 'I don't think they can take more than about twenty minutes,' the principal had told me; but after ten minutes the murmuring in the audience had nearly drowned my words. I continued to speak, glancing at my watch and then brought the proceedings to an end. Any questions?

'How much money do you make?' asked a boy in the front row.

'What's it like in Africa?' asked a girl.

'Why bother to take a train all that way?' was the last question. 'I mean, if it takes so wicked long?'

I said, 'Because you can take a six-pack of beer in your compartment and guzzle it and by the time you've sobered up you've arrived.'

This seemed to satisfy them. They howled and stamped and then booed me loudly.

'Your, um, students,' I said to the principal afterwards, 'are rather, um –'

'They're real nice kids,' he said, thwarting my attempt to be critical. 'But I thought when I came down here that I'd find some real sophisticated kids. This is a foreign country – maybe they'd be cosmopolitan, I figured. The funny thing is, they're less sophisticated than the kids back home.'

'Ah, yes, unsophisticated,' I said. 'I couldn't help noticing that they've dumped red paint on the bust of Balboa in front of your school.'

'That's the school colour,' he said.

'Do they study Panama's history?'

This gave him a pause. He thought a moment and then said uncertainly, 'No, but when they're in the sixth grade they have a few classes in social studies.'

'Good old social studies!'

'But Panama history – it's not what you'd call a subject or anything like that.'

I said, 'How long have you been here?'

'Sixteen years,' he said. 'I consider this my home. Some people here have houses in the States. They go home every summer. I don't do that. I plan to stay here. Back in 1964 a teacher of ours ran away – he thought it was the end. Remember the flag-burning? If he had stayed he would have had nearly thirty years service and a good pension. But he didn't. I'm going to see what happens here. You never know – this treaty business is far from settled.'

Another teacher, a young woman, had wandered over to hear what the principal was saying. When he finished, she said, 'This isn't home for me. I've been here ten years and I've always felt, well, *temporary*. Sometimes I wake up in the morning and open the curtains and see those palm trees and I think, "Oh, heavens!"'

'What'd you think of the students?' asked a male teacher, smiling, as he accompanied me out of the building.

'Pretty noisy,' I said.

'They were behaving themselves,' he said. 'I was surprised – I expected trouble. They've been raising hell recently.'

Behind us, I heard the unmistakable sound of glass breaking, and youthful laughter, and a teacher's exasperated yell.

It was the high school students who nick-named this train 'The Balboa Bullet'. Like the canal, it is American in character, of solid appearance, efficiently-run and well-maintained. Boarding at Balboa Heights you could not be blamed for thinking that this was the old train to Worcester. In the way tickets are sold and conductors in pill-box hats punch them and hand you a seat-stub (*Keep This Check in Sight*) it is slightly old-fangled and very dependable. But that too is like the Canal: both Canal and railway have worn well, lasting through the modern age without having to be modernized. It travels from the Atlantic to the Pacific in under an hour and a half, and it is nearly always on time.

I had been in Panama long enough to be able to recognize some of the landmarks – 'The Building' overlooking Stevens Circle, the mansion houses on Balboa Heights, and Fort Clayton which has the look of a maximum security prison. Most of the houses had a monotonous sameness – the two trees, the flower-bed, the boat in the breezeway. There are no pedestrians on the side-walks – in most places there are no pavements. Only the servants lounging at kitchen doors break the monotony and hint at life being lived.

The first stop was Miraflores: 'Mirror-floors,' in the corrupt Zonian pronunciation. And then the Canal drops behind a hill and does not reappear until Pedro Miguel where, at that set of locks, there are dredgers whose shape and smoke-stacks gave them the look of old Mississippi riverboats.

The train, unlike any other train in Latin America, contains a cross-section of the country's society. In the air-conditioned cars are the American army officers, the better-paid Zonians, tourists, and the businessmen from France and Japan who, at this crucial time, have come down to make a killing in real estate or imports. I was in the non-air-conditioned car by preference, with an ill-assorted group of Panamanians and Zonians, enlisted men, canal workers on the afternoon shift, blacks in velvet caps and some with Rastafarian dreadlocks and octoroons in pig-tails and whole families – black, white and all the intermediate racial hues.

In the air-conditioned car the passengers were looking out of the windows, marvelling at the Canal; but here in the cheaper seats many of the passengers were asleep and no one seemed to notice that we were passing through woods which thickened and, shadier and with hanging vines, turned into half-tame rain-forest. It became jungle, but it remained to the east; on the west, next to the Canal, there was a golf course, with brown tussocky fairways and forlorn golfers marching towards the rough – snakes and scorpions plague the duffers on this course. There are no billboards, no signs at all on the roads, no litter, no hamburger stands or petrol stations: this is an American suburb in apotheosis, the triumph of banality, a permanent encampment of no-nonsense houses and no-nonsense railway stations and no-nonsense churches, and even no-nonsense prisons, for here, in Gamboa, is the Canal Zone Penitentiary and it looks no better or worse than the barracks at Fort Clayton or the Zonian houses at Balboa. The severity is given emphasis by a policeman in a state trooper's Stetson leaning against the fender of his squad car, filing his nails.

Only in the tunnels was I reminded that I was in Central America: people screamed.

Out of the tunnel deeper jungle began, tree jammed next to tree, vine creeping on vine, pathless and dark. It bears no rela-tion to the Canal; it is primeval jungle, teeming with birds. That is the margin of the Zonian's world, where Panama re-sumes after the interrupting ribbon of the Zone. And it is in its wildness as unreal as the military manicure of the Zone. It does not matter that there are alligators and Indians there, because there are puppy-dogs and policemen here, and everything you need to ignore the jungle that does not stop until the Andes begin.

At Culebra we crossed the continental divide, and two ships were passing in the Cut. For these two ships to be sliding sleepily along, seven years of digging were necessary; it was, said Lord Bryce, 'the greatest liberty ever taken with nature'. The details are in David McCullough's canal history, *The Path Between The*

Seas: to dig nine miles and remove 96 million cubic yards of earth it cost $90 million; 61 million pounds of dynamite were used to blast open the canal, and much of it was used right here at Culebra. But it was a hot sunny afternoon; the birds were singing; Culebra seemed little more than a natural river in the tropics. The Canal's history is unimaginable from what it is possible to see in the Zone; most of it is underwater, in any case. Bunau-Varilla's remark that 'the cradle of the Panama Republic' was Room 1162 of the Waldorf-Astoria Hotel in New York City is true, but seems, like all the other historical details connected with the Canal, monstrous and fanciful.

And what could be odder than the sight of a great sea-going ship in the jungle? Inland, swamps and lagoons were more frequent, and then the lake began. Gatun Lake was formed by the Canal; until the sluice gates opened in 1914 there was only a narrow river, the Chagres. Now there is a vast lake, bigger than Moosehead Lake in Maine. Near Frijoles, a cool breeze blew across it and whitened the water and made it choppy. I could see Barro Colorado Island. As water filled the valley to create the lake the animals made for Barro Colorado, the birds flew to its trees, and so this hill was turned into an ark. It remains a wild-life sanctuary.

All the transistor radios – there were five – in my car were playing a current hit, *Stayin' Alive*, as the train crossed the causeway from Monte Liro to the Gatun side. It was like being in Louisiana, not merely because of the blacks and their radios and that music; but most Zonians had been recruited out of New Orleans, and this passage was practically identical to crossing the long lacustrine bridge on Lake Pontchartrain on the Chicago train called, not entirely by coincidence, 'The Panama Limited'. The islands in Gatun Lake are so young they still look like hilltops in flood-time, but there is no time to examine them. Here, the train does sixty, going clickety-click across the causeway. I regretted that it was not going farther, that I could not simply sit where I was, puffing my pipe, and be taken to Colombia and Ecuador. But no good train ever goes far enough, just as no bad train ever reaches its destination soon enough.

The last set of locks at Gatun, and the surrounding buildings, the camp, the houses, the military signs – all this jogged a memory in me I thought I had lost. It put my Panama experience into perspective. I had felt at Balboa High a familiar melancholy. It had been like my high school. But one American high school is much like another; they all have a timeless gamesmanship, a pretence of study and a rather comic look of skirmish between student and teacher. And the atmosphere is always the same, the smell of textbook glue and paper, corridor wax, chalk dust and sneaker rubber; the distant strongbox clang of locker-doors, the shouts and giggles. It was no aid to perception to be in Balboa High.

But Gatun moved me. Gatun was a piece of my past I thought I had lost; I had forgotten it, and it was not until we passed through that I realized how special it was. Except for this trip, the memory might have been irrecoverable. Round about 1953, when I was twelve and skinny and too near-sighted to catch a baseball, my uncle – an army surgeon – did me the favour of inviting me to spend the summer with him and my aunt and cousins at Fort Lee in Virginia. He was an officer. Punished-looking privates picking up gum-wrappers at the roadside used to salute his car, even when my aunt was driving it – saluting the insignia, I suppose. We were always going to the pool when this happened, to the Fort Lee Officers Open Mess. We usually went to the pool. There was a boy my age there, named Miller. He had a yellow stain on his swimming trunks. 'That's pickle juice,' he said. 'I spilled it in Germany.' It seemed an amazing explanation, but I believed him: he owned a German bayonet. Miller had been in Virginia long enough to ignore the heat. I had never known such temperatures. I volunteered to caddy for my uncle, but after six holes I had to sit in the shade and wait for him to return for the thirteenth, which was nearby. I tried to acclimatize myself like Miller, but invariably I ended up in the shade of a tree. My uncle said I probably had dropsy. 'This is my nephew,' he would say to his golf partner. 'He's got dropsy.' The nickname 'Dropsy' dogged me throughout the summer. Fort Lee was an army camp, but it did not match the stereotype I had seen in war movies; it looked like a state prison that was being used as a country club. Apart from the soldiers –

saluting, saluting – there were blacks, lurking everywhere, gardening, idling at the Tastee-Freez ice-cream parlour, walking down the unshaded roads, driving the DDT spraying truck which tore through the back yards leaving a cloud of poison as pretty as fog and, afterwards, piles of dead grass-hoppers. The woods were thin and piney, the earth redder than any I had ever seen, the houses cool (my aunt had 'coffee mornings'). At the restaurants near the camp there were small rectangular signs near the doors, like the tin name-plates in Boston that said DUFFY or JONES; but here, the name – I innocently believed it was a name – was always WHITE. A train ran nearby, to Hopewell and Petersburg; the insects were as loud in the daytime as at night, the buildings pale yellow, with red-tile roofs, and fences, and stencilled signs – like this.

As the train approached Gatun, and stopped, I was back in Fort Lee, returned to a moment twenty-five years before, when I had watched with the same sense of fear and excitement the military buildings and the stunted trees in the red soil, the unaccountably bright flowers, the WACs, the yellow school bus, the row of olive-drab Fords, the baseball diamond and the black people, the Little League field, the cemetery, the young soldiers who looked aimless whenever they were not marching, the dust settling in the heat. The two worlds met; here it was rural Virginia, and still the Fifties, and the smell was the same and the memory so clear, I thought: *The next stop must be Petersburg.*

It was Mount Hope, but Mount Hope was a continuation of the same memory. It is not often that I have travelled so far and been able, so easily, to uncover a fragment of the past that had remained lost to me. And as in all recollection there is something that looks inexact, like the memory of the name-plate WHITE. The perspective of years allowed me to see how old and small that other world was, and how I had been fooled.

The spell was broken at Colón. Colón had a divided look I could never grow used to. It was colonial in such a naked way: the tenements of the poor on one side of the tracks – what passed for the native quarter; and the military symmetries of the imperial buildings on the other side, the yacht club, the offices, the houses set in gardens. Here the governors, there the governed.

It is the old form of colonialism because, unlike the equally grasping multi-national corporations which are so often invisible, you can see at a glance from the appearance of things that you are in a colony, and the make of every car tells you that it is an American colony.

The tenements were like those I had seen in Panama City, decaying antiques. With a coat of paint and a dose of rust-remover they would have looked like the houses in New Orlean's French Quarter or those in the older parts of Singapore. If Gatun and so much else in the Zone looked like Fort Lee, Virginia, circa 1953, what lay just outside it seemed like the hectic and faintly reeking commercial districts of pre-war Singapore – the sour tangs of the bazaar, the cloth and curio emporiums, the provisioners, the ships' chandlers who, in Colón as in Singapore, were Indians and Chinese.

I had been told that the Indians in the Zone had come from India to work on the railway. It is not an easy fact to authenticate – workers are workers: they are the silent men in history books – but the labour supply in the building of the Canal was drawn from ninety-seven countries; India must have been one of them. I could not find any Indian in Colón who had come for this reason. Mr Gulchand seemed to be typical. He was a Sindhi, and a Hindu – he had a coloured portrait of the Mahatma in his shop. After the partition of India, the province of Sindh became part of Pakistan, and fearing Muslim rule, Mr Gulchand went to Bombay. It wasn't home, but at least it was Hindu. He started an import-export business and, in the course of this enterprise, had occasion to deal with Filipinos. He visited the Philippines. He liked it well enough to move his business there in the Sixties. The Vietnam war created a brief boom in the Philippines. Mr Gulchand's business prospered. His move accomplished several things: it estranged him from the Anglo-Indian sphere of influence and put him in close touch with Americans. And he learned to speak Spanish. He was now halfway across the world. Only the Pacific Ocean separated him from the emporium of Colón and the promise of greater wealth in Panama, more import-export, Central American connections and the city all Latin Americans regard as their metropolis: Miami. He had been in Colón for five years. He hated it. He longed for the more comprehensible disorder of Bombay, the more familiar anarchy.

'Business is slack,' said Mr Gulchand. He blamed the Canal Treaty. It was an old story: the colony about to collapse around the shopkeepers' ears; recessional; bolting whites; prices down. *I can't give this stuff away.*

What did he think of Colón?

'Wiolent,' said Mr Gulchand. 'And darty.'

He told me to take my watch off. I said I would. Then, trying to find the post office, I asked a black man the way. 'I will show you the way,' he said. 'But that,' he went on, tapping my watch crystal, 'you must remove it or you will lose it.' So I took it off.

The shop-signs were variations on the same theme: *Liquidation Sale, Everything Must Go!, Total Liquidation, Close-Down Sale Today.* 'I don't know what's going to happen,' Mr Reiss had said in the Gorgas Mortuary, speaking of the treaty. But it was clear from these shop-signs in Colón that it would be ratified and these shops soon empty.

I asked another Indian what he would do if the treaty was ratified.

'Find new premises,' he said. 'Other country.'

The Indians said the blacks were violent; the blacks said the Indians were thieves. But the blacks did not deny that some blacks were thieves. They blamed the young, the Rastas, the unemployed. Everyone in Colón looks unemployed, even the shopkeepers: not a customer in sight. But if business *is* slack – and it certainly seemed slack to me – it might be understandable. Look at the merchandise: Japanese pipes that look as if they're for blowing soap-bubbles; computerized radios and ridiculously complicated cameras; dinner services for twenty-four and purple sofas; leather neckties, plastic kimonos, switchblades and bowie knives; and stuffed alligators in eight sizes, the smallest for $2, the largest – four feet long – for $65; stuffed armadilloes for $35, and even a stuffed toad, like a cricket ball with legs, for a dollar. And junk: letter-openers, onyx eggs, flimsy baskets, and pokerwork mats turned out by the thousand by the derelict Cuña Indians. Who needs this stuff?

'It is not quality of merchandise,' said another Hindu shop-keeper. 'It is absence of customer. They are not coming.'

I was thirsty. I went into a bar and ordered a beer. A Panamanian policeman was standing near the juke-box. He pressed buttons. *Stayin' Alive* soon filled the bar. He turned to me and said, 'This is not a safe place.'

I went into the French Wax Museum. The bleeding head of Christ led me to think it might be devotional; and there was also a martyr in the window. Inside, it became more anatomical, with two hundred corpses and exhibits. There were fetuses in wax, and sex organs, Siamese twins, lepers, syphilitics and an entire Caesarean section. *Know the truth about the transformation from a man to a woman!* said the brochure. The exhibit was androgynous and yellow. *See Cancer of the Liver, the Heart and Other Organs! See the Miracle of Birth!* A note in the brochure said that this Wax Museum was operated to benefit the Panama Red Cross.

If I was to stay in Colón I would have to choose between the chaos and violence of the native quarter or the colonial antisepsis of the Zone. I took the easy way out, bought a ticket back to Panama City and boarded the 5:15. As soon as we pulled out of the station, the skies darkened and it began to rain. This was the Caribbean: it might rain anytime here. Fifty miles away, on the Pacific, it was the Dry Season; it was not due to rain for six weeks. The Isthmus may be narrow, but the coasts are as distinct as if a great continent lay between them. The rain came down hard and swept across the fields; it blackened the canal and wrinkled it with wind; and it splashed the sides of the coach and ran down the windows. With the first drops the passengers had shut the windows and now we sat perspiring, as if soaked by the downpour.

'I said, "*Where's your ticket?*" '

It was the conductor, fussing down the aisle, using his Louisiana drawl on a black.

'You cooperate with me, buddy – you're on my train!'

He spoke in English. This, after all, was the Zone. But these were not Zonians – they were canal workers, most of them the blacks who had been reclassified as 'Panamanian'. So it seemed

246

especially incongruous for this American conductor, irritably tugging his peaked railway cap and busy with his ticket-punching, coming to rest before a Spanish-speaker with a ticket stub and saying, 'That'll be five cents more – fares went up a year ago.'

He moved along: another ticket problem. 'Don't give me *that* crap!'

At the height of the empire in the Dutch East Indies, men just like this one – but Dutchmen – wore blue uniforms and ran the trams and trains through Medan. This was in North Sumatra, a world away from Amsterdam. But they had learned their trade in Amsterdam. They wore leather pouches and sold tickets and punched them and rang the tram-bells. Then the archipelago became Indonesia and most of the trains and all of the trams stopped running, because the Sumatrans and the Javanese had never run them.

You're on my train: it was a colonial cry. But I would be doing this conductor a disservice if I did not say that after he had dealt with all the passengers he relaxed; he joked with a cackling black girl and he chatted with a family which filled three long seats. And for the amusement of the passengers hanging out of the window – they were now open: it had stopped raining three miles out of Colón – he chased five small boys who were playing on the platform at Frijoles. He stamped his feet and shouted, 'Git! Git! Git! Git! Git! Git!' Then he talked to the men who stood near the train holding bunches of fish they had caught in the lake, which was twenty feet from the railway line.

In Balboa and Panama City, the early evening baseball games had started in the parks; we passed three in a row, then another pair. And the American tourists, who had occupied every seat of the air-conditioned coach, tottered out of the train and walked across the platform to their air-conditioned bus. It struck me that we must have the most geriatric tourists in the world; and, even though they were treated like kindergarteners, they were curious about the world. For them, bless their yellow pants and blue shoes, travel was part of growing old.

All over the Zone it was Club-going Hour. At the officer's mess and the VFW, the American Legion and the Elks, at the Church of God Servicemen's Center, the Shriners Club, the Masons, the golf clubs, the Star of Eden Lodge No. 9, of the Ancient and Illustrious Star of Bethlehem, the Buffaloes, and the Moose, and at the Lord Kitchener Lodge No. 25, and the Company cafeteria in Balboa the day's work was done and clubby colonials of the Zone were talking. There was only one subject, the treaty. It was seven o'clock in the Zone, but the year – who could tell? It was not the present. It was the past that mattered to the Zonian; the present was what most Zonians objected to, and they had succeeded so far in stopping the clock, even as they kept the canal running.

At Balboa High some students were waiting for it to grow dark enough so that in stealth they could drive nails again into the locks, and jam them, and prevent school from opening. At midnight the arts teacher suddenly remembered that she had left a kiln on and was afraid the school would burn down. She phoned the principal and he changed out of his pyjamas and checked. But there was no danger: the kiln had been left unplugged. Nor were the locks successfully jammed. The next day, school opened as usual, and all was well in the Zone. I was asked to stay longer, to go to a party, to discuss the treaty, to see the Indians. But my time was getting short; already it was March, and I had not yet set foot in South America. In a few days, there was a national election in Colombia, 'and they're expecting trouble,' said Miss McKinven at the Embassy. These considerations, as Gulliver wrote, moved me to hasten my departure sooner than I intended.

13 The Expreso de Sol to Bogotá

When strangers asked me where I was going I often replied, 'Nowhere.' Vagueness can become a habit, and travel a form of idleness. For example, I could not remember why I had come to Barranquilla.

True, I had to fly somewhere from Panama – there is no road or rail link through the Darién Gap between Panama and Colombia; but why I chose Barranquilla I did not know. Perhaps the name was printed in large type on the map; perhaps it had seemed important; perhaps someone had told me that it was the right place to go in order to catch the train to Bogotá. But none of these suppositions had much basis in fact. Barranquilla was inconvenient and filthy, and I was at an additional disadvantage in arriving in this rat-hole the day before the national senatorial elections. There would be riots, I was assured; mob violence was expected; farmers were being bussed in from the mountains – they had sold their votes for 200 pesos (about £2.50) and for this they got a free ride to the polling stations. The man I was talking to had no teeth. If one learns a foreign language one never quite reckons on speech defects; it was difficult for me to understand this man's Spanish through his champings. But I got the message. For two days, no liquor would be sold; all the bars would be shut and, once polling had begun, no taxis or buses would be allowed to leave the city, which was near the mouth of the Magdalena River, on the Caribbean. You will have to wait, the man said. And while I waited I tried to think why I had come to Barranquilla. I drank soda water and five-cent cups of coffee. I started Boswell's *Life of Johnson* under a palm tree in the hotel garden. I listened to the honking cars. Several times I walked through town and saw truckloads of supporters with the names of their candidates on their banners and tee-shirts, or much fuller trucks carrying armed soldiers. It looked as though armies were massing for battle. I retreated to sit under the palm tree with Boswell and tried to remember why I had not gone straight to Santa Marta, where the train leaves for Bogotá.

In my meanderings around Barranquilla I had met an American foreign service official. He felt that he had been marooned in the place; he ran the cultural centre; his name was Dudley Symes. On election day, he telephoned me at my hotel and asked whether I wanted to see the people voting. Was it safe? I asked.

'We'll see,' he said. 'I figure if we keep a very low profile, no one will bother us.'

I trimmed my moustache and put on a wrinkled short-sleeved shirt, dark trousers and my leakproof shoes: I would blend perfectly, I thought. But it was pointless. Dudley wore sandals and bright plaid Bermuda shorts, and his car, a great lumbering Chevrolet, was unlike any other I saw in Barranquilla. *A low profile*, he had said, but people stared at us wherever we went, and the car was nearly unmanageable on the narrow broken roads in the middle of town. Almost immediately we were in a traffic jam. And the people who had sold their votes, whose homeward-bound buses could not leave for another day, milled around wearing the paper hats of their particular candidate; they looked curiously into our car. There was shouting, and singing, and at various campaign headquarters – store-fronts draped in bunting – hundreds of supporters (tee-shirt, paper hat) chanted candidates' names and awaited the results. (In the event, the votes were not correctly counted for two weeks.) The voters were clearly identified as supporting this party or that party; it would not have been hard for any of the opposing parties to pick a fight. But the soldiers were numerous, and the only blood-curdling sounds I heard were those of the twanging tin-drum music and braying voices – one party headquarters trying to drown out another.

Dudley manoeuvred his car down a back street, cursing the pot-holes and blowing his horn at the crowds. It was hot and humid; the faces of these people were shining with perspiration.

'See any violence?' said Dudley.

I said no.

'These people,' he said – and he might have been speaking about the boys who were now thumping the rear fenders of his car with their fists – 'are known as "the happy people of Colombia".'

Happy was not precisely the word I would have used. They looked hysterical; their voices were shrill; they wiped their faces on their campaign tee-shirts, darkening the face of the man already printed there; they cat-called from cars, and we saw one new car run smack into the rear of a jeep and drive it into a tree. The new car's radiator burst and water dribbled into the street.

'His daddy will buy him a new one,' said Dudley.

'Who calls them the happy people of Colombia?' I asked.

'Everyone,' said Dudley. 'That's why nothing ever happens here. The government doesn't do anything here. They don't have to. They know the people are happy, so they don't give them anything.'

Some of the cars, and all the buses and trucks, had thick bunches of palm fronds tied to the bumpers just ahead of the tyres. They looked like tropical decorations. They were no such thing. In election time, playful Colombians sprinkled broken glass and nails on the roads; a vehicle without the palm fronds would have its tyres punctured, and then the occupants could easily be robbed or intimidated. But if the palm fronds were tied correctly they swept the glass and nails aside.

'Now if I was a little smarter,' said Dudley, 'I would have put some of those things on my car. I will, next time, if I live that long.'

Dudley was black. He had worked for a number of years in Nigeria and Mexico. He spoke Spanish with a drawl. He said Barranquilla was the worst place he had ever been, and he wondered sometimes if he would not be better off back home in Georgia.

'You seen enough of this election?'

I said I had. And I had seen enough of Barranquilla. The city had no centre. It was no more than hundreds of dusty roads running at right angles; a traffic jam at every corner, a rally on every street; soldiers positioned at polling stations, policemen aimlessly tweeting their whistles. Music, and mobs. The editorial in the morning *Chronicle* had said, 'Living in a democracy often makes one take its liberties for granted.' This might have been a democracy – it certainly looked chaotic enough to be one. The voting was unreadably busy and the crowds in the streets looked as if they expected something momentous to happen.

But nothing happened. The next morning, all the parties claimed a victory of some sort. Perhaps that was the answer. In a dictatorship only one party wins; in a Latin American democracy all the parties win; and such victories can only end in squabbles. It was like a Latin American football game. The score, the playing, the strategy mattered very little; the mob satisfaction mattered most. And it had to be a free-for-all because, no matter what happened, Barranquilla would remain Barranquilla. 'I once went to Buenaventura,' an American said to me. 'Someone told me that Buenaventura was the worst place in Colombia, and I couldn't believe that anything could be worse than Barranquilla. It was pretty bad, but it wasn't anything like this.'

While the election was going on, the Germans, the British, the Lebanese, the Americans, the sunbathing Japanese – all the communities that live in Barranquilla, all members of the Cabana Club – were observing the curfew from the swimming pool and patio of the Prado Hotel. The women read old copies of *Vogue*, the girls played radios, the men twirled the gold crucifixes around their necks; they flirted and idled. A mile away, in town, the farmers sat down in doorways, with the money in their pockets from the votes they had sold, and they waited until the curfew was lifted, so that they could go back to the mountains.

One commodity links all the people in Barranquilla: dope. Some grow it, some sell it, some buy it, some smoke it. Many people are in Barranquilla's jail for trafficking in dope (Henri Charrier, 'Papillon', spent a year in the same jail after he left Devil's Island), but far more have become millionaires by trading in marijuana. They even have a group name: they are *marijuaneros* – marijuana-ists. The profit is obvious in Barranquilla – more obvious than in any other city in South America, because Barranquilla is poorer than any other city. Less than a mile from the littered streets of downtown Barranquilla, on gentle hills that have a view of the Magdalena mudflats and the haze which hangs over the Caribbean shore, there was street after street of the strangest houses I had ever seen. They are the houses of the smugglers and drug peddlers who are known imprecisely as 'the Mafia'. The houses are built like bank vaults. They have high walls or unclimbable fences surrounding them. Most are faced with marble slabs and many have no windows. Windows here are long slits, six inches wide. They are more than burglar-proof; they are capable of withstanding a siege. These houses make the fortified suburb of the Bel-Air Estate in California look positively friendly and unprotected. And how, one asks, do the citizens of such a poor town find the money to build such prisons, each house a series of slabs arranged mausoleum-style? Why so many guard dogs, air-conditioners, coils of barbed wire?

It helps to look at the map to find the answer. Barranquilla is strategically located. It has a port. Between the mountains to the east are many flat hidden valleys, where planes can land and take off without being detected. The mountains rise to a high peninsula called the Guajira. The weather is perfect on the Guajira for growing marijuana, and the Guajira is a one-crop economy. Pot-smokers the world over recognize the taste of its product, known as Colombian Gold. Most of the houses in that Barranquilla suburb belong to farmers who have made their pile in the drug trade. The profits are vast for both farmer and smuggler. It is not unusual for a plane to leave with a ton of raw marijuana, and the smuggling has become such an institution that Barranquilla is the centre of the cocaine trade as well. The coca leaves are grown in Peru, smuggled into southern Colombia, processed in Cali, packaged in Bogotá, freighted to the coast, and by the time they arrive in Barranquilla it is ready for consumption. A kilo is worth half a million dollars in the States. The risks are high, but so are the rewards.

The planes are chartered in Miami; the small ones make refuelling stops in the Caribbean, the larger ones fly direct to the Guajira. Occasionally, arrests are made – flying an empty plane into Colombia is a criminal offence – but only the small-fry are sent to jail. The rest buy their way out or pull strings in Bogotá – only the most naive person balks at the suggestion that many Colombian politicians are closely involved in the drug trade. The successful American smuggler can make millions in this way; the

Colombians use their money by buying expensive houses, or cars, refrigerators, hi-fi sets and deep freezes in Miami; they set themselves up in Barranquilla as gentry. But, apart from their unusual houses, they try to remain inconspicuous. One drug dealer imported a Rolls-Royce Corniche at a cost of $400,000; but the other dealers would not let him drive it on the streets of Barranquilla – they felt it was too ostentatious, and that reprisals would be made against them. As for the small-fry who are caught and jailed – not much can be done for them. Their money is confiscated and they serve long sentences. There were twenty Americans in the Barranquilla prison when I passed through, and the American consulate which had been closed for a number of years had reopened solely to deal with them. But the consulate also issues visas: the demand for American visas increased a hundred-fold after the Barranquillans became rich in the drug trade.

The election was over, but the Bogotá train was not leaving until the next day. With a day to kill I did what most people do with time on their hands: I went sight-seeing. I took a dreadful local bus west along the coast road to the old – it was founded in 1533 – city of Cartagena. Cartagena had been what Barranquilla is now, a place of smugglers, pirates and adventurers, and the fortifications are like the Barranquilla houses on a large scale. If you can ignore the pitiful huts along the way, and the scary road, and the scream of the horn, and the heat, Cartagena is charming. It is venerable and attractive, a museum in the open air. The castle, the sea walls, the plazas and churches and convents are all pretty and well-preserved. But it is boredom and idleness that motivate sightseers, and even in this fine city there was not enough to take away my feelings of restlessness. I wandered into the Hotel Bolivar. The upstairs dining room was empty, but cool; four fans turned on the ceiling and the boughs of trees rattled against the balcony. I had fresh hearts of palm and a dish of Cuban rice and wrote a letter to my wife on the hotel's note-paper, and at once it seemed a day well-spent.

On my way to the post office to mail my letter I passed the curio shops. The curios were identical to the ones I had seen all through Central America: leather goods, Indian embroidery (it struck me once again that the Indians had been subverted, if not blinded, by having been turned into seamstresses: or was the crocheting of table napkins a native art?), clumsy carvings, cow-hoofs made into ashtrays and alligators into lamp stands and more stuffed toads with glass eyes. Trade was brisk. Here was a line of tourists near a cash register: one carried a coconut mask, another a stitched tablecloth, and others fibre mats and alliga-tors. The last, a rather abstracted woman in a sweat-stained frock, held a coiled whip.

One street in Cartagena I found worthy of study. Here there was nothing but pawnshops, each with the sign *We Buy And Sell Everything*. It was not the old clothes, the toasters, the watches and used boots that interested me; it was the tools. Half the merchandise in these pawnshops was builders' equipment. There were wrenches, drills, screwdrivers in many sizes, awls, claw-hammers, planes, axes, monkey-wrenches, plumb-bobs, spirit-levels, plasterers' hods and spikes and trowels. All had been pawned, all were for sale. And I began to understand why no one was working on those half-built houses between Cartagena and Barranquilla: the workers had pawned their tools. If there had been a few tools in each shop, or only a few shops selling tools, it would not have seemed so remarkable. But these pawnshops were like hardware stores, and the signs said that the pawned goods would be kept for three months and then sold; this was resignation and no mistake. There were enough tools in the shops to rebuild Colombia, and enough idle people, too. But it was a smuggling, thieving society; a hammer or a saw was not a tool – it was a form of currency, an article of trade.

But, so far, what had I seen? Only this small stretch of coast. I decided to move on; I might, I thought, find something differ-ent. I began to seek information about the train and I redis-covered, after that pleasant train-ride in Panama, the difficulties of train travel in Latin America. It was never simple. And it was not the poor service or the bad trains, but rather the fact that no one knew anything about them. The general routes are well-known from Mexico to South America; many people travel from capital to capital. But they fly, and the poorer travellers take the bus. Few people seem to know that the railways exist, and those who claim to know have never taken them. One person says it takes twelve hours from Santa Marta to Bogotá, another swears it is twenty-four hours; I was told there was no sleeper, but the Cook's *Timetable* listed one. Was there a diner, did I need a sleeping bag, was it air-conditioned? 'Do yourself a favour,' I was told. 'Take the plane. That's what Colombians do.'

I found that I was always travelling to a popular place by an unknown route. I seldom had any idea of how much it would cost, or how long it would take, or even whether I would arrive. This made for a certain anxiety, since I was always presuming or drawing on my own conclusions from the thin black line that signified a railway on the map. I knew I was not in Europe, but this train service was less dependable than any in Asia. No time-tables were published locally, little information was available, and what there was to know could only be found out at the station itself, if I had the good luck to locate it ('The *railway* station – are you sure you want the *railway* station?' I was asked by any number of vague locals). The information I needed I usually got from a man sweeping out the waiting room or a mango seller at the door. Before each journey, I inquired at the station from these people (who knew the answer because they were always there: they saw the trains come and go); I found out the times of the trains. But I was still uneasy; I had seen nothing in writing, I had no ticket, no official confirmation. Ticket windows were only opened a few hours before the train was to go. The mystery was not solved until the day of travel. I would arrive at the ticket window and give my destination, and the ticket seller would be surprised to see me, and a little incredulous, as if I had penetrated his secret by some devious stratagem. He would hesitate and giggle; but the game was over – I had won by finding him. He had no choice but to sell me a ticket.

And it did seem something like an elaborate game in which I was pursuing something that often eluded me; discovering the train, finding the station, buying the ticket, boarding and dropping into a seat became an end in itself. The travel was epilogue when it was not anti-climax. I was so preoccupied with this ticket-business that I frequently forgot where I was going, and, on being asked, found the question of dubious pertinence and said, 'Nowhere.'

A Colombian song goes,

> Santa Maria has a train,
> But it hasn't got a tram!

Santa Marta, where Simon Bolívar died penniless in a borrowed shirt, is the oldest town in Colombia. In the past few years it has become a resort, but the expensive hotels are outside town, away from the bars and pool halls. The town makes strenuous claims to being Bolívar's shrine, and like every other town of size in Latin America it has an impressive statue of the liberator. There is a corrosive irony in this Bolívar-worship, but it is quite in key with the other misapprehensions on the continent. Bolívar came to Santa Marta because he was in danger of being assassinated in Bogotá. He was regarded as a dictator in Peru, a traitor in Colombia, and in Venezuela – his birthplace – he was declared an outlaw. For setting Latin America free, his reward was penury and vilification. The monuments are an afterthought and the words chiselled onto them the battle cries he uttered when the revolution seemed a success. Which town council could raise a subscription to engrave his last judgements on any of these marmoreal plinths? 'America is ungovernable,' he wrote to Flores. 'Those who serve the revolution plough the sea. The only thing to do in America is to emigrate.'

Bolívar had come here to Santa Marta with the intention of fleeing the country. It could not have been much of a place in 1830; it was very little now: a small town, a beach, some cafés, a brothel ('*Mister*!'), a strip of shoreline on the flat blue Caribbean. On this cloudless March day, sanctified by sunlight, the town was very empty. I got off the Barranquilla bus and walked along the sea front, asking passers-by for directions to the station. The girls in the brothel, so pleased when I entered, howled in annoyance at me when I said I was merely inquiring the way to the railway station.

The ticket window was closed, but on it, sellotaped to the glass and scribbled in ballpoint, were the times of the trains: one departed, one arrived; and the name of the departing train, *Expreso de Sol*. I sat on a bench and waited for the window to open. Then I heard shouting and saw four policemen chasing a young man through the lobby. They wrestled him to the floor and wrapped chains around his legs and wrists. Then, they sat him next to me. He had wild hair and fresh wounds on his face and was breathing hard, but once he sat down he did not move. I stood up and walked to a different bench. If he decided to make a break for it, one of those armed policemen might feel impelled to shoot. I made sure I was out of the line of fire.

A tiny old lady with a shopping bag (she too was on her way to Bogotá) walked over to the prisoner. She put her face close to his, then exchanged a few words with the policemen. She chose to sit near me.

'What is he?' I asked. 'A thief?'

She looked at me and screwed up one eye. She had thick glasses that distorted her eyes and she wore a rather mad expression.

'Crazy!' she hissed.

The ticket window opened. I went over and asked for a sleeper to Bogotá.

'You have a family?'

'Yes.'

'They are travelling with you?'

'They are in Great Britain.'

'Then I cannot sell you a bed,' she said. 'Those compartments are for families. Six people or more.'

I bought an ordinary ticket and asked, 'What time does the train arrive?'

She smiled, but looked doubtful. 'Tomorrow?'

'And a bed is impossible, is that right?'

'If you really want one, ask the conductor when you get on the train. He might sell you one.'

I'll bribe the conductor, I thought; but when I saw the train and examined the sleepers – small dirty rooms with padded shelves – I was not encouraged. I hurried down the street and bought some loaves of bread, some cheese and what the girl called 'eastern baloney'. There was no point in bribing my way into a sleeper: there was no bedding, no water, no locks on the doors. I would take my chances here in the open car, in a sloping plastic seat. Something told me this was going to be a long trip.

We left at sunset, and at once I had an urge to get off the train. Already I was uncomfortable, and the journey was not worth this discomfort. Children were crying in their mothers' arms and as soon as we left the station people began complaining loudly about the broken lights and the crowds and the heat. *You're sitting in my place!* a boy yelled at an old man, who was travelling with his elderly wife. *I'm not moving*, said the man. Everyone was perspiring and muttering. *I can hardly breathe*, said a woman. *What a smell!* said a cruel-looking man into his hand. I had been moved by the tenderness on the platform, the fathers kissing their children good-bye, the boys hugging their girl-friends, the husband and wife holding hands. But now these same people were squawking irritably and I loathed them. I thought: They have to be here. They have a purpose. They're going home, or to work, or to meet friends. I had no such justification.

I was a victim of my plans. I had got this far and had boarded the train for no other reason than to be on the train. It was going to Bogotá, so I was. But Bogotá meant nothing to me: I was going there in order to leave it. At the best of times such a trip could be a lark, but this one had begun joylessly. It was too late to get off the train; we were moving away from the sunset, into darkness; the whistle was blowing and the passengers, quieted by the racket of the wheels, were smiling rather sadly. I was sorry that the train was not taking me out of Colombia, but only deeper into it, on a route that everyone had warned me about – the heat, the mosquitoes, the Magdalena swamps – to a capital no one praised.

Out of Santa Marta we crossed a green plain at the far end of which were mountains of pale velvet, a nap of shrubbery which was yellow in the salmon-coloured light that shone from the hinge of sun. Then, along the Caribbean for several miles, and the pink sky made the swamps pink and the still pools mirrored the new stars. This, with the palms and the fertile fields, gave me a little hope. The tidal pools were stirred by the breeze and lost their colour.

The train was almost full, but at Cienaga, the first stop, a cry went up from the crowd waiting at the platform, and fights broke out as the people pushed into the cars. 'Colombia has taken ardently to the air,' says *The South American Handbook*. 'No one rides the trains' I was told in Barranquilla. Some people denied that the train even existed; and I had had to search for days to get information about it. How, then, to explain these crowds? Perhaps it was very easy. Despite the protestations that it was a rich civilized country, it was actually a country of semi-literate peasants, most of whom lived in inaccessible areas. Such conditions – poverty, illiteracy, remoteness – created an oral tradition, and it was this, the hearsay of the bush telegraph, that conveyed information about the trains. We were late arriving at Cienaga, but the people had been there on the platform all day: it had been said that a train was due. Now they scrambled to the few empty seats, dragging boxes and suitcases after them. But the rest – and there were many – simply stood in the aisle, or sat on their cardboard boxes. The aisle was jammed. It was like a homeward-bound commuter train of exhausted strap-hangers. The difference was that this train was going 750 miles to Bogotá.

There was no air in the car. It had begun to rain, a warm night-time drizzle; the passengers had shut the windows. The lights flickered, the train lurched, and the passengers were so closely packed that the slightest lurch had them yelling in complaint. *Now*, I thought, *someone is going to turn on a radio*. But, before the thought came whole, the music started, an awful trumpeting and harmonizing, the Latin quick-step that was like acid in my ears. The rain, the music, the hot steamy car; and the mosquitoes, the dim lightbulbs that looked like withered tangerines. I propped my window up and pulled out Boswell, but I had not read two sentences when the lights failed entirely. We were in darkness.

Darkness proved better than dim light. These were country people: darkness put them to sleep. Soon the car was quiet, the rain let up, the moon was as round and yellow as a wheel of cheddar, and out of the window – mine was the only one open – I could see the flat swampy plain, and some huts with fires burning outside. The bog-dark land smelled of mud and rain; the passengers slept or stood silently rocking in the aisle. The darkness was pure and serene. I thought: *I am alive.*

At nine o'clock, or just after, we passed Aracataca. The novelist Gabriel Garcia Marquez was born here; this was the Macondo of *Leaf-Storm* and *One Hundred Years of Solitude*. In the light of fires and lanterns I could see mud huts, the silhouettes of palms and banana trees, and glow-worms in the tall grass. It was not late, but there were few people awake; glassy-eyed youths who had stayed up watched the train go by. 'It's coming,' says a woman in Marquez's Macondo, when she sees the first train approach the little town. 'Something frightful, like a kitchen dragging a village behind it.'

I made myself a baloney sandwich, drank two of the beers I had bought in Santa Marta and went to sleep. The noise, the rhythm of the clicking on the rails, was a soporific; it was silence and a stillness in the car that woke me. At midnight, I came awake: the train had stopped. I did not know where we were, but it must have been a fairly large place because most of the people in the car – including the man next to me – got off. But an equal number boarded here, so we were no less crowded. Children woke and cried, and people pushed and fought for the empty seats. An Indian girl sat next to me; her plump profile, outlined by the station lights, was unmistakable. She wore a baseball cap and a jersey and slacks, and her luggage was three cardboard boxes and an empty oil-drum. When the train started, she snuggled up to me and went to sleep. My shirt was damp with sweat, but the humid breeze was no help; and I knew we would not be out of this swamp until late the next day. I fell asleep, but when I woke again at another lonely station – a low building, a man, a lantern – I saw that the girl had moved across the aisle and was snuggling against a murmuring man.

Dawn was tropical, the sun a grey puffball in a humid cloud. I made sure I had not been robbed in the night: my passport and money were safe in my leather pouch. And, studying my map, I saw that we were about an hour out of Barrancabermeja. The land was thinly populated, savannah giving on to swamp. We were as yet too far from the Magdalena to be able to see it, and the hot clouds obscured the mountains. This was simply a small

261

train on a straight track, labouring through a region where there were no roads, only huts, and an occasional bull in the grass, and vultures and herons. And the huts were poor, no more than mud shelters with grass roofs.

'How about a coffee?'

It was a man carrying a tray of filled cups. I bought two and gave him the Colombian equivalent of a penny. With an empty seat next to me I could spread out, drink coffee, light my pipe and read Boswell. This was not so bad; and I had that same sense of virtue I had experienced in Mexico, having endured a hideous night in a cramped seat.

It remained cloudy for most of the morning, which was just as well. I had been told that when the sun broke through the heat would be unbearable. Perhaps that was no more than talk: everything else people had told me was wrong. They said there would be jungles, but I had seen no jungles. This was all swamp and nearby were low hills with odd worn-down configurations, as if a great flood had washed over them and made them small and smooth. People said there would be mosquitoes. There were, but the flying beetles were much worse – they not only bit fiercely, but got tangled in my hair. And the heat was no worse than Santa Marta's, and nothing like as bad as Zacapa's. They said we would run out of ice, but indeed there was no ice at all on this train; and even at the time the threat had not seemed to me particularly dire. So after eighteen hours on this swampland express I could truthfully say that I had seen worse trains in my life. It was not praise, but neither did I hold the conviction that the train should be insured and wrecked.

I wished to remain sane on this trip, so, in a businesslike way, I brought my diary up to date, writing until lunch-time. Then I walked the length of the train, carrying my sandwich ingredients, and finding an empty table in the unused dining car, made myself a submarine sandwich. Another walk, and finally I settled down with Boswell. The sun had come out, the swamps shimmered; and the book was perfect. Doctor Johnson remarks on everything, including travel. Boswell is off to Corsica: 'When giving me advice as to my travels, Dr Johnson did not dwell upon cities, and palaces, and pictures, and shows, and Arcadian scenes. He was of Lord Essex's opinion, who advises his kinsman Roger Earl of Rutland, "rather to go an hundred miles to speak with one wise man, than five miles to see a fair town." '

The book became my life-line. There was no landscape in it. I had all the landscape I wanted out the window. What I lacked was talk, and this was brilliant talk, sage advice, funny remarks. I could identify with Boswell ('Why is a fox's tail bushy, Sir?'), and the combination of this train and the Magdalena valley, and Boswell on my lap, was just the ticket. I think if I had not had that book to read as I made my way through Colombia, the trip would have been unendurable.

But it was demeaning, after those conversations at Mrs Thrale's and at the Mitre, to enter into discussions with the rest of the passengers. I had thought I was the only foreigner on the train. I was wrong – I should have known the moment I saw his cut-off dungarees, his full beard, his earring, his maps and rucksack that he was a fellow-traveller. He was French. He had a sore throat. A French traveller with a sore throat is a wonderful thing to behold, but it takes more than tonsillitis to prevent a Frenchman from boasting.

He looked contemptuously at my drip-dry shirt, my leakproof shoes, my sunglasses.

'You're a tourist?' he said.

'Like you,' I said in a friendly way.

'I am travelling,' he said, forcing the distinction. 'I have come from San Andres Island. Before that, I journeyed through the States.'

'So did I. But I came through Central America.'

'You saw Tikal?'

'No, but I saw Zacapa. No one goes to Zacapa.'

'I have seen Tikal. Very beautiful. You should have seen it. How long have you been travelling?'

'A little over a month.'

'Five months I have been travelling! *Five*. I left Paris in October. I spent one month in New York City.'

'Travelling in New York City?'

This stung him. 'Going here and there,' he said. 'Where are you going?'

'Bogotá.'

'Yes, but after that.'

'Southern Argentina.'

'*Patagone.*' He was making tracings with his finger on his French map. 'I am going here,' he said, tapping a green bulge in Brazil. 'Down the Amazon, from Leticia. It will take fifteen days, or more, by river.' He looked up at me. 'Argentina has a bad government.'

'Brazil has a wonderful government,' I said. 'Ask those Indians on the Amazon, they'll tell you.'

He stroked his beard, not sure whether I was mocking him. 'Chile and Argentina are worse. That's why I'm not going there. You are taking this train all the way to Bogotá?'

'That's right.'

'I am not. I am getting off at La Dorada. Then by bus.'

'Is that quicker?'

'No, but you save money – five dollars or more.'

'I've got five dollars,' I said. He started to cough. He stood up to give himself room, and coughed, bowing from the waist each time. I said, 'You should do something about that throat. Want an aspirin?'

'No,' he said. 'It is not serious.'

I went back to Boswell, then dozed and looked out of the window. The landscape did not change. The valley was so flat, so broad, it had no sides that were visible; and the foliage was too dense to be clearly discernible. But later in the day the savannah reasserted itself, and I could make out the faint pencillings of hills, and cattle grazed nearer the track, and horses, which broke into a gallop at the sight of the train. Flocks of white herons blew across the grass tips like flecks of paper in a breeze.

At one town there was a bar; it was called 'The Blue Danube' in Spanish, this bar near the much-mightier Magdalena. Outside it was a hitching post, with three saddled horses tied to it; the riders were at the window, drinking beer. It was an appropriate wild-west scene in this poor empty land, the settlers' shacks and the pig-pens and the rumours of emeralds. It was no better in the train. The passengers were either asleep or sitting silently, traumatized by the heat. Half of them were flat-faced Indians in shawls or felt hats.

In the late afternoon, we had word at one station that near

Bogotá there had been a derailment, probably caused by a landslide. The Frenchman confirmed this, but said that he didn't mind – he was getting off at La Dorada. The news of this derailment did not really surprise me. In Barranquilla, Dudley had put me in touch with an American who was working on transport problems. This fellow had shown me the latest statistics for derailments on the line between Santa Marta and Bogotá. He only had the figures up to 1972, but these were enough: in 1970 there were 7,116 derailments, in 1971 there were 5,969, in 1972 there were 4,368. He said the situation was getting worse; so I set out from Santa Marta expecting to be derailed, or to be held up by one. (It is also said that bandits stop this train and rob the passengers, but the Colombians on the train denied that this was so.)

'You think we're going to make it?' I asked the conductor.

'You will be in Bogotá tonight,' he said. 'That is the truth.'

Soon after, the mountains appeared, the cordillera of the Andean chain; and with them the brown Magdalena River on which men paddled dugout canoes or fished from the shore with contraptions that looked like butterfly nets. The mountains were at first scattered buttes and solitary peaks, and some were like citadels, squarish with fortress-like buildings planted around the summits. But it was an illusion – there were no buildings. My eye, unprepared for these heights, was misled, and made the strangeness into familiar shapes. The train rolled straight at these blue, grey, green peaks, and what I took to be loops of cloud – faint tracings in the sky – were mountains, too; and everything around me which had seemed no more than vapour had substance.

The train started to climb towards the vapour and fog. Here, it was still hot and dry; there, it was raining. We entered the rain, which was a cold zone in a drenching downpour. The fields and gardens were bright green, and here were villas the likes of which I had never seen before. They were on the hillsides, behind hedges and walls, with names like 'Seville' and 'The Refuge'. They had swimming pools and flower gardens and lawns as evenly-coloured as carpets. Some were like castles, and some were built like Swiss chalets, and one was made entirely of orange tiles, like a fairy-tale house with conical roofs. The Indians and the ragged people in the Expreso de Sol, who had come from the coast, watched these houses pass with astonishment and something like alarm. I wondered whether they realized that single families occupied these grand houses on the mountainside. The houses seemed fantastic to me; what, then, would a person from a Magdalena village think of them?

I asked one of the passengers. He gaped through the window, his face was wet with rain. It was cold, but he was in his shirtsleeves. 'Who lives in these houses?'

'The bosses,' he said in Spanish.

But this was Colombia. There was no swamp without a mountain, no mansion without a cluster of huts. The huts were nearer the tracks, and in the villages hunched-over peasants hurried through the rain. It was cold, but we had moved from the plain to the mountains with such rapidity that my shirt was still damp with sweat, and now it chilled me to the bone. I put on my leather coat and still I shivered.

Then, on this mountainside, the train stopped. As if by a pre-arranged signal everyone got off. There were buses waiting. No announcement had been made about the derailed train ahead, the landslide; but everyone knew. We went the last few miles in an old bus, skidding on the rain-slick mountain roads. For the first time on this trip I felt I was in mortal danger. We arrived in the high rainy city in darkness.

The mournful countenance of Bogotá's antique buildings is pure Spanish, but the gloom of its setting is Andean and all its own. Even on a sunny day, the three peaks – the convent, the cross, the Christ statue – are wet and dark; the city is spread across a gigantic shelf of granite. Over a mile and a half high, it experiences mountain weather; it rained for most of the time I was there, and this cold drizzle imprisoned it in dreary solemnity. My mood was no better. The height gave me the staggers. I tottered from one end of the city to the other, slightly dizzy and feeling palpitations.

Before the skyscrapers were put up, Bogotá's church spires must have given the place a sullen beauty. They are the best examples of the golden age of Spanish architecture, and what with a climate like that of north-west Spain it is not hard to believe in some parts of the city that you are, as Boswell puts it, 'perambulating Salamanca'. Bogotá's contact with Spain was considerable, since for hundreds of years it was easier to get to Spain – sailing down the Magdalena to the sea – than to anywhere else in Colombia. Culturally and geographically, Bogotá was aloof from South America and its own hinterland. It remains so, a lofty city with an unscalable class system. Cows crop grass in Bogotá's parks, but this hint of the pastoral is all but obscured, like the church spires, by Bogotá's ugly office buildings.

With the sight of my first Indian in Bogotá, my Spanish images quickly faded from mind. There are 365 Indian tribes in Colombia; some climb to Bogotá, seeking work; some were there to meet the Spanish and never left. I saw an Indian woman and decided to follow her. She wore a felt hat, the sort detectives and newspapermen wear in Hollywood movies. She had a black shawl, a full skirt and scandals, and, at the end of her rope, two donkeys. The donkeys were heavily laden with metal containers and bales of rags. But that was not the most unusual feature of this Indian woman with her two donkeys in Bogotá. Because the traffic was so bad they were travelling down the pavement, past the smartly dressed ladies and the beggars, past the art galleries displaying rubbishy graphics (South America must lead the world in the production of third-rate abstract art, undoubtedly the result of having a vulgar moneyed class and the rise of the interior decorator – you can go to an opening nearly every night even in a dump like Barranquilla); the Indian woman did not spare a glance for the paintings, but continued past the Bank of Bogotá, the plaza (Bolívar again, his sword implanted at his feet), past the curio shops with leather goods and junk carvings, and jewellers showing trays of emeralds to tourists. She starts across the street, the donkeys plodding under their loads, and the cars honk and swerve and the people make way for her. This could be a wonderful documentary film, the poor woman and her animals in the stern city of four million; she is a reproach to everything in view, though few people see her and no one turns. If this was filmed, with no more elaborate scenario than she was walking from one side of Bogotá to the other, it would win a prize; if she was a detail in a painting it would be a masterpiece (but no one in South America paints the human figure with any conviction). It is as if 450 years have not happened. The woman is not walking in a city: she is walking across a mountainside with sure-footed animals. She is in the Andes, she is home; everyone else is in Spain.

She walked, without looking up, past a man selling posters, past the beggars near an old church. And, glancing at the posters, examining the beggars, I lost her. I paused, looked aside, and then she was gone. So I contented myself with the posters. They were of Bolívar, Christ and Che Guevara; but they were hard to tell apart. They seemed like versions of the same person: the same sorrowing eyes, the same mulish good looks and heroic posture. The political posters in Barranquilla had been similarly emblematic – the right-wing candidates had looked fat and complacent, while those of the left resembled a composite of this patriot, saviour and revolutionary. The other posters were of blonde nudes, Jane Fonda, Joseph Stalin (bearing a warning about 'Yankys'), Marlon Brando and Donald Duck. The one I bought was the best of the bunch. It showed Christ on the cross, but he had managed to pull his hand away from one nail, and still hanging crucified, but with his free arm around the shoulder of a praying guerilla fighter, Christ was saying, 'I also was persecuted, my determined guerrilla.'

The beggars were everywhere, but they tended to linger near the churches and holy places, much as in Calcutta, to catch people when they are conscience-stricken. They were blind, lame, palsied; children, women, old men, infants – naked in the cold – being dangled on the knees of cringing hags. Here were two sisters, one in an orange crate with a scribbled sign saying she is paralysed (*And this is my sister . . .*). Some are not begging, but merely camped out on a traffic island in the middle of the city, boiling grey liquid in tin cans; or holed up next to a wall, or living (like the young boy I saw every day I was in Bogotá) in the rubble of deserted buildings. The signs the importuning beggars carry are pathetically blunt: *I am a leper* and *I am sick* and *We are orphans*, and some carry placards with potted histories of bad luck and disease. The ones who do tricks draw crowds – the Indian contortionists, the blind musicians.

> See the blind beggar dance, the cripple sing,
> The sot a hero, lunatic a king.

To remark on the numbers of beggars is perhaps to make an observation of no great insight, like saying it is a continent of soldiers and shoeshine boys. One could even say that, in Colombia as elsewhere, it takes a degree of organization to beg. But why, I wondered, were so many of them children? Not sick or lame, and not carrying signs, they lived among the ruined buildings and ran in packs through the streets. They were lively, but they lived like rats. I asked several Colombians about them, and the Colombians were surprised by the ignorance of my question. They were gamins, they said – the word is the same in Spanish and English; and I ought to be careful of them, for most were pickpockets and sneak-thieves. It does not occur to the wealthy Colombian that these urchins are anything but vermin, and why house them or feed them when it is so much cheaper to put up a high fence around the house to keep them out?

I spent my days in Bogotá church-going (elegant interiors with a touch of voodoo: ladies jostle in line to collect pints of holy water; *No Jugs, Only Bottles* reads the sign), and climbing the hills, and admiring the old American cars – here a Nash, there a Studebaker – until I began to lust after one myself and regret that my father had sold his 1938 Pontiac. It struck me that the next great craze in America will be these indestructible cars of the 40s and 50s, restored to perfect condition. And when I grew tired of suspicious-looking youths who approached me ('Ay, meester, joo from New Jork?'), and depressed by the beggars and gamins, I turned to Boswell for cheer. It was in Bogotá, one grey afternoon that I read the following passage: 'Where a great proportion of the people are suffered to languish in helpless misery, that country must be ill-policed and wretchedly governed: a decent provision for the poor is the true test of civilization.' Gentlemen of education, he observed, were pretty much the same in all countries; the condition of the lower orders, the poor especially, was the true mark of national discrimination.

14 The Expreso Calima

There is very good reason for the Bogotá railway to end at the town of Ibagué. After Ibagué there is such a precipitous pass that, to imagine it, you would have to picture the Grand Canyon covered with greenery – deep green gorges and green peaks and ledges and cliffs. The genius for building railways through such places disappeared around the turn of the century. Not long ago, the Colombians extended the railway from Girardot to Ibagué, but having got that far they were flummoxed by the Quindio Pass. There are impassable rapids in it, and high mountains around it; the walls of the gorge are vertical. It is remarkable that a road exists, but it is not much of a road. It takes six hours to go the 65 miles from Ibagué to Armenia, where the train resumes, heading south to Cali and Popayán; from there, it is a short hop to Ecuador.

Descending the cordillera from Bogotá, I felt I had recovered my health. My head cleared at this lower altitude, the trench between two mountain ranges. The hills were fine-textured, like great soft piles of green sand, poured on the plain beside the tracks. Telegraph lines ran by the railway, and the district was so humid that small plants had taken root on the slack wires. They grew in the air like clusters of orchids, their blossoms and leaves dangling.

At Girardot the train stopped. Everyone got out. I stayed in my seat reading Boswell.

'We have arrived,' said the conductor. He was on the platform; he spoke to me through the window.

'I have not arrived,' I said. 'I am going to Ibagué.'

'You will have to take the bus. This train does not go there.'

'They did not tell me that in Bogotá.'

'What do they know in Bogotá? Ha!'

Cursing, I walked to the bus station. The Ibagué bus had already left, but there was another bus to Armenia leaving in a few hours. That would take me through the Quindio Pass; a night in Armenia, then chug-chug to Cali. I bought my ticket and went to have lunch. I had left Bogotá too early to have breakfast, so I was ravenously hungry.

The restaurant was small and dirty. I asked to see the menu. There was no menu. I asked the waitress what there was to eat.

'Dish of the day,' she said. 'Today it is beans Antioch-style.'

Beans Antioch-style: it did not sound bad. We were in the province of Antioquia. Perhaps this was a local delicacy? But names can be so misleading. They could call this dish anything they pleased but I knew hog-jowls when I saw them. Flies buzzed around me, around the fatty maw in my plate. I ate the beans and a slice of bread and handed it back.

Girardot lies on the upper reaches of the Magdalena River, but here the river is too shallow to be navigable by anything larger than a canoe. And the bridge over it was being painted. The bus became stationary in traffic and for an hour and a half it did not move. This meant a late arrival in Armenia and, what was much worse, a dangerous night-time ride along the hairpin curves of the Quindio Pass. The Colombians are good-tempered people. They are used to waiting for buses that are late, used to riding buses and trains that do not arrive. They do not complain; they rarely speak. I complained, but got no response. So I read about Doctor Johnson. 'He used frequently to observe, that there was more to be endured than enjoyed, in the general condition of human life ... For his part, he said, he never passed that week in his life which he would wish to repeat, were an angel to make the proposal to him.' And I thought: A week ago I was in Barranquilla.

I looked up. Our bus had not moved: that same sign advertising beer; the child still in the doorway with his tray of fried cakes; the piles of broken brick; and on the road the line of trucks and buses.

'This is terrible,' I said.

The man next to me smiled.

We were nowhere. We had come from nowhere. Ibagué,

Armenia, Cali: they were names on the map, no more than that.

'Where are you from, sir?'

I told him.

'Very far,' he said.

'And you are from?'

'Armenia.' He gestured at the sky. His poncho was folded on his lap. It was very hot.

'Do you think we will get there?'

He smiled, he shrugged.

I said, 'I wish I was home. I have been travelling, but I keep asking myself if it is worth the trouble.'

The man laughed. If my Spanish had been better I would have translated what I had just read: *He never passed that week in his life which he would wish to repeat.*

We talked about the men painting the bridge. For this trivial chore the traffic in Girardot had halted and no vehicle was allowed across the bridge. Painting was difficult, said the man; was it not? They were trying to do a good job. He sat and sweated and mocked. The coastal Colombians had been loud and effusive, but these mountain people were stoical and sometimes wry.

'It doesn't matter,' said the man. 'I'm going home. I will be inside my house tonight.'

'You are lucky,' I said. 'You could walk home if you wanted to.'

'No. I could not walk through the Quindío Pass.'

More waiting, more Boswell. 'Mr Elphinstone talked of a new book that was much admired and asked Dr Johnson if he had read it. Johnson: "I have looked into it." "What, (said Elphinstone) have you not read it through?" Johnson, offended at being thus pressed, and so obliged to own his cursory mode of reading, answered tartly, "No, Sir, do *you* read books *through*?" '

We began to move – slowly, but I was grateful for the motion after this purgatorial waiting in the sun. It was not only the painters who had held up traffic, but a police patrol, boarding buses and inspecting trucks for drugs. Or it might not have been drugs. They climbed onto our bus and walked up and down the aisles with their hands on their pistols. Then they singled out half a dozen people and made them empty their suitcases at the roadside. This happened four times in the trip from Girardot to Armenia, and one of the times I was asked to empty my suitcase. 'What are you looking for?' I asked. The policeman did not reply. Inside the bus, the man next to me said, 'You should not have asked the policeman that question. You see, he is not looking for anything. He is just making trouble.'

The mountains were as yet still distant. The stretch between Girardot and Ibagué was surrounded by green hills and shady meadows and farms: corn, cattle and well-watered valleys. It seemed idyllic, and at every house the bougainvillea was in blossom, purple and orange. The colour alone seemed a form of wealth. The landscape was gentle, and the deep green grass made me feel mellower: to have seen this was to have discovered a part of this poor country in which people lived in contentment, with space and a mild climate. I was still reading, looking up from time to time. Boswell was just right for this trip, and often in these uplands of Colombia I was given clarification by the book, or emphasis; or – as it happened in this pleasant valley – a kind of deflation.

'The modes of living in different countries, and the various views with which men travel in quest of new scenes, having been talked of, a learned gentleman ... expatiated on the happiness of a savage life; and mentioned an instance of an officer who had actually lived for some time in the wilds of America, of whom, when in that state, he quoted this reflection with an air of admiration, as if it had been deeply philosophical: "Here am I, free and unrestrained, amidst the rude magnificence of Nature, with this Indian woman by my side, and this gun with which I can procure food when I want it: what more can be desired for human happiness?" ... Johnson: "Do not allow yourself, Sir, to be imposed upon by such gross absurdity. It is sad stuff; it is brutish. If a bull could speak, he might as well exclaim, – Here am I with this cow and this grass; what being can enjoy greater felicity?"'

It was true; I could not presume on the contentment of these Colombian peasants. It helped to have Doctor Johnson nearby to strike a cautionary note.

We stopped in Ibagué to endure a police search, and then

headed out of town. We had not gone a hundred yards before we started to climb a mountainside. We turned and turned again, gaining altitude; and in minutes Ibagué was beneath us, rooftops and steeples and chimneys. We had entered the Quindío Pass.

In my travel-weary frame of mind, it took a great deal to tear me away from the charms of Boswell and Johnson. But at the Quindío Pass I put the book aside and did not pick it up again for several days. I had seen nothing to compare with this, well, rude magnificence of nature. Not even the Central American chain of volcanoes, or Death Valley near Zacapa, or the wild heights of Chiapas were as grand as this. In this green canyon, deep down, ran a river; but the river was white and unreachable. What houses and small farms there were in the canyon were fixed somehow to the cliffsides; and the cliffs were so steep the huts seemed painted there, primitive two-dimensional splashes of huts and plots. The straight-down precipice meant that the bean furrows ran one above the other, like the grooves on a vertical washboard. I saw no people venturing out; it looked as though they would simply fall down as soon as they left their front door, and how they hoed their washboard gardens I could not tell.

There were only the gardens; there were no animals – there was no room for them, nothing flat enough to hold a chicken, much less a pig. And the farms were few – a dozen vertiginous small-holdings and the rest green steepnesses and plunging ravines of thin air. The road was cut into the mountainside and it was so narrow that the buildings which faced onto it – nearly all of them were bars – were propped over the ravine, underpinned by timber scaffolding. Birds nested in these lofty beams.

The one town on the way, Cajamarca, lay on a small ledge. I could not see it until we were in it, but a moment later the houses dropped away, and Cajamarca was rusty roofs and hat-brims, a hamlet magnetized to a cliff. The tortuous road helped to explain Bogotá's remoteness. This was the only way south and west, to the coffee regions and the main port of Buenaventura. Flying back and forth over Colombia, one would have no idea of the difficulty in getting petrol and food to Bogotá, and the longer I travelled overland here the more Bogotá seemed a fastness in the

Andes which bore no relation to the other towns. And it was still a country in which river and mule-track mattered. In the rainy season a road like this through the Quindio Pass – it was only partly paved – seemed unthinkable. Even on this dry bright afternoon five trucks lay wrecked on the road, and the drivers perhaps sceptical that any help would arrive had built small camps beside the trucks, the way pygmies do when they manage to kill an elephant they cannot move.

It was probably less the splendour of the heights than the depthless terror of the empty space beside them that silenced the passengers. Most were Indians, with dark sulky faces under porkpie hats and wrapped in ponchos for the cold. They were impassive and did not move except to stuff bits of goat's cheese into their mouths. After the disgusting meal at Girardot, I had got hungry, and as we waited on a bend for a truck to pass us a boy had come up to the bus yelling, 'Cheese! Cheese! Cheese!' The word echoed against the ravine walls. Lumps of it, the texture of unrisen dough, were wrapped in banana leaves. I bought a lump and ate it, pinch by pinch. It was salty and tasted of goat, but it was no worse than Gorgonzola.

Four hours passed in this way in the labouring bus: cheese, curves, and occasionally glimpses of the ravine that took my breath away.

At the highest point in the pass we were in cloud. Not tufts of it billowing in the genie-shapes I had seen near Bogotá that morning, but a formless white vapour we had entered and become lost in. It was a void and it had taken away the road. It dripped into the bus and it obscured the ravine; it veiled the peaks in some places and obliterated others further on. It shut out the sun, or rather dimmed it, giving it a bulbous pearly stare. The vapour changed from white to grey and there was no road, no valley, no mountains, no sky, only a grey sea-kingdom of mist, like the horror scene that greets Arthur Pym at the end of his voyage. It was a species of blindness, of blind flight, like a children's tale of a rattletrap bus that takes to the air, of enchantment so pure and unexplainable – and now we were buffeted by wind – that I lost all sense of space and time. It was most of all like an experience of death; as if, try as I might, I could see nothing beyond the silly immediacy of this bus but a grave featureless vapour, my senses in collapse.

The grey turned white, became discoloured and bits of green were thrown up. We were descending now. The green was almost black in the damp cloud; then it was olive, the unfenced margin of road beside the gorge which a skid would land us into. No one would see us drop; there would be no sound but a gulp as we were swallowed at the pit of that mile-deep gullet.

The bus door was open – broken on its hinge. The bus swerved, and at one bend there was a thump. An Indian on one of the front seats had been holding a bundle on his lap; the bundle had bounced out of his hands, rolled across the floor and out of the open door.

The Indian stood up.

'Please sir,' he said. 'I have five pesos in that.'

About fifteen cents. The driver slowed down.

'And some of my things,' said the Indian.

The driver stopped in the middle of the road. He could hardly have pulled off to the side – five feet to the right there was only emptiness. The Indian got out and, poncho flapping, he ran down the road for his bundle.

'Five pesos,' said the driver. 'That is valuable, eh?' He pulled at his moustache and the passengers roared with laughter. The driver was encouraged. 'What does it matter if we have to travel in the darkness? That fellow needs his bundle and his five pesos, eh?'

The passengers were still burbling when the Indian returned. He put the bundle on his seat and thumped it and sat on it. We continued through segments of cloud which filtered the sun and made it pale yellow and dripped this yellow colour onto the trees and the grass. Ahead, in another valley, lay a yellow town flanked by yellow fields and yellow hills. This was Armenia.

Armenia, Antioquia, and not far away the town of Circasia. The names were Asiatic and baffling, but I was too tired to wonder at them. The bus rumbled through town, and though it was dark I saw a large hotel in the middle of a block. I asked the driver to stop, then walked back to that hotel and checked in. I thought that working on my diary until midnight would put me to sleep, but the altitude and the cold made me wakeful. I decided to go for a walk and see a bit of Armenia.

If the town had been dark or in any way threatening, I would not have gone out alone. But it was well-lighted and as it was a Friday night – Saturday was market-day – it was full of country folk who had come into town to sell their vegetables. There were crowds of people standing in front of the windows of electrical shops, watching television. They were mainly farmers, Indians and peasants from villages which had no lights, let alone televisions. I watched with one group. The programme was a documentary about Australian aborigines. Many of the aborigines were naked, but an equal number wore slouch hats and cast-off clothes that were not very different from those worn by these fascinated watchers in Armenia.

'. . . *these paleolithic people,*' said the narrator; and the aborigines were shown building lean-tos, and overturning logs and gathering witchetty-grubs, and impaling lizards and roasting them over fires. The aborigines, seen from this Colombian valley, did not seem so badly off. It was sunny there in the Australian outback and, stalking a kangaroo, the aborigines looked alert and full of hunter's cunning. And here were the aborigine children. The narrator made some condescending remarks about their health and their history, and in Bogotá this probably did seem like the dawn of the world and a scratching settlement of cavemen. But the people in Armenia marvelled only at the nakedness, the lank penis, the fallen breasts. They laughed in embarrassment. The know-it-all voice of the narrator droned on, calling attention to the meal of maggots, the dwellings of twigs, the crude digging tools.

'Look, look,' said the watchers here in front of the electrical shop. 'Where is this place? Is it Africa?'

'Far,' said one man. 'Very far away.'

Five minutes later, walking back to the hotel, I paused on the pavement to light my pipe. I heard coughing; it came from a dark doorway, and it was the coughing of a child. An adult's cough is frequently an annoyance, a child's is always helpless and pathetic. I peered into the doorway and said, 'Are you all right?'

Three children jumped to their feet. The tallest was black and wore a man's suit-jacket which came to his knees; the others, in torn shirts and shorts, were sleepy-eyed Spanish-looking boys. They said hello. I asked them their ages. The black boy was ten, the others were both nine; it was one of the nine-year-olds – a thin, sickly boy – who had been coughing.

'I was just doing this arithmetic,' said the other nine-year-old. He showed me a scrap of paper with a column of figures written on it; they were neatly-done in pencil and covered the paper. 'Look, I made a million.'

'Good for you,' I said. 'Your teacher will like that.'

They laughed. The black boy said, 'We don't have a teacher.'

'No school?'

'We used to go.'

'Where do you come from?'

The black boy's village was unintelligible to me. He said his parents were there, but they had sent him away because there were too many children at home. How many? I asked. More than ten, he said. The house was small, there was no food.

The second boy said, 'My mother and father are in Cali. That is where my house is. I have a lot of brothers and sisters. But there was a problem. My father was always hitting me and beating me. I was afraid, so one day I came here to Armenia.'

I said, 'Is this your brother?'

The third boy giggled and began again to cough.

'That is my friend.'

'Look,' I said, 'if I give you some money, will you share it?'

'Yes,' said the second boy. He put his arm around the black boy. 'This is my best friend.'

'What about him?' I indicated the third boy.

He was the smallest and the most ragged, he wore no shoes, his arms were thin and dirty; he raised them as he coughed.

The black boy said, 'He is with us, too. He wants to stay with us. He is afraid to be alone.' The black boy was a bit doubtful. I could tell from his tone that this frail boy was considered a burden.

I gave them some money and told them to share it, then I asked (but I knew what the answer would be), 'What are you doing out so late?'

The second boy said, 'We were trying to sleep.'

'Where do you sleep?'

'Here.' They pointed to the doorway, where a rectangle of cardboard, a small flattened box, lay like a doormat next to the sidewalk. It was a damp chilly night and this side street in Armenia – all the shop-windows shuttered – was as dark and windswept as a mountain pass.

'Where do you eat?'

'People give us food.'

I said, 'You should go home.'

'That is worse,' said the second boy.

'We can't go home,' said the black boy. 'It is too far and too difficult. We can live here.'

'It is not a good idea to live here, is it?'

'We have to.'

It was past midnight, but their replies were prompt; their intelligence was obvious and, for moments, it was possible to forget that they were small children. They were street-wise and as alert as adults; but there was nothing in this doorway they inhabited but that piece of cardboard. I had seen children begging in India, the mechanical request for a rupee, the rehearsed story; they were as poor and as lost. But the Indian beggar is unapproachable; he is fearful and cringing, and there is the language barrier. My Spanish was adequate for me to inquire about the lives of these little boys and every reply broke my heart. Though they spoke about themselves with an air of independence, they could not know how they looked, so sad and waif-like. What hope could they possibly have, living outside on this street? Of course, they would die; and anyone who used their small corpses to illustrate his outrage would be accused of having Bolshevik sympathies. This was a democracy, was it not? The election was last week; and there was no shortage of Colombians in Bogotá to tell me what a rich and pleasant country this was if you were careful and steered clear of muggers and gamins. What utter crap that was, and how monstrous that children should be killed this way.

We talked some more, but people passing had begun to stare at me. What was this, some pervert cajoling homeless boys into performing unspeakable acts? I went away, but I did not go far. About fifteen minutes later I walked by. The children were in the doorway, lying down. They slept over-lapping each other, like sardines, the smallest boy in the middle, the black boy using the flap of his jacket to keep out the cold – wrapping it around the other two. I was wearing my leather jacket; I was not warm. I watched the boys from a distance. They were restless and fidgeting, their bare legs outstretched. I walked to the corner and paused to let a car pass. When its sound died out I heard the smallest boy's cough, a deep dragging tubercular cough, followed by a harsh gasp.

Such children are not news. Armenia had a paper, and on the front page the next morning, with the news of the election – the votes were still being counted – was an item about an incident that had taken place in Columbus, Ohio. It triumphantly announced that a seven-hour operation had been performed to separate a pair of Siamese twins. Mark and Matthew Myers were now in satisfactory condition, said the doctor. 'Mark is kicking perfectly.' This was news: the freakish element suited the readers of this provincial paper – freaks had an abiding popularity all over Latin America. But it seemed more remarkable to me that children should sleep on cold nights in doorways, on strips of cardboard. They were not mentioned; they were not noticed: after all, the child in the doorway had the singular misfortune of having been born without two heads. There was nothing strange in Colombia about homeless children; because it was commonplace it had ceased to be seen as savage.

I turned the page. Here was a full-page advertisement for an expensive housing estate. *Who Says You Have To Leave The Country To Live California-style?* That was the headline. The houses were being built a mile from Armenia, a mile from that doorway. They were described in lush detail. They had 'fabulous interiors' and two-car garages. And for safety and convenience, the text went on, the estate would be completely walled-in.

The railway station in Armenia is a substantial yellow chunk of South American turn-of-the-century architecture, a Roman villa which, enhanced by shabby neglect, looks even more like a Roman villa. This railway gave Armenia, Medellin, and – by a circuitous route – Bogotá, access to the seaport of Buenaventura.

The trouble with the railway station – the trouble with so much in Colombia – was that people warned me away from it. 'Do not go there alone,' said the lady in the hotel. 'I would not go there alone.'

But I was travelling alone, I said.

'It is very dangerous.'

I asked why.

'Thieves.'

There were thieves, people told me, at the railway stations, at the bus stations, in the markets, the parks, on the hill paths, on the back streets, on the main streets. When I asked directions to a particular part of town, no directions were given. 'Do not go,' they said. On the Expreso de Sol, I was told Bogotá was dangerous. In Bogotá I said I was going to Armenia. 'Do not go – it is dangerous.' The railway station? 'Dangerous.' But the train was leaving at six in the morning. 'That is the worst time – the thieves will rob you in the dark.' How, then, should I get to Cali? 'Do not go to Cali – Cali is more dangerous than Armenia.'

I did not take these stories lightly. A tourist's warning is like the mugging story in New York: it is a whisper of fear rather than a report of actual experience. But a Colombian's warning about a place he knows well is something to heed. He has every reason to reassure the stranger and persuade him to linger. But the message of most Colombians was: Get out of town, hire a taxi, take a plane, go home.

This was impossible. I took the precaution of removing my watch when I went out. But as I never stayed more than a few nights anywhere I was usually on the move, with my suitcase and (credit cards were no help in the hinterland) several thousand dollars. I was easy game: I knew that, and this was why I had grown a moustache – that and my slicked-down hair would make me anonymous. The thieves, I was told, approached you in pairs. They stuck a knife in your ribs or they slashed open your suitcase. And I had been approached ('Con ere, meesta. Leesen – joo my fren . . .'); it annoyed me to be singled out, after having taken trouble with my disguise. But I was lucky – I ran, or I ducked out of sight. I was never robbed, in Colombia or anywhere else.

The persistent warnings about this threat of thieves gave me a fantasy that entertained me throughout Colombia. I was walking down a dark street with a pistol in my pocket. A thief accosted me and held a stiletto at me. Your money, he said. I pulled out my pistol and, getting the drop on him, robbed him of his last peso. So long, sucker. I chucked a cigarette at him and watched him creep away, pleading for his life.

But without this imaginary pistol I was nervous in Armenia. It was dangerous. I woke early and hurried through the dark slum to the far side of town. That was dangerous. The railway station, on its side street, contained huddled Indians and indistinct shadows. That was dangerous, too. I bought my ticket, jumped onto the train, found a corner seat and kept my head down until the train left. This Colombian train, by Colombian standards, was luxurious – much better than the Expreso de Sol which had taken me on that long haul from the coast. There were net curtains on the windows, and at this hour it was not crowded. With any luck I would meet the boastful Amazon-bound Frenchman in Cali and I would tell him that the train was thirty-five cents cheaper than the bus.

The hills had been visible from the streets of Armenia; the train drew out and we were in them, and I could see how, beyond this range of green ones, was another range of blue ones, and a third range of black ones, much higher and more sharply defined. We travelled through the Cauca Valley, past groves of fern-like bamboos: they were clumped against the river which ran the length of the country. I could see the road, too. The road crossed the railway and climbed the hillsides, but the railway kept to the straight line of the riverbank. The buses on the road heaved back and forth, then shot out of sight; the train moved at its turtle pace, chugging south, stopping frequently. We travelled into heat; I was encouraged, because this was the way to Patagonia, this rumbling south. It was the delays, and easterly and westerly traverses that exasperated me and made me think how mistaken I had been in Boston to assume that I could board a local train and arrive in Patagonia within a couple of months. I had been gone well over a month and where was I? On a sleepy train in a green and distant country. The people here had no notion of where Patagonia was.

This was a lush place – bananas and coffee growing together, cultivation as far as the eye could see. Where were the owners of these estates? I saw only the peasants: small huts, pigs, skinny horses, people living dustily among garbage, all of Colombia's blameless savagery. The grazing cows had trimmed the hills and meadows, so that the grass looked newly mowed, and each expanse had the manicure of a golf course. But this was hyperbole; unless it rained soon the entire area would become over-grazed and unable to support these herds.

At Tulua Station I bought a bottle of 'British'-brand soda water. I drank it on the train after we got underway. An old lady was watching me.

'It is hot here,' I said, self-conscious under her gaze.

She said, 'It is much hotter in Cali.'

'Really? I thought it was cool there.'

'Very hot. You will not like it.'

'You are from Cali?'

She smiled. 'Venezuela.'

'How long have you been travelling?' I asked.

'Two days. I flew to Bogotá. The bus to Armenia, and now this train. I am going to visit my sister. Why are you going to Cali?'

I had no answer for this. I had no good reason for going to Cali, other than the fact that it was south of Bogotá and on the way to Ecuador. If I told her my ultimate destination I felt she would ask me more unanswerable questions.

I said, 'I have a friend in Cali.'

The lie depressed me. I had no friend in Cali. Apart from some distant relations in Ecuador I did not know a single soul anywhere on this continent. I had been offered the addresses of people, but one of my rules of travel was to avoid looking up my friends' friends. In the past, I had done so reluctantly, and the results had been awkward, not to say disastrous. But travelling alone, a selfish addiction, is very hard to justify or explain.

'That is good,' said the woman. 'You will need a friend in Cali.'

This made my depression complete.

It was too hot to read. I had packed Boswell in my suitcase with my watch and my ring. I finished my soda water and looked at the men washing their trucks in the middle of the Rio Barragan. It was a tropical habit, the washing of motor vehicles in rivers; but this zone was both tropical and temperate. The green hills would not have looked unusual in the Catskills, except for the tall straight palms on their slopes, and the bananas, and that pig. We crossed into lower hills of shaggy green: bananas, chickens, and more pigs – it was impossible to look out of the window without thinking of breakfast.

After forty miles the hills became wilder still, and at sixty the climate had changed utterly. Now the hills were brown and overgrazed, and all the landscape sun-scorched, and no green thing anywhere. The bald hills, stripped of all foliage, were rounded on their slopes and had little wave-like shapes beating across them. It was a brown sea of hills, as if a tide of mud had been agitated and left to dry in plump peaks; this was the moment before they crumbled into cakes and dunes and dust slides. Glimmering beyond them was pastel flatness of diluted green – the cane fields which lie between the two cordilleras. From here to Cali, the cane fields widened, and at level crossings there were cane-cutters standing – there were too many of them to sit down – on the backs of articulated trucks, like convict labour. They had been up before dawn. It was four o'clock, and they were being taken home, through the fields they had cleared

What towns I had seen, from the forecourts of railway stations, had seemed unprepossessing. There were a few factories at Bugalagrande and dried-out fields of shrivelled corn. Every town's hills had a distinctive shape – Bugalagrande's were great slumping circus tents. At Tulua I saw two churches, one with the dome of Saint Peter's, the other like Rheims; but Tulua was an otherwise dismal-looking place, like the Moslem railway junctions in eastern Turkey, all dust and sun and huts and a mosque or two. There were signs near these Colombian stations, indicating a place or giving a traffic warning, and all included a piece of advertising. The effect could be odd: *National Police Institute Drink Coca-Cola; No Passing Smoke Hombre Cigarettes; Drive Slowly Bank of Colombia.* After the town of Buga (a grand old station, with waiting rooms lettered First Class and Second Class – but they were both equally empty and derelict), the tracks became perfectly straight; such straight tracks were always an indication that, with no hills ahead, we were moving directly into the heat, across the plains with nothing ahead but a wiggling mirage cast up from the swamp-scalded earth.

The sun was blazing through the net curtains. I could not change my seat, so I walked to the rear of the train and found an open shady door where I sat and smoked my pipe and watched the cane fields pass. Another man had the same idea. We talked awhile. He wore a crumpled hat, a faded shirt; no shoes. He said he was a coffee picker. He worked in Cali, but did not like picking coffee in Cali. The pay was poor and the coffee was not much good either. 'Armenia is where the best coffee comes from,' he said. 'It is the best in the whole of Colombia.' In Armenia the pay was better – the highest prices went for Armenia's coffee.

'How much do you earn in Cali?'

'Eighty pesos.' This was less than three dollars.

'A week? A day? A basket?'

'Eighty a day.'

'Why don't you get paid by the basket?'

'In some places they do. Not in Cali.'

'Is it hard work?'

'It is work,' he said, and smiled. 'I can tell you it is very hot.'

'How much did you make a day last year?'

'Sixty-four pesos.' Two dollars.

'And the year before that?'

'Fifty-six pesos.' A dollar fifty.

I said, 'So you get more every year.'

'But not enough. Do you know what it costs to buy meat, flour, eggs, vegetables?'

'You might get a hundred next year.'

'They get a hundred in Armenia now,' he said. 'Sometimes a hundred and fifty. That is why I went up there. I want to work in Armenia.'

'How many hours do you work?'

'All day.'

'You start early?'

'Oh, yes. We start early, we finish late.'

'I am sorry to ask you so many questions,' I said.

He used a nice Spanish phrase to excuse me. 'I am at your command, sir.'

'How much do you pay for half a kilo of coffee?' I asked.

'If you work on an estate it does not cost much,' he said.

Then I told him what a pound of coffee costs in the United States. At first he did not believe me, then he said, 'But, no matter what you say, we are still very poor in Colombia. Everything is expensive here and it just gets worse.' He shook his head. 'Look, that is Palmira. We will be in Cali soon.'

I had been glad to have my leather jacket in Bogotá and Armenia. Now, in this heat, it seemed absurdly out of place. At Cali I was so hot I inadvertently left it on the train and had to run back and retrieve it. I was walking across the platform when I noticed a porter talking rapidly and angrily to an old man with a sack of oranges. I pretended to tie my shoe-lace, and listened.

'I helped you with that thing,' said the porter. 'The least you can do is give me something.'

'I am not giving you anything. You did not do anything.'

'Five pesos,' said the porter. 'Give it!'

The old man turned away.

The porter, wringing his hands, walked ten steps. But he did not say anything.

The old man turned and showed his teeth. 'You are a son of a whore.'

The porter heard him. He turned. 'You are a whore and your mother was a black whore.' He saw me staring and said, 'Look at that stupid man!'

Cali ('Very dangerous') was so dull that, simply to keep myself occupied one afternoon, I bought a roll of dental floss and carefully flossed my teeth. Nor was I lucky with Cali's hotels; I stayed three nights in the city and each morning checked out of the madhouse I had slept in the night before and set off in search of a new one. I toured the churches and watched long lines of little old ladies waiting to have their confessions heard. What could their sins possibly be? *I have had evil thoughts, Father*. I inquired into Cali's recreations. 'If I were you I would go up to

Armenia,' said a Colombian in my second hotel. 'That is a lovely little town.' I told him I had already been to Armenia and that it had reminded me of the most poverty-stricken parts of India. This was always a conversation-stopper: no matter how poor the Colombian believed himself to be, he felt libelled by any comparison with another poor country.

There were hills to the south and west. On my last day in Cali, I bought a map of the district and plunged into the country-side, keeping to the mule-tracks and by-passing the highest hill, a sort of local Golgotha with three crosses erected on its peak. I hiked throughout the morning and when the sun was directly overhead saw a stream splashing into a gully. I had sandwiches but no water, so I hurried to this stream for a drink. On the far side was a shack, with a goat tethered to one wall. An old man stood near the shack, pitching stones into the stream. He seemed Wordsworthian until his aim grew better and I realized that he was throwing the stones at me. I went no farther. Now the man was mumbling and shouting; he was either a lunatic or had taken me for a tax-collector. I headed towards a different path and eventually found some water.

There were shacks all over these hills, in the most unlikely places, built against boulders and cave entrances, and at the bottom of sand pits. I came to fear them, because at each one there was a mangy dog which ran out and yapped at me, snarling into its paws. I was genuinely frightened of being bitten by one of these mutts: they had a crazy rabid look, and a bark from one excited barks from other dogs hidden all over the stony hillside. Giving these dogs a wide berth, I strayed from the mule-tracks; and then my map was no help. I guided myself back to Cali using the crosses on Golgotha as my landmarks.

I mentioned the dogs to a Colombian that evening. There seemed to be a lot of mutts in the hills, I said. Were they dangerous?

'*Some* of the dogs are dangerous,' he said. 'But *all* the snakes are deadly poisonous.'

'I did not see any snakes.'

'Maybe not. But they saw you.'

To celebrate my departure from Cali, I went to an expensive

Sunday-night buffet at one of the fancy restaurants. There was a group of American missionaries in the place, perhaps spending a weekend away from their mission. There were two enormous men, and two fat women, a pot-bellied boy and some smaller children; they were the sort of Bible-punching Baptists who are sometimes found bristling with poisoned arrows on a tributary of the upper Amazon, meddlesome mid-westerners groping and preaching their way through the blankest part of the South American map, only to meet, just in time for the church news-letter back home, a peculiarly grisly martyrdom. But tonight they were having a whale of a time: they made repeated trips to the buffet table, seconds, thirds, and then dessert. 'That pie is scrumptious!' The waiters looked on in bewilderment and in-credulity as they were asked to dismember another chicken or hack another cake apart. I wanted very badly to talk to the missionaries, but they kept to themselves – all ten of them, at a long table. In Costa Rica, on the Mosquito Coast, I had found the setting for a story about castaways; here, across the room at this hotel in southern Colombia, I saw who those castaways might be. God had sent them here.

The centrepiece of the buffet was a three-foot ice carving, a lyre-shaped object which melted slowly and dripped onto the tablecloth as the evening passed. It was interesting, because in the Cali slums and in the villages I had seen that afternoon there was no ice, and in some places nearby no water. Here, ice was frivolous decoration, and I found its foolish shape objectionable. Studying this piece of ice sculpture, I was accosted by a fat woman. At first, I thought she might be one of the missionaries. But no, she was speaking Spanish.

'What do you call these in English?' she asked.

'Oranges,' I said, feeling once again that my moustache was a failure.

'Narrishes,' she said, in Spanish, 'I want to learn English. You can teach me. These?'

'Grapes.'

'Crepes.'

'Good evening.' It was a man in black, with a dog-collar – a priest. 'Get your food, Maria,' he said. The woman smiled at me and then walked to the far end of the buffet table. 'She talks to everyone,' said the priest. 'You must forgive her. She is retarded.'

The woman was heaping her plate with food. She had a broad plain face and pale eyes, and the sort of unusual bulk, the benjy-fat you see in the mad and housebound, who do nothing but stare out of the window.

'Her father was very rich. He died two years ago,' said the priest. 'Extremely rich.' The priest made a noise, a slurp of pity.

'Is Maria in your parish?'

'Ah, no. She is all alone,' said the priest. 'I look after her.'

The priest had a matador's thin face and dark stare; he glanced at Maria, he glanced at me. He had an anxious smile and lines of suspicion set this smile in parenthesis. We were soon joined by a solemn man in a blue shirt.

'This is Father Padilla,' said the first priest. 'He is a Capuchin. Father Padilla, this gentleman is an American. You must excuse me while I see to Maria.' He hurried to the buffet; Maria had begun to talk to another stranger.

I turned to Father Padilla and said, 'You are not dressed like a priest.'

'We do not wear those clothes anymore,' he said. 'In Colombia it is not the custom.'

'Capuchins?'

'All.'

'But your friend,' I said, indicating the man in black, helping Maria with her plate, 'he is wearing his collar.'

Father Padilla frowned. 'He is not a priest.'

Strange: the priest in a sports shirt, the layman in a dog-collar. I said, 'He seems to be one.'

'He is a sort of helper, but not in my parish.'

The black-suited man looked up. Seeing that he had stopped filling her plate, Maria scolded him. The man jerked the tines of his fork into a slab of ham.

'She is rich?' I said.

'Very rich,' said Father Padilla. 'But in my district everyone is poor. They have nothing.'

I told him what I had seen in Armenia – the children in the doorway. How could such a situation be allowed to continue?

He said, 'It is incomprehensible to me that some people in this country are so rich and others so poor. It is a terrible situation. There are tens of thousands of children who live like that. Why is this so? I cannot explain it.'

The bogus priest came over with Maria. He guided her as if he was a zoo-keeper with a rare clumsy animal. He said, 'She wants to ask you a question.'

Maria was drooling. She held a silver implement in her hand. 'How do you say this in English?'

'Spoon.'

'Boon.' It was an infant's utterance. 'Come with me. You must eat with us at our table. You can teach me English.'

'I am sorry,' I said. 'I have to go.'

The bogus priest led her away.

Father Padilla watched them go. Then he said, 'I want you to know that I do not come here often. This is perhaps the second time. You understand?'

'Yes,' I said.

'Good luck on your travels,' he said. 'God be with you.'

15 The Autoferro to Guayaquil

In Central America and Colombia I had met a number of people, who were travelling north, who told me of the excitements of the Guayaquil and Quito Railway – the 'G and Q', or 'the Good and Quick', as it is known to those who have not ridden on it. It had taken thirty-seven years to build (it was finished in 1908), although it was less than 300 miles long. From an altitude of over 9,000 feet at Quito, the Autoferro – a converted bus welded to a railway undercarriage – rises another 3,000 feet at Urbina and then drops down a series of confined switchbacks and loops (the Devil's Nose double zig-zag! the Alausi Loop!) to sea-level at the steamy southern port of Guayaquil. I had no difficulty getting information about it; the station was nearby, service was frequent and a ticket cost no more than a few dollars. I was confident that this trip would be easy; confidence made me procrastinate. I agreed to give a lecture in Quito; people at that lecture invited me to parties; I went to the parties and tried to be amusing. The train could wait: I would be on it any day now.

The weather in Quito was a source of wonder to me. It made ceaseless adjustments throughout the day. There were times when the cloud hung so low over the city that it seemed as if I could reach up and peel wisps of vapour from the ceiling of the sky. I lived on a hill and could see a zone of clear air and, just above it, this lowering cloud. The mornings were often sunny, the afternoons grey, and in the evening some cloud settled and another tide of it rolled across the city, putting out the lights in houses, blurring the neon signs, and finally obscuring the yellow street-lamps, until Quito seemed an uninhabited place, or less, merely a chute of air down which whorls of opaque fluff tumbled. One morning it drizzled, and very tiny birds – the size of cuckoos in cuckoo clocks: but they were hummingbirds – crouched in the branches of a bush, each bird requiring no more than the shelter of a small leaf to keep it dry.

In spite of the cold, and the altitude that made me breathless, I enjoyed Quito. Of all the mountain-top cities in South America, Quito struck me as being the happiest, and in retrospect Bogotá seemed a cruel towering place, like an eagle's nest now inhabited by vultures and their dying prey. Quito looked altogether cheerier, a plateau of church steeples, with light-coloured houses scattered across the slopes of the mountain which rose above it, and on the higher harder-to-reach slopes of Pichincha were the huts of the very poor who could see Peru from their doorways. But Quito had subtleties that were not discernible to me; a month after I had decided that it was one of the pleasantest places I had seen, and one of the fairest (there were no political prisoners in Ecuador), bus fares were raised to six cents and every bus in the city was destroyed by rioters.

'You must not judge people by their country,' a lady advised me. 'In South America, it is always wise to judge people by their altitude.'

She was from Bolivia herself. She explained that there were fewer national characteristics than|high-level characteristics. The mountain people who lived on the heights of the Andes were formal and unapproachable; the valley people were much more hospitable, and the sea-level folk were the sweetest of all, though rather idle and lazy. Someone who lived at an altitude of about 4,000 feet was just about ideal, a really good scout, whether he lived in Ecuador, Peru, Bolivia, or wherever.

I gave a lecture in Quito and dined out on it for days, meeting writers and teachers and Coca-Cola salesmen. Quito has one of the best bookshops in South America, but I bought no books: my new friends pressed books into my hands, and instead of catching the train to Guayaquil I read the books and stared at humming-birds. A few days after I arrived I expressed a vague wish to see some of Quito's churches (there are eighty-six), and immediately found myself being chauffeured around to these holy places.

In the Italian-style, Jesuit church, called La Compañia, there was a painting of Hell. From a little distance this mural seemed to me an accurate representation of a night-time football game in

El Salvador, but on closer inspection it was pure Bosch, Hell's great amphitheatre depicted in detail. Schoolchildren in Quito are brought to the church and shown this mural, so that suitably terrified they will stay on the straight and narrow. Each sin is labelled and the sinners receive appropriate punishment: the shrieking adulteress is being eaten by a wild hog; the impure man is having fire poured through a funnel in his mouth, and a fire-breathing dog is scorching his genitals with flames; the vain woman wears a necklace of scorpions, the drunkard is made to guzzle boiling oil, the tongue of the gossip is bitten by a snake, a giant scorpion smothers the unjust man; money-lenders, with unmistakably Semitic faces, are made into mincemeat, embezzlers chopped into bits, gluttons choking on garbage, liars stretched on the rack. Lettered in gold across the top of the mural was a quotation from Luke (13:3) in Spanish: *Unless you repent, you will all likewise perish.*

The horror of the punishments is much greater than anything in Dante's Hell. The impartial beastliness more likely derives from that described by Saint Teresa of Avila, the Spanish nun whose *Confessions* include a terrifying vision of hell. Saint Teresa was canonized the same year the Compañia church was founded, 1622. I imagined that such a mural was most effective in persuading Indians to keep the faith. Indians, certainly, comprised the largest number of church-goers in Quito, and there were Indian – that is, Inca – touches in the artistry of these churches. A quarter of the decoration in the Church of San Francisco was Inca. The church itself was built on the site of Atahuallpa's summer residence; the Inca motifs occur throughout the church – two sun gods carved on gold discs as soon as you enter the door are repeated on the walls of the interior, with fruit and flowers, the Inca harvest symbols decorating saints and crucifixion scenes. The Stations of the Cross are Spanish, the masks fixed to the walls above them are the large gold faces, some with headdresses that one sees in miniature on Inca jewellery – with exaggerated up-turned or down-turned mouths, like masks of comedy and tragedy.

These churches were filled with Indians on their knees, praying in ponchos and shawls, carrying papooses. In the Church of

Santo Domingo they were lighting candles, in San Francisco they were doing the stations on their knees, and at La Compañia they were venerating the guitar of Ecuador's first saint – Saint Mariana de Jesus – who was so beautiful she went through life wearing a dark veil. It is said that a man once lifted this veil and beneath it he saw the grinning skull of Saint Mariana, which was God's way of showing him that he had trespassed. No one could explain the guitar; a guitar requires no explanation in South America. The Indians gazed on it; they were small, stout, bandy-legged, with thick black hair, like kindly trolls. They walked bent-over even when they were carrying nothing: it is a carrier's posture.

Almost half the population of Ecuador are Indians, but it seems like more than that, for the nature of their jobs makes them conspicuous. They sell tangerines and relics, cigarettes, sweets, and matches on every street; they work as cooks, gardeners, and day-labourers on building sites – living in the half-made house until it is finished, and then moving to the foundations of one being planned. In the smartest suburban street, father, mother and child can be seen gathering firewood and picking through dustbins. In a crowd of Ecuadorians the Indians can be spotted immediately: they are the burdened ones and are known by their bundles.

'Someone should do something about them,' a man said to me. 'You see a little man and he's always got a band around his head and carrying a huge bundle and walking uphill. If only there was something they could be given to help them.'

'Wheels?' someone suggested.

'Wheels wouldn't work on those mountain paths,' said the first man.

'A sort of sled,' said a woman. 'They could pull it.'

'Never get it uphill,' said the man.

I said, ' I suppose they could be provided with another Indian.'

My mocking suggestion was treated with the utmost seriousness.

'What you've got to understand,' said another man, 'is that as soon as an Indian puts on a pair of shoes he's not an Indian anymore.'

The Ecuadorian writer, Jorge Icaza, told me that it was the Indianness in Ecuadorian novels that made them Ecuadorian. Everything else was fakery and imitation. His own novel, *Huasipungo*, is full of Indian folklore and locutions: deliberately so, he said – he did not want to write a Spanish American novel or a European-style novel, but rather a truly South American epic. For this, he said, he had to invent an idiom and thereby start a tradition. 'I can tell you, this did not please the Academy at all.'

I had planned to ride the train to Guayaquil on this day, too, but it had not taken much to persuade me to change my plans and have lunch with three elderly Ecuadorian writers instead. Besides Icaza, who trembled and brooded and told me he had given up on North American writers ('These books say nothing to me'), there was Benjamin Carrión and Alfredo Pareja. Pareja, the youngest, looked like a Kentucky colonel and had travelled widely in the States. Carrión was in his eighties and reminded me of the actor Alastair Sim, the venerable and the gaga intermingled on his wondering face. They wore pinstripe suits and carried canes. In my drip-dry shirt and leakproof shoes I felt like a very small stockholder who had been granted an interview by the chairman of the board. Indeed, Carrión was the chairman of a daily newspaper he had founded.

They were in agreement on one point: the last interesting writer that America had produced was John Steinbeck. After that, all American writing had become unreadable.

Before I could get my shovel in, Icaza said that all literature was a struggle, each word was a struggle; and he described the composition of *Huasipungo*.

I mentioned Borges.

'No, no, no,' said Icaza.

'Borges said that the Argentine tradition was the whole of Western culture,' I said.

'Borges is mistaken,' said Carrión.

'We don't think much of Borges,' said Icaza.

Pareja looked unsure, but said nothing.

I said, 'I've always wanted to meet him.'

'Look,' said Carrión, 'it is the sales that matter. You have to be accepted. You have to make your name known or no one will look at you.'

He enlarged on this theme, and it really was like the board-room of a South American company which had not shown much profit lately. Icaza and Pareja deferred to Carrión who was saying that critics' praise meant nothing if no one read your books. Publishing was a business, publishers were businessmen and had to make money to survive. And of course authors had to sell their books in order to be recognized. He knew. He was on the Latin American panel of the Nobel Prize Committee. He had put forward many worthy authors, but the Nobel Prize people always said, 'Who is this fellow? We've never heard of him.'

It was a problem, said Icaza.

Yes, that was a serious problem, said Pareja. It ought to be looked into.

I wanted to mention Borges again, but I felt I would get a dusty answer. Then I realized that Pareja was talking to me. The trouble with American writers, he said, was that he always identified them with American politics – with the United States government, Nixon, Vietnam. He did not find anything of interest in American politics, so he found the books unrewarding.

I said that American novels – the good ones – were quite separate from American politics.

'To me they are the same,' he said.

'Aren't you confusing the hunter with the fox?' I said.

No, he didn't think so. The others agreed with him, so on this note the board meeting was adjourned.

'Maybe they thought you were criticizing them,' an American political officer told me the next day.

I said I had tried to be tactful and had only mentioned Borges out of an abiding admiration for his work.

'Latin Americans are funny,' he said. 'They hate to be criticized. They can't take it – so don't do it. They loathe criticism, or what they *think* is criticism. The Ecuadorian government is a kind of triumvirate of dictators – the army, the navy, the air force – three generals. When they think they're being criticized they plant dynamite near the critic's house and make an explosion.'

That sounded serious, I said.

'No, no,' he said. 'No one gets hurt. It's just a reminder. The only fatality so far was a critic who had a heart attack when he heard the blast.'

On this man's office wall there was a map of Ecuador. But it did not resemble in the least my map of Ecuador. The man explained that it was an Ecuadorian map and that half the territory was actually Peru. The Ecuadorian maps of Peru and the Peruvian maps of Ecuador were also radically different, each country showing itself as very large and in possession of an Amazonian province.

This man was such a fund of information, I asked him about the Indians. Well, he said, there were very few Inca noblemen and they used the Indians as cheap labour. The Spaniards conquered and replaced the Inca noblemen, using the Indians in the same way. The situation had not changed very much: the Indians were still on the bottom, and because they were mostly illiterate they could not vote.

'I'm surprised the Indians don't strangle these people,' I said.

There had been stranglings in Quito ever since I had arrived. The next day the strangler was caught. The story was in the newspaper *El Universo* under the title *Obsessed With Ties*. The murderer was a homosexual, but there were greater revelations. He found his victims by dressing as a woman (he was shown wearing an assortment of female wigs in a series of photographs). He had strangled four men. His statement to the police was paraphrased by the paper: 'When he had a sexual relationship with a distinguished person, or one wearing a tie, he had a desire to strangle him, while with other people he was perfectly normal.'

'Things are looking up,' said the American writer Moritz Thomsen. The author of *Living Poor* and *The Farm on the River of Emeralds* – two superb books that put Thomsen in a class with the Patagonian resident, W. H. Hudson – he has lived in one of the wilder districts of Ecuador for fourteen years. 'If you drive in some parts of Ecuador the Indians throw rocks at you. Lots of people get their windshields broken.' He grinned and narrowed his blue eyes. 'So I guess there's hope for a revolution.'

It was Moritz who said to me one afternoon on a Quito street,

'I don't get it, Paul. How do you write a travel book if all you do is go to parties?'

'Write about the parties?' I said. But he was dead right, and I was ashamed of myself. I vowed to take the train to Guayaquil the next day.

There was no train the next day. Mr Keiderling at the American Embassy had the solution. I would be flown to Guayaquil providing I gave a lecture there. He would cable the office in Guayaquil and ask them to get a ticket for me on the Autoferro back to Quito. 'It's the same train,' he said. 'It's just a different direction.'

That seemed all right to me, so I flew to Guayaquil.

Visitors to Guayaquil are urged to raise their eyes, for on a clear day it is possible to see the snowy hood of Mount Chimborazo from the humid streets of this stinking city; and, if you look down, all you see is rats. Chimborazo was shrouded in dense yellow-brown air which throughout the day spat discoloured rain and kept pedestrians sheltering under the shops that overhung the pavements. There were torrents of rain at night, but neither the spittle nor the downpour had any effect on the rats. Rats can swim, they can tread water for three days and gnaw through cinder blocks and climb vertical walls; they can live for days without food and can endure extremes of heat and cold; they are vicious, fearless and robust, and their breeding habits make them very nearly indestructible. They are probably alone among vermin in being noisy creatures: they have no real stealth. They don't sneak, but rather stumble carelessly with a kind of tottering half-derailed motion. Rats within thirty yards or so announce themselves: they chatter and squabble constantly, leaping at each other. They are too evil to require any cunning.

In Guayaquil, they are of the species *Rattus rattus*, the black or ship rat, which carried the Black Death – bubonic plague – from Asia to Europe. The plague was intermittent in Europe for four hundred years, and in the late eighteenth century it began to move back, via the Middle East, to Asia. It is thought that the plague ended in Europe because the black rats were driven out by a hardier unsociable species, but one less dangerous to humans, the brown rat (*Rattus norvegicus*). The black, flea-ridden rats boarded ships and in the hot, wet, port cities of Africa and South America they thrived, bringing plague, which is still endemic on these continents. I could get no figures on death by plague in Guayaquil – the question was considered discourteous – but people do die there from the bite of the rat-flea. It is a short, horrible sickness: you are bitten and two days later you die.

There was a louvred panel on the upper wall of my Guayaquil hotel room. For two nights I was kept awake by the chirp of a fan belt. It would start in the darkness, the chirping of a band slipping on an un-oiled wheel. I mentioned this to the manager.

'There is no fan in your room,' he said.

I went back to the room and stood on a chair and held a match to the louvred panel. What I had taken to be an air-conditioning device was a nest of rats – there were three of them, pattering and chirping in the dirt behind the panel.

'There are rats in my room,' I said to the manager.

'Ah, yes,' he said. He was not surprised. I waited for him to say more, but he only smiled.

I said, 'Suppose we give the rats that room. They seem very happy there.'

'Yes,' said the manager in a tentative way. He didn't see my irony at all.

'The rats can have that one, and I'll move to a different one.'

'You want to change your room, is that it?'

But all the rooms in this expensive hotel (it was named after a famous rat-hunting German explorer and naturalist) smelled of rats. It was a smell of chewed clothes and droppings and damp, and it was in every corner. And one could easily see where the rats had gnawed through walls and ceilings.

I had been eager to go to Guayaquil: I had distant relatives there. In 1901, my great-grandfather had left his village of Agazzano near Piacenza in northern Italy and gone to New York with his wife and four children. His name was Francesco Calesa, and he found New York disgusting and America a great disappointment. Twenty days on the steamship *Sicilia* had been bad enough, Christmas on Ellis Island was purgatorial; New York was pure hell. He had been heading for a farming job in Argentina, but a yellow fever outbreak in Buenos Aires made him change his plans. Perhaps he had hoped to do some farming in America, but he was fifty-two and had no money. His situation was hopeless. When he could bear it no longer he made plans to go back to Italy. His wife, Ermengilda, resisted and finally refused to go with him. So the marriage was fractured: he returned to Piacenza where his married daughter was living (she had fled America with her husband a year before); his wife stayed in New York City, raised the rest of the children alone, and introduced a strain of stubborn singlemindedness into the family. My greataunt, who remained in Italy, had a daughter Maria Ceruti, who married into a Chiavari family called Norero. The Noreros were distinguished as doctors and they had risen by establishing themselves in Ecuador – in Guayaquil, where they manufactured biscuits, sweets, pasta and spaghetti. They became prominent in Ecuador, and they brought this notoriety back to Chiavari. I had no problem finding them in Guayaquil. Everyone knew the Noreros. The only surprise was that I, a stranger, should be related to this now powerful family.

I met Domingo Norero at the family factory, La Universal. It was a large building – the city had few of them. A strikingly beautiful Italian girl was with him: his sister, Annamaria, on a visit from Italy. It was not easy to explain the family connection, but the place-name Chiavari was like a password. Annamaria lived in Chiavari, Domingo too had a house there, and their mother was there at the moment.

In his third-floor office, which was penetrated with the smell of chocolate biscuits, we had a family reunion. Domingo, a tall, thin, rather English-looking fellow, remembered my grandmother's visit to Italy. His grandfather had started the factory in Guayaquil, and on the death of this pioneer the business had passed to Vicente, Domingo's father. Ill-health, and an interest in Inca history, caused Vicente to retire; now he added to his already large collection of Pre-Colombian art and he wrote historical monographs on the subject – he had recently published, in Italian, *Pre-Colombian Ecuador*, a history. Domingo, only twenty-seven, had married at nineteen; his wife was blonde and bird-like, their two children as handsome as princelings. His yacht, the *Vayra*, was moored on the River Guayas, his Chevy Impala was parked at the factory, his jeep and his Mercedes were at his villa in the outskirts of town. But he was, for all his wealth, a modest person, if a bit rueful that the running of the entire business had fallen to him.

'I had no idea I had so many relatives in the States,' he said. 'But do you know how many cousins you have in South America? There are Noreros all over the continent – Chile is full of them.'

It gave me pause. These tycoons and walled-in businessmen I had seen, and cursed, in Colombia and Ecuador – they were perhaps my own flesh and blood. The proof was the Villa Norero. It was the sort of estate I had been seeing all through Central America and this part of South America, and it had made me doubtful that the old order would change. This one was Moorish in design, with Arabian tiles and pillars, and a swimming pool in the landscaped grounds – lemon trees, palms, and formal flower beds. The motto over the door on the family crest read: *Deus Lo Vulte* – 'God Wishes It' or 'God's Will'.

We had a drink, and I talked with old Vicente, a dignified man who was president of the Guayaquil branch of the Garibaldi Club. Vicente was the spitting-image of Giorgio Viola, the Garibaldino of Conrad's *Nostromo*. Conrad, in his previous incarnation – Captain Korzeniowski – had been here, and in *Nostromo* he reinvented Ecuador as Costaguana, Guayaquil as Sulaco and the volcano Chimborazo as Mount Higuerota. No one looked more at home in Ecuador than Vicente Norero, and he would not have looked out of place in Conrad's novel, either. He inscribed one of his books for me and we set off in two cars for the Guayaquil Yacht Club. The previous day I had passed it alone and had not seen a club; the rats tumbling out of bushes and screeching around the river-front path had held my attention.

Lunch lasted the afternoon. As we talked and ate I could see the river out of the window. It was wide, and great tufted mats of weed – 'lettuces' as the locals call them – floated on its surface, and logs and tree branches. Such flotsam and jetsam made it seem more a monsoon flood carrying the landscape away, than a river. But, though Guayaquil seemed a thoroughly nasty place, the family reunion had taken away much of its sting, even if it reminded me of my link with these adventurers. We were all profiteering in the New World, even I with my leakproof shoes and my notebooks was plundering the place with my eyes and hoping to export a few impressions.

Annamaria was in business, too. Her husband and two children were in Italy. This was a business trip, she told me, in Genoese-accented Italian. 'I do a lot of business,' she said. I make parts for toilets, and also disposable injections – one jab and you throw them away. And these.' She shook ringlets out of her eyes and reached across the table, picking up an empty bottle with delicate fingers. 'I make bottles. I make everything.'

'You make money?' I asked.

'Yes, money – I make money,' she said, and laughed. 'But I like to cook very much at home.'

'You haven't said why you came to Guayaquil,' said Domingo to me.

My train explanation was too complicated. I said I was giving a lecture at the local cultural centre and then planned to take the Autoferro back to Guayaquil.

'That's nice,' said Annamaria, 'if you only do it once.'

They pointed out the railway station, which was across the messy river, in Duran. They said that they had never taken the train themselves, but this did not surprise me. I had been in Latin America long enough by now to know that there was a class stigma attached to the trains. Only the semi-destitute, the limpers, the barefoot ones, the Indians, and the half-cracked yokels took the trains, or knew anything about them. For this reason, it was a good introduction to the social miseries and scenic splendours of the continent.

'I hope you come to Guayaquil again,' said Domingo, and then we parted: the Noreros to their profitable pursuits and I to profitless gassing – a lecture on American literature.

And the ticket I had been promised? 'We tried to get you a seat,' said the embassy's man in Guayaquil. 'But it's full for the next few days. If you want to stick around Guayaquil for a while we could probably get you on, but don't hold me to it.'

'Why is this train so popular?' I asked.

'It's not popular, it's just small.'

One night in Guayaquil, a middle-aged Irishman in a loud check suit said to me, 'You probably won't believe what I'm going to tell you.'

'Give me a chance,' I said. His manner was benign, his voice gentle, and he had the sartorial inelegance of a man not used to matching the suit with the tie. With his directness was a whispered intimacy, of a soulful searching kind. I guessed that he had been a priest.

'I was a Jesuit priest,' he said. 'In the priesthood for fifteen years, I was. I served my novitiate in Ireland and Rome, and after I was ordained I went to the States. I was in Ecuador for a while as a missionary, then I had a parish in New York. I used to go to Belfast every now and then to see my family. It was very bad in '72 – "Bloody Sunday", British atrocities. My brother was tortured, my sister burned out of her house. I was really shaken. "Preach love to your fellow-men," they say, but how could I preach love to my fellow-men after what I had seen? Of course, it didn't all happen like that – it didn't hit me overnight. I had had doubts for seven years, but after that trip I was in bad shape. When I got back to New York, I went to my bishop and told him I wanted to have a six-month leave of absence. It's quite a normal thing, you know. Priests are human. They drink too much sometimes, they have personal problems – they need time to sort themselves out. With a leave of absence I would have no duties. I didn't have to say mass, only assist at mass. You know what I'm telling you.

'My bishop was flabbergasted. He couldn't believe what I was telling him. He said he had made a list of doubtful priests. He had actually drawn up this list of priests – fellers he thought would be leaving the priesthood sooner or later. And the funny thing was – I wasn't on the list. But he gave me a leave of absence all the same, and he said to me, "You'll be back."

'I had time on my hands – assisting at mass didn't take any

time at all. So I got a job selling insurance. Was I good at it! I sold policies all over New York. Being a priest helped, I suppose – you can't beat the sincere manner if you want to sell insurance. I didn't care much about the money. It was the people that interested me, talking to them in their homes. And they didn't know I was a priest. I was a salesman you see, flogging my policies.

'At the end of six months I went back to my bishop and asked him for another leave of absence. He was surprised, oh yes, but I hadn't been on his list. He even smiled at me and said again, "I know you'll be back." But I knew I wouldn't.

'It's so easy to be a priest, isn't it? Well, you wouldn't know about that. But it is easy. All your needs are taken care of. There's no rent to pay, no food to buy. No cooking, no cleaning. You get presents. "Need a car, Father?" "Here's a little something for you, Father." "Anything we can do, Father? Just name it." I didn't want that, and I didn't want to go on selling insurance – in a way, that was like being a priest, too. I couldn't go home, and I couldn't stay in New York. I knew one thing – I wanted out.

'I made a last visit to Belfast, saw the family, and the political things were just as bad as ever. My brother saw me to the plane, and as we were walking along I thought: You'll never see me again. That was the hardest thing I've ever done. It was harder than leaving the priesthood – turning my back on my brother and walking to the plane.

'I came straight to Ecuador. I had always been happy here and I had friends here. That was five years ago. I married an Ecuadorian. I've never been so happy in all my life. We have a child of fourteen months and one on the way – that's why my wife isn't with me tonight.

'Do I go to church? Of course, I do. I left the priesthood – I didn't leave the church. I never miss mass. I go to confession. You see, when I go to confession I'm not talking to the priest, I'm talking to God. I've got a job here. It's not a very important job, but I'll be here for some time.

'The hardest thing is not being able to tell anyone. How do you say, "I left the priesthood. I am married. I have children"? No one knows. It would be terrible for my mother. But funny things happen, strange things. My sister wrote to me a few years ago. She said, "If you ever decide to go over the wall, we'll understand." Why did she say that? And last Christmas, my other sister sent me some money. "You might need this," she says. She had never done that before – priests don't need money. But I can't face my mother. I think I have always taken suffering on myself to save other people from suffering. Would my mother understand this? I don't understand the depth of her under-standing. You know what I'm telling you. It's a great pity. I dream about going home. In one of these dreams, I'm in Belfast. I see my old house and I walk up to the front door. But I can't go in – I'm frozen there on the steps, and I have to walk away. I have this dream every week.

'Oh, yes, I write home all the time. My letters – these letters about myself in Ecuador, the parish and so forth – they're masterpieces. Not a word of truth in them. I know my brother and sisters would understand, but I think it would kill my mother. She's over eighty, you see. She wanted me to be a priest. She lives for me. But, when she dies, I'll leave for Belfast the next day – I'll be on that plane like a shot. That's what hurts me most. That she can't know about me. And I can't ever see her again.

'Do you think I should write about it? I wish I could, but I can't write. I'll tell you what, Paul – you write it. It would make a good story, wouldn't it?'

To that Irishman, the Indians were sorely-pressed people who had not been given a chance; to Jorge Icaza, the Indians had the key to all culture; to my distant cousins, the Noreros, the Indians had real distinction and their past had been glorious; to most others, the Indians were hewers of wood and drawers of water and, on the whole, bumpkins.

I heard another view in Guayaquil. Mr Medina was a spinster-ish and rather thorny Ecuadorian, with a thin moustache and a narrow head and severe grey eyes. His tie was tightly knotted, his trousers perfectly creased, the toes of his shoes polished and very sharp – it was hard to believe that there were five toes under those claw-like points. We had begun by talking about rats. Some people poisoned the rats, or trapped them, he said, but there was a better method. You used a high-pitched whine that was not audible to the human ear. It had the effect of driving the rats away – they found the noise unbearable. The local flour mills had been beset by rats, but this high-pitched whine – I think he called it 'sonar' – had been a success. Sometimes, rats were locked into rooms with the sound, and in the morning they were found dead: the sound had tortured them to death.

'Juke-boxes have that effect on me,' I said. 'Especially Ecuadorian juke-boxes.'

'You cannot hear this sound, though apparently it gives some women headaches,' he said. 'I wish there was something like this they could use on the Indians.'

'What a neighbourly idea,' I said.

He gave me a thin smile. 'Ecuador's problem is a race problem,' he said. 'The Indians are lazy. They are not like your Indians. Sometimes they cut their hair and work, but not often. There are no poor people in Ecuador – there are only Indians. They are uneducated and unhealthy.'

'Why don't you educate them, then? Provide doctors and schools. That's why they're wandering forlornly around Quito and Guayaquil – they think that they can find in the cities what they lack in the countryside.'

'They have no idea why they come to Guayaquil. They don't know what to do here. They sell a few things, they beg, some work, but they are all lost. They were always lost.'

'Even before the Spanish came?'

'Definitely. The Inca Empire was over-rated.'

'Who agrees with you?' I asked.

'Most people do, but they are afraid to say it. If you stayed here longer you would agree with me. The Incas – who were they? They had no great culture, no literature, nothing. It did not impress the Spaniards, it does not impress me even now. I don't know what these people are talking about when they show these pots and masks. Can't they see how crude these things are? The Incas weren't warriors – they didn't fight the Spaniards. They were simply overpowered.'

I said that the Spaniards had arrived at a period of civil war. Atahuallpa had usurped the Inca throne from his brother. The people were fatalistic – they thought the Spaniards had been sent to punish them. It wasn't hard to conquer people who believed they were guilty already.

'They were a degenerate race,' said Mr Medina.

'The Incas had a system of social security that was a damn sight better than anything Ecuador has produced.'

'They were what you see – lazy people with a different mentality.'

'Different from yours, you mean?'

'And from yours. This talk about the Incas in Ecuador is nonsense – Ecuador history is Spanish history, not Indian history.'

'That sounds like an epitaph,' I said. 'Whose grave will it be written on?'

Mr Medina was growing impatient with me. He gathered his fingers together and rapped the table and said, 'Do you know what fetishism is? That is their religion – fetishism. They have to see the statue and touch the cross. It comes from their own religion and it is horrible to see. They do not believe what they can't see. That is why they touch the holy things and grovel in the church.'

I said, 'People do that in Boston, Massachusetts.'

'Stay in Guayaquil,' he said. 'You will change your mind.'

But I could not think of any reason for staying in Guayaquil. Moreover, the Autoferro on which I was supposed to have a seat remained booked up. If I went back to Quito, I was told, I could then take the Autoferro back to Guayaquil and fly to Peru. I decided to do this and left the very next day, and it was arriving in Quito on that plane that reminded me of the hopelessness of air travel and how futile it would be if every arrival and departure were recorded in the out-of-the-window glimpse: *Beneath us, lay the folded fabric of ploughed fields, the toy-town appearance of a city in the Andes* . . . No, anything but that. If I was to travel it would be overland, where every sight and every place had its own smell; and I knew that if I wrote about what was minuscule out of the window of a jet I would sound like a man on the moon.

Back in Quito, the people I had met the previous week welcomed me as if I was an old friend. The temporariness of travel often intensifies friendship and turns it into intimacy. But this is fatal for a man with a train to catch. It sounds, as I write this, as if I am coyly hinting that I enjoyed a passionate affair that was keeping me from moving on. ('Just one more day, my darling, and then you may break my heart and go . . .') It wasn't that. It was a simpler, tidier business, but it still meant delay. I could handle strangers, but friends required attention and made me feel conspicuous. It was easier to travel in solitary anonymity, twirling my moustache, puffing my pipe, shipping out of town at dawn; and South America was a problem in geography that could only be understood if one kept moving: to stay put was to be baffled. People complained of the barbarism of the places, but as far as I was concerned they were not barbarous enough.

'Ecuador is nice, in its tiny way,' the writer V. S. Pritchett had told me before I set off. It is, and I felt certain that I would return, for when at last I got my train ticket, the Autoferro left without me.

16 The Tren de la Sierra

The name of the lovely cream-coloured railway station in Lima is Desamparados, which means 'forsaken'. But the word seems a piece of baseless gloom until the Tren de la Sierra has crossed the plains to Chosica and climbed the pink walls of the narrow Rimac Valley; here, the passengers begin to fall ill. I knew from my palpitations in Bogotá and my wheezy indolence in Quito that I was a candidate for altitude sickness; the rising gorge I experienced on the way to Ticlio was as much a feature of the landscape as a physical symptom: I suffered as we ascended the Andes, and I decided that no railway journey on earth can be so aptly described as going on *ad nauseam*.

A strike was threatened by the railway workers in Peru, but though this was no more than a rumour, the warning was substantiated by streaks of graffiti dripping from the mellow outside walls of churches and cloisters: *Down with the Imperialists and Oppressors, Support the Railway Workers* and *More Money!* Repeatedly in this large impromptu script was the word *Strike*, but the Spanish word for strike is also the word for rest or leisure, so all over Lima the exhortation could also be read as *Relax!* If the railway workers had been undeserving louts using a period of political confusion in order to make unreasonable demands, I would have been more confident of my chances to see the strike forestalled by the intervention of some sweet-talking arbitrators. But this was not play-acting; the railway workers – indeed, workers all over Peru – were grossly underpaid. Elsewhere in Latin America, the provocations or simple pleas of workers had been checked; where the charade of elections failed, the soldiers and police succeeded. Peru, once a golden kingdom occupying a third of the continent, had taken a mighty tumble and in defeat looked incapable of supplying those muttering workers with any hope. Few great cities in the world look more plundered and bankrupt than Lima. It is the look of Rangoon, the same heat and colonial relics and corpse-odours: the imperial parades have long ago marched away from its avenues and left the spectators to scavenge and beg. Ever since Mexico, the description 'formerly an important Spanish city, famous for its architecture' made me stiffen in apprehension, but no city had fallen as far as Lima. Like a violated tomb in which only the sorry mummy of withered nationalism is left, and just enough religion to console a patient multitude with the promise of happier pickings beyond the grave, Lima – epitomizing Peru – was a glum example of obnoxious mismanagement. Official government rhetoric was dispirited and self-deceiving, but the railway workers' anger was sharpened by their sense of betrayal, and their hunger.

I felt that any strike here would be a protracted affair, and so I left Lima on the train to Huancayo the first chance I got. After arriving at that railhead in the mountains I would make my way by road via Ayacucho to Cuzco and there begin my long descent through Bolivia and Argentina to the end of the line in Patagonia. It was a hasty plan, but how could I know that in three days I would be back in Lima trying to find another route to Cuzco?

The Rimac river flowed past the railway station. At seven in the morning it was black; it became grey as the sun moved above the foothills of the Andes. The sandy mountains at the city's edge give Lima the feel of a desert city hemmed-in on one side by hot plateaux. It is only a few miles from the Pacific Ocean, but the land is too flat to permit a view of the sea, and there are no sea breezes in the day-time. It seldom rains in Lima. If it did, the huts – several thousand of them – in the shanty town on the bank of the Rimac would need roofs. The slum is odd in another way; besides being entirely roofless, the huts in this (to use the Peruvian euphemism) 'young village' are woven from straw and split bamboo and cane. They are small frail baskets, open to the stars and sun, and planted beside the river which, some miles from the station, is cocoa-coloured. The people wash in this river water; they drink it and cook with it;

and when their dogs die, or there are chickens' entrails to be disposed of, the river receives this refuse.

'Not that they eat chickens very often,' explained the Peruvian in the train. The river, he said, was their life-line and their sewer.

Travelling across this plain it is not immediately apparent how any penetration can possibly be made into the escarpment at the far end – it seems too steep, too bare, too high; the valleys are no more than vertical cracks and there is no evidence of trees or men anywhere in these mountains. They have been burned clean of vegetation and have the soft bulge of naked rock. For twenty-five miles the mountain walls remain in the distance; the train seems deceptively quick, rolling along the river, and then at Chosica it stops. It resumes after five minutes, but never again on the trip does it regain that first burst of speed.

We entered the valley and zig-zagged on the walls. It was hardly a valley. It was a cut in the rock, a slash so narrow that the diesel's hooter hardly echoed: the walls were too close to sustain an answering sound. We were due at Huancayo at four o'clock; by mid-morning I thought we might arrive early, but at noon our progress had been so slow I wondered whether we would get to Huancayo that day. And long before Ticlio I had intimations of altitude sickness. I was not alone; a number of other passengers, some of them Indians, looked distinctly ghastly.

It begins as dizziness and a slight headache. I had been standing by the door inhaling the cool air of these shady ledges. Feeling wobbly, I sat down, and if the train had not been full I would have lain across the seat. After an hour I was perspiring and, although I had not stirred from my seat, I was short of breath. The evaporation of this sweat in the dry air gave me a sickening chill. The other passengers were limp, their heads bobbed, no one spoke, no one ate. I dug some aspirin out of my suitcase and chewed them, but only felt queasier; and my headache did not abate. The worst thing about feeling so ill in transit is that you know that if something goes wrong with the train – a derailment or a crash – you will be too weak to save yourself. I had a more horrible thought: we were perhaps a third of the way to Huancayo, but Huancayo was higher than this. I dreaded to think what I would feel like at that altitude.

I considered getting off the train at Matucana, but there was nothing at Matucana – a few goats and some Indians and tin-roofed shacks on the stony ground. None of the stops contained anything that looked like relief or refuge. But this altitude sickness had another punishing aspect: it ruined what could have been a trip of astonishing beauty. I had never seen cliffs like these or been on a railway quite so spectacular. Why was it, in this landscape of such unbelievable loveliness, that I felt as sick as a dog? If only I had had the strength to concentrate – I would have been dazzled; but, as it was, the beauty became an extra-ordinary annoyance.

The pale rose-coloured mountains had the dark stripes and mottled marks of the shells of the most delicate snails. To be ill among them, to be slumped in my seat watching the reddish gravel slides stilled in the crevasses, and the configuration of cliff-faces changing with each change in altitude, was torture so acute that I began to associate the very beautiful with the very painful. These pretty heights were the cause of my sickness. And now my teeth hurt, one molar in particular began to ache as if the nerve had caught fire. I did not know then how a cavity in a bad tooth becomes sore at a high altitude. The air in this blocked hole expands and creates pressure on the nerve, and it is agony. The dentist who told me this had been in the air force. Once, in a sharply descending plane, the cockpit became depressurized and an airman, the navigator, screamed in pain and then one of his teeth exploded.

Some train passengers had begun to vomit. They did it in the pitiful unembarrassed way that people do when they are help-lessly ill. They puked on the floor, and they puked out of the windows and they made my own nausea greater. Some, I noticed, were staggering through the cars. I thought they were looking for a place to puke, but they returned with balloons. *Balloons?* Then they sat and held their noses and breathed the air from the balloon nozzle.

I stood unsteadily and made for the rear of the train, where I found a Peruvian in a smock filling balloons from a tank of oxy-gen. He handed these out to distressed-looking passengers who gratefully gulped from them. I took my place in the queue and discovered that a few whiffs of oxygen made my head clear and helped my breathing.

There was a boy in this oxygen car. He had an oxygen balloon, too, and wore a handsome cowboy hat decorated with a band of Inca pokerwork.

'If I had thought it was going to be anything like this,' he said, 'I would never have come.'

'You took the words out of my mouth.'

'This oxygen's an improvement. Boy, do I feel shitty.'

We sipped from our balloons.

'You from the States?'

'Massachusetts,' I said.

'I'm from Minnesota. Been in Lima long?'

'One day,' I said.

'It's not that bad,' he said. 'I was there a month. It's one of the cheapest places in South America. They say Cuzco's even cheaper. I figure I'll spend a month or so there, then go back to Lima – get a job on a ship.' He looked at me. 'You're smart to have those warm clothes. I wish I had a jacket like that. All I have is these Lima things. I'll buy a sweater when we get to Huancayo – they make them there. You can get alpaca ones for practically nothing. Jesus, do I feel shitty.'

We entered a tunnel. We had been through other tunnels, but this one was long, and it had a certain distinction: it was, at 15,848 feet, the highest railway tunnel in the world. The train was loud – deafening, in fact, and I don't think I had ever felt sicker in my life. I sprayed the last of my balloon gas into my mouth, swallowed, and got another one. 'I feel like throwing up,' said the fellow from Minnesota. In the weak yellow light, with his cowboy hat over his eyes, he looked limp and fatally stricken. I did not feel so well myself, but when we emerged from the Galera Tunnel I knew we were past the highest point, and having survived that I was sure I would make it to Huancayo.

'This ship,' I said. 'The one you're going to get a job on. Where do you plan to go?'

'Home,' he said. 'I'll get one to the States. If I'm lucky I'll be back the end of April. I really want to see Minneapolis in the spring.'

'Is it as pretty as this?'

'It's better than this.'

We were now high enough to be able to see across the Andes, the whole range of mountains which, on some curves, were visible for hundreds of miles. They are not solitary peaks, but rather closely packed summits which, surprisingly, grow lighter as the distance deepens. I asked the Minnesotan how he planned to get to Cuzco. He had been in Lima for a month; his information would be good, I thought. He said there was a bus and if I was interested we could take it together. It didn't cost much, but he had heard it sometimes took four or five days to reach Cuzco. It depended on the road. This was the rainy season: the road through Ayacucho would be bad.

At La Oroya, where the line branches – the other line goes north to the tin and copper mines of Cerro de Pasco – our train was delayed. La Oroya itself was desolate and cold. Children came to the platform to beg, and sacks were loaded. Walking made my throat burn, so I sat and wondered whether I should eat anything. There were Indians selling knitted goods – mufflers and ponchos – and also fried cakes and burned bits of meat. I drank a cup of sour tea and took some more aspirin. I was rather eager to get back on the train, so that I could get another balloon of oxygen.

When we boarded, an old Indian woman stumbled on the platform. She had three bundles – cloth, packets of greasy newspaper, a kerosene lamp. I helped her up. She thanked me and told me in Spanish that she was going to Huancavelica, some miles beyond Huancayo. 'And where are you going?'

I told her, and then I asked her if the people here spoke Quechua, the Inca language.

'Yes,' she said. 'That is my language. Everyone speaks Quechua here. You will see in Cuzco.'

We crawled the rest of the afternoon towards Huancayo, and the longer we went the more I marvelled at the achievement of this mountain railway. It is commonly thought that it was planned by the American Henry Meiggs, but it was actually a Peruvian, Ernesto Malinowski, who surveyed the route; Meiggs supervised and promoted it, from its beginning in 1870 until his death in 1877. But it was another twenty years before the railway reached Huancayo. A trans-Andean line, from Huancayo to Cuzco, although proposed and surveyed in 1907, had never been built. If it had been, my arrival at the muddy mountain town would have been more hopeful; as it was, I felt too sick to eat, too dazed to go on or do anything but lie shivering in bed, still wearing my leather jacket, reading the poems and devotions of John Donne. It was comfortless stuff for a cold night in the Andes: 'As sickness is the greatest misery, so the greatest misery of sickness is solitude; when the infectiousness of the disease deters them who should assist from coming; even the physician dares scarce come. Solitude is a torment which is not threatened in hell itself.'

There was something about the damp walls of every room in this town, and the muddy roads leading out of it, that made its isolation palpable; its chill conveyed a physical feeling of remoteness. I did not have to look at the map to know I was at the back of beyond. But I woke the next day with an idea. Instead of inquiring about the way to Cuzco from the people who lived in the town, I would go to the bus station and talk to people who had just come by bus along the Andean roads from Cuzco. I was somewhat happier to be in a doubtful frame of mind; I had thought there was only one way to Cuzco and I had been determined to pursue this trans-Andean route; but, realizing that several choices were open to me, I could take the best one, the easiest, even if it meant my turning back. The trip to Huancayo had been bad, but what if the onward journey was worse?

I spent the better part of the morning chatting to passengers who had disembarked from the Ayacucho buses. Many were vague, rendered stuporous by the long trip, but the lucid ones told me that they had been delayed by rain and landslides; they had had to sleep on their buses, and only two people I talked to had actually been to Cuzco. They had come here by road because it was the only way for them – they lived in Huancayo.

There was a bar quite near to where the buses stopped. Peruvian bars are medieval. They have rough wooden tables and moist walls and dirt floors. You see dogs and chickens in Peruvian bars. Bottled beer is sold, but most drinkers in the Andes here prefer a fermented brew which is a soupy broth and very bitter. It is served in plastic beakers. It is almost identical to the sort of beer drunk in villages in East Africa, the maize beer that is ladled out of greasy pots; indeed, one mouthful of the Huancayo stuff brought me memories of dear old Bundibugyo.

'We want to know the best way to Cuzco?' said a man in this bar. He was a student, he said, from Lima, and was hoping there would be a general strike to do something about the rising prices. 'You say you just came from Lima, and you probably don't want to go back there – it seems far, right? But Lima is closer to Cuzco than Huancayo is.'

'But Cuzco is right through those mountains,' I said.

'That is the difficulty, eh?' He swigged his beer. I noticed he was not drinking the local brew, but like me had a bottle of lager. 'It is easier to go over them than through them. You take the morning train to Lima. You get a plane ticket and, bam, you are in Cuzco.'

'I thought only tourists took the plane.'

'But you are a tourist.'

'Not exactly.'

'Listen, even some Indians' – he whispered the word – 'even they take the plane.'

I took the train back to Lima the next day, leaving in the fog and cold, arriving at Desamparados in withering heat. This train-trip was shorter, and we arrived on time, but then, it was downhill all the way.

'Isn't Peru awful?' said a Peruvian to me one day in Lima. It was a very un-South American sentiment: no one so far had run down his own country in my presence. Even the most rebellious Colombians praised their coffee, and Ecuadorians said they had tasty bananas. I wondered whether this Peruvian was fishing for a compliment, so I expressed mild surprise and wary disagreement. He insisted that I was wrong: Peru was cruelly governed, hostile to its neighbours and falling completely to pieces. He was not fishing for compliments. I said, 'Yes, now that you mention it, it is rather awful.'

'Peru is dying. Terrible things are going to happen here.' He was very cross.

I said that I saw his point entirely.

'I hope when you come to Peru again it will be different,' he said.

He was more critical than I was. I had begun to appreciate Lima; I had developed a toleration for its squalor. It was nothing like home: there were no reminders here of anything familiar. I only got homesick in places where people were buying vacuum cleaners or paying light bills. Like me, the people in Lima were all a bit lost; they took walks or lounged around the plazas because there was nothing else to do, and when they visited museums and churches their motive was the same as mine: sheer boredom. I knew I was an alien; but these people? They were poor, and the poor are always aliens in their own country. For quite different reasons we were placeless.

And life in Lima was obvious, because it was lived outdoors. There were wealthy suburbs, but the rich kept behind their walls; it was dangerous in such a poor city to expose yourself as strong or well off. In Lima, people in fancy cars were often shouted at by ragged passers-by. The rest of society had spilled into the street, and there they sat, amid the stink of sewers and the pervasive half-sweetish odour of human excrement. Some rain might have washed the city clean, but it does not rain much in Lima. The warmth allows the people to live outside, and so it is possible to walk through the city and assess the population as poor and idle and youthful. The poverty has prevented Lima from having a traffic problem (the avenues are wide: they were built for victory parades), but it also means that the buses are very old and always full. In the central part of the city there are seven large plazas and parks. They teem with people; most simply sit or sleep, but others sell oranges, sweets, sunglasses, or they carry contraptions that resemble a panjandrum's sedan chair onto the pavements and on these they shine shoes. More enterprising ones are box-camera men, pulling fairly good likenesses out of crates cobbled together to look like camera obscuras or Kodak Brownies. Here is another man operating a stand where, for ten cents, you can look at Viewmaster slides of Snow White and the Seven Dwarfs, Singapore, New York, Rome, Bambi, or Wild Animals; there is an organ grinder with a parakeet and a crazed monkey; over here, five girls dressed like gypsies, telling fortunes with playing cards. 'You have come from very far away, Mister,' I was told. 'I see a woman – she is talking to you, she is not your wife.' (The woman proved to be Elvera Howie, from Chicago, who was in Cuzco with her husband Bert; she drank a great deal, but offered me nothing in the way of romance.) Families also lived in the parks, with all their cooking pots and their meagre bedding; mothers suckled infants, other children cried pitifully, urchins yelped, and I saw one skinny boy sleeping on the littered grass next to a skinny dog. And prostitutes, gangs of men, lovers, beggars – 'all the world,' as the Spanish describe crowds. They were people with nothing to do.

A Solution To The Crisis: Popular War! The paint on this splashed message near the Plaza de Armas was still fresh; but it looked as though the war had come and gone. The thousands of people in the parks and plazas could have been the dead and wounded left behind after a bitter conflict; most could accurately be described as refugees. And no buildings in South America looked more bombed and battle-scarred than those in Lima. But the pocked façades were not the result of bullets or cannon balls: this was wear and tear. Class warfare proceeds without bugle calls; it creates stinks and murmurs, not the noisy grandeur of armies heroically wrecking themselves on battlefields.

Peru is too poor to fix its cracked buildings; and it cannot afford to tear them down. They are faded and broken, but some with porticoes and balconies are still lovely, and those that have not been boarded up and left to rot are turned into dance halls and bars, and what looks like a bread-line is a mob of Peruvians waiting for the doors of a once-elegant mansion to open and admit them to a violent movie or (in the middle of the afternoon) a dance. But I had the impression that Peruvian disgust was so keen that if it were to be combined with wealth the city of Lima would be destroyed and rebuilt to match the misguided modernity of Bogotá.

I walked from the Cathedral (the mummy on view is not that of Francisco Pizarro: his skeleton has recently been found in a lead box in the crypt) to the University Park, and then made a circuit of the city, finally stopping at the Plaza Bolognesi where I sat and reflected on the melodrama of General Bolognesi's monument. It was the most bizarre statue I had seen so far. It was eighty feet high, and at its front was a copy of the Winged Victory; soldiers marched on its panels, and on one ledge was the statue of a man falling from a horse – the horse was there, life-sized, twisted onto its side. Another detachment of soldiers reconnoitred another ledge with drawn swords; eagles, wreaths and cannons in marble and bronze lifted the column higher, and still it rose, with a large grieving woman pressing her body against an upper pillar; more rifles, more flags, more troops – battles on all sides – defeat here, victory there – and higher up two marble nymphs with wings soared, their feet sticking into the air, their wings out, their arms held high and reaching towards the top where Bolognesi himself, in bronze, rushes forward, a pistol in one hand, a flag in the other, facing the wide avenue, the dance halls, the screaming children, the overloaded buses.

'Want to buy some pictures?'

It was a Peruvian, with an old photograph album: tin-miners, old cars, snow-drifts, churches, trains. They were eighty years old. I bought two old train photographs, a dollar apiece, and we talked.

'You will believe me, I hope, if I tell you I have spent some years in your country,' he said in Spanish. He was very ragged and wore a felt hat. 'I lived in Washington, D.C.'

'How did you like it?'

'I should never have left. Lima is no place to live.' He reached into his rags and took out a tattered piece of paper. It was a coupon stating that he had filed a tax-return in 1976. 'I am fully paid up,' he said. 'They will let me back if I choose to go.'

'Why don't you choose to go?'

'I got into trouble here not long ago. There was a man who was drinking too much. He wanted to fight me. So I fought him.

I cannot go anywhere. I have to appear in court. But who knows when they will hear the case?'

'You will be all right,' I said. 'After the trial, you can go back to Washington.'

'No,' he said. He thought for a moment, moved his lips as if practising a phrase and then said in English, 'I'm flat broke. Like my country.'

17 The Train to Machu Picchu

Peru is the poorest country in South America. Peru is also the country most visited by tourists. The two facts are related; even the dimmest tourist can count in Spanish – low numbers especially trip off his tongue – and he knows that Peru's gigantic ruins and threadbare currency are a bargain. The student I had met in Huancayo was right: there were some Quechua Indians on the plane to Cuzco, but the others were all tourists. They had arrived in Lima the day before and had been whisked around the city. In their hotel was a schedule: '4:00 AM – Wake-Up Call! 4:45 AM – Luggage in Corridor! 5:00 – Breakfast! 5:30 – Meet in Lobby! . . .' At eight in the morning, some men with shaving cream still stuck to their earlobes, they arrived in Cuzco and fought their way past the Indians (who carried tin pots and greasy bundles of food and lanterns, much as they had on the train) to a waiting bus, congratulating themselves on the cheapness of the place. They are unaware that it is almost axiomatic that air travel has wished tourists on only the most moth-eaten countries in the world: tourism, never more energetically pursued than in static societies, is usually the mobile rich making a blind blundering visitation on the inert poor.

> Let Observation with extensive view
> Survey Mankind, from China to Peru;
> Remark each anxious Toil, each eager Strife,
> And watch the busy scenes of crouded Life.

The result is frequently maddening to both parties.

The visitors wore badges, *Samba South America*; the badges also served as name-tags. At this early hour in the thin grey air and high altitude drizzle, the haggard faces did not match the tittupping names: Hildy Wicker, Bert and Elvera Howie,

Charles P. Clapp, Morrie Upbraid, the Prells, the Goodchucks, Bernie Khoosh, the Avatarians, Jack Hammerman, Nick and Lurleen Poznan, Harold and Winnie Casey, the Lewgards, Wally Clemons, and little old Merry Mackworth. They were a certain age; they had humps and braces and wooden legs and two walked with crutches – amazing to see this performance in the high Andes – and none looked well. What with the heat in Lima and the cold here, the delays, the shuffling up and down stairs – and they had yet to climb the vertical Inca staircases ('I don't know which is worse, going up or going down') – they were suffering. You had to admire them, because in two days they would be on the same plane flying back to Lima, waking again at four in the morning, and that day arriving in another godawful place like Guayaquil or Cali.

The arrival in Cuzco made me feel wobbly and I felt much worse after lunch. But I decided not to give in to altitude sickness. Feeling slightly sea-sick, a combination of nausea and dizziness, I stumbled around town. The place had a dark brown look of isolation, and there were still signs of the earthquake that had hit it thirty years ago. Virtually the only buildings that did not fall down were the outlying Inca forts and temples, which are indestructible. Indians were selling alpaca sweaters, rugs, ponchos and knitted caps on every street corner. The Indians have a broadbased look, like chess pieces, particularly the women, who wear three skirts, one over the other, and heavy knee-socks; they are stocky and squat and you think, looking at them, that they would be impossible to tip over. They are warmly dressed because they are such expert knitters and get the raw material – the alpaca wool – from their own domestic animals. Only the hat is not woven; one seldom sees an Indian without a hat, usually of raw felt. For the past few weeks I had been asking people why the Indians were so fond of these hats; the explanations were neither ingenious nor interesting and none really explained why European hats were popular. I heard two tourists remarking on this subject in Cuzco.

'I still don't understand about those hats,' said the first man.

'It's like postage stamps, isn't it?'

'Is it?'

'Sure. Everybody licks postage stamps, but there has never been a study to determine if it's harmful to your health. It's the same thing with those hats.'

For the first time since leaving the United States on this aimless trip I saw other aimless travellers. I had been passing myself off as a teacher; they called themselves students. There were advantages in being a student: student fares, student rates, student hostels, student entry fees. Great hairy middle-aged buffoons complained at ticket counters and shouted, 'Look, I'm a student! Do me a favour! He doesn't believe I'm a fucking student. Hey –' They were cut-priced tourists, idlers, vagabonds, freebooters, who had gravitated to this impoverished place because they wanted to save money. Their conversation was predictable and was wholly concerned with prices, the exchange rate, the cheapest hotel, the cheapest bus, how someone ('Was he a gringo?') got a meal for fifteen cents, or an alpaca sweater for a dollar or bunked with some Aymara Indians in a benighted village. They were Americans, but they were also Dutch, German, French, British and Scandinavian; they spoke the same language, always money. Their boast was always how long they had managed to hang on here in the Peruvian Andes and beat the system.

To an Indian selling Chiclets (it was either sweaters or Chiclets) such travellers could be demoralizing. Unemployment was very high in Peru, jobs were scarce, streets were lined with beggars and homeless people. How, then, to account for these thousands of poncho-wearing foreigners who lounged around and lived well but had no visible means of support? The tourists were easy to understand; they came, they went, they made no fuss. But the rucksack brigade were the cause of alarm and despondency.

They had several effects in Peru. For one thing, they kept the crime rate down. They did not carry much money, but what they did have they protected ferociously. The Peruvian pickpockets or street thieves who made the mistake of trying to rob one of these travellers always came out worse in the fight that inevitably ensued. A number of times in and around Cuzco I heard a scream and saw an infuriated Dutchman or a maddened

American with a Peruvian by the throat. The mistake the Peruvian made was in thinking that these people were solitary travellers; in fact, they were like tribesmen – they had friends who came to the rescue. It was not hard to rob me, or to mug Merry Mackworth; but the bearded lout with a poncho over his *California Is For Lovers* tee-shirt, and the knapsack and only his busfare back to Lima, was a different story altogether; he was tough, and he was not afraid to hit back.

They also kept the prices down. They did not tip or buy anything that was very expensive. They haggled in the market like the Peruvians themselves, buying tomatoes or fruit at the going rate and not paying a centavo more than they had to. Their very presence in a place indicated that there was cheap food and lodging to be had: they kept to one district in Lima, they stayed away from Huancayo, they were numerous in Cuzco. The tourist will pay any price, if forced to: he does not plan to stay long. These other travellers were unshakable skinflints; they had no marked effect on Peru, they certainly did not improve it, but perhaps this was better than a bungling attempt to colonize it with expensive hotels. The argument that five-star hotels benefit a country by producing employment is a silly and even subversive one – it turns nationals into waiters and scullery maids, and that is about all.

The rucksack brigade was very ruin-conscious. It was for many of them one of the justifications of Cuzco. I wondered what it was about the ruins that attracted them. They were not archaeologists and, despite their protestations to the contrary, they were not students either. From their conversations I concluded that they felt a spiritual affinity with the sun-worshipping Incas, and a kind of social affinity – this was almost pure fakery – with the Indians. The Indians made baskets and pots and wove cloth; these were the enthusiasms, either real or imagined, of their well-wishers. In one respect were they un-Indian: they did not go to church. Not only did they not to to mass – all the Indians did so – but also they did not tour the Catholic convents, the cloisters or chapels. The cloisters could be interesting. Apart from the paintings and statues there were instruments of flagellation, whips, iron lashes, the cat, bracelets of barbed wire and steel headbands that had been worn by Santa Catalina and Rose of Lima in painful and bloody mortification (the band was tightened until it drew blood). But the freebooters and tough, bearded students did not go to the cloisters. They preferred to walk six dizzying miles to see the Fortress of Sacsahuaman – a fort designed to imitate the shape of a puma's jaws – or the Amphitheatre of Qengo with its dark interior altars ('Far out'), or the bubbling spring at the shrine of Tambo Machay farther up the road. The tourists went by bus; these other people used the Inca road, a precipitous path along the mountains north of Cuzco. They came not to reflect on the Spaniards but to live among the remnants of the Incas. It is to them still an Inca city. The Plaza de Armas is not the site of two magnificent churches, but the spot where during 'Corpse Carrying Month' the Incas displayed the mummies they hauled out of the Temple of the Sun. It is no use pointing out that there is no Temple of the Sun in the plaza, for the stones are there: they were incorporated into the Church of Santo Domingo. Every Spanish building was once an Inca building, the roads Inca walkways, the grand houses Inca palaces.

I had neither a tourist badge nor a rucksack. I trod a narrow implausible line between the two and found myself in the company of Mexicans, who considered themselves tourists but who were taken for hippies or, even worse, for Peruvians. 'Take a good look, Paul,' a Mexican said to me one evening. 'Do I look like a Peruvian?'

'Absolutely not,' I said.

'What is wrong with these people? I am in Cuzco for two days and they stop me in the street and ask me directions! I will tell you one thing – two more days and I am back in Mexico. It may be dirty, but it is not dirty like this.'

The next day, just before nightfall, the Mexicans and I were taking a short cut through some back streets in Cuzco and found ourselves in a damp shadowy courtyard. There were no lights in the low buildings; some laundry hung on a rope. A limping puppy made its way to a puddle and drank, a large tom turkey chortled at us, and two Indian women sat on a bench, drinking maize beer out of plastic beakers.

'I hear music,' said one Mexican. His face lit up, and he went closer to the sound: a dark doorway at the side of the courtyard. He entered, but a moment later he hurried out. 'It is a typical bar.'

'Shall we go in?' I said.

'There are no seats,' he said. He seemed anxious to leave. 'I will have my beer at the hotel.'

Off they went, the three Mexicans. I entered the bar, and I understood their hurry. The bar was almost underground; it had a low ceiling and was lighted by six sooty lanterns. In this lantern light I could see ragged Indians, grinning drunkenly and guzzling maize beer from dented tankards. The bar was shaped like a trough. At one end an old man and a very small boy were playing stringed instruments; the boy was singing sweetly in Quechua. At the other end of the trough, a fat Indian woman was frying meat over a log fire – the smoke circled in the room. She cooked with her hands, throwing the meat in, turning it with her hands, picking it up to examine it, then taking a cooked hunk in each hand and carrying it to a plate. An infant crawled near the fire; it was nearly naked, not more than six months old, and like a soft toy. I had had my look, but before I could leave I noticed three men beckoning to me.

'Here is a seat,' said one in Spanish, and he made room on the bench.

That man was drinking maize beer. He urged me to try some. I said I had had some in Huancayo. It was different here, he said. But it did not taste any different to me. It was the same sour taste of rancid porridge.

'It is like African beer,' I said.

'No!' he cried. 'This is good stuff.'

I ordered a regular beer and introduced myself, privately justifying the lie that I was a teacher by telling myself that it was easier to explain what a teacher teaches than what a writer writes. Writing is an impossible profession to describe. And even when the disclosure does not produce bewilderment, it causes exaggerated respect and tends to make conversations into interviews. A geography teacher has a harmless excuse for being practically anywhere.

They were, they said, from the Ministry of Works. Gustavo and Abelardo were architects, and the third, whose name was Napoleon Prentice ('It is a good English name, but I cannot speak English') was a civil engineer. The jobs sounded impressive, but the men were poorly dressed and looked rather gloomy.

'You may not speak English,' I said to Napoleon, 'but I am sure your Quechua is better than mine.'

'I cannot speak Quechua,' said Napoleon.

Gustavo said, 'I know a few words, but that is all. You will have no touble learning it. It is just like English.'

'Quechua is like English?'

'The grammar is exactly the same. For example, in Spanish we say "a book red", but in Quechua they say "a red book". Like English. Go ahead, say it.'

'Red book,' I said in English.

They smiled at the phrase, an English stutter in this sonorous Spanish conversation.

Gustavo said, 'You will have no touble with Quechua.'

They were not from Cuzco. They were, all three, from Lima. They had been sent here by their ministry to design a housing scheme at Quillabamba, beyond Machu Picchu, on the Urubamba River. Abelardo had just arrived; the other two had been in Cuzco for some months.

'How long will you be here, Abelardo?' I asked.

'A year,' he said, and glanced at the others, shaking his head. Without much conviction he added, 'It is not too bad.'

Napoleon said, 'All the ruins! Interesting!'

I said, 'Are you interested in ruins?'

'No,' said Napoleon. I could tell from their laughter that he spoke for all of them.

'What do your wives think of your being away for so long?' I asked. It was the question everyone asked me. I wondered whether they had a clever reply that I might use later on.

'We are not married,' said Gustavo. 'Do you think married people would go to places like Cuzco and Quillabamba?'

'I am married and I went to Huancayo.'

'That is your affair, my friend. If I was married I would stay home.'

I said, 'I do – more or less.'

'More or less!' screamed Gustavo. He was shaking with laughter. 'That is really funny.'

Abelardo said, 'It is only single fellows like us who get sent to the terrible places, like Iquitos and Puerto Maldonado.'

'Isn't Iquitos in Ecuador?' I asked.

'Sometimes it is, and sometimes it isn't,' said Gustavo, laughing. 'These days it is.'

'I was in Maldonado,' said Napoleon. 'It was awful – hotter than Brazil.'

Abelardo said, 'Lima is nice. Did you like Lima? Yes? There is always something to do in Lima.'

It was clearly going to be a long year for him in Quillabamba.

'But think of all the ruins in Cuzco,' said Napoleon.

Abelardo uttered an obscenity, something like, 'Oh, piss on God's balls!'

'What other countries do you know?' asked Gustavo. 'What about France? Look, how much would I need to live in Paris? How many dollars a day?'

I said, 'About forty.'

He looked discouraged. 'How about London?'

'Maybe thirty,' I said.

'Go to Lima,' said Abelardo. 'It will only cost four.'

'Go to Maldonado,' said Napoleon. 'It will only cost one.'

'And the girls in Lima,' said Abelardo, mournfully.

'There are plenty of girls here,' said Gustavo. 'American, German, Japanese. Pretty ones, too. Take your pick.'

'You will be all right,' I said.

'Certainly,' said Gustavo. 'We will be happy in Quillabamba. We will exchange ideas.'

The small boy and the old man had been playing sad twanging music. It seemed so melancholy, this barefoot boy singing in such a low-down place. The music stopped. The boy took off his cloth cap and went among the tables, collecting coins. We gave him. He bowed, then returned to his songs.

'He is poor,' I said.

'Seventy percent of Peru is poor,' said Gustavo. 'Like that boy.'

We continued to drink, but at this altitude alcohol has a paralysing effect. I felt leaden and stupid, and refused a third bottle of beer. The others began to eat plates of fried meat. I tasted some, but I saved my appetite for later; I had been in Cuzco long enough to know that I could get a good steak and a stuffed avocado for a dollar fifty. I left the men discussing Peru's chances in the World Cup. 'We are not very good,' said Napoleon. 'I think we will lose.' I did not argue with him; the only way to handle a Peruvian is to agree with his pessimism.

After dinner, I felt too ill to go for a walk. I went back to my hotel – which was not a hotel but only a few rooms above the plaza; and nosing around the dining room I found an old phonograph. It was literally a Victrola, a 1904 Victor, and near it was a stack of 78 rpm records. Most of them were cracked. I found one that was not cracked and read the label: *Ben Bernie and the Lads*, it said, *Shanghai Lil* (*Warner Bros.*, '*Footlight Parade*'). I turned the crank and set the disc in motion.

> I've travelled every little highway,
> I've climbed every little hill;
> I've been looking high,
> I've been looking low,
> Looking for my Shanghai Lil.

There were lights on in the plaza. The leper I had seen that afternoon shuffling on bleeding feet, like the Pobble who had no toes, was curled up near the fountain. On the far side was the beautiful Jesuit church, and beyond that the Andes as black and high-crowned as the hats of the Indians who were also bunking down in the plaza.

> I've been trying to forget her,
> But what's the use – I never will.
> I've been looking high,
> I've been looking low –

It was cold. My leather coat was not enough, and I was indoors. But it was quiet: no honking horns, no cars, no radios, no screams; only the church bells and the Victrola.

> Looking for my Shanghai Lil.

At four o'clock every weekday morning the Cuzco church bells ring. They ring again at 4:15 and 4:30. Because there are so many churches, and the valley is walled-in by mountains, the tolling of church bells, from four to five in the morning, has a celebratory sound. They summon all people to mass, but only Indians respond. They flock to five o'clock mass in the Cathedral, and just before six the great doors of the Cathedral open on the cold cloudy mountain dawn and hundreds of Indians pour into the plaza, so many of them in bright red ponchos that the visual effect is of a fiesta about to begin. They look happy; they have performed a sacrament. All Catholics leave mass feeling light-hearted, and though these Indians are habitually dour – their faces wrinkled into frowns – at this early hour after mass most of them are smiling.

The tourists wake with the Indians, but the tourists head for Santa Ana Station to catch the train to Machu Picchu. They carry packed lunches, umbrellas, raincoats and cameras. They are disgusted, and they have every right to be so. They were led to believe that if they got to the station at six, they would have a seat on the seven o'clock train. But now it was seven and the station doors had not opened. A light rain had started and the crowd of tourists numbered two hundred or more. There is no order at the station.

The tourists know this and they hate it. They were woken early yesterday for the Cuzco flight and found a mob at the airport. They were woken early for the Machu Picchu train, and this mob is worse. They do not jostle or push. They stand in the grey dawn, clutching their lunches and muttering. Most are on a twelve-day tour of South America; they have spent much of the time just like this, waiting for something to happen, and they don't like it one bit. They don't want to complain because they know Americans are famous for complaining. But they are disgusted. I stand in the mob and wait for a chance to say *I don't blame you*.

'You'd think they'd at least open the doors and let us into the station,' says one of the Goodchucks.

'That's too simple for them. They'd rather keep us waiting,' says Charles P. Clapp.

'I'm awful sick of this,' says Hildy, who really does look ill. The poor woman is over seventy and here she is in the middle of the Andes, standing behind the filthy Cuzco market on the steps of the station. At her feet is an Indian woman with a crying child, selling Chiclets and cigarettes, and another pitifully dirty man with a pile of bruised peaches. Hildy is from – where? A neat suburb in the mid-West, where the trains run on time and polite people offer her their seat. She did not know how hard it would be here. She has my sympathy, even my admiration; at her age this counts as bravery. 'If they don't open the doors pretty quick I'm going straight back to the hotel.'

'I don't blame you.'

She says, 'I haven't been right since La Paz.'

'Marquette got beat,' says Morrie Upbraid, a stout man from Baton Rouge, who talks with his teeth locked together.

'Texas got a real good team this year,' says Jack Hammerman.

'What happened to Notre Dame?'

They talk about football: wins, losses, and the coloured fella who is over six foot eight. This is contentment of sorts and takes the curse off waiting in the drizzle in Cuzco. Men talk to men; the women stand and fret.

'I want to see LSU knock the stew out of them,' says Mr Hammerman.

'You'd think they'd at least open the doors,' says Mrs Goodchuck.

At last the station doors open. There is a general surge forward. The elderly tourists shuffle but do not push. A mob is awkward, and they feel they are being tested, as if too violent a response on their part will turn them into Peruvians. Shame and disapproval make them exercise some restraint, and it is only an Argentine honeymoon couple – a dark unapologetic man and his skinny clinging wife – who shove their way to the front. It is easy for them. They elbow past the gentler Americans and are probably surprised that they are through the door so quickly.

'Just sort of lean back,' cautions Charles P. Clapp. 'That way you won't get trampled.'

Hearing this, the Americans lean back.

There were seats for everyone except three Indian women

with papooses and cloth bundles, and two freebooters dressed as Indians, in slouch hats and ponchos. The rest of us sat with our box lunches on our laps. An hour of this, and as it passed the timid speculation as to whether the train was going to leave at all became loud discouragement. There was a general sigh of relief as the train started out of the station. It was still cloudy, the mountainsides softened in greeny mist. The motor road is high, but the train stays low, circling the mountains through a series of gorges in which rushing water runs alongside the tracks. There were few vistas here: we were too deep in the mountains to see anything but overhanging cliffs. Where a gorge floor was flat there were mud huts built near the ingenious Inca walls, the careful stonework of neatly fitted boulders, Inca terraces which had become Indian villages. The mud-block huts were recent, the Inca walls were old, and yet the walls had been built without the use of wheels, the surfaces smoothed and joined with stone tools.

Seeing this stonework, Bert Howie chants, 'Inca! Inca! Inca! Everywhere you look – Inca!'

'Now this reminds me of Wyoming,' says Harold Casey. He directs our attention to the rocky bluffs, the falling water, the green hillsides.

It reminds the Lewgards of parts of Maine. The Prells say it is nothing like Indiana and raise a laugh. Someone else says it is similar to Ecuador. The rest are annoyed: Ecuador is their next stop.

Bert and Elvera Howie listen to these comparisons and then say it is like Africa. Parts of Africa are just like this. We look out of the window and see llamas and smaller fluffier alpacas and very hairy pigs and women in tall hats and shawls and kneesocks gathering firewood. *Africa*? Elvera insists that it is so. She is surprised, she says, because Bert was saying that morning that their hotel – out of the window of the cocktail lounge on the top floor – reminds them of Florence, Italy: all the orange-tiled roofs, all the churches, the light.

'I've always wanted to go to Africa.' This is Hildy, who looks fresher, having sat down.

Bert says, 'We were the last people out of Uganda.'

'It must have been terrible.'

'Those poor Hindus. Took their earrings off at the airport.'

Elvera says, 'It was scary. I liked it.'

'You saw mountains like this, and African women walking down them with things on their heads.'

'Bert went fishing.'

'In the Nile.' As he says it, and smiles, the Peruvian river running beside the train, the funny little Anta River, looks homely: what is this to the Nile? 'I caught huge things – Nile Perch they call them. The water was as black at that seat there.'

Mr Upbraid says, 'Look at the poverty.'

This is the village beyond the town of Anta: some mud huts, some pigs, an alpaca with matted fur, small girls carrying infants, and children with their hands out crying, 'Monis! Monis!'

'Haiti,' says Bert. 'Ever been to Haiti? That's poverty. That's squalor. This is nothing. These people have farms – everyone has an acre or two. Grow their own food. Roof over their heads. They're all right. But Haiti? They're just starving there. Or Jamaica? Even worse.'

No one can contradict him. We looked out of the window. Bert has made it seem all rather prosperous.

Bert says, 'That's not poverty.'

It is no good my telling him that these are tenant farms and that these people own nothing but the clothes on their backs. The huts leak. The plots of vegetables are high on the hillsides, some on Inca terraces, others like light green patches stitched against the cliffs at a sixty-degree angle. I am tempted to tell him this, that no one owns anything here, that these Indians themselves are owned. But information confuses these tourists: they like to guess at the meanings of things. 'Looks like a kind of cave – I suppose they lived in places like that, years ago' and 'Sort of a stairway – must lead to a kind of look-out.'

'It's a sunny day, but it's real dark here.'

'That's because we're in the valley.'

The conversation, pure Thornberry, went its rackety way as we slid past the rumps of these squatting mountains.

'Look. More Indians.'

There were two, in red pie-plate hats and shawls; one tugging a llama out of a field, the other – perhaps for the benefit of the tourists – ostentatiously making yarn from a spindle of rough wool and twisting the stuff in her fingers.

'Did you get a picture of that, Bert?' asked Elvera.

'Just a minute.'

Bert took out his camera and snapped a picture of the two Indians. A man named Fountain was watching him. Bert saw Mr Fountain and said, 'That's the new Canon – just on the market.'

He did not say how much he paid for it, or stress that it was his. It was an oblique piece of bragging: *That's the new Canon*.

Mr Fountain took the camera, weighed it in his hand, looked through the viewfinder and said, 'Handy.'

'Compact,' said Bert. 'I wish I'd had one of these when we were on our Christmas trip.'

There were a few murmurs, but not much real interest.

Bert said, 'Know what a Force Twelve gale is?'

Ignorance often seems wrapped like a package. The murmurs were like the rustlings of the wrapper of that plain thing. No one knew.

'It was a cruise,' said Bert. 'We're one day out of Acapulco. Nice sunny day. Suddenly it clouds up. Pretty soon it's a Force Twelve. Everyone was sick. Lasted forty-eight hours. Elvera went over to the bar and sat there – just held on for two days.'

'It was my security blanket.'

'Couldn't sleep, couldn't eat. See, Dramamine only works if you take it *before* you start to puke. It was awful. I walked around for two days saying, "I just don't believe it. I just don't believe it."'

There was more. For ten minutes, Bert and Elvera Howie told their hurricane story, and even in their monotonous narration – they took turns, interrupting each other to add details – it was a terrifying report, like a page of *Arthur Gordon Pym*. It was a story of high waves and wild winds, sickness and cowardice and loss of sleep. The old people on the ship (and this alarmed the old people on this train) were thrown around so badly they suffered broken arms and fractured legs. 'And one old fellow – nice old guy – busted his hip. Some people were hurt so bad we didn't see them for the rest of the trip.' Bert said it was chaos; Elvera blamed the English captain: he hadn't given them any warning – 'He must have known *something*.' Afterwards, the captain had said that in all his years at sea it was the worst storm he had ever known.

Elvera had been glancing at me with a kind of sour mistrust. Finally, she said, 'You English people.'

'I'm not English, actually.'

'Actually,' she said, and made a face.

Bert was still talking about the hurricane, the wind, the broken bones. The effect of his tale was to make this light rain falling into a canyon in the Andes seem a spring shower, and this railway journey no more than a joyride. Bert and Elvera had known days of storm in the Pacific; this train ride was a Sunday outing and almost beneath notice.

'I want a drink,' said Elvera. 'Instead of telling these people about our other trip, why don't you concentrate on this one and find me a drink?'

'Funny thing,' said Bert. 'I don't speak a word of Spanish. I don't speak anything but English. But I can always make myself understood. Even in Nairobi. Even in Italy. Know how I do it? I sit there and say, "Me – want – a – drink." It always does the trick.'

He soon had a chance to prove that he could hurdle the language barrier. A conductor entered our car. Bert smiled and tapped him on the arm. He said, 'Me – want – a – drink.'

The conductor grunted and walked away.

'That's the first time I ever –'

'Look.'

Ahead, through a black gateway of pinnacles, was a wide flat valley filled with sunlight; birds were slanted in the sky and on ledges like the diacritical marks on vowels, and there were green streaks, wind-flattened bushes, on the steep mountains beyond. In the centre of the valley, coursing beside fuchsias and white orchids, was a turbulent brown river. This was the Vilcanota River, running north to Machu Picchu, where it becomes the Urubamba and continues north-east to join a tributary of the Amazon. The river flowed from Sicuani, past the glaciers above the crumbling town of Pisaq, and here, where our train was tooting, had formed the Sacred Valley of the Incas. The shape of this valley – so flat and green and hidden – in such a towering place, had attracted the Incas. Many had been here before the Spaniards entered Cuzco, and here others fled, fighting a rearguard action after Cuzco fell. The valley became an Inca stronghold, and long after the Spaniards believed they had wiped out or subdued this pious and highly civilized empire, the Incas continued to live on in the fastnesses of these canyons. In 1570, a pair of Augustinian missionaries – the friars Marcos and Diego – had the fanatical faith to take them over the mountains and through this valley. The friars led a motley band of Indian converts who carried torches and set fire to the shrines at which Incas were still worshipping. Their triumph was at Chuquipalta, near Vitcos, where for the greater glory of God (the Devil had made appearances here, so the Incas said) they put their torches to the House of the Sun. Some missions were established along the river (Marcos eventually suffered a horrendous martyrdom), but farther on, where the mountains and sky seemed scarcely distinguishable, the ruins were not re-entered. The valleys slept. They were not penetrated again until 1911, when the Yale man, Hiram Bingham, with the words of Kipling's 'Explorer' running through his head ('Something hidden. Go and find it. Go and look behind the Ranges – / Something lost behind the ranges. Lost and waiting for you. Go!') found the vast mountain-top city he named Machu Picchu. He believed he had found the lost city of the Incas, but John Hemming writes in *The Conquest of the Incas* that an even more remote place to the west, Espiritu Pampa, has the greater claim to the title.

It was part of the Inca genius to seal themselves into hidden valleys, past rockslides and at the far end of precipitous trails that were lost behind the ranges. Their grasp of advanced masonry allowed them to build secure fortresses and posting stations out of these natural battlements. A few miles after we entered the Vilcanota Valley we came to Ollantaytambo, and if I had not made a separate visit to this place I would not have known how perfectly it had been sited, how the terraces, and the temple walls, could not be seen until one was on top of them.

They are all but hidden from the railway tracks and the river, and what you see and think are habitations are Inca watch-towers, hundreds of feet up, tall thick-walled cottages on cliffs which aided the besieged warriors in warning them of Spanish attacks. Ollantaytambo was a success of sorts; over four hundred years ago, a regiment of Spanish soldiers led by Hernando Pizarro attacked this town, and they were defeated. 'When we reached Tambo,' wrote one Spaniard, 'we found it so well forti-fied that it was a horrifying sight.' The battle was bloody, and the Spaniards were beaten off by Inca slingers, Amazonian bow-men and Incas armed with weapons and wearing helmets and bucklers they had captured from their enemy.

Inca symmetries have a graceful Biblical magnificence: behind these walls there are hanging gardens crowned by twenty-ton megaliths that were quarried several miles away and lifted to this summit. It was not specifically a fortress; it had first been a royal garden.

'They must be for landslides,' said Mr Fountain, going by.

Bert Howie said, 'Hey, what a terrific pair of shoes!'

He was marvelling at my feet.

'Leakproof,' I said.

'Hey, honey,' said Bert to Elvera, 'have a look at these terrific shoes.'

But Elvera was still looking at Ollantaytambo. She mistook the clock-tower in the village square for a church and said she was reminded of the churches in Cuzco. The others mentioned churches in Lima, in Quito, Caracas, La Paz and even further afield; and so, as we travelled through the Sacred Valley of the Incas, no one remarked on the fields of wheat and corn, or the staggering heights of these cliffsides which had been plumbed by glaciation, or our progress into the sun beside this loud brown river. The mention of churches produced a discussion about religion, and with it, a torrent of muddled opinion.

Those gold altars really get me, said one. I don't understand why they don't melt them down and feed some of these starving people. And the statues, said another: they're so exaggerated, always bloody and skinny. Everyone was shouting and argufying at once: the Christ statues were the worst, really gory; the Mary

337

ones were chubby and dressed up like dolls in lace and velvet; Jesus on the cross looked horrible among the gold carvings, his ribs sticking out; you'd think they'd at least make them look human. It went on: blood, gold, suffering, and people on their knees. Why did they have to exaggerate, said one man, when it only ended up looking vulgar?

I had been hearing quite a lot of this. There was patronizing mockery in the pretence of bafflement and disgust. *I just can't understand it*, they said, but they used their incomprehension to amplify their ignorance. Ignorance licensed them to indulge in this jeering.

I felt my moment had come to speak. I had also seen those churches, and I had reached several conclusions. I cleared my throat.

'It *looks* exaggerated because it *is* exaggerated,' I said. 'It's possible that the churches here have bloodier Christs than those in Spain, and they're certainly a lot bloodier than anything you'd see in the United States. But life is bloodier here, isn't it? In order to believe that Christ suffered you have to know that he suffered more than you. In the United States the Christ statue looks a bit bruised, a few tear-drops, some mild abrasions. But here? How is it possible to suffer more than these Indians? They've seen all sorts of pain. Incas were peace-loving and pious, but if anyone broke the law he got unbelievable punishment – he might be buried alive, clubbed to death, staked out on the ground and ritually trampled, or tortured. High officials who committed an offence had heavy stones dropped on their backs from a high cliff, and virgins caught speaking to a man were hung by their hair. Pain wasn't brought here by the Spanish priests, but a crucified Christ was part of the liturgical scheme. The Indians were taught that Christ suffered, and they had to be persuaded that his suffering was worse than theirs. And by the same token that Mary, the world's mother, was healthier and better dressed than any woman in their society. So, yes, the statues are exaggerations of their lives, because these images represent God and the Holy Mother. Right?'

Convinced I was right, I warmed to my theme. Mary in the Church of San Francisco in Lima, in her spangled cape and brocade gown and holding a silver basket, had to outshine any Inca noble and, at last, any Spanish woman of fashion. These divine figures had to be seen to exceed the Spaniard or Peruvian in suffering or wealth – they had to seem braver, more tortured, richer or bloodier in order to seem blessed. Christ in any church was more battered than the very battered leper in the plaza: he had to be. The lesson of the Peruvian – perhaps Latin American – Church demonstrated the extraordinariness of the Saviour. In the same way, the statues of Buddha as a mendicant showed a man who was hungrier and skinnier than the skinniest Buddhist. In order for you to believe in God it was necessary to see that God had endured a greater torment than you. And Mary had to look more motherly, more fecund and rich, than any other mother. Religion demanded this intensity in order to produce piety. A believer could not venerate someone like himself – he had to be given a reason for the holiness of the God statue. And he responded by praising it in the most appropriate way, by enshrining it in gold.

After this, no one mentioned religion. They stared out of the window and said, 'More pigs' or 'Look, is that a rainbow?' And they went on talking in the off-hand Thornberry way that distracted them from what had become for them a dull and eventless train ride.

There *was* a rainbow poised across the Urubamba. The Incas were the only people on earth, as far as we know, who worshipped the rainbow. And now we were close to what Hiram Bingham called 'the last Inca capital'. The train stopped. Macchu Pichu was above us, hidden behind cliffs and outcrops of rock. The tourists were still chattering. I had foolishly told Bert Howie about the Victrola in my hotel and how I had played 'Shanghai Lil' on it. Bert said that Ben Bernie had been a Chicago boy, and he began to reminisce as he laboured up the path. High above Bert's yakking head, the sun priests in beautiful robes had stood facing east every dawn on this steepest side, and when the sun, their god, began to blaze above the Andes, the priests extended their arms to it and (wrote Father Calancha in 1639) 'threw kisses to it . . . a ceremony of the most profound resignation and reverence.' But we had not gone far; we were still near the river, which is troubled and dark, because it reflects the spongy foliage of the overhanging rock, not the sky. 'The water looks black and forbidding,' said Bingham, 'even to unsuperstitious Yankees.'

We continued to climb the steepness. The tourists chattered, stopping only to gasp; the gasping turned to complaint. It was not until the last step, at the brow of the hill, that the whole city was revealed. It sprawled across the peak, like a vast broken skeleton picked clean by condors. For once, the tourists were silent.

18 El Panamericano

The Panamerican Express is one of South America's great trains, travelling over 1,000 miles from La Paz in Bolivia to the Argentine city of Tucuman. It crosses a national frontier – few in this hemisphere do – and railway travel is never more interesting than when it involves a border crossing. The frontier is nearly always a no-man's land in which fascinating pieces of fraudulent theatre are enacted – the passport stamping ceremony, the suspicious looks, the bullying at customs, the foolishly patriotic pique, and the unexplained delays. I had walked across the Rio Grande from Texas to Mexico, and hiked from Guatemala into El Salvador. I was looking forward to boarding a train in Bolivia and ending up, after three days on the Andean high-plains, in the heart of Argentina.

But first I had to find my way out of Peru. By now, the railway strike had taken hold. Only one line was in operation; the train to Machu Picchu was being manned by the Peruvian army. This was strictly for the tourists' benefit – too bad if you were an Indian who wanted to go home on any of the other routes. The miners were also on strike, and the municipal workers had occupied the city hall in Lima. The peaceful demonstrations had become angry mobs, and there were threats of sabotage on the Machu Picchu train. The workers' demand was for £1.50 more a month. In Peru, two pounds of meat costs £1.50, and two pounds is all the average Peruvian family can afford each month. I was warned that if I did not leave Peru soon the buses, too, would be strike-bound; and though I had vowed in Colombia that I would not set foot on another South American bus – good heavens, I had a wife and children! – I had no choice but to take one to Puno.

By train the trip would have been simple and enjoyable; by

bus, it was dusty and harrowing, over a corrugated road. I could not read on this bus, and that day I abandoned my diary. We reached Lake Titicaca at sundown and crossed it in the steamer *M.V. Ollanta* in the dead of night. People tell you that this is one of the most enchanting trips on the continent. But I saw nothing: it was night. The last leg, from Guaqui to La Paz, was too brief to be memorable. I recall a puzzled Indian standing among boulders with a llama watching us pass. The llama was a special reproach to me.

> The llama is a woolly sort of fleecy hairy goat,
> With an indolent expression and an undulating throat,
> Like an unsuccessful literary man.

Just above La Paz, as the train rises and travels across the ridge before descending into the city, there are coal-black peaks covered with snow. The snow has a dry ghostly permanent look to it, a far cry from the radiant slush you see in New England.

The bareness of Bolivia had been apparent as soon as we reached the south end of the lake. It was not the cookie crumb bareness of Mexico or the snail shell bareness of Peru or the withered aridity of Guatemala; Bolivia's bareness was the gritty undercrust of the earth, a topography of stony fossils: the top-soil had simply blown away, exposing the country to its old bones. The place could not have looked colder or fiercer. And yet, all the Bolivians on the Guaqui train were friendly, and the hat-style of the Indians – here a brown derby was favoured – gave them a jaunty look. 'You should stay here awhile,' said a Bolivian, and he pointed to the snowy peaks. 'You can go skiing over there.'

The clouds were grey and creased with black, and as we made our descent into La Paz – the city grew larger and uglier as we neared the valley floor – there was a blue-white crack of lightning from the collapsing clouds. Then a thunderclap; and it began to hail. The hailstones bobbled against the train windows; they were the size of marbles – it was a wonder they did not shatter the glass.

I did not feel well. I had slept badly in Cuzco, I had dozed on the bus to Puno; the furious boilers on the *M.V. Ollanta* had kept me awake crossing Lake Titicaca. I had stomach trouble, and for once my English cement, which was spiked with morphine, did no good. And of course there was the altitude: La Paz was over 12,000 feet, and the train had gone even higher in order to make its way into the city. I had a groggy half-awake feeling, dizzyness and shortness of breath. Altitude sickness had penetrated to my entrails, and though I kept swigging cement and chewing my cloves – my teeth had begun to ache again – I knew I would not feel any better until I left La Paz on the Panamerican express.

I had another affliction, too, but this turned out to be an advantage. I cannot remember how I found a hotel in La Paz – I think I just saw a likely one and walked in. In any case, I was taking some aspirin shortly after finding my room and dropped the water tumbler into the sink. My hand went to it, propelled by instinct, and then I saw that I was holding broken glass and blood. It was my scribbling hand, and now the blood was running down my arm. I stepped into the corridor, bandaging the wound with a towel, and called to the room lady who was sweeping the floor. She clucked: the blood had begun to leak through the towel. She took a rubber band out of her apron pocket.

'Put this around your wrist,' she said. 'That will stop the blood.'

I recalled that tourniquets had been discredited. I asked her the address of the nearest pharmacy.

'Maybe you should go to the doctor,' she said.

'No,' I said. 'I am sure it will stop.'

But I had not gone two blocks when the new towel I had wrapped around my hand was soaked with blood. It did not hurt, but it looked dreadful. I hid it under my arm so as not to alarm pedestrians. Then the blood dripped on the pavement and I thought: Goddamn. It was deeply embarrassing to be walking through this large grey city with a blood-soaked towel on my hand. I began to wish that I had tried the rubber band. I left spatters of blood on the crosswalk, and more spatters on the plaza. I asked directions to the pharmacy and saw, when I looked back, that there was a pool of blood where I had paused and a

343

horrified Bolivian watching me. I tried not to run: running makes your heart beat faster and you bleed more.

The pharmacy was run by five Chinese girls, who spoke Spanish in the twanging gum-chewing way that they speak English. I held my dripping paw over a waste-paper basket and said, 'I have a problem here.' Before leaving the hotel, I had looked up the Spanish words for wound, antiseptic, bandage, tape and gauze.

'Is it still coming out, the blood?' asked one of the Chinese girls.

'I think so.'

'Take that bandage off.'

I unwound the soaked towel. Blood poured out of the slice in my palm: it was a neat cut in my flesh, slightly parted, and with a steady trickle of blood flowing out of it. Now I was bleeding on the counter. The girl moved briskly, got some cotton, dunked it in alcohol and pressed it painfully to the cut. Moments later the cotton was crimson.

She said, 'It is still coming out.'

The other Chinese girls and some customers came over to look.

'What a shame,' said one.

'It does not hurt,' I said. 'I am sorry for making a mess.'

Without saying a word, another Chinese girl twisted a rubber tube around my wrist and tightened it. More cotton was applied to the cut. This cotton stayed white.

The second Chinese girl said, 'Now it is not coming out.'

But my hand had gone numb and I saw that it was turning grey. This gave me a fright. I undid the rubber tube. The blood flowed again down my elbow.

'You should have left the rubber on.'

'I think that is dangerous,' I said.

They tried everything. They poured alcohol on it from the bottle, they squeezed it, they dyed it with Mercurochrome, they sprinkled white powder on it – and now my hand looked like a Bolivian pastry. But nothing worked; direct pressure seemed to make the blood flow faster.

'Put the rubber on again.'

344

'No,' I said. 'It is no good.'

'It is good. It will work.'

The other girl said in amazement, 'It is still coming!'

'You need stitches,' said a third girl.

'It is not that big,' I said.

'Yes. Go to the doctor. He is across the street.'

I went to the doctor's office, but it was shut: out for lunch. Back in the pharmacy and, still bleeding, I said, 'Forget the rubber tube. Just sell me a bandage and some antiseptic. I know it will stop – they always stop, sooner or later.'

A different Chinese girl broke open a bandage and helped me wrap my hand, then she gave me all the odds and ends of tape and bottles we had used and I went to the cash desk and paid for them.

It leaked some more – not too much, but enough to soak the gauze bandage and look quite horrible, like the joke shop bandage children wear to frighten their friends. The bandage was thick, the blood bright red. But I was fairly certain it had stopped. Buying a sugary coffee to restore my health, I held my bandaged hand in my lap.

'Yugh. How did that happen?' asked the waiter.

'An accident,' I said lightly.

And at the bank, changing some money, I rested my wounded hand on the counter. The teller was quick; she sorted the bills, asked no questions, averted her eyes from my hand, and off I went: it was the fastest bank transaction I had made in months.

I went to the railway agency. The clerk was elderly but full of beans. He kept saying in Spanish a word that means 'Ready!' or 'Check!' He told me to sit down. I did so, placing my right hand on his desk and pretending to ignore it.

'One ticket to Buenos Aires, via Tucuman, please.'

'Check!'

'A First Class sleeper, and I would like to go as soon as possible.'

'Check!'

He shuffled papers, and as he wrote out my ticket he said, 'The wound – is it big?'

'Very.'

'Check,' he said, giving me a wheeze of sympathy. No ticket had ever been easier for me to buy. I was so encouraged by the Bolivian response to my wounded hand that I did not change the bandage until the next day. I was treated with great promptness, I was asked questions about it – did it hurt? how had it happened? was it large? My hand became a wonderful conversation piece, and everyone who passed by me stared at my white mitten. In Lima I had tried to buy a painting, but the price was ridiculously high and I had given up in frustration. In La Paz, I saw a better painting, a pious portrait of Saint Dominic, done in Potosi in the mid-eighteenth century. I haggled for less than an hour, using my bandaged hand to gesture with, and walked out of the shop with the painting under my arm.

'Better keep that painting in your suitcase,' said the lady in the shop. 'It is illegal to take such works of art out of the country.'

The wounded hand turned out to be one of my most satisfying experiences in South America. But later I thought I might be pushing my luck. I began to worry that the cut would become infected and my hand would drop off.

It was a city that seemed suited to ghastliness of this kind; it suffered itself, from a sort of urban gangrene, and if any city looked blighted to the point of being wounded – it even had a scabrous cankered colour – it was La Paz. Its extreme ugliness was woeful enough to be endearing, and I found it on further inspection to be a likable place. It was a city of cement and stale bread, of ice storms that produced a Bulgarian aroma of wet tweeds, built above the timber-line in a high pass in the Andes. The people in La Paz had heavy dignified faces and none of the predatory watchfulness I had seen in Colombia and Peru. In the wood-panelled coffee shops in La Paz, with their white-jacketed waiters and espresso machines and gooey pastries and mirrors, scowling matrons at one table, thickset men in baggy ill-fitting suits at other tables, it was hard to believe I was not in eastern Europe; it was only when I went outside and saw a stocky Indian chewing coca leaves in the shelter of a cement mixer that I was reminded where I was.

It drizzled constantly: cold rain, ice slivers, hail. But most people were dressed for the weather. They wore thick overcoats and heavy sweaters, wool hats, and even mittens and gloves. The Indians had a bulky rounded look, and some wore earflaps under their derby hats. I saw the sun once. It appeared one morning between a break in the mist that hung over the canyon, and it was powerfully bright without being warm, simply a blinding flash that was soon eclipsed by more mist. The weather report in the daily paper was usually the same: *Cloudy, fog, some rain, no change*, like a certain season in northern Maine, except that here I was never able to elude my feeling of the bends or my nausea. I was tired but could not sleep; I had no appetite, one drink and I was staggering. And it is hard to be a stranger in a cold city: the people stay indoors, the streets are empty after the stores close, no one lounges in the parks, and the purposefulness – or what looks like it – in a cold climate is always a reproach to an idle traveller. I rolled up my painting, hid it in my suitcase and made preparations to leave.

The sun came out just as the Panamerican left the precincts of the railway station and began to travel in tight circles through the eucalyptus groves on the slopes north of the city. They were the only trees I was to see for several days. Ragged toothy boys ran from behind the trees and hitched on the train, and after a few minutes jumped off and hurried, shouting, into the frail foliage. Then they were lost among the tall slender trees, the stringy bark. There were mud huts on the lower slopes, but as we climbed higher there were no more huts, only abandoned earthworks and an Indian or two. In spite of the steady rain of the previous days the steep creekbeds were dry and stony, cut deep in the waterless mountainside. Littered with rocks and sand, the soil could not have looked more infertile. But we were very high now, perhaps 13,000 feet and still climbing above the back of the city to the dry grey lip of the plateau that hangs over it. On this steep grade the train was tilted at a sharp angle; on the right a mountainside, on the left a deep ravine of clumsily made roofs.

After almost an hour we were still in sight of La Paz. It was there below us; we had gone back and forth on the mountainside,

347

passing and repassing the city which had become large and spectacularly shabby. Behind the city were the Andes, snowy mountains with clouds smoking on their summits. We were up among the daisies and the weeds and the twittering birds; it was cold and bright, and clear enough to see for a hundred miles. There were plateaux and peaks on three sides of the city, and as we passed it for the last time – we had now reached an open plain – it looked strip-mined with roads and ditches, a reddened ledge rising to green slopes, black cliffs, white peaks.

Chased by rabid dogs, the train picked up speed and crossed the grey plain to the first station, Illimani, at 13,500 feet. There were sheep on the tracks and Indian women selling oranges for a penny each. I bought six oranges and boarded quickly as the train began to move. After the slow climb to this station it was surprising for the train to pick up speed and begin racing across the high plains.

It was a Bolivian train. Most of the coaches were wooden Second Class boxes crammed with Indians on their way south. These coaches, and the dining car and the one Bolivian sleeping car, would go no farther than the border at Villazon. My sleeping car belonged to Argentine Railways and was going all the way to Tucuman. This solid British-made pullman was about fifty years old, each compartment fitted with cupboards and a sink and a chamberpot. There were two berths in my compartment. Fernando, a journalism student, had the upper berth; I had the lower one and was privileged, because this gave me the window seat and the table.

'You are a teacher and all you do is write,' said Fernando. 'Me, I'm supposed to be the journalist and I haven't even got a pen! You should be a journalist!'

'A geography teacher,' I said, pausing in my note-taking. 'And, you see, this is rather unusual geography.'

'This?'

We stared out the window.

'That mountain, for example.'

'Ah, yes,' he said. 'That is a big mountain.'

It was Nevada de Illimani, four miles high, dark brutal bulk surmounted by wind-whipped snow. And it lay beyond the plain where grey grass had been trampled flat by storms.

Fernando smiled. He had not seen my point at all. He said, 'I am so glad you are happy in my country.' And he left the compartment.

The mountain was soon far behind us; we were sprinting towards an irregular wall of rainclouds and hills, past wheatfields and pepper patches. The eastern horizon was white and domed, like the skyline of an Arabian city idealized in a fable; it was the far edge of the high plains, this range of mosque-like peaks buried to their domes and squat minarets, and it was so thin and yet so marvellously shaped that at times it appeared as oddly beautiful as a mirage. Nearer the railway line – but very far apart – were small mud huts. They had mud-block courtyards and some had corrals, but none of them had any windows. They were shut; there were no lights; they were no more than hovels, and they looked forlorn. At Viacha, which was a village, we stopped to take on passengers. Now there was only standing room in Second Class, the battered green coaches were filled to overflowing, and on the curves I could see three or four faces at every window. I had tried to walk through the train to these coaches, but they were impassable – the Second Class corridors were jammed with people and their belongings. There was no greater contrast than this glow-worm stuffed with Bolivians and those empty plains.

> It is equal to living in a tragic land
> To live in a tragic time.
> Regard now the sloping mountainous rocks
> And the river that batters its way over stones,
> Regard the hovels of those that live in this battered land.

There were no cars in the villages, no roads, no trees; only mud huts and cows, and Indians wrapped up against the cold. Except for the llamas which frisked when they saw the train, and the very shaggy mules which took no notice, travelling across the high plains was a bit like travelling through Texas. The hills were distant and slightly rounded – rain poured on one, the sun was setting on another – and the sky was enormous. The tracks

349

from now on were perfectly straight, and just before the daylight was entirely gone the air became very cold. In this empty land an Indian pushed a bicycle along a path and then cut across a barren field, and later I saw a woman watching some still sheep. In the gathering dusk, some miles further on, an Indian woman and two small children laboured across the plain leading five mules which were carrying loads of farm tools, shovels and hoes. In a cloudy sunset, the village of Ayoayo – mud houses and a church – looked like a distant outpost from another age; it lay in the middle of the plain and it was so small the train did not stop.

The land became hillier, and a range of rugged bare mountains appeared – so high they were brightly lit by the setting sun, although we were travelling in near darkness. And the condors, too, flew so high they caught the light. The last Indian I saw that day was walking away from the train through a gulch. He wore sandals, but – in spite of the cold – no socks.

I saw what I thought at first was a Christ statue, but as we grew near it changed from the shape of a man to the shape of a bottle. It *was* a bottle, and it was twenty feet high and made of wood. It stood in utter emptiness and the large letters on its side said *Inka-Cola*.

By then I had brought my diary up to date. I was pleased with myself: my work was done for the day, and I was well settled in this sleeping car and moving south towards the border. I went to the dining car, and there I found Fernando, who was drinking beer with his friend Victor and a third man – either drunk or naturally surly – whose name I did not catch. They invited me to join them and they asked me the usual South American questions: Where was I from? Where had I been? Was I a Catholic? What did I think of their country?

They hate to be criticized, the man in Ecuador had told me. *Never criticize them.* This advice had not worked in Peru, where praise only antagonized Peruvians and made them think that I sympathized with their rotten government. But Bolivians – if Fernando and his friends were anything to go by – clearly wanted to be praised.

'Bolivia's a wonderful country,' I said.

'It is, isn't it?' said Victor. He smiled coldly. The others agreed. Surely, we knew we were lying?

'Take Peru,' said Fernando.

The three Bolivians ran down Peru for a minute.

I said, 'Most Peruvians would agree with you.'

'Chile is the worst of all,' said Victor.

'What about Ecuador?' asked the surly man.

'They have a military dictatorship,' said Fernando.

It was an uninspired remark. Every country that had been mentioned, including Bolivia, had a military dictatorship.

I said, 'Ecuador is going to hold an election.'

'So are we,' said Victor.

Four months later the Bolivian election was held. There were shootings all over the country, mysterious machine-gunnings, and stuffed ballot boxes. It was generally agreed that the election had been rigged, and then the head of state, General Banzer, 'annulled' the election. A state of siege was declared and a new government was formed in what was officially termed a 'bloodless coup'. Within five months there was a counter-coup and another promise to hold elections.

Peru was backward, said Fernando. Chile's black market was so bad you couldn't buy a tube of toothpaste, said Victor. The surly man said that they were massacring Indians in Brazil. Fernando said he knew a thing or two about newspapers: Bolivia's papers were the best in South America, but Argentina's seldom printed foreign news. The rest was hearsay: Paraguay was an unspeakable swamp, Colombia was full of thieves, and the Panamanians were so stupid and had such a tyrannical leader they didn't deserve the canal.

We went on drinking beer and the Bolivians went on belittling their neighbours. I suggested that they shared some national characteristics and recounted what the lady in Ecuador had told me about altitude being a factor in the South American consciousness. They said this was nonsense; they were insistent in exaggerating the differences. Oddest of all, they had not said much about Bolivia – and Bolivia could not have been nearer: it was this old-fashioned dining car and hurrying waiters; it was the Indians who were hunkered down in the doorway, and the cold downpour on the high plains out of the window. Perhaps reading my mind, Victor said, 'We have one problem in Bolivia.'

'Only one?' I asked.

'One major problem,' he said. 'The sea. The Chileans ought to let us have a bit – or the Peruvians. We need a seaport of our own. It is because we don't have one that we have so many other problems. What can you do without a seaport?'

'He likes Bolivian beer,' said Fernando.

'Yes,' I said, 'it's very nice.'

'Look at that man,' said Victor.

At a side table a man was drinking beer. One look told me he was an American. He wore lumberjack shoes and the sort of woollen plaid forester's shirt that graduate students in state universities especially favour. His shirt-tails hung down, his beard was shaggy; he drank his beer straight from the bottle, tipping it up and then wiping his mouth with his forearm and belching.

'That is ugly,' said Victor.

'He could have asked the waiter for a glass,' said Fernando.

The surly man had started to smile. 'Look at that! Glug-glug' – he mimicked with his thumb – 'right out of the bottle!'

'Very ugly,' said Victor.

'I think he is an American,' I said.

'He must be a German,' said Victor. 'Germans drink beer like that.'

We were speaking in Spanish – incautiously, it turned out, for a moment later the man stood up and said in fluent, American-accented Spanish, 'I am an American and this is the way Americans drink beer.' He drained his bottle, belched and walked towards Second Class.

While we were eating, I got a severe stomach cramp. I excused myself and went back to my compartment. The train had stopped. This was Oruro, a fairly large city, mostly Indian, near Lake Uru Uru. The rain had intensified; it beat against the window in a torrent made silver by the arc-lamps of the station. I got into bed and turned off the light and curled up to ease my cramp. I woke at about midnight. It was very cold in the compartment and so dusty – the dust seemed an effect of the train's rapid motion – I could barely breathe. I tried the lights, but they didn't work. I struggled to open the door – it seemed locked from the outside. I was choking, freezing and doubled up with stomach pains. I had no choice but to remain calm. I took four swigs of my stomach cement, and then buried my face in my blanket and waited for the morphine to work.

At dawn, I saw why I had not been able to get the door open: it had been bolted top and bottom by Fernando, who was still asleep in the upper berth. And I still felt terrible. I had imagined that after fifteen hours we would be off the high plains and perhaps rumbling through a valley nearer sea-level. I had been mistaken. We were still at 12,000 feet and travelling across a gaunt moonscape of dry rocks and empty craters. Alcohol worsens the symptoms of altitude sickness; and a hang-over at a high altitude makes one feel close to death. The landscape was cheerless and full of hard sharp rocks, a plain of tormented flint. There were not even Indians here in the cold Cordillera de Chichas. The few pools of water I saw looked gelid, and then I noticed that these were crusts of dusty ice, and further on dirt-speckled swatches of snow, like hanks and rags of torn underwear. Snow!

Over breakfast of dry toast and tea, I talked with Victor. It seemed that he and Fernando (the surly man had disappeared) had decided to get away from it all. They had chosen a town in Southern Bolivia; the train would stop there later in the day. What did they plan to do there?

'Nothing,' said Victor.

I said I knew exactly what he meant.

'And maybe read,' said Victor. 'I love to read American novels.'

'Who are your favourite authors?'

'E. Bing Walla,' he said without hesitation. 'Also Artur Ailie and Tyla Cowdway.'

'Never heard of them,' I said.

The paperbacks were in his briefcase, Spanish translations of Irving Wallace, Arthur Hailey and Taylor Caldwell. 'This,' he said, picking up the Taylor Caldwell novel, 'is about Cicero. But I am sure you have read these authors.'

'I have never read a single word of any of them.'

'What is your book?'

It was a Jack London novel, *The Assassination Bureau*. I had not been enjoying it. 'It has a bad smell. In English we say, "It stinks".'

'Eet sdeenks,' he repeated.

'I feel terrible,' I said. 'It's this altitude, I think I should go back to bed.'

I went and lay down on my bunk, propped by a pillow, and watched our progress through creased mountains the colour of gunpowder. I guessed that we must by now be descending from the high plains. What settlements I could see were derelict, with ruined churches and collapsed fences, but otherwise there was nothing for miles but scrub and rock and small brown creeks. Fernando and Victor came into the compartment from time to time. Are you all right? they asked. I said I was fine, but I still felt crummy, and I was growing worried: I had drunk the last of my cement, and still my stomach cramps had not gone away.

The hours passed and the train rocked enraging the porcupine which now lived in my abdomen. Then we came to Tupiza, and Fernando and Victor said good-bye. Even in sunshine Tupiza, a heap of brown houses on a hillside, looked as forlorn as Dogpatch. There were condors circling it and some curious Indians squinting at the two new arrivals, who would be spending several weeks with them. Just the thought of standing on the platform in such a place, and watching the train depart as silence sifted down on the village, was enough to make me shudder.

We moved off at the speed of a jogger and for the next few hours followed the west bank of a wide muddy river, the Camblaya. There were bushes here, and cactus growing like cudgels, and even some cornfields between the dry hills. I thought then that we had descended to a lower altitude, but really it had not changed much. I was deceived by the disappearance of my cramps; feeling slightly better I believed we had left the high plains. But only this river valley was fertile – the rest was dry and mountainous desert, the maddeningly unfriendly landscape of a nightmare. It was an immense and empty country. There were brambles and small willows near the diminished river, but the rest was dusty blue – the hills, the gorges, the twisted knots of cactus.

The hills grew flatter, the river was lost from view, and for miles ahead there was only this wasteland. The train did not vary its speed. It crept slowly along, under a clear sky, across this repeating aridity. The only interesting landscape was elsewhere: to the west, where there were canyons; to the east, a mountain range of snowcapped peaks, with the same elusive sparkle of a mirage that I had detected the day before outside La Paz. The Andes, people call them; but the name means nothing. It seemed remarkable to me that mountains so huge and snowy should have such a simple general name and not be known by individual names. But this variegated desert, a thousand miles of plateau and strange shapes, was known by no other name than the high plains. And even the map is notoriously without names or descriptions. The train rolled through cloud-land; there were a half dozen stops, but the rest was unknown. Now everyone on this train was travelling to the frontier town, which had a name.

Nearer Villazon the train had speeded up and sent grazing burros scampering away. We came to the station: the altitude was given – we were as high here as we had been at La Paz. The Argentine sleeping car was shunted onto a siding, and the rest of the train rolled down a hill and out of sight. There were five of us in this sleeping car, but no one knew when we would be taken across the border. I found the conductor, who was swatting flies in the corridor; and I asked him.

'We will be here a long time,' he said. He made it sound like years.

The town was not a town. It was a few buildings necessitated by the frontier post. It was one street, unpaved, of low hut-like stores. They were all shut. Near the small railway station, about twenty women had set up square home-made umbrellas and were selling fruit and bread and shoelaces. On arriving at the station, the mob of Indians had descended from the train, and there had been something like excitement; but the people were now gone, the train was gone. The market women had no customers and nothing moved but the flies above the mud puddles. It made me gasp to walk the length of the platform, but perhaps I had walked too fast – at the far end an old crazy Indian woman was screaming and crying beside a tree stump. No one took any notice of her. I bought half a pound of peanuts and sat on a station bench, shelling them. 'Are you in that sleeping car?' asked a man hurrying towards me. He was shabbily dressed and indignant.

I told him I was.

'What time is it leaving?'

I said, 'I wish I knew.'

He said, 'I am going to get some answers.'

He went into the station and rapped on a door. From within the building a voice roared, 'Go away!'

The man came out of the station. He said, 'These people are all whores.' He walked through the puddles back to the sleeping car.

The Indian woman was still screaming, but after an hour or two I grew accustomed to it, and the screams were like part of the silence of Villazon. The sleeping car looked very silly, stranded on the track. And there was no train in sight, no other coach or railway car. We were on a bluff. A mile south, across a bridge and up another hill was the Argentine town of La Quiaca. It too was nowhere, but it was there that we were headed, somehow, sometime.

A pig came over and sucked at the puddle near my feet and sniffed at the peanut shells. The clouds built up, massing over Villazon, and a heavy truck rattled by, blowing its horn for no reason, raising dust, and heading into Bolivia. Still the Indian woman screamed. The market women packed their boxes and left. It was dusk, and the place seemed deader than ever.

Night fell. I went to the sleeping car. It lay in darkness: no electricity, no lights. The corridor was thick with flies. The conductor beat a towel at them.

'What time are we going?'

'I do not know,' he said.

I wanted to go home.

But it was pointless to be impatient. I had to admit that this was unavoidable emptiness, a hollow zone which lay between the more graspable experience of travel. What good would it do to lose my temper or seek to shorten this time? I would have to stick it out. But time passes slowly in the darkness. The Indian woman screamed; the conductor cursed the flies.

I left the sleeping car and walked towards a low lighted building which I guessed might be a bar. There were no trees here, and little moonlight: the distances were deceptive. It took me half an hour to reach the building. And I was right: it was a coffee shop. I ordered a coffee and sat in the empty room waiting for it to come. Then I heard a train whistle.

A frail barefoot Indian girl put the coffee cup down.

'What train is that?'

'It is the train to La Quiaca.'

'Shit!' I put some money down and without touching the coffee ran all the way back to the sleeping car. When I arrived, the engine was being coupled to the coach, and my throat burned from the effort of running at such a high altitude. My heart was pounding. I threw myself onto my bed and panted.

Outside, a signalman was speaking to one of the passengers.

'The tracks up to Tucuman are in bad shape,' he said. 'You might not get there for days.'

Damn this trip, I thought.

We were taken across the border to the Argentine station over the hill. Then the sleeping car was detached and we were again left on a siding. Three hours passed. There was no food at the station, but I found an Indian woman who was watching a tea-pot boil over a fire. She was surprised that I should ask her to sell me a cup, and she took the money with elaborate grace. It was past midnight, and at the station there were people huddled in blankets and sitting on their luggage and holding children in their arms. Now it started to rain, but just as I began to be exasperated I remembered that these people were the Second Class passengers, and it was their cruel fate to have to sit at the dead centre of this continent waiting for the train to arrive. I was much luckier than they. I had a berth and a First Class ticket. And there was nothing to be done about the delay.

So I did what any sensible person would do, stuck on the Bolivia–Argentine frontier on a rainy night. I went to my compartment and washed my face; I put on my pyjamas and went to bed.

There was a knock on the compartment door: the conductor.

'Tickets please.'

'Where are we?'

'La Quiaca.'

Still on the border.

'When are we leaving?'

'In a few minutes.'

Sure, I thought, and went back to sleep. Despair and impatience had a soporific effect. But I was woken some time later by a train whistle and a grunting of metal, then the anvil noises of the coupling. At last we were on our way.

I slept for twelve hours. I woke again at six in the morning, and saw that we had come to a station. There were three poplars outside the window. In the early afternoon I woke again. The three poplars were still outside the window. We had not moved.

This was Humahuaca, a small town in northern Argentina. We had travelled no more than 100 miles since leaving La Quiaca, and had dropped about 1,000 feet. The day was cool and sunny, with a crackle of insects and a joyful sound of church bells. It was Sunday, and the place looked serene. I was unused to seeing flower gardens – rows of chrysanthemums – and a kind of dogged prosperity. It was the first railway station I had seen for weeks that did not have at least one pig snuffling near the tracks or chickens clucking in the station master's office. I was encouraged by this appearance of order: this was obviously a different country, and the filthy train with its fly-blown coaches looked out of place here.

A glamorous woman of about forty was showing a pretty girl around the station. She said in Spanish, 'This is the train to Tucuman – it came all the way from Bolivia. Aren't you glad we came by car?'

The girl winced at the Panamerican.

I wanted to see the town, but I was afraid of being duffilled.

Humahuaca was a nice place, but it was miles from anywhere; and there would not be another train for three days.

I asked the sleeping car attendant what was up.

The tracks, he said. Somewhere down the line there was a break in the tracks, either flooding or a landslide. It could not be fixed earlier because the men could not work at night. It was serious: something to do with a volcano.

'We cannot leave for hours,' he said.

I went for a stroll in the town and saw Indians returning from church with wilted flowers. Then I remembered that it was Palm Sunday. There was great contentment on the faces of these people, a kind of after-church radiance, the pure joy that goes under the name of holiness. There were hundreds of them, and each one carried a flower.

But the rest of the town was shut, the restaurants closed, the bus depot deserted. I made a circuit of the town park and then returned to the railway station.

In the hours that had elapsed since the Panamerican had arrived at the station the atmosphere had changed. The train had brought squalor to the station and transformed it into a muck-heap. There were orange peels and banana skins under every window – the station was too respectable to have pigs nearby to eat them; and water poured from beneath the coaches, and there were heaps of shit under each toilet pipe. The sun had grown stronger, and flies collected around the coaches. This express train, so dramatic when it was on the move, became foul when it was stationary.

I thought that I was the only foreigner on the train. I should have known better. Experience had shown me that there was always a German in Second Class, slumbering on his pack-frame and spitting orange pips out of the window. At Humahuaca, it was Wolfgang. He had boarded the Bolivian segment of the train in the cold downpour at Oruro and he had suffered in Second Class ever since. I had not seen him, though he said he had seen me, buying tea from the Indian woman in La Quiaca. He had been travelling for months through Central and South America, and had only the vaguest idea of where he was going. He was certain of one thing: if he did not have the luck to find a

359

job in Buenos Aires he would be in Argentina for the rest of his life. Frankly, he was eager to go home, he said.

Sometimes, in the presence of such a person – I had met many – I felt rather ashamed that I had travelled so swiftly from Boston. Two months before, I had boarded the Lake Shore Limited in South Station and after a few snowy days I had been rattling under clear skies to Mexico. I had not been robbed or fallen seriously ill; I had seen pretty places and met pleasant people. I had filled hundreds of pages of my diary and now I felt certain that I would make it to Esquel in Patagonia, the small town I had seen on my map which had become an arbitrary destination. I had breezed through most of the countries, and I was always brought up short when I met another traveller who said he was planning to spend a month in, say, Barranquilla or Cuzco. 'I didn't like Ecuador,' an American told me in Peru. 'Maybe I didn't give it enough time.' He had been there two months, which seemed an eternity to me.

Wolfgang's story was the same – a month here, a month there, two months somewhere else. He had been practically a resident in these places; he was like a man looking for a new life. I knew I was merely skimming south, a bird of passage generalizing on the immediate. But because I had no camera, and had written so much, my impressions of what I had seen were vivid. I could call up Mexico or Costa Rica by glancing at the conversations I had written, and from the particularities of the railway journey from Santa Marta to Bogotá I felt I could reinvent Colombia. Travel was, above all, a test of memory.

So, partly to kill time – the train was still stalled at Humahuaca – and partly to relieve myself of the guilt I felt with someone who regarded me as no more than a tourist, I asked Wolfgang what he remembered of the places he had been.

'This is a quiz,' I said. 'I'll say the name of a place and you tell me what you remember best about it. Pretend I'm someone who has never travelled anywhere – I want to know what these places are like. Okay?'

'It's a good game,' he said.

'Ready? Here goes. Mexico.'

'Americans have a lot of trouble there,' said Wolfgang.

'Guatemala.'

'I missed the bus to San Salvador, but my pack was still on it, so my passport too. I spent three dollars on phone calls. It was terrible.'

'Nicaragua.'

'I should not have gone there.'

'Costa Rica.'

'Dull.'

'Colombia.'

'Lots of nice food in the markets, but I got sick there.'

'Maybe it was the food,' I said. 'What about Ecuador?'

'One month I am there, trying to take the buses.'

'Peru.'

'Nice and cheap.'

'Bolivia.'

'All the people in Bolivia are stupid.'

'Argentina.'

'I will be here for some weeks or months,' he said 'So? I have passed the test?'

'You flunked, Wolfgang.'

He only became concrete when the conversation turned to the exchange rate. Here it was 670 pesos to the dollar, but there were towns where you could get 680. The difference was much less than a cent, but Wolfgang was the embodiment of the maxim I had devised earlier in this trip: It is the raggedest traveller who has the most precise notion of the exchange rate. Wolfgang wasn't looking for another life. Travel for him, as for many others, was just another way of saving money.

Without any warning, the train began to move. We ran from where we were standing on the platform and jumped on to the train, Wolfgang to Second, I to First. I did not see him again until two days later, in Tucuman.

The Panamerican travelled along a flat green valley, beside a nearly dry but very wide river – the Rio Grande de Jujuy. Mountains rose swiftly out of the valley. They were old and cracked and extremely high, a whole range of them without a single tree. The cliffs, where they had been exposed to wind, were pink, smeared with maroon and orange – these were the high cliffs and peaks; the hills nearer the river were like mounds of mud. These hillocks, and the fact that the mountains were without any foliage, gave the mountain range a look of brutal authority: the contours were exposed, the flanks were pitted with rock-slides and clawed white by erosion, and the rounded peaks of the lower slopes looked like collapsed tents, or the blankets – with the same folds – that the Indians used to cover their belongings. A brown stream ran through the centre of the sluiced-out trough of river – this was all that was left of the Rio Grande; and on each bank there were poplars and willows and cactuses and mud-block houses at the periphery of ploughed fields. It was a strange sight, the bare mountains above the green valley, the wide river bed that had so little water in it, and the only human figure an old man, like the stereotype of the grizzled prospector, stumbling from bank to bank.

There were cornfields, tomato gardens and sunflowers, and fields of blue cabbage that looked much grander than the colourless huts. We were moving slowly through Argentina, but this was a more agreeable altitude. I could feel the change in myself, and I had slept well. I liked the look of Argentina. The landscape was wide-open and fertile. It seemed underpopulated, awaiting settlement, and it was easy to understand why Welshmen and Germans and Italians had come here and disappeared, carting their culture into a mountain valley and ignoring the rest of the world.

Dust flew through the window of my compartment. My worry was my wounded hand. I washed it and changed the bandage. I was sure that if dust got into my unhealed cut it would become infected. The dust storm ceased at Tilcara, which lay under poplars on the side of a mountain. There were people picnicking here, and it looked like a remote part of Italy. The people were almost certainly Italian settlers, the old women in black, the pot-bellied men standing in the shade of apple trees. But Tilcara was an oasis. A hundred yards outside the town, after a notice *Do Not Destroy the Trees* (perversely enough, it was like a sign of civilization), the dust began to fly, and the naked mountains were streaked with yellow sandstone.

We crossed the Tropic of Capricorn. The line was actual, a

fissure that ran over the mountains which were themselves marked with stratified stripes as on a topographical map, pink, orange, green; indeed, the landscape was as simple and clearly coloured as a map, accurately reproduced on the paper square before me – black railway line running through brown valley edged in green, pink and orange contours in their proper places. This was near Maimara. There were only a few houses to be seen, but the yellow chapel had been built in the mid-seventeenth century. The people in these Argentine towns looked as if they were there to stay, while in Bolivia the towns had the look of imminent desertion.

A lame dog in Maimara reminded me that, since leaving the United States, I had not seen a dog that wasn't lame, or a woman who wasn't carrying something, or an Indian without a hat, or – anywhere – a cat.

We were supposed to have been in Maimara for three minutes, no more, but after an hour we were still there, in the late afternoon sunshine. I sat on the steps of the platform and smoked my pipe. Seeing me, a man on a path by the railway tracks came over and asked me where I was going. He was short, and very dark, with slits for eyes, a broad face and chubby hands. I assumed he was Indian, or half Indian – the Incas had come this far, and even beyond, as far as Jujuy.

I told him I was going to Tucuman on this train.

There was a volcano farther south, he said; it had caused a mudslide and ripped the tracks apart. It seemed that they were trying to fix it, but in any case it was four hours to Jujuy, and I certainly would not be in Tucuman until tomorrow.

'What's the point of travelling?' said this swarthy provincial. 'I've been around the country – Jujuy, La Quiaca, all the places. But none of them is as good as Maimara. We've got apples, corn, pears – everything you need. It's easy to grow things here, and it's a pretty town. I saw Villazon once – it was really ugly. I would hate to live there. Here, I have everything I need.'

'Good for you.'

'You should stay here,' he said.

'The train doesn't seem to be going, so I guess I am staying here.'

'It is the volcano – it wrecked the tracks. Where are you headed after Tucuman?'

'Buenos Aires, and then Patagonia.'

'Patagonia! That's so far away they speak differently there.' He grinned at me. 'So you were at La Quiaca and you're going to Patagonia. They are at opposite ends of Argentina. I would never go to those places. I would rather stay home.'

'After Patagonia, I will go home.'

'That's the idea!' he said. 'It must be terrible to be so far away from home on a nice Sunday afternoon like this.'

'It is sunny here,' I said. 'I am sure it is rainy at home.'

'That's interesting,' he said, and thanked me. He disappeared beyond the rattling poplars.

Just south of Purmamarca, in a dry river bed – the wide valley was surrounded by clouded mountains – I saw a Palm Sunday procession. I guessed it was that, but it might have been anything. There were easily 2,000 people making their way down the river bed. Many were on horseback, some waved banners and flags, and there was a smartly dressed band, the source of a lugubrious braying. Near the front of the procession some people carried a white box, a coffin, either emblematic or real. And what made this group especially strange was the sky lowering upon them. They were a multitude of tiny figures in a gigantic mural, in which the important feature was the granite muscle in this toppling cloud.

The train moved on, and the cloud continued to drop. It slid down the mountains and into the valley and down the river bed. It hovered at the tree-tops and the afternoon darkened. In fifteen minutes the landscape had changed from an overpowering vista of Argentina to a weeping late-afternoon in New England. The visibility was about fifty yards; it was warm and dimly white, a world of sudden ghostliness.

It began to drizzle and beside the track there were cleared mudslides. The damage was obvious: wrecked walls and tipped-over culverts, and water rushing at sand-bags. I hung out of the door to look at the land-slip and behind me the sleeping car attendant said, 'This is the volcano.'

'I didn't realize there were volcanoes here.'

'No, the town is called Volcano.'

I had got it wrong: what I had taken to be a volcano – the descriptions I had heard up the line – was just the name of the town.

'How are we doing?' I asked.

'We will be a day and a half late in arriving in Buenos Aires.'

I spent the rest of the daylight hours reading Friedrich Dürrenmatt's *End of the Game*. Its original title, a better one, was *The Judge and His Hangman*. After Jack London's feeble and preposterous plot, Dürrenmatt's struck me as brilliant; and necessary, too, since he had little insight. Such order made him seem like a sage. For railway reading, the best book is the plottiest, a way of endowing the haphazardness of the journey with order.

At Jujuy I saw that the river which had been dry some miles north was in full flood. Here the Rio Grande deserved its name. Along its banks were leafy trees and flowers, and an evening mist hung over the water. Jujuy looked peaceful and damp; it was just high enough to be pleasant without giving one a case of the bends. The rain on the blossoms perfumed the dark air and a fresh breeze blew from the river. It seemed idyllic, and yet later I heard that Jujuy was so badly flooded that thousands of people had to be evacuated from their homes. It is not possible to see everything from a train.

The station was full of Indians, who had come to welcome the Indians on this train from the border. This was the last place in Argentina where I saw so many Indians, and there were people in Argentina who denied that they existed in this country in any great number. So Jujuy seemed a frontier of sorts, the end of the old Inca trail. It was green, a town buried – so it seemed – in lush depthless spinach.

I would gladly have stayed here, and nearly did, but as I stood on the platform I saw twenty new coaches being hitched to our train and, with them, an attractive dining car. I felt wonderful now: no cramps, no altitude sickness; my appetite had returned (and only the day before I had been sitting in Villazon, eating peanuts), and with it a thirst. I went to the dining car and ordered a carafe of wine. The waiter, dressed in a black uniform, set all the tables – tablecloths, silver, vases of flowers. But his exertions were premature. I was the only customer that night.

Dinner – now we were proceeding via the town of General Miguel Martin de Guemes to Tucuman – was five courses: home-made noodle soup, sausage and polenta, veal cutlets, ham salad and dessert. Although the waiter stood nearby, supplying me with a new carafe of wine every so often, after I finished and lit my pipe he sat down with me, clinked glasses and we talked.

He spoke Spanish with a strong Italian accent – many people did in Argentina. But his Italian was poor. 'I'm an Italian,' he said, but he said it in the way Americans say they are Polish or Armenian: it is the immigrant's claim, or excuse, in an undefined country.

'We are lucky to get through on this train,' he said. 'This is the first train in two weeks that's made it past Volcano. Did you see the landslide?'

I had: the hill of mud had moved sideways across the track.

'Several trains tried to get through it when it was only half cleared and, *tweet*, off the tracks they came – derailed. So they stopped taking chances. I've been sitting for two weeks waiting for the train to arrive.'

What a fate: this steward waits two weeks in Jujuy for the Panamerican, and then it comes, they hitch up his dining car and all he gets is one customer – me. Yet he did not seem especially downhearted.

'What countries have you seen?'

I told him.

'And, of all of them, which one do you like most?'

They hate criticism.

'Argentina,' I said.

'The rest of them are so poor,' he said. 'Know how much the best steak costs here? Take a guess.'

I guessed too low; I gave him the peso equivalent of fifty cents. He said – and he was slightly annoyed – that a pound of filet mignon cost seventy-five cents.

It seemed a specious argument for prosperity in a country where the annual inflation rate was between 300 and 400 per

366

cent. Every day, the peso was worth less, and everything but steak rose in price. Most Argentines had steak twice a day, and even the lowliest clerk ordered a great shoe of it, with french fries, at lunch time. And it reminded me that the most violently critical pieces I had read about Argentina were by V. S. Naipaul. His articles appeared in *The New York Review of Books*, and they aroused a certain amount of controversy. No one had made the obvious point about Naipaul's loathing of Argentina, but then perhaps it was not commonly known that he was a vegetarian.

'What do you think of this train?'

Whatever you do, don't criticize them.

'It is one of the best trains I've ever seen in my life.'

'It *should* be the best. It's got good equipment – reclining chairs, lots of space and comfort. But look at the people! They're in First Class and they spit on the floor, hang their clothes on the light fixtures, stick their feet up on the nice chairs.' He made mocking Italian gestures and mimicked the slobs he was describing; the cooks, who had also come over to sit with us, found this very funny. 'You see them? What can we do? They don't know how to ride on a train, that's all.'

His blame was general. He did not single out a group, and what was more interesting, he did not mention Indians. I found this a relief. One of the pleasures of Argentina – it had also been one in Costa Rica – was that one could be wholly anonymous. The faces on the Panamerican at this point were the faces one might see on any train in the United States, or Europe for that matter. It was possible to enter a crowd in Argentina and vanish. It was very restful for anonymity to be available to me; it simplified travel and allowed me to stare at people for long periods without being detected.

I slept well that night, but woke to hear the attendant pounding on my compartment door.

'Wake up,' he cried. 'We're at Tucuman! You have to get up!'

I opened the door.

'Hurry, sir. All the other passengers have left.'

'How do I get to Buenos Aires?'

'You missed the train. You'll have to catch the North Star

tonight. See,' he said, pulling my suitcase out of the door, 'we should have been here last night. All the other passengers have the same problem.'

He helped me out into the grey dawn of Belgrano Station in Tucuman. The morning coolness was already condensing into humidity. There was fog giving an eeriness to the palm trees in the station garden. I checked my suitcase in at the Left Luggage window and went to have breakfast.

19 La Estrella del Norte ('The North Star') to Buenos Aires

Necessity kissed me with luck. There was no better way to leave the high plains – that world of kitty litter – than to slip across Argentina's simple frontier at night, make the acquaintance of its empty quarter the next day and, the following morning, arrive at a large provincial capital and to walk its streets while the city slept. It was only seven-thirty; not even the coffee shops were open. The royal palms and the dark green araucarias dripped in the mist. The day was mine; if nothing in the city of Tucuman persuaded me to stay, I could board the North Star that evening on a sleeper and wake up in Buenos Aires. There was a risk on this route. In my notebook, I had a clipping which I had cut out of a Bogotá newspaper. *Railway Catastrophe in Argentina: 50 Dead*, ran the Spanish headline. 'The train "The North Star", said the police, was leaving the province of Tucuman when it charged a heavy truck at a level crossing.' The incident, which was reported with all the enthusiasm Latin Americans have for disasters, had happened only a month before. 'You will have no difficulty getting a berth on that train,' a station porter told me in Tucuman. 'Ever since it crashed, people have been frightened to take it.'

Tucuman was older, flatter, cleaner and a great deal duller than I had expected. It was the ultimate provincial town, self-contained and remote, and being an Argentine town it was thoroughly European in a rather old-fashioned way, from the pin-striped suits and black moustaches of the old men idling in the cafés or having their shoes shined in the plaza, to the baggy, shapeless school uniforms of the girls stopping on their way to the convent school to squeeze – it was an expression of piety – the knee of Christ on the cathedral crucifix. Old Europe was evident in the façades of the houses in the centre of the city, in

369

all the paperwork at the bank (every transaction recorded in triplicate), in the contrived glamour of the women shopping and in the vain posturing and hair-combing of the young men. The houses were French, the official buildings Italian baroque, the monuments and statues pure South American – they seemed to get more outlandish as one moved south, the goddesses and sprites got nakeder, the heroes sterner and more truculently posed.

After the barrel-chested Indians living among wind-haunted rocks in the high plains, and the farmers in the tumbledown villages near the border, and the yawning cracked-open river valleys of the north, I was prepared for anything but Tucuman. It was gloomy, but gloom was part of the Argentine temper; it was not a dramatic blackness, but rather a dampness of soul, the hang-dog melancholy immigrants feel on rainy afternoons far from home. There was no desolation, and if there were barbarities they remained dark secrets and were enacted in the torture chambers of the police stations or in the cramped workers' quarters of the sugar planations. It was four in the afternoon before I found a bar – Tucuman was that proper.

I spent the day walking. It was cloudy and humid, and the light was so poor, the box-camera man in the Plaza Independencia (Argentina's independence was declared in Tucuman in 1816) could not get a likeness of me until he had made two tries. And what was it – perhaps the sombre tones of a Buñuel movie? – that made me think of Tucuman as the sort of place a sad innocent child would be sent to spend a terrifying week with his maiden aunt, among her dusty heirlooms. I imagined pretty, persecuted servant girls in the narrow houses, and the steady tick of ormolu clocks in high-ceilinged parlours. But this was fantasy, a stroller's embroidery. I found a tourist office. The lady gave me three brochures, each urging me to leave Tucuman: to go to the mountains, to the woods outside town, or – and this amused me – to visit Jujuy. One of the attractions of Tucuman, it appeared, was that it was a day's drive from Jujuy.

The curios in Tucuman were versions of gaucho kitsch – sets of bolas, toy horse-whips, overpriced daggers; and there were also salt shakers, aprons, calendars and little boxes made out of cactus fibre, all stamped *Tucuman*. The bookshelves were vastly more impressive than any I had seen on this trip, or was this a stubborn bias I had formed after seeing three of my own titles on display in Spanish translation? I made a note of the publisher's address in Buenos Aires: I would look him up when I arrived.

I did little else in Tucuman but buy a pizza – a thick Neapolitan-style pizza, garnished with anchovies. This reminded me of a sad remark I had heard in Peru. 'Times are so bad in Peru,' a man said, 'even the anchovy has left our waters and swum away.' As the day wore on I became firmer in my resolve to leave Tucuman on the North Star. I ran into Wolfgang later in the day and we walked together to the railway station. He was happy. In twenty-four hours the dollar had risen five pesos, 'and tomorrow it will be more.' He was delighted with the way things were going, and I saw him in Buenos Aires, waking each morning to examine the rise in the inflation rate. For Wolfgang, inflation was a great dividend.

The North Star was waiting at the platform.

Wolfgang sighed. 'After this,' he said, 'I take no more trains.'

'Want something to read?' I took out the Dürrenmatt novel and handed it to him.

'I have read it before, in German,' he said, after examining it. But he kept it all the same: 'I can practise my English language.'

Oswaldo, who had the lower berth in my compartment on the North Star, was a jumpy, fast-talking salesman on his way to Rosario to sell some meat. He had wanted to take a plane, but his company said it was too expensive. 'This same train crashed about a month ago. Lots of people got killed – the coaches were burning, it was terrible.' He looked out of the window, jerking the curtains apart. 'I hope it doesn't happen to us. I don't want to be in a train crash. But I have a very bad feeling about this train.'

His conversation was so depressing that I took myself to the dining car and sat at a table with the Tucuman newspaper and a bottle of beer. There was a gloating report in the paper about the right-wing parties having won in the French elections and about kidnappings in Italy. ('Our terrorists have all gone to Europe,' an Argentine man said to me in Buenos Aires. There was something vindictive in his commiseration. 'Now you will have a taste of what we've been through.') The press in Argentina made political capital out of reporting other countries' news.

'With your permission,' said Oswaldo, seating himself at my table. He carried a comic book. It was a Spanish one, about an inch thick, and its title was *D'Artagnan* – the name of the goonish swashbuckler in the cover story. It seemed fairly unambitious reading, even for a meat salesman.

I ignored him and looked out of the window. We left Tucuman, the city, then the province, and entered the adjacent province of Santiago de Estero. In the misty dusk, the cane fields and orange groves were richly green, like Ireland at twilight. There were fires in some of the farmyards, and enough light for me to make out the cane-cutters' brick sheds in a terrace row, and far-off the roofs and pillars of the owner's mansion, and the beautiful horses standing by the fence. Then night fell on the cane fields and the only sign of life was the yellow headlamps of cars wobbling down the country roads.

'This is where it happened,' said Oswaldo. He had put down his comic book. 'The crash.'

He braced himself against the table, as if he expected to be thrown off his chair. But the train continued to rock through Argentina and a man was singing in the kitchen.

Dinner was served at ten o'clock – four courses, including a fat steak, for two dollars. It was the sort of dining car where the waiters and stewards were dressed more formally than the people eating. All the tables were full, a well-fed noisy crowd of mock-Europeans. Two men had joined Oswaldo and me, and after a decent pause and some wine, one of them began talking about his reason for going to Buenos Aires: his father had just had a heart attack.

He spoke in slushy Argentine Spanish, turning every double-L into a Russian *zha* sound. 'My father's eighty-five years old,' said the man, stuffing his mouth with bread. 'Never got sick a day in his life. He smokes all the time, practically eats cigarettes. He's very strong and healthy. I was surprised when they called me up and told me he'd had a heart attack. I said, "That man's never been sick a day in his life."'

'My father was the same,' said the second man. 'Very tough, a real old-timer. He didn't die of a heart attack. With him it was his liver.'

Oswaldo said, 'Well, my father –'

The first man was smoking and eating compulsively; smoke trickled out of his nostrils as he chewed bread. Every so often he'd call out, 'Boss!'

'Boss!' he yelled. 'Bring me an ashtray. I need an ashtray when I eat.'

He ate all the bread in the basket.

'Boss! More bread – I'm hungry. And, while you're at it, another beer – I'm thirsty.'

They had a lot of swagger, these men; they were full of talk and rather deficient in humour. They were not idle; in fact, they struck me as being hard-working. But, of all the people I met in South America, the Argentines were the least interested in the outside world or in any subject that did not directly concern Argentina. They shared this quality with white South Africans; they seemed to imply that they were stuck at the bottom of the world and surrounded by savages. They had a bluff bullying tone, even when they spoke to one another, and they were philistines to the core. This was my assessment on the North Star. It was not until I arrived in Buenos Aires that I met sweeter-natured people, and even intellectuals, and had to revise my opinion.

For the next half-hour Oswaldo and the other two talked about football. Argentina had just beaten Peru, and they were confident about Argentina's chances in the World Cup in July.

'Do you speak Spanish?' It was the first man, whose father had had the heart attack. He held a segment of bread near his mouth.

'Yes,' I said. 'I think it's adequate.'

'You don't say very much. That's why I'm asking.'

'I'm not interested in football.'

He smirked at the others. 'I mean, you don't join the conversation.'

'What conversation?'

'This one,' he said, growing impatient.

'About football.'

'No, about everything. We talk – you don't. You just sit there.'

'So what?' I said.

'Maybe something is wrong.'

So that was it: suspicion, fear, the sense that my silence meant disapproval; the old South American insecurity.

I said, 'Nothing is wrong. I am very happy to be here. Argentina is a wonderful country.'

'He is happy,' said the man. He still held the segment of bread in his hand. He moved his wine glass closer and said, 'Want to know what they do in Spain? Watch. This is what they do. Ready? They dunk their piece of bread in like this.' He dunked his piece of bread in the wine. 'Then they eat it. Like this.' He ate the soggy bread and, still chewing, he said, 'See? They put bread into wine. In Spain.'

I said, 'If you think that's strange, listen to this.'

They smiled: I had joined the conversation.

'The Italians put fruit into wine,' I went on. 'They chop up pears, peaches, bananas, and put them into a wine glass. They stir it, eat the fruit, and then drink the wine. Imagine doing that to a glass of wine!'

This did not go down well. They stared at me.

Finally, Oswaldo said, 'We do that, too.'

The meal ended with coffee and creme caramel, and then the second man launched into a boring description of what bread was called in different parts of Argentina. 'Now this, in Tucuman, we call a bun. But if you go to Cordoba they'll call it a roll. Over in Salta they call it a cake. But loaf – that's what they call it in –'

He went on and on, and the others chipped in with their regional differences. I felt I could add nothing to this. I said good night and walked through the speeding train and went to bed.

A dream claimed me. I was with a lovely sly woman in an Edwardian house. The house shook, the floor dipped and bobbed like a raft, and cracks made their way up the walls. The woman pleaded with me to explain this shaking. I looked out of the shattered front window, and then walked into the yard. There was such a wobble in the yard I could barely stand up; but it had to be felt – it could not be seen. The woman was at the window, and all the bricks around her were split.

'You are over a magnetic field,' I said. 'There is a wire down there loaded with electricity.' I was balancing unsteadily as I spoke. 'This magnetism is causing the house to shake –'

I woke up. The train was shaking like the yard in my dream, and I no longer remembered the woman's name.

It was a sunny day, and moments later we stopped at San Lorenzo on the Parana River. Across the river was the province of Entre Rios, and beyond that Uruguay. The land was flat, the fences entwined with morning glories, and horses cropped grass in the open pastures.

Oswaldo was packing. 'Those fellows we were having dinner with last night,' he said. 'They got interesting after you left. You should not have gone to bed so soon.'

'I didn't have anything to say.'

'You could have listened,' said Oswaldo. 'It was interesting. One of them is in the meat business. He knew me! Well, not personally, but he had heard of me.'

Oswaldo was very pleased with this. He finished packing. His comic book still lay on the seat.

'Want my book?'

I picked it up and glanced through it. *D'Artagnan* was a Spanish comic, luridly illustrated. *Super Album*, it said. *Ten Complete Stories in Full Colour*. I looked at the stories: 'Goodbye California,' 'We, The Legion,' 'Or-Grund, Viking Killer.' It was cowboys, detectives, cave men, soldiers, and ads for learning how to fix televisions in your spare time.

'I've got a book,' I said.

'I'm offering it to you for nothing,' said Oswaldo.

'I don't read comics.'

'This one is beautiful.'

Comics are for kids and illiterates, I wanted to say, but one was not supposed to criticize these people.

'Thank you,' I said. 'Do you ever read Argentine authors?'

'This,' he said, tapping the comic book in my hand, 'is an Argentine book. It is from Buenos Aires.'

'I was thinking of the other kind of books. Without pictures.'

'Stories?'

'Yes. Borges, for example.'

'Which Borges?'

'Jorge Luis.'

'I don't know him.'

He was bored by this and rather annoyed that I hadn't enthused when he had given me his comic book. He said good-bye a bit curtly and got off the train when we drew into Rosario. Rosario was industrial, suburban, and also on the Parana. These smells were mingled: factory smoke, flowering trees, the hot river. It was in one of these solid middle-class villas, in 1928, that Che Guevara was born. But it was not Rosario that made him a revolutionary, it was his experience in Guatemala – when the CIA gave Arbenz the push in 1954 – that provoked in him the conviction that South America was badly in need of another liberator. My peregrinations through these countries had led me to the same conclusions. In a way, Guevara's fate was worse than Bolívar's. Guevara's collapse was complete; his intentions were forgotten, but his style was taken up by boutique owners (one of the fanciest clothes boutiques in London is called Che Guevara). There is no faster way of destroying a man, or mocking his ideas, than making him fashionable. That Guevara succeeded in influencing dress-designers was part of his tragedy.

There was a look of September in the fields beyond Rosario, the depleted furrows, the litter of corn husks, the harvesters fuddling with hay bales. Farther on, the farming ceased and the grazing land took over, cattle stilled on green grass, windbreaks of gum trees. It could not have looked quieter or more orderly.

Here was an army camp, a suburb, a factory. Elsewhere in South America army camps could look as menacing as prisons, but this one was unfortified, and the soldiers on manoeuvres – they were attacking a tank in a field near the tracks – looked like boy scouts. The suburb did not look stifling, nor was the factory a blot on the landscape. It was easy to be fooled by appearances, but after what I had seen I needed the reassurance of this order, the lightness of this air, the glimpse of this hawk steadying itself in the sky.

There were many small stations here on the line, but the North Star did not stop at them. The land grew swampier – rivers, tributaries of the Parana, were brimming their banks and flooding the dirt roads. The flooding showed in the greenery it had produced: very tall blue-gums and thick woods. The ranch houses had elegance and space, but there were small square bungalows, too, each on its own fenced-in plot, the tiny house, tiny garden, tiny swimming pool.

Then the houses began to pile up – sheds at the marsh's edge, bigger houses and buildings farther on, water towers and church steeples. It was lunch time. Schoolgirls in white uniforms skipped on the pavements, and at the station called J. L. Suarez there were suburbanites waiting for the local train, and beyond them, beyond the graffiti (*Give Peron the Power*), were stern little houses in tight streets, and hedges, and, purely for decoration, banana trees. The cooks and waiters from the dining car got off at San Martin, where nearly all the houses were one-storey affairs; and, at Miguelete, more people got off and walked past the golf club – here a player waited for the train to pull out before making his putt.

The city itself, I knew, could not be far away. The houses became more splendid and with this splendour was a haunted look, like the ghostly houses in Borges' stories. They were built in the French style and had gothic grille-work and balconies and bolted shutters. They were the colour of a cobweb and just as fragile-seeming and half hidden by trees. The next open space was a park in a burst of sunlight. then a boulevard, and a glimpse of Europe and the hurry and fine clothes of people on a busy pavement. It was as if I had been travelling in a tunnel for months and had just popped out of the other end, at the far side of the earth, in a place that was maddeningly familiar, as venerable as Boston but much bigger.

Retiro Station was English-made and built to an English design, with a high, curved roof supported by girders forged in a Liverpool ironworks, and marble pillars and floors, ornately carved canopies, shafts of sunlight emphasizing its height and, indeed, everything of a cathedral but altars and pews. The stations and railways in Argentina are British in appearance for a very good reason: most of them were built and run by the British until, in 1947, in what was surely one of the worst business deals ever, Juan Peron bought them. If he had waited a few years, the British railway companies – which were losing money – would have given them to him for nothing. The Argentine Railways have been losing money ever since. But the equipment remains, and it was a relief to me, after such a long trip, to arrive at this station, in the heart of a complex and beautiful city. It reminded me that I had travelled a great distance, and this kind of arrival mattered more than the unearthly sights of the Andes and the high plains. It was not enough for me to know that I was in uninhabited altitudes; I needed to be reassured that I had reached a hospitable culture that was explainable and worth the trouble.

Buenos Aires is at first glance, and for days afterwards, a most civilized ant-hill. It has all the elegance of the old world in its buildings and streets, and in its people all the vulgarity and frank good health of the new world. All the news-stands and book shops – what a literate place, one thinks; what wealth, what good looks. The women in Buenos Aires were well-dressed, studiously chic, in a way that has been abandoned in Europe. I had expected a fairly prosperous place, cattle and gauchos, and a merciless dictatorship; I had not counted on its being charming, on the seductions of its architecture, or the vigour of its appeal. It was a wonderful city for walking, and walking I decided it would be a pleasant city to live in. I had been prepared for Panama and Cuzco, but Buenos Aires was not what I had expected. In the story 'Eveline' in James Joyce's *Dubliners*, the eponymous heroine reflects on her tedious life and her chance to leave Dublin with Frank: 'He had fallen on his feet in Buenos Ayres, he said, and had come over to the old country just for a holiday.' Frank is an adventurer in the new world and is full of stories ('he told her stories of the terrible Patagonians'); soon, he proposes marriage, and he urges her to make her escape from Dublin. She is determined to leave, but at the last moment – 'All the seas of the world tumbled about her heart' – her nerve fails her. Frank boards the boat-train and she remains in Dublin, 'like a helpless animal'.

The stories in *Dubliners* are sad – there are few sadder in literature – but 'Eveline' did not seem to me such a chronicle of thwarted opportunity until I saw the city she missed. There had seemed to me to be no great tragedy in failing to get to Buenos Aires; I assumed that Joyce used the city for its name, to leave the stinks of Dublin for the 'good airs' of South America. But the first girl I met in Buenos Aires was Irish, a rancher, and she spoke Spanish with a brogue. She had come in from Mendoza to compete in the World Hockey Championships and she asked me – though I would have thought the answer obvious – whether I too was a hockey player. In America, the Irish became priests, politicians, policemen – they looked for conventional status and took jobs that would guarantee them a degree of respect. In Argentina, the Irish became farmers and left the Italians to direct traffic. Clearly, Eveline had missed the boat.

In the immigrant free-for-all in Buenos Aires, in which a full third of Argentina's population lives, I looked in vain for what I considered to be seizable South American characteristics. I had become used to the burial-ground features of ruined cities, the beggars' culture, the hacienda economy, the complacent and well-heeled families squatting on Indians, government by nepotism, the pig on the railway platform. The primary colours of such crudities had made my eye unsubtle and spoiled my sense of discrimination. After the starving children of Colombia and the decrepitude of Peru, which were observable facts, it was hard to become exercised about press censorship in Argentina, which was ambiguous and arguable and mainly an idea. I had been dealing with enlarged visual simplicities; I found theory rarified and, here, in a city that seemed to work, was less certain of my ground. And yet, taking the measure of it by walking its streets, restoring my circulation – I had not really walked much since I had left Cuzco – it did not seem so very strange to me that this place had produced a dozen world-class concert violinists, and Fanny Foxe, the stripper; Che Guevara, Jorge Luis Borges, and Adolf Eichmann had all felt equally at home here.

There was a hint of this cultural overlay in the composition of the city. The pink-flowered 'drunken branch' trees of the pampas grew in the parks, but the parks were English and Italian, and this told in their names, Britannia Park, Palermo Park. The downtown section was architecturally French, the industrial parts German, the harbour Italian. Only the scale of the city was American; its dimensions, its sense of space, gave it a familiarity. It was a clean city. No one slept in its doorways or parks – this, in a South American context, is almost shocking to behold. I found the city safe to walk in at all hours and at three o'clock in the morning there were still crowds in the streets. Because of the day-time humidity, groups of boys played football in the floodlit parks until well after midnight. It was a city without significant Indian population – few, it seemed, strayed south of Tucuman, and what Indians existed came from Paraguay, or just across the Rio de la Plata in Uruguay. They worked as domestics, they lived in outlying slums, they were given little encouragement to stay.

It was a divided culture, but it was also a divided country. The Argentines I met said it was two countries – the uplands of the north, full of folklore and mountains and semi-barbarous settlers; and the 'humid pampas' of the south, with its cattle ranches and its emptiness, a great deal of it still virgin territory (pampas derives from an Aymara word meaning space). You have to travel a thousand miles for this division to be apparent, and Argentines – in spite of what they claim is their adventurous spirit – only travel along selected routes. They know Chile. Some know Brazil. They spend weekends at the fleshpots of Montevideo. The richer ones own second homes in the Patagonian oasis of Bariloche. But they do not travel much in the north of Argentina, and they don't know, or even care, very much about the rest of South America. Mention Quito and they will tell you it is hellish, small, poor and primitive. A trip to Bolivia is unthinkable. Their connections tend to be with Europe. They fancy themselves Frenchified and have been told so often that their capital is like Paris they feel no need to verify it with a visit to France. They prefer to maintain their ancestral links with Europe; many go to Spain, but almost a quarter of a million visit Italy every year. The more enterprising are Anglophile.

They are unsure of the United States, and their uncertainty makes them scorn it.

'But what do you know about Argentina?' they asked me, and by way of forestalling their lectures – they seemed deeply embarrassed about their political record – I said things like, 'Well, when I was in Jujuy –' or 'Now, Humahuaca's awfully nice –' or 'What struck me about La Quiaca –.' No one I met had been to La Quiaca or taken the train across the border. The person in Buenos Aires who wishes to speak of the squalor of the distant provinces tells you about the size of the cockroaches in near-by Rosario.

I had arrived in Buenos Aires exhausted at the beginning of a heatwave which people said was the Argentine autumn. Five days and nights on the train from La Paz had left me limp. I had a bad cold, my wounded hand throbbed, and for several days I did nothing but convalesce; I read, I drank wine, and I played billiards until I was completely myself again.

At last, I felt well enough to see my Argentine publisher. But I had no luck with the telephone. The receiver honked and buzzed, but no human voice could be heard on it. I decided to see the hall porter at my hotel about it.

'I am having difficulty calling this number,' I said.

'Buenos Aires?'

'Yes. A company on Carlos Pellegrini.'

'But Carlos Pellegrini is only four blocks from here!'

'I wanted to call them.'

He said, 'You will find it much quicker to walk.'

I walked to the office and introduced myself as the author of the three titles I had seen in the book stores in Tucuman.

'We were expecting someone much older,' said Mr Naveiro, the managing director of the firm.

'After what I've been through, I feel eighty years old,' I said.

Hearing that I had arrived, a lady entered Mr Naveiro's office and said, 'There is a certain general in the government who has read your books. He is Minister of Transportation, and he would like you to take the train to Salta.'

381

I said that I had already been to Salta, or at least a few miles away.

'He would like you to take the train from Salta to Antafagosta in Chile.'

I said that I would prefer not to.

'The general was also wondering where else you would like to go.'

I said south, to Patagonia.

'He will give you tickets. When do you wish to go?'

Like that, the arrangements were made.

'We hope you will enjoy your stay in Argentina,' said Mr Naveiro. 'We have passed through terrible times, but things are better now.'

It seemed so. There had not been a political kidnapping for two years. My friend Bruce Chatwin, who had recently returned from Patagonia, said that the urban guerillas were on holiday in Uruguay or skiing in Switzerland. Isabel Peron had been overthrown; disarmed, she lived under house arrest in a remote valley with her pet canaries and her maid. I was more sceptical about the official reports of political prisoners. 'There are no political prisoners in all of the Argentine Republic,' said Colonel Dotti, Director of the National Prison System. 'They are subversive delinquents, not political prisoners.' Shortly after I arrived, sixty 'subversive delinquents' died in a prison riot in Buenos Aires; some had been shot, others had been asphyxiated.

I could not draw Mr Naveiro on this issue, and it seemed rude to insist. He was anxious to please. Did I want to send anyone a telex? Did I wish to dictate some letters to his lovely secretary? Was my hotel comfortable? Was there anyone in Argentina I wished to meet? Did I want someone to fly to Patagonia to make arrangements for me there?

'My idea,' he said, 'is to get someone to take a plane to Patagonia. You take the train. When you get there, you will have someone on hand, if any problem arises. All you have to do is say yes and it will be done.'

I explained that this might have been helpful in the mountains of Colombia, but that I did not anticipate any difficulties in Patagonia.

'Well, then,' he said, 'I suppose you know that this is the country of meat. You must have a big piece of meat to celebrate your arrival in Buenos Aires.'

It was the biggest steak I had ever seen, the shape of a size twelve football boot and tender as a boiled turnip. In this particular restaurant it was necessary to specify the cut as well as the steer. You said rump, then long-horn; or tenderloin and short-horn.

'Yes, things are very quiet at the moment,' said Mr Naveiro, pouring the wine. He said that Isabel Peron had been a disaster, but that most people regarded her as pathetic rather than malicious. General Videla, a man so corpselike in appearance he was known as 'The Skull' or 'The Bone', was a shy, cautious man whom most people hoped would return Argentina to civilian rule.

It struck me that Argentina was bureaucratic and ungovernable in the same way that Italy was. This was a developed country which was attached geographically to the Third World, but it was under-developed politically, with a distrust of government and a contempt for politics. Patriotism, without a tempering faith in legality or free elections, had become muddled aggression and seedy provincialism. Politics was seen to be a cheat because it was ineffectual. With the highest literacy rate in Latin America, and one of the highest in the world (91.4 per cent), there was really no excuse for Argentina to be a tyranny. Even the most charitable witness had to find a carelessness in the attitude that tolerated authoritarianism and said that the alternative was anarchy. Wasn't this, I suggested, rather infantile?

'I don't know,' said Mr Naveiro. 'But I will tell you what I suspect. This is a very rich country. We have resources. We have a very high standard of living – even in the north where you have been it is quite all right. And I think I am right in saying that we work hard. Some people here work very hard. But we have one great defect. Can you guess what it is?'

I said no, I couldn't.

'Everyone works well separately, but we cannot work with one another. I don't know why this is so, but we just cannot work together as a team.'

'I wouldn't have thought a self-appointed government of generals was much inspiration for people to work together,' I said. 'Why don't they hold an election?'

'We keep hoping,' said Mr Naveiro. 'I would like to change the subject, with your permission.'

'Fine.'

'I have been reading your essay on Rudyard Kipling. It is very good.'

It was a book review, but a long one, which had appeared a few weeks before on the cover of *The New York Times Book Review*. I was surprised that Mr Naveiro had seen it – I had not seen it myself; but, unlike Mr Naveiro, I did not have an airmail subscription, and anyway I had been in Peru or Bolivia when it was published.

Mr Naveiro said, 'Do you know who would be interested in your views on Kipling? Borges.'

'Really? I've always wanted to meet him.'

'We publish him,' said Mr Naveiro. 'I'm sure it can be arranged.'

I did not hear from Mr Naveiro immediately. In the meantime, his publicity director sent a reporter to my hotel to interview me. The reporter was small, thin and anxious to know what I thought about Argentina. I hardly knew where to begin. Apart from the difficulty of expressing political complexities in Spanish (how did one say 'muddled aggression and seedy provincialism'?), there was the caution I had been usually scrupulous about observing: *Don't criticize them – they hate to be criticized*.

The reporter took my hesitation for timidity. He prompted me.

'Argentina is cultured, eh?' he said.

'Oh, yes, very cultured.'

He wrote this on his pad.

'Civilized – true?'

'Absolutely.'

He scribbled; he was very pleased.

'Good trains – English trains?'

'You said it.'

'Pretty girls?' he said, still smiling, still writing.

'Ravishing.'

'And Buenos Aires? It's like —'

'Paris,' I said.

'Of course,' he said, and screwed the cap back onto his pen. The interview was over.

That night I went to a party with the man who had translated my books into Spanish for the Argentine editions. He had earned my admiration by finding the source of a quotation I had mischievously left unattributed in the text of one. It was two lines from Thomas Moore's *Intercepted Letters*. But, then, Rolando Costa Picazo had taught in Ohio and Michigan, where such things were common knowledge. He too urged me to meet Borges.

'The question is not whether I want to meet Borges, but whether Borges wants to meet me.'

'He is reading your Kipling piece at the moment. If he likes it, he will want to meet you,' said Rolando. 'Now, here is someone you must meet,' he added, easing me towards an elderly gentleman.

The man smiled and shook my hand and said in Spanish, 'Delighted to meet you.'

Rolando said, 'He has translated Ezra Pound into Spanish.'

In English — the man was a translator after all — I said, 'It must be difficult to translate Pound into Spanish.'

The man smiled. He said nothing.

'The *Cantos*,' I said. 'They're difficult.' And I thought: difficult, if not complete balderdash.

The man said, 'Yes. The *Cantos*.'

'Which ones do you like best?'

He shrugged. He smiled at Rolando now, but he was seeking help. And it was only after the longest time that I realized that this man, who had been recommended to me as an Argentine intellectual and translator, could not speak English. But how appropriate for a translator of Ezra Pound, I thought. Surely this ignorance was a great advantage, and I had no doubt that his versions were more felicitous than the originals.

Late the next afternoon, my phone rang.

'Borges wants to see you.'

'Wonderful,' I said. 'When?'

'In fifteen minutes.'

20 The Buenos Aires Subterranean

Despite its eerie name, the Buenos Aires Subterranean is an efficient five-line network of subway trains. The same size as Boston's subway, it was built five years later, in 1913 (making it older than Chicago's or Moscow's), and as in Boston it quickly put the tram cars out of business. The apartment of Jorge Luis Borges was on Maipú, around the corner from Plaza General San Martín Station, on the Retiro–Constitucion line.

I had been eager to take the Subterranean ever since I heard of its existence; and I had greatly wished to talk to Borges. He was to me what Lady Hester Stanhope had been to Alexander Kinglake: 'in all society, the standing topic of interest', an eccentric genius, perhaps more than a prophet, hidden in the depths of an unholy country. In *Eothen*, one of my favourite travel books (' "Eothen" is, I hope, almost the only hard word to be found in the book,' says the author, 'and signifies ... "From the East" '), Kinglake devotes an entire chapter to his meeting with Lady Hester. I felt I could do no less with Borges. I entered the Subterranean and, after a short ride, easily found his house.

The brass plaque on the landing of the sixth floor said *Borges*. I rang the bell and was admitted by a child of about seven. When he saw me he sucked his finger in embarrassment. He was the maid's child. The maid was Paraguayan, a well-fleshed Indian, who invited me in, then left me in the foyer with a large white cat. There was one dim light burning in the foyer, but the rest of the apartment was dark. The darkness reminded me that Borges was blind.

Curiosity and unease led me into a small parlour. Though the curtains were drawn and the shutters closed, I could make out a candelabra, the family silver Borges mentions in one of his

386

stories, some paintings, old photographs and books. There was little furniture – a sofa and two chairs by the window, a dining table pushed against one wall, and a wall and a half of bookcases. Something brushed my legs. I switched on a lamp: the cat had followed me here.

There was no carpet on the floor to trip the blind man, no intrusive furniture he could barge into. The parquet floor gleamed; there was not a speck of dust anywhere. The paintings were amorphous, but the three steel engravings were precise. I recognized them as Piranesi's 'Views of Rome'. The most Borges-like one was 'The Pyramid of Cestius' and could have been an illustration from Borges' own *Ficciones*. Piranesi's biographer Bianconi called him 'the Rembrandt of the ruins'. 'I need to produce great ideas,' said Piranesi. 'I believe that were I given the planning of a new universe I would be mad enough to undertake it.' It was something Borges himself might have said.

The books were a mixed lot. One corner was mostly Everyman editions, the classics in English translation – Homer, Dante, Virgil. There were shelves of poetry in no particular order – Tennyson and E. E. Cummings, Byron, Poe, Wordsworth, Hardy. There were reference books, Harvey's *English Literature*, *The Oxford Book of Quotations*, various dictionaries – including Doctor Johnson's – and an old leatherbound encyclopaedia. They were not fine editions; the spines were worn, the cloth had faded; but they had the look of having been read. They were well-thumbed, they sprouted paper page-markers. Reading alters the appearance of a book. Once it has been read, it never looks the same again, and people leave their individual imprint on a book they have read. One of the pleasures of reading is seeing this alteration on the pages, and the way, by reading it, you have made the book yours.

There was a sound of scuffing in the corridor, and a distinct grunt. Borges emerged from the dimly-lighted foyer, feeling his way along the wall. He was dressed formally, in a dark blue suit and dark tie; his black shoes were loosely tied, and a watch chain depended from his pocket. He was taller than I had expected, and there was an English cast to his face, a pale seriousness in his jaw and forehead. His eyes were swollen, staring, and sightless. But for his faltering, and the slight tremble in his hands, he was in excellent health. He had the fussy precision of a chemist. His skin was clear – there were no age-blotches on his hands – and there was a firmness in his face. People had told me he was 'about eighty'. He was then in his seventy-ninth year, but he looked ten years younger. 'When you get to my age,' he tells his double in the story 'The Other', 'you will have lost your eyesight almost completely. You'll still make out the colour yellow and lights and shadows. Don't worry. Gradual blindness is not a tragedy. It's like a slow summer dusk.'

'Yes,' he said, groping for my hand. Squeezing it, he guided me to a chair. 'Please sit down. There's a chair here somewhere. Please make yourself at home.'

He spoke so rapidly that I was not aware of an accent until he had finished speaking. He seemed breathless. He spoke in bursts, but without hesitation, except when starting a new subject. Then, stuttering, he raised his trembling hands and seemed to claw the subject out of the air and shake ideas from it as he went on.

'You're from New England,' he said. 'That's wonderful. That's the best place to be from. It all began there – Emerson, Thoreau, Melville, Hawthorne, Longfellow. They started it. If it weren't for them there would be nothing. I was there – it was beautiful.'

'I've read your poem about it,' I said. Borges' 'New England 1967' begins, 'They have changed the shapes of my dream . . .'

'Yes, yes.' he said. He moved his hands impatiently, like a man shaking dice. He would not talk about his work; he was almost dismissive. 'I was lecturing at Harvard. I hate lecturing – I love teaching. I enjoyed the States – New England. And Texas is something special. I was there with my mother. She was old, over eighty. We went to see the Alamo.' Borges' mother had died not long before, at the great age of ninety-nine. Her room is as she left it in death. 'Do you know Austin?'

I said I had taken the train from Boston to Fort Worth and that I had not thought much of Fort Worth.

'You should have gone to Austin,' said Borges. 'The rest of

it is nothing to me – the mid-West, Ohio, Chicago. Sandburg is the poet of Chicago, but what is he? He's just noisy – he got it all from Whitman. Whitman was great, Sandburg is nothing. And the rest of it,' he said, shaking his fingers at an imaginary map of North America. 'Canada? Tell me, what has Canada produced? Nothing. But the South is interesting. What a pity they lost the Civil War – don't you think it is a pity, eh?'

I said I thought defeat had been inevitable for the South. They had been backward-looking and complacent, and now they were the only people in the States who ever talked about the Civil War. People in the North never spoke of it. If the South had won, we might have been spared some of these Confederate reminiscences.

'Of course they talk about it,' said Borges. 'It was a terrible defeat for them. Yet they had to lose. They were agrarian. But I wonder – is defeat so bad? In *The Seven Pillars of Wisdom*, doesn't he say something about "the shamefulness of victory"? The Southerners were courageous, but perhaps a man of courage does not make a good soldier. What do you think?'

Courage alone could not make you a good soldier, I said, not any more than patience alone could make you a good fisherman. Courage might make a man blind to risk, and an excess of courage, without caution, could be fatal.

'But people respect soldiers,' said Borges. 'That's why no one really thinks much of the Americans. If America were a military power instead of a commercial empire, people would look up to it. Who respects businessmen? No one. People look at America and all they see are travelling salesmen. So they laugh.'

He fluttered his hands, snatched with them, and changed the subject. 'How did you come to Argentina?'

'After Texas, I took the train to Mexico.'

'What do you think of Mexico?'

'Ramshackle, but pleasant.'

Borges said, 'I dislike Mexico and the Mexicans. They are so nationalistic. And they hate the Spanish. What can happen to them if they feel that way? And they have nothing. They are just playing – playing at being nationalistic. But what they like especially is playing at being Red Indians. They like to play.

They have nothing at all. And they can't fight, eh? They are very poor soldiers – they always lose. Look what a few American soldiers could do in Mexico! No, I don't like Mexico at all.'

He paused and leaned forward. His eyes bulged. He found my knee and tapped it for emphasis.

'I don't have this complex,' he said. 'I don't hate the Spanish. Although I much prefer the English. After I lost my sight in 1955 I decided to do something altogether new. So I learned Anglo-Saxon. Listen –'

He recited the entire Lord's Prayer in Anglo-Saxon.

'That was the Lord's Prayer. Now this – do you know this?'

He recited the opening lines of *The Seafarer*.

'*The Seafarer*,' he said. 'Isn't it beautiful? I am partly English. My grandmother came from Northumberland, and there are other relatives from Staffordshire. "Saxon and Celt and Dane" – isn't that how it goes? We always spoke English at home. My father spoke to me in English. Perhaps I'm partly Norwegian – the Vikings were in Northumberland. And York – York is a beautiful city, eh? My ancestors were there, too.'

'Robinson Crusoe was from York,' I said.

'Was he?'

' "I was born in the year something-something, in the city of York, of a good family . . ." '

'Yes, yes, I had forgotten that.'

I said there were Norse names all over the north of England, and gave as an example the name Thorpe. It was a place-name and a surname.

Borges said, 'Like the German *dorf*.'

'Or Dutch *dorp*.'

'This is strange. I will tell you something. I am writing a story in which the main character's name is Thorpe.'

'That's your Northumberland ancestry stirring.'

'Perhaps. The English are wonderful people. But timid. They didn't want an empire. It was forced upon them by the French and the Spanish. And so they had their empire. It was a great thing, eh? They left so much behind. Look what they gave India – Kipling! One of the greatest writers.'

I said that sometimes a Kipling story was only a plot, or an exercise in Irish dialect, or a howling gaffe, like the climax of 'At the End of the Passage', where a man photographs the bogeyman on a dead man's retina and then burns the pictures because they are so frightening. But how did the bogeyman get there?

'It doesn't matter – he's always good. My favourite is "The Church that was at Antioch." What a marvellous story that is. And what a great poet. I know you agree with me – I read your piece in the *New York Times*. What I want you to do is read me some of Kipling's poems. Come with me,' he said, getting to his feet and leading me to a bookshelf. 'On that shelf – you see all the Kipling books? Now on the left is the *Collected Poems*. It's a big book.'

He was conjuring with his hands as I ran my eye across the Elephant Head Edition of Kipling. I found the book and carried it back to the sofa.

Borges said, 'Read me "Harp Song of the Dane Women".'

I did as I was told.

> What is a woman that you forsake her,
> And the hearth-fire and the home-acre,
> To go with the old grey Widow-maker?

' "The old grey Widow-maker," ' he said. 'That is so good. You can't say things like that in Spanish. But I'm interrupting – go on.'

I began again, but at the third stanza he stopped me. ' "the ten-times fingering weed to hold you" – how beautiful!' I went on reading this reproach to a traveller – just the reading of it made me feel homesick – and every few stanzas Borges exclaimed how perfect a particular phrase was. He was quite in awe of these English compounds. Such locutions were impossible in Spanish. A simple poetic phrase such as 'world-weary flesh' must be rendered in Spanish as 'this flesh made weary by the world'. The ambiguity and delicacy is lost in Spanish, and Borges was infuriated that he could not attempt lines like Kipling's.

Borges said, 'Now for my next favourite, "The Ballad of East and West".'

391

There proved to be even more interruption-fodder in this ballad than there had been in 'The Harp Song', but though it had never been one of my favourites, Borges drew my attention to the good lines, chimed in on several couplets and continued to say, 'You can't do that in Spanish.'

'Read me another one,' he said.

'How about "The Way Through the Woods"?' I said, and read it and got goose pimples.

Borges said, 'It's like Hardy. Hardy was a great poet, but I can't read his novels. He should have stuck to poetry.'

'He did, in the end. He gave up writing novels.'

'He should never have started,' said Borges. 'Want to see something interesting?' He took me back to the shelves and showed me his *Encyclopaedia Britannica*. It was the rare eleventh edition, not a book of facts but a work of literature. He told me to look at *India* and to examine the signature on the illustrated plates. It was that of Lockwood Kipling. 'Rudyard Kipling's father – you see?'

We went on a tour through his bookshelves. He was especially proud of his copy of Johnson's *Dictionary* ('It was sent to me from Sing-Sing Prison, by an anonymous person'), his *Moby Dick*, his translation by Sir Richard Burton of *The Thousand and One Nights*. He scrabbled at the shelves and pulled out more books; he led me to his study and showed me his set of Thomas De Quincey, his Beowulf – touching it, he began to quote – his Icelandic sagas.

'This is the best collection of Anglo-Saxon books in Buenos Aires,' he said.

'If not in South America.'

'Yes, I suppose so.'

We went back to the parlour library. He had forgotten to show me his edition of Poe. I said that I had recently read *The Narrative of Arthur Gordon Pym*.

'I was talking about *Pym* just last night to Bioy Casares,' said Borges. Bioy Casares had been a collaborator on a sequence of stories. 'The ending of that book is so strange – the dark and the light.'

'And the ship with the corpses on it.'

'Yes,' said Borges a bit uncertainly. 'I read it so long ago, before I lost my sight. It is Poe's greatest book.'

'I'd be glad to read it to you.'

'Come tomorrow night,' said Borges. 'Come at seven-thirty. You can read me some chapters of *Pym* and then we'll have dinner.'

I got my jacket from the chair. The white cat had been chewing the sleeve. The sleeve was wet, but now the cat was asleep. It slept on its back, as if it wanted its belly scratched. Its eyes were tightly shut.

It was Good Friday. All over Latin America there were sombre processions, people carrying images of Christ, lugging crosses up volcanic mountains, wearing black shrouds, flagellating themselves, saying the Stations of the Cross on their knees, parading with skulls. But in Buenos Aires there was little of this penitential activity to be seen. Devotion, in this secular city, took the form of movie-going. *Julia*, which had won a number of Oscars, opened on Good Friday, but the theatre was empty. Across the street, at the Electric, *The Ten Commandments* – the Fifties Bible-epic – was showing. The box-office line was two blocks away. And there was such a crowd at Zeffirelli's *Jesus of Nazareth* that theatre-goers, five hundred or more, were standing piously in the rain.

I had spent the day transcribing the notes I had made on my lap the night before. Borges' blindness had enabled me to write unselfconsciously as he spoke. Again I boarded the Buenos Aires Subterranean to keep our appointment.

This time, the lights in Borges' apartment were on. His loose shuffling shoes announced him and he appeared as over-dressed in the humid night heat as he had the previous evening.

'Time for Poe,' he said. 'Please take a seat.'

The Poe volume was on the seat of a nearby chair. I picked it up and found *Pym*, but before I could begin, Borges said, 'I've been thinking about *The Seven Pillars of Wisdom*. Every page of it is very fine, and yet it is a dull book. I wonder why.'

'He wanted to write a great book. George Bernard Shaw told him to use a lot of semi-colons. Lawrence set out to be exhaustive, believing that if it was monumentally ponderous it would be regarded as great. But it's dull, and there's no humour in it. How can a book on the Arabs not be funny?'

'*Huckleberry Finn* is a great book,' said Borges. 'And funny. But the ending is no good. Tom Sawyer appears and it becomes bad. And there's Nigger Jim' – Borges had begun to search the air with his hands – 'yes, we had a slave market here at Retiro. My family wasn't very wealthy. We had only five or six slaves. But some families had thirty or forty.'

I had read that a quarter of Argentina's population had once been black. There were no blacks in Argentina now. I asked Borges why this was so.

'It is a mystery. But I remember seeing many of them.' Borges looked so youthful that it was easy to forget that he was as old as the century. I could not vouch for his reliability, but he was the most articulate witness I had met on my trip. 'They were cooks, gardeners, handymen,' he said. 'I don't know what happened to them.'

'People say they died of TB.'

'Why didn't they die of TB in Montevideo? It's just over there, eh? There is another story, equally silly, that they fought the Indians, and the Indians and the Negroes killed each other. That would have been in 1850 or so, but it isn't true. In 1914, there were still many Negroes in Buenos Aires – they were very common. Perhaps I should say 1910, to be sure.' He laughed suddenly. 'They didn't work very hard. It was considered wonderful to have Indian blood, but black blood is not so good a thing, eh? There are some prominent families in Buenos Aires that have it – a touch of the tar-brush, eh? My uncle used to tell me, "Jorge, you're as lazy as a nigger after lunch." You see, they didn't do much work in the afternoon. I don't know why there are so few here, but in Uruguay, or Brazil – in Brazil you might run into a white man now and then, eh? If you're lucky, eh? Ha!'

Borges was laughing in a pitying, self-amused way. His face lit up.

'They thought they were natives! I overheard a black woman saying to an Argentine woman, "Well, at least we didn't come here on a ship!" She meant that she considered the Spanish to be immigrants. "At least we didn't come here on a ship!"'

'When did you hear this?'

'So many years ago,' said Borges. 'But the Negroes were good soldiers. They fought in the War of Independence.'

'So they did in the United States,' I said. 'But a lot were on the British side. The British promised them their freedom for serving in the British infantry. One Southern regiment was all black – Lord Dunmore's Ethiopians, it was called. They ended up in Canada.'

'Our blacks won the Battle of Cerrito. They fought in the war against Brazil. They were very good infantrymen. The gauchos fought on horseback, the Negroes didn't ride. There was a regiment – the Sixth. They called it – not the Regiment of Mulattoes and Blacks, but in Spanish "the Regiment of Brownies and Darkies". So as not to offend them. In *Martin Fierro*, they are called "men of humble colour" ... well, enough, enough. Let's read *Arthur Gordon Pym*.'

'Which chapter? How about the one where the ship approaches full of corpses and birds?'

'No, I want the last one. About the dark and the light.'

I read the last chapter, where the canoe drifts into the Antarctic, the water growing warmer and then very hot, the white fall of ashes, the vapour, the appearance of the white giant. Borges interrupted from time to time, saying in Spanish, 'That is enchanting,' 'That is lovely' and 'How beautiful!'

When I finished, he said, 'Read the last chapter but one.'

I read Chapter 24, Pym's escape from the island, the pursuit of the maddened savages, the vivid description of vertigo. That long terrifying passage delighted Borges, and he clapped his hands at the end.

Borges said, 'Now how about some Kipling? Shall we puzzle out "Mrs Bathurst" and try to see if it is a good story?'

I said, 'I must tell you that I don't like "Mrs Bathurst" at all.'

'Fine. It must be bad. *Plain Tales from the Hills* then. Read "Beyond the Pale".'

I read 'Beyond the Pale', and when I got to the part where

Bisesa sings a love song to Trejago, her English lover, Borges interrupted, reciting,

> 'Alone upon the housetops, to the North
> I turn and watch the lightning in the sky, –
> The glamour of thy footsteps in the North,
> Come back to me, Beloved, or I die!'

'My father used to recite that one,' said Borges. When I had finished the story, he said, 'Now you choose one.'

I read him the opium-smoker's story, 'The Gate of the Hundred Sorrows'.

'How sad that is,' said Borges. 'It is terrible. The man can do nothing. But notice how Kipling repeats the same lines. It has no plot at all, but it is lovely.' He touched his suit jacket. 'What time is it?' He drew out his pocket watch and touched the hands. 'Nine-thirty – we should eat.'

As I was putting the Kipling book back into its place – Borges insisted that the books must be returned to their exact place – I said, 'Do you ever re-read your own work?'

'Never. I am not happy with my work. The critics have greatly exaggerated its importance. I would rather read' – he lunged at the bookshelves and made a gathering motion with his hands – 'real writers. Ha!' He turned to me and said, 'Do you re-read my work?'

'Yes. "Pierre Menard" – '

'That was the first story I ever wrote. I was thirty-six or thirty-seven at the time. My father said, "Read a lot, write a lot, and don't rush into print" – those were his exact words. The best story I ever wrote was "The Intruder". And "South" is also good. It's only a few pages. I'm lazy – a few pages and I'm finished. But "Pierre Menard" is a joke, not a story.'

'I used to give my Chinese students "The Wall and the Books" to read.'

'Chinese students? I suppose they thought it was full of howlers. I think it is. It is an unimportant piece, hardly worth reading. Let's eat.'

He got his stick from the sofa in the parlour and we went out, down in the narrow lift, and through the wrought-iron gates. The restaurant was around the corner – I could not see it, but Borges knew the way. So the blind man led me. Walking down this Buenos Aires street with Borges was like being led through Alexandria by Cavafy, or through Lahore by Kipling. The city belonged to him, and he had had a hand in inventing it.

The restaurant was full this Good Friday night, and it was extremely noisy. But as soon as Borges entered, tapping his stick, feeling his way through the tables he obviously knew well, a hush fell upon the diners. Borges was recognized, and at his entrance all talking and eating ceased. It was both a reverential and curious silence, and it was maintained until Borges took his seat and gave the waiter our order.

We had hearts of palm, and fish, and grapes. I drank wine, Borges stuck to water. He cocked his head sideways to eat, trying to spear the sections of palm with his fork. He tried a spoon next, and then despairingly used his fingers.

'Do you know the big mistake that people make when they try to film *Doctor Jekyll and Mister Hyde*?' he said. 'They use the same actor for both men. They should use two different actors. That is what Stevenson intended. Jekyll was two men. And you don't find out until the end that it is the same man. You should get that hammerstroke at the end. Another thing. Why do directors always make Hyde a womanizer? He was actually very cruel.'

I said, 'Hyde tramples on a child and Stevenson describes the sound of the bones breaking.'

'Yes, Stevenson hated cruelty, but he had nothing against physical passion.'

'Do you read modern authors?'

'I never cease to read them. Anthony Burgess is good – a very generous man, by the way. We are the same – Borges, Burgess. It's the same name.'

'Any others?'

'Robert Browning,' said Borges, and I wondered if he was pulling my leg. 'Now, he should have been a short story writer. If he had, he would have been greater than Henry James, and people would still read him.' Borges had started on his grapes. 'The food is good in Buenos Aires, don't you think?'

'In most ways, it seems a civilized place.'

He looked up. 'That may be so, but there are bombs every day.'

'They don't mention them in the paper.'

'They're afraid to print the news.'

'How do you know there are bombs?'

'Easy. I hear them,' he said.

Indeed, three days later there was a fire which destroyed much of the new colour television studio which had been built for the World Cup broadcasts. This was called 'an electrical fault'. Five days later two trains were bombed in Lomas de Zamora and Bernal. A week later a government minister was murdered; his corpse was found in a Buenos Aires street, and pinned to it was a note reading, *A gift from the Montoneros.*

'But the government is not so bad,' said Borges. 'Videla is a well-meaning military man.' Borges smiled and said slowly, 'He is not very bright, but at least he is a gentleman.'

'What about Peron?'

'Peron was a scoundrel. My mother was in prison under Peron. My sister was in prison. My cousin. Peron was a bad leader and, also, I suspect, a coward. He looted the country. His wife was a prostitute.'

'Evita?'

'A common prostitute.'

We had coffee. Borges called the waiter and said in Spanish, 'Help me to the toilet.' He said to me, 'I have to go and shake the bishop's hand. Ha!'

Walking back through the streets, he stopped at a hotel entrance and gave the metal awning posts two whacks with his stick. Perhaps he was not as blind as he pretended, perhaps it was a familiar landmark. He had not swung timidly. He said, 'That's for luck.'

As we turned the corner into Maipú he said, 'My father used to say, "What a rubbish story the Jesus story is. That this man was dying for the sins of the world. Who could believe that?" It is nonsense, isn't it?'

I said, 'That's a timely thought for Good Friday.'

'I hadn't thought of that! Oh, yes!' He laughed so nard he startled two passers-by.

As he fished out his door-key, I asked him about Patagonia.

'I have been there,' he said. 'But I don't know it well. I'll tell you this, though. It's a dreary place. A very dreary place.'

'I was planning to take the train tomorrow.'

'Don't go tomorrow. Come and see me. I like your reading.'

'I suppose I can go to Patagonia next week.'

'It's dreary,' said Borges. He had got the door open, and now he shuffled to the lift and pulled open its metal gates. 'The gate of the hundred sorrows,' he said, and entered, chuckling.

Borges was tireless. He urged me to visit him again and again. He stayed up late, eager to talk, eager to be read to; and he was good company. By degrees, he turned me into Boswell. Each morning when I woke I sat down and wrote the conversations that had taken place the night before; then I walked around the city, and at nightfall I boarded the Subterranean. Borges said that he seldom went out. 'I don't go to the embassies, I don't go to parties – I hate to stand around and drink.'

I had been warned that he could be severe or bad tempered. But what I saw was close to angelic. There was something of the charlatan in him – he had a way of speechifying, and I knew he was repeating something he had said a hundred times before. He had the beginnings of a stutter, but he calmed that with his hands. He was occasionally magisterial, but he could be the opposite, a kind of student, his face elfin with attentiveness, his fingers locked together. His face became aristocratic in repose, and when he bared his yellow teeth in the exaggerated grin he used to show pleasure – he laughed hard at his own jokes – his face came alight and he looked like a French actor who has realized that he has successfully stolen the show. ('Stolen the show!' Borges would say. 'You can't say *that* in Spanish. That's why Spanish literature is so dull.') His was the perfect face for a sage, and yet, working his features a certain way, he could look like a clown, but never a fool. He was the gentlest of men; there was no violence in his talk and none in his gestures.

'I don't understand revenge,' he said. 'I have never felt it. And I don't write about it.'

'What about "Emma Zunz"?'

'Yes, that's the only one. But the story was given to me and I don't even think it's very good.'

'So you don't approve of getting even – of taking revenge for something that was done to you?'

'Revenge does not alter what was done to you. Neither does forgiveness. Revenge and forgiveness are irrelevant.'

'What can you do?'

'Forget,' said Borges. 'That is all you can do. When something bad is done to me, I pretend that it happened a long time ago, to someone else.'

'Does that work?'

'More or less.' He showed his yellow teeth. 'Less rather than more.'

Talking about the futility of revenge, he reached and his hands trembled with a new subject, but a related one, the Second World War.

'When I was in Germany just after the war,' he said, 'I never heard a word spoken against Hitler. In Berlin, the Germans said to me' – now he spoke in German – ' "Well, what do you think of our ruins?" The Germans like to be pitied – isn't that horrible? They showed me their ruins. They wanted me to pity them. But why should I indulge them? I said' – he uttered the sentence in German – ' "I have seen London." '

We continued to talk about Europe; the conversation turned to the Scandinavian countries and, inevitably, the Nobel Prize. I did not say the obvious thing, that Borges himself had been mentioned as a possible candidate. But, quite off his own bat, he said, 'If I were offered it, I would rush up and grasp it in two hands. But which American writers have got it?'

'Steinbeck,' I said.

'No. I don't believe that.'

'It's true.'

'I can't believe that Steinbeck got it. And yet Tagore got it, and he was an atrocious writer. He wrote corny poems – moons, gardens. Kitsch poems.'

'Maybe they lose something when they're translated from Bengali into English.'

'They could only gain by that. But they're corny.' He smiled, and his face became beatific – the more so because of his blindness. It frequently went this way: I could watch him studying a memory. He said, 'Tagore came to Buenos Aires.'

'Was this after he won the Nobel Prize?'

'It must have been. I can't imagine Vittoria Ocampo inviting him unless he had won it.' He cackled at that. 'And we quarrelled. Tagore and I.'

'What did you quarrel about?'

Borges had a mock-pompous voice. He reserved it for certain statements of freezing dismissiveness. Now he threw his head back and said in that voice, 'He uttered heresies about Kipling.'

We had met this evening to read the Kipling story, 'Dayspring Mishandled', but we never got to it. It had grown late, it was nearly dinnertime; we talked about Kipling's stories and then about horror stories in general.

' "They" is a very fine story. I like Lovecraft's horror stories. His plots are very good, but his style is atrocious. I once dedicated a story to him. But it is not as good as "They" – that is very *triste*.'

'I think Kipling was writing about his own dead children. His daughter died in New York, his son was killed in the war. And he never went back to the States.'

'Well,' said Borges, 'he had that fight with his brother-in-law.'

I said, 'But they laughed him out of court.'

' "Laughed him out of court" – you can't say that in Spanish!' He was gleeful, then he pretended to be morose. 'You can't say anything in Spanish.'

We went out to eat. He asked me what I had been doing in South America. I said that I had given some lectures on American literature, and that twice in describing myself as a feminist to Spanish-speaking audiences I had been taken for a man confessing a kind of deviation. Borges said that I must remember that the Latin Americans were not very subtle on this point. I went on to say that I had spoken about Mark Twain, Faulkner, Poe, and Hemingway.

'What about Hemingway?' he asked.

'He had one great fault,' I said. 'I think it is a serious one. He admired bullies.'

Borges said, 'I could not agree more.'

It was a pleasant meal, and afterwards, walking back to his apartment house – again he whacked the awning posts at the hotel – he said, 'Yes, I think you and I agree on most things, don't we? Eh?'

'Maybe,' I said. 'But one of these days I have to go to Patagonia.'

'We don't say Patagonia,' said Borges. 'We say "Chubut" or "Santa Cruz". We never say Patagonia.'

'W. H. Hudson said Patagonia.'

'What did he know? *Idle Days in Patagonia* is not a bad book, but you notice there are no people in it – only birds and flowers. That's the way it is in Patagonia. There are no people there. The trouble with Hudson was that he lied all the time. That book is full of lies. But he believed his lies, and soon he couldn't tell the difference between what was true and what was false.' Borges thought a moment, then said, 'There is nothing in Patagonia. It's not the Sahara, but it's as close as you can get to it in Argentina. No, there is nothing in Patagonia.'

If so, I thought – if there is really nothing there – then it is the perfect place to end this book.

21 The 'Lagos del Sur' (Lakes of the South) Express

Patagonia was also the way home. I had cancelled several train reservations in order to spend more time with Borges, but now I stopped procrastinating and made firm plans to head south. I had a few days in hand before I could leave Buenos Aires but, excluded from the Argentine intimacy of the long Easter holiday, I roamed the city on my own. It now depressed me. Some of the gloom the natives had temporarily dispelled entered my own soul and dampened it. It was partly the effect of La Boca, the Italian district near the harbour; there were boys swimming in the oily, evil-smelling harbour, and I saw more fakery than charm in the Sicilian-style houses and restaurants; some of the squalor was affectation, the rest was real dirt. I went to the Chacarita Cemetery – everyone seemed to be doing that. I found Peron's tomb and saw women kissing his bronze creepy face and twining carnations around the handle on the mausoleum door ('Fanatics!' said a man standing near by. 'It is like football,' whispered his wife). One night, driving towards a suburb with Rolando, we were overtaken by a policeman on a motorcycle, who waved us to the roadside. Rolando did the talking. The policeman said that we had gone through a red light. Rolando insisted the light had been green. At last, the policeman agreed: the light had been green. 'But it is your word against mine,' said the policeman, in a voice coyly extortionate. 'Do you want to be here all night, or do you want to settle this now?' Rolando gave him about seven dollars' worth of pesos. The policeman saluted and wished us a happy Easter.

'I'm leaving,' I told Rolando.

'You don't like Buenos Aires?'

'No, I like it,' I said. 'But I want to leave before I have to change my mind.'

*

It took an hour for the Lakes of the South Express to dis-entangle itself from the city. We had left at five, on a sunny afternoon, but when we began speeding across the pampas, a cool immense pasture, it was growing dark. Then the afterglow of sunset was gone, and in the half-dark the grass was grey, the trees black; some cattle were as reposeful as boulders and in one field five white cows were as luminous as laundry.

This was the General Roca Railway. It had recently been bombed, but such a line was easy to bomb. It ran through the provinces of La Pampa and Rio Negro, through empty grassland and desert and across the Great Plateau of Patagonia. It took very little skill to blow up trains in these scarcely inhabited places. Anyone could be a terrorist here. But the sleeping car attendant said that I would have nothing to worry about. For some reason, the terrorists preferred freight trains – perhaps there was more damage to be done on freight trains; but this was entirely a passenger train. 'Relax,' he said. 'Enjoy yourself. Let us do the worrying. It is our job to worry.'

The sleeping car was an unusual shape. It was old, and wooden, and the wood panelling of the interior was dark polished maho-gany. It was very long, and in the middle there was a lobby, a sort of sitting room, with upholstered chairs and card tables. There were doors here, too; this was where the passengers – most of them elderly – congregated and talked about how cold it was in Patagonia. I had been given a First-Class ticket. I kept to my compartment, wrote about Buenos Aires and Borges and regretted that I had not asked him in my Boswell role, 'Why is a fox's tail bushy, Sir?'

At dinner that first evening – wine, two salads, the statutory steak – a fellow in an army uniform was seated at my table. It was purely for the waiter's convenience – there were only six of us eating in the dining car, but we were gathered together to save the waiter running the length of the car to serve us. The soldier was young. I asked him where he was going.

'Comodoro Rivadavia,' he said. 'It is an ugly place.'

'So you're going to Patagonia, too.'

'I don't have any choice,' he said, tugging at his uniform. 'I'm in the service.'

'You have to do it?'

'Everyone does – for a year.'

'It could be worse,' I said. 'You don't have a war.'

'Not a war, but a problem – with Chile, over the Beagle Channel. It had to be this year! This is an ugly year to be in the service. I might have to fight.'

'I see. You don't want to fight the Chileans?'

'I don't want to fight anyone. I want to be in Buenos Aires. What did you think of it? Beautiful, eh? Pretty girls, eh?'

'What sort of an army does Chile have?'

'No good – not very big. But the Chilean navy is huge. They've got ships, boats, cannons, everything. I'm not worried about the army – it's the navy that scares me. Where are you going?'

'Esquel,' I said.

He snorted. 'Why there?'

'The train goes there.'

'The train goes to Bariloche, too. That's where you should go. Mountains, lakes, snow, pretty houses. It's like Switzerland or Austria.'

'I've been to Switzerland and Austria.'

'The snow is fantastic.'

'I came to South America to get away from snow. It was ten feet deep where I come from.'

'What I'm saying is that Esquel is only a little bit pretty, but Bariloche is fantastic.'

'Maybe I'll take your advice and go to Bariloche after Esquel.'

'Forget Esquel. Forget Patagonia. They're ugly. I'm telling you, Buenos Aires is the place to be.'

So even here, within striking distance of the little town I had circled on my map in Boston, they were trying to discourage me.

Hearing frog-croaks that night, I peered out of the window and saw fireflies. I slept badly – the wine gave me insomnia (was this the reason the Argentines always diluted it by mixing it with water?) – but, wakeful, I was comforted by a great orange disc of moon. Towards dawn I began to drowse; I slept through Bahia Blanca, a city I had wanted to see, and did not wake until

405

we started to cross the Rio Colorado. Some people take this to be the frontier of Patagonia, and indeed there was nothing to be seen after we reached the far bank. Nothingness, I had been told, was the prevailing feature of Patagonia. But grassland intervened, and with it, cattle grazing under an empty sky. For the next few hours, this was all: grass, cattle, sky. And it was chilly. The towns were small, no more than clusters of flat-roofed farm buildings which quickly diminished to specks as the train moved on.

Just after eleven that morning we came to the town of Carmen de Patagones, on the north bank of the Rio Negro. At the other end of the bridge was Viedma. This river I took to be the true dividing line between the fertile part of Argentina and the dusty Patagonian plateau. Hudson begins his book on Patagonia with a description of this river valley, and the inaccuracy of its name was consistent with all the misnamed landscape features I had seen since Mexico. 'The river was certainly miscalled Cusar-leofú, or Black River, by the aborigines,' says Hudson, 'unless the epithet referred only to its swiftness and dangerous character; for it is not black at all in appearance ... The water, which flows from the Andes across a continent of stone and gravel, is wonderfully pure, in colour a clear sea-green.' We remained on the north bank, at a station on the bluff. A lady in a shed was selling stacks of bright red apples, five at a time. She looked like the sort of brisk enterprising woman you see on a fall day in a country town in Vermont – her hair in a bun, rosy cheeks, a brown sweater and heavy skirt. I bought some apples and asked if they were Patagonian. Yes, she said, they were grown right here. And then, 'Isn't it a beautiful day!'

It was sunny, with a stiff breeze riffling the Lombardy poplars. We were delayed for about an hour, but I didn't mind. In fact, the longer we were delayed the better, since I was scheduled to get off the train at Jacobacci at the inconvenient hour of one-thirty in the morning. The connecting train to Esquel was not leaving until six AM, so it hardly mattered what time I got to Jacobacci.

With 'the aid of a bright sun', said Charles Darwin, who had come to Carmen on the *Beagle*, the view was 'almost picturesque'.

But he had found the town squalid. 'These Spanish colonies do not, like our British ones, carry within themselves the elements of growth.'

We crossed the river; it was only a few hundred yards wide, but the experience, even after so many repetitions in South America, was startling to me: on the far bank we entered a different land. The soil was sand and gravel, there was no shade, the land was brown. Over in Carmen de Patagones there were cattle grazing and poplars grew and the grass was green. But there was no grass beyond Viedma. There was scrub and dust, and at once a pair of dust-devils rose up and staggered towards the horizon.

I was in the dining car, eating my lunch. A plastics salesman, on his way to the Welsh settlement at Trelew, chucked his hand disgustedly at the window and said, 'There is just more and more and more of this, all the way to Jacobacci.'

You might at first mistake it for a fertile place. At the horizon there is a stripe of rich unbroken green, with the bumps of bushes showing. In the middle distance it is greeny yellow, paling to a bumpier zone with patches of brown. Up close, in the foreground, you see the deception: these sparse, small-leaved thorn bushes create the illusion of green, and it is these dry brittle things that cover the plain. The thorn bushes are rooted in dust, and the other bushes are lichen-coloured and nearly fungoid in appearance. There are not even weeds on the ground, only these bushes, and they might well be dead. The birds are too high to identify. There are no insects at all. There is no smell.

And this was only the beginning of Patagonia. We were as yet still travelling along the coast, around the Gulf of San Matias. One would hardly have known the sea to be so near, although in the middle of the afternoon what first appeared to be a lake came into view, grew fuller and bluer and proved to be the Atlantic Ocean. The land continued scrubby, the old salt water tides had made the soil more desolate by poisoning it.

We passed villages; they were named as towns on the map, but in reality no name would do. What were they? Six flat weatherbeaten buildings, of which three were latrines; four widely spaced trees, a lame dog, a few chickens, and the wind blowing so hard a pair of ladies' bloomers were flapping horizontal from a clothesline. And sometimes, in the middle of the desert, there were solitary houses, made out of mud blocks or dusty bricks. These were a riddle; they had the starkness of cartoons. The picket fence of branches and sticks – what were they enclosing? what were they shutting out? – was no aid to fathoming the purpose of such huts.

We came to San Antonio Oeste, a small town on the blue waters of the Gulf of San Matias, with the look of an oasis. About forty people got off the train here, since they could catch buses at the local depot to the towns farther down the coast of Patagonia, Comodoro and Puerto Madryn. Seeing that we were stalled, I got off and hiked up and down in the wind.

The waiter leaned out of the window of the dining car.

'Where are you going?'

'Esquel.'

'No!'

'Via Jacobacci.'

'No! That train is only this big!' He measured a small distance with his fingers.

In the United States and Mexico I had avoided telling people where I was going: I had not thought their credulity could take it. Then, in South America, I had mentioned Patagonia: the news was received politely. But here, the closer I got to Esquel, the more distant it was made to seem, and now it could have been farther away than ever. I got the message: no one ended a journey in such a place; Esquel was where journeys began. But I had known all along that I had no intention of writing about being in a place – that took the skill of a miniaturist. I was more interested in the going and the getting there, in the poetry of departures. And I had got here by boarding a subway train filled with Boston commuters, who had left me and the train and had gone to work. I had stayed on and now I was in San Antonio Oeste in the Patagonian province of Rio Negro. The travel had been a satisfaction; being in this station was a bore.

We continued south-west, making for the province of Chubut. The landscape was no longer green, even in that illusory way.

It was halftones of brown and grey and the low ugly thorn bushes were sparser, with fewer leaves. There were small stiffer plants beneath them, as hard and fan-like as coral. The soil was not pulverized enough to make mud-blocks. At great intervals there were houses, but these were made of logs; and it was surprising to see logs in a place where there were no trees. Hudson and other Patagonian travellers mention the bird-life – Hudson goes on for pages about the birdsong in the desert – but I saw nothing but oversize swallows and one hawk all afternoon. There were supposed to be rheas, flamingoes and egrets here, but when I grumbled to myself about not seeing them I was reminded of Thornberry in Costa Rica ('Where are the parrots and monkeys?') and stopped looking for them. It was astonishing how empty a place it was. Borges had called it dreary. It was not dreary. It was hardly anything. There was not enough substance in it for it to have a mood. A desert is an empty canvas; it is you who gives it features and a mood, who work at creating the mirage and making it live. But I was incurious; the desert was deserted, as empty as I felt.

Fine dust poured through the windows and billowed in the corridor and settled in the little lobby at the centre of the sleeping car. There were men in the lobby, but those near the wall of the car were almost obscured by it. They were seven feet from me. I had never minded dust very much, but I found this hard to take. It had a way of trickling through the door-jambs and the cracks in the window frames and swelling in the car.

There were some surprises. I had given up all hope of seeing something growing in Patagonia when, at the town of Valcheta, I saw poplar fencing in a field of grapevines – a vineyard here in the desolate land; and an apple orchard. The small river at Valcheta explained it – it flowed from the south, from the volcanic tableland of the plateau. But Valcheta was a village, and it was clear from the villages farther east that they were there because of this northbound river. They had been founded where wells could be dug.

I had been getting out of the train at each stop, simply so that I could draw a breath. But as the day wore on it grew chillier, and now it was almost cold. The passengers remarked on the cold; they were used to the heavy air of Buenos Aires. They remained wrapped up in the dusty lobby, some with handkerchiefs over their mouths, making small-talk.

'How is the weather in Bariloche?'

'Rainy – very rainy.'

'Oh, sir, you are not telling the truth! You are being very cruel!'

'All right, the weather is lovely.'

'I know it is. Bariloche is so pretty. And we'll be there Tuesday morning!'

They had cameras. I almost laughed out loud at the thought of anyone bringing a camera here with the intention of taking snapshots of the sights. The very idea! You see an unusual feature of the landscape and you realize it is a mud puddle, given ribs by a breeze. The sun near seven was bright and low, and for a few minutes the foul stunted thorn bushes were beautifully lit and cast long shadows across the desert. There were scoops and eruptions far off, and the landscape became familiar. It was the brown eroded landscape you see in the illustrations on the back pages of a school Bible. 'Palestine,' says the caption, or 'The Holy Land', and you look: dust, withered bushes, blue sky, kitty litter.

At dinner that night I was joined by a young couple who had recently been to Brazil. They hailed from Buenos Aires, and I guessed they were on their honeymoon. It was sunset, the sky bright blue, bright yellow, the landscape black; and we had just arrived at the windblown station of Ministero Ramos Mexia. It was not on the map. The woman was talking: they ate hearty breakfasts in Brazil; there were a lot of black people there; everything was expensive. And outside the window, on the platform of Ministero, boys were selling walnuts and grapes.

Then the sun was gone. It was immediately cold and very dark, and the people near the train walked to the overbright lights which were hung on the station posts. They moved out of the darkness and settled near the light like moths.

Our dusty dining car seemed luxurious in comparison with this remote station. The young couple – a moment before they had been talking about the poverty in Brazil – became self-conscious.

Outside, a boy sang, 'Grapes! Grapes! Grapes!' He hoisted his basket to the window.

'They are so poor here,' said the lady. The waiter had just served us with steaks, but none of us had begun to eat.

'They are forgotten,' said her husband.

The people on the station platform were laughing and pointing. For a moment, I thought we might be cheated out of our guilt – the people in Ministero seemed fairly jolly. The train moved on, and then we attacked our steaks.

When this couple left and went back to their compartment, the conductor asked if he could sit down. 'By all means,' I said, and poured him a glass of wine.

'I have been meaning to ask you,' he said. 'Where did you get your free pass?'

I said, 'From a certain general.'

He did not pursue the subject. 'Argentina's expensive, eh? Guess how much I earn.'

A man in Buenos Aires had told me the average wage in Argentina was about £50 a month. It seemed rather low, but here I had a chance to verify it. I translated £50 into pesos and said that I guessed he earned this much a month.

'Less,' said the conductor. 'Much less.' He said he earned about £40 a month. 'How much do they earn in the States?'

I did not have the heart to tell him the truth. I decided to soften the blow and said that a conductor earned about £50 a week.

'I thought so,' he said. 'You see? Much more than we do.'

'But food is expensive in the States,' I said. 'It is cheap here.'

'A little bit cheap. But everything else is expensive. You want clothes? You want shoes? They're expensive. And yet you might think it is just Argentina that is this way. No, it is the whole of South America. There are countries that are much worse off than we are.'

He poured himself another glass of my wine, splashed some soda into it and muttered, 'When the people come to see the World Cup in July they will be very surprised. Like you, eh? "What a wonderful civilized city this is!" That is what they'll say. Then they'll see how expensive it is. They will want to go home!'

'Are you interested in football?' I asked.

'No,' he snapped. Then he reflected a moment and said very slowly, 'No. I hate football. I don't know why exactly. In this respect, I am a very unusual person. Most people are crazy about it. But want to know my real objection?'

'Yes, go ahead.'

'It is too dirty. It is unfair. Watch a football game – you will see. They are always kicking each other in the ankles. The referees don't care at all. Kick, kick – punch, punch. It is stupid. It is unfair. People love the game for its roughness. They like to see fights, bleeding ankles.' He swigged the wine. 'Me? I like to see skill. Now tennis is a nice clean and safe sport, and basketball is very good. No fights, no kicking. The referee writes down the fouls – three infractions and out you go.'

We went on talking. He told me he had been working on the railway for thirty-two years.

'Have you been to Patagonia?' I asked.

'This is Patagonia.' He tapped on the window. It was dark outside, but the dust was pouring through the crack between the sill and the frame. He might have been gesturing at that dust.

'I take it you worked for the British then.'

'Ah, the British! I liked them, even though I am a German.'

'You are a German?'

'Sure.'

But he was speaking as Americans do. *We're English*, say some citizens of Charlottesville, Virginia, referring to the fact that their ancestors abandoned soot-grimed mining towns in Yorkshire and made enough money raising pigs to set up as gentry and keep Jews out of the local hunt clubs. At my high school, a boy who was good at algebra explained that it was because he was Albanian.

Some of this raw uncertainty, this fumbling with pedigrees was evident in Argentina. The Argentine conductor told me his surname. It was German. 'Listen,' he said, 'my first name is Otto!' He did not of course speak German. Mr DiAngelo and his chunky-faced mates in the dining car did not speak Italian. Mr Kovacs the ticket-puncher did not speak Hungarian. The one immigrant in Argentina I met who had yet to become deracinated was an Armenian – I thought of him as Mr Totalitarian: he was a believer in dictators, and Totalitarian had an appropriately Armenian ring to it. He dressed in a smock and a little blue cap and every day he read his Armenian newspaper, which was published in Buenos Aires. He had left Armenia sixty years before.

The conductor – Otto – said, 'You are getting out at Jacobacci?'

'Yes. What time do we arrive?'

'About two, tomorrow morning.'

'What do I do at Jacobacci?'

'Wait,' he said. 'The train to Esquel does not leave until five-thirty.'

'You've taken that one, have you?'

Otto's expression said, *You must be joking!* But he had a tender conscience and the presence of mind to say, 'No, there is no sleeping car on that train.' He thought a moment, sipping wine. 'There is not very much on that train, you know. It is small.' He used the Spanish double-diminutive: 'It is teeny-weeny. It takes hours and hours. But go to bed, sir. I will wake you up when we get there.'

He drank the last of his wine and soda water. Then he rattled the ice cubes in his glass and tossed them into his mouth. Then he stood up and looked out of the black window at black Patagonia and the yellow moon which, being misshapen, was a perfect example of a gibbous moon. He chewed the ice, crunch-crunch on his molars. When I could not stand the sound any longer I went to bed. There are few things more abrasive to the human spirit, even in Patagonia, than someone standing behind you chomping and sucking ice-cubes.

22 The Old Patagonian Express

It was not necessary for Otto to wake me up; the dust did that. It filled my compartment, and as the Lakes of the South Express hurried across the plateau where it seldom rains (what good were leakproof shoes here?), the dust was raised, and our speed forced it through the rattling windows and the jiggling door. I woke feeling suffocated and made a face mask of my bed sheet in order to breathe. When I opened the door a cloud of dust blew against me. It was no ordinary dust storm, more like a disaster in a mine shaft: the noise of the train, the darkness, the dust, the cold. There was no danger of my sleeping through Ingeniero Jacobacci. I was fully awake just after midnight. I gritted my teeth and sand grains crunched in my molars.

I put my suitcase in order, stuffed my pockets with the apples I had bought in Carmen de Patagones and went to the vestibule to wait for Otto's signal. There I sat. The dust whirled out of the corridor and gusted around the light-bulbs and covered the mirrors and windows with hamster fur. I held a handkerchief against my face. It was no use washing; there was no soap, and the water was ice cold.

Otto appeared some time later. He had put on his railwayman's uniform over his pyjamas and looked haggard. He tapped his wristwatch and in a groggy voice said, 'Jacobacci, twenty minutes.'

I wanted to go back to bed. The last thing I wanted was to leave the safety of this train for the uncertainty outside. The train was only dusty, and I had a nest here; out there was emptiness, and nothing was certain. Every person I had met had warned me against taking the train to Esquel. But what could I do? I had to go to Esquel to go home.

I had expected that I would be the only person to get out at

Ingeniero Jacobacci. I was wrong. There was a pair of old men carrying large oil drums as part of their luggage, a woman with one child around her neck and another tagging along behind her, a couple whose suitcase was bound with string and belts, and others who were shadows. The station was small – there was just about room for all of us on the platform. The faces of the people in the second class coaches, who had been woken by the jolt of the stop, the station lights, were fatigued and bloodless. For half an hour the train hissed at the platform, and then it drew out very slowly. It left dust and dim light and silence. It seemed to take the world with it.

That express train – and how I yearned to be back on it – had blurred distance and altitude. The statistics were given at Jacobacci. We were over a thousand miles from Buenos Aires, and since Carmen de Patagones, which was at sea-level, we had climbed to over 3,000 feet, on a plateau that did not descend again until the Straits of Magellan. In this wind, at this altitude, at this time of night – two in the morning – it was very cold in Jacobacci. *No one stops at Jacobacci*, people had said. I could disprove that. Passengers had got off the train. I assumed that, like me, they would be waiting for the train to Esquel. I looked around for them. They were gone.

Where? Into that wind, that darkness, those huts in the desert. They were not changing trains – they lived in Jacobacci. Later I judged it to be a naive thought, but at the time I reflected on how strange it was that there were people – immigrants and the children of immigrants – who had chosen to live here, of all places. There was no water, no shade, the roads were terrible, and little paid employment was possible. However tough the people, they did not have the stamina and ingenuity of the Indians who, in any case, had never lived in this part of Patagonia. To the north-east were the fertile grasslands of Bahia Blanca, to the west the lakes – the Tyrolean paradise of Bariloche. For the sake of a few sheep and cattle, and a baffling stubbornness, people lived in this tiny Patagonian town, where the rail line divided, a railway junction in the desert. But it was a naive thought. Some people required space much more than they required grass or trees, and for them cities and forests were stews of confusion. You can be yourself here, a Welshman told me in Patagonia. Well, that much was true.

I left my suitcase on the platform, paced for a while and smoked my pipe. There would not be a train to Buenos Aires for three days. A Unesco poster nailed to the station wall told me about malnutrition in Latin America. As in Guatemala, a sign said *Use The Train – It Is Cheaper!* And another said, *The Train Is Your Friend – Be A Friend of The Train!* Hanging from a platform post was a bronze bell, like an old school bell. The station master had rung it just before the Lakes of the South Express had pulled out, but no one had boarded.

The train had gone in one direction, the Jacobacci passengers in another. So only I was left, like Ishmael: 'And I only am escaped alone to tell thee.' It was cold in this dismal place, but I had no choice but to wait four hours for the teeny-weeny steam train to Esquel. But I also thought: *It's perfect.* If one of the objects of travel was to give yourself the explorer's thrill that you were alone, that after fifteen or twenty thousand miles you had outrun everyone else and were embarked on a solitary mission of discovery in a remote place, then I had accomplished the traveller's dream. The train travels a thousand miles from Buenos Aires, stops in the middle of the desert and you get out. You look around; you're alone. It is like arriving. In itself it is like discovery – it has that singularity. The sky was full of stars in unfamiliar constellations, and even the moon was distorted, like an antipodean version of the one I was used to. This was all new. In the best travel books the word *alone* is implied on every exciting page, as subtle and ineradicable as a watermark. The conceit of this, the idea of being able to report it – for I had deliberately set out to write a book, hadn't I? – made up for the discomfort. Alone, alone: it was like proof of my success. I had had to travel very far to arrive at this solitary condition.

A voice, a frog-croak, said, 'Tea?'

It was the station master. He wore a winter coat and a scarf and cracked boots and had a silver General Roca Railways badge on his coat collar. The tiny gas stove in his office afforded some heat, and a small dented tea kettle rocked on an improvised wire grill.

I thought I had better explain. I said, 'I am waiting for the train to Esquel.'

'Esquel is a very nice place.'

This was the view from Jacobacci. He was the first person I had met to praise Esquel. But having seen a bit of Jacobacci I could understand why. People in Belchertown, Massachusetts, always have a good word for Holyoke.

He had packed maté leaves (they are from an evergreen tree, the Ilex) into a small cup and inserted a silver straw. The cup was bone, a cow's horn with crude ornamental writing on it.

He said, 'There is lots to do in Esquel. Hotels, restaurants. There are big farms. Go about fifty kilometres and you will find a lovely park – trees, grass, everything. Yes, Esquel is a nice place.'

He poured boiling water over the leaves and handed me the tea.

'You like it?'

'Very good. I like maté.' He had put too much sugar in it. It tasted disgusting.

'I mean, the cup.'

I looked at the cup.

'A cow's horn,' he said. 'It is from Paraguay.'

The scratches on the horn said as much. I told him I admired it.

'You have been to Paraguay?'

He shrugged. 'My wife. Her brother is there. She went there last year.' He grinned. 'In a plane.'

He was nodding, making another cup of tea. I asked him questions about Jacobacci, and the train, and Patagonia. His replies were not interesting. He wanted to talk about money. How much had my suitcase cost? How much was a house in the United States? What did I earn? How much did a new car cost? By way of reply I told him how much a pound of steak cost in Massachusetts. That took his breath away. He stopped complaining and began to boast about the price of sirloin.

If only he had said, *Want to hear something strange?* He was old enough to know a good story. But he was half asleep, and it was cold, and nearly three in the morning. So I left him alone and went outside. I walked up the tracks, away from the lights of the station. The wind in the thorn bushes rasped like sand in a chute. The air smelled of dust. The moon on the bushes shone blue across the bumpy monotony of Patagonia.

I heard a growl. There was a low black hut about thirty yards away, and I suppose my footsteps on the gravel of the railway line had woken the dog. He began to bark. His bark woke one nearby and this nearer one yapped loudly. I have never managed to overcome my childhood fear of being bitten by a dog, and large barking dogs petrify me. There are Irish wolfhounds slavering in my worst nightmares. The most aggressive dogs are owned by old people and lovely women and ugly midget men and childless couples. *He won't hurt you*, say these people, enjoying my terror, and I want to say, *Maybe not, but I might hurt him.* In South America – the fact is well-known – many of the dogs are rabid. They are not the cowering pariahs I had seen in Ceylon and Burma, but sleeker, fangy wolf-like creatures which were encouraged by the natives. There were always dogs in the Indian villages in Peru and Bolivia, looking much more alert than the Indians themselves. The silly things had chased the train. I was afraid of getting rabies. 'The cure is as bad as the disease.' It was not an irrational fear: I had seen notices warning people of the dangers of mad dogs.

One dog, smaller than his bark suggested – about the size of a satchel – pushed through the thorn bushes and hurried onto the track. He crouched and snarled, summoning the other one. I put my hands into my pockets and started walking backwards. I glanced back at the lighted station – I was stupid to have strayed so far. The dogs were now together on the tracks and approaching me, but warily, rushing forward and barking loudly and keeping themselves low. I looked for a stick to beat them with (would a beating madden them and make them killers, or would it drive them away?), but this was the desert. Apart from the few poplars at the station there was not a tree for hundreds of miles. I wanted to run, but I knew they would understand this as a sign of cowardice and pounce on me. I continued to walk backwards, keeping my eye on them and fearing them too much to hate them. Nearer the station I was given hope by the poplars – at least I could climb one and be safe. But there was light here, too; the light seemed to worry the dogs. They kept in the shadows, darting between the railway cars, and when they saw I was safe on the platform they chased each other. They were small, stupid, pathetic and crippled; and from my position of safety I hated them.

The station master had heard the commotion. He said, 'Don't go out there very far. There are a lot of dogs around.'

I dragged my suitcase to a wooden bench. I had discarded every book but Boswell, and this I started to re-read. My hands were cold. I tucked the book away and put on another sweater, and with my hands in my pockets I lay on the bench, under the sign *The Train Is Your Friend*. I stared at the lightbulb and gave thanks for not having been bitten by a rabid dog.

Rational or not, it was my fear. There are many satisfactions in solitary travel, but there are just as many fears. The worst is the most constant: it is the fear of death. It is impossible to spend months travelling alone and arrive in Patagonia and not feel as if one has done something very foolish. In the cold hours before dawn in such a desolate place, the whole idea seems fool-hardy, an unnecessary risk, and thoroughly pointless. I had arrived alone and had nearly reached my destination, but what was the point? I had intended to enjoy myself; I had no point to prove. And yet every day I know this fear. Passing a car crash, reading of a train wreck, seeing a hearse or a graveyard; in the back of a swerving bus or noticing a firedoor that was locked (the firedoors in most hotels I stayed in were kept pad-locked at night to prevent thieves from entering), or scribbling a post card and seeing the ambiguity in my sentence *This is my last trip* – all of it started a solemn death-knell at the back of my brain.

I had left a safe place and had journeyed to a dangerous one. The risk was death and it seemed even more imminent because, so far, no bad thing had befallen me. It seemed that to travel here, in this way, was asking for trouble. Landslides, plane crashes, food poisoning, riots, blow-outs, sharks, cholera, floods, mad dogs: they were everyday events in this neck of the woods – you needed a charmed life to avoid them. And, lying there on the bench, I did not congratulate myself on how far I had come, that I was within an ace of my destination. Rather, I understood the people who had sniggered when I had told them where I was headed. They were right to mock; in their simple way, they had seen the futility of it. Mr Thornberry, in the Costa Rican jungle, had said, 'I know what I want to see. Parrots and monkeys! Where are they?' There were guanacos in Patagonia ('Guanacos spit at you!'). But really, was it worth risking your life to see a guanaco? Or, to put it another way, was it worth even one night half-frozen on a wooden bench in a Patagonian railway station, to hear the trill of the celebrated Flute-bird? I did not think so then. Later, it seemed such a diverting story I forgot my fear. But I was lucky. Usually, throughout this trip, I had looked out of a train window and thought: What a terrible place to die in.

I was also worried about losing my passport, my ticket home, or being robbed of all my money; of catching hepatitis and spending two months in a hospital in a desperate place like Guayaquil or Villazón. These were informed fears. 'We risk our lives every day, just crossing the street,' friendly people say, to reassure us. But there are greater risks in the Andes and in primitive countries, and anyone who thinks otherwise is a fool.

And yet, on that bench at Jacobacci, I was glad I had left everyone else behind. Although this was a town with a main street and a railway station, and people and dogs and electric lights, it was near enough to the end of the earth to give me the impression that I was a solitary explorer in a strange land. That illusion (which is also an illusion in the South Pole and at the headwaters of the Nile) was enough of a satisfaction to make me want to go forward.

I dozed, but when I did I woke up cold. I tried to stay awake and warm. I went for three more walks, giving the dogs a wide berth. There were cockcrows, but no signs of dawn; and the only sound was the wind, pushing against the station.

I had arrived at Ingeniero Jacobacci in darkness. It was still dark when I boarded the train. The station master gave me more tea and said I could get into the coach. It was as small as I had been warned it would be, and it was filled with dust that had blown through the windows. But at least I had a seat. At five, people started to gather. Incredibly, at this hour, they were seeing friends and family off. I had noticed this custom all over Bolivia and Argentina, this send-off, lots of kisses, hugs, and waves, and at the larger stations weeping men parting from their wives and children. I found it touching, and at odds with their ridiculously masculine self-appraisal.

There was a whistle, a steam-whistle – a shrill fluting pipe. The station bell was rung. Well-wishers scrambled from the train, passengers boarded; and, just before six, we were off.

The moon was bright in a blue sky. There was no sun, and the land around Jacobacci was blue-grey and pale brown. We were out of town before the eastern sky began to glow. I was gladdened by the hills. In the darkness of our arrival I had assumed it would be as flat as the land I had seen at twilight, that wasteland around the village of Ministero Ramos Mexia, where grapeselling boys hopped and chirped in the dust. But this was different, and there were no clouds in the sky, so I had some assurance that it would be a warm day. I ate an apple and took out Boswell, and when the sun came up I went quietly to sleep.

It was an old train, and although by this time I ought to have been inured to the strangeness of South American railways, I still found it strange. There was a boy across the aisle, watching me yawn.

'Does this train have a name?' I asked.

'I don't understand.'

'The train I took to Buenos Aires was called "The North Star", and the Bariloche express is called "The Lakes of the South". The one to Mendoza is called "The Liberator". That sort of name.'

He laughed. 'This train is too insignificant to have a name. The government is talking about getting rid of it.'

'Isn't it called "The Esquel Arrow" or something like that?'

He shook his head.

'Or "The Patagonian Express"?'

'The *Old* Patagonian Express,' he said. 'But express trains are supposed to go very fast.'

'They never do,' I said. 'I was on an express to Tucumán

that arrived a day late. It took us six hours to leave one station, up in Humahuaca.'

'Floods,' said the boy. 'Rain. It doesn't rain here, but it is still a slow train. It's these hills. See, we're going around and around.'

We were. The hills and dales of Patagonia which I had welcomed for their variation and their undeniable beauty were the cause of our slow progress. On a straight track this trip would not have taken more than three hours, but we were not due to arrive in Esquel until 8.30 – nearly a fourteen-hour ride. The hills were not so much hills as they were failed soufflés.

It was a steam train, and for the first time since leaving home I wished I had brought a camera, to take its picture. It was a kind of demented samovar on wheels, with iron patches on its boiler and leaking pipes on its underside and dribbling valves and metal elbows that shot jets of vapour sideways. It was fuelled by oil, so it did not belch black smoke, but it had bronchial trouble, respirating in chokes and gasps on grades and wheezing oddly down the slopes when it seemed out of control. It was narrow gauge, the small carriages were wooden. First was no cleaner than Second, though First had higher back-rests on the seats. The whole contraption creaked, and when it was travelling fast, which was seldom, it made such a racket of bumping couplings and rattling windows and groaning wood that I had the impression it was on the verge of bursting apart – just blowing into splinters and dropping there in one of the dry ravines.

The landscape had a prehistoric look, the sort that forms a painted backdrop for a dinosaur skeleton in a museum: simple terrible hills and gullies; thorn bushes and rocks; and everything smoothed by the wind and looking as if a great flood had denuded it, washed it of all its particular features. Still the wind worked on it, kept the trees from growing, blew the soil west, uncovered more rock and even uprooted those ugly bushes.

The people in the train did not look out of the window, except at the stations, and only then to buy grapes or bread. One of the virtues of train travel is that you know where you are by looking out of the window. No sign-boards are necessary. A hill, a river, a meadow – the landmarks tell you how far you have come. But this place had no landmarks, or rather, it was all landmarks, one indistinguishable from the other – thousands of hills and dry riverbeds, and a billion bushes, all the same. I dozed and woke; hours passed; the scenery at the window did not alter. And the stations were interchangeable – a shed, a concrete platform, staring men, boys with baskets, the dogs, the battered pick-up trucks.

I looked for guanacos. I had nothing better to do. There were no guanacos. But there were other creatures – birds of all sorts, small twittering ones, swifts and sparrows, and dark falcons and hawks. Patagonia is, if nothing else, a bird sanctuary. There were owls here, too, and nearer the Andes great eagles; and, in the far south, albatrosses of enormous size. The ugliness of the landscape continued without let-up, and I had no wish to stir from this train. 'Here also we are grateful to the train, as to some god who conducts us swiftly through these shades and by so many hidden perils,' wrote Robert Louis Stevenson. 'So lightly do we skim these horrible lands; as the gull, who wings safely through the hurricane and past the shark.'

The fellow across the aisle was sleeping. I looked at him and the others, and I was struck by their resemblance to me. I had decided quite early in my trip that I was an implausible traveller – no credit cards, no rucksack, I was not well-dressed enough to be a tourist on a ten-day jaunt through ruins and cathedrals; nor was I dirty or frazzled enough to be a wanderer. People asked me what I did, and when I said I was a geography teacher ('Easter vacation!') they doubted me. I mentioned my wife and children: but why was I here and they there? I had no ready answer to that one. Tourists regarded me as a back-slider, wanderers seemed to think I was an intruder, and natives did not understand me. It was hard to convince anyone that I did not have an ulterior motive, that I wasn't on the run, a con-artist, a man with a scheme. I *had* a scheme – that was the worst of it – but I did not wish to disclose it. If I had told Thorn-berry, or Wolfgang, or the lady in Veracruz, or Bert and Elvera Howie, that I was a writer they would have either bolted or, as Bert Howie phrased it, 'put a couple of layers of shit in my ear'.

423

But on this train, the Old Patagonian Express, I looked like everyone else; slightly unshaven, fairly presentable, with a battered suitcase, vaguely European, moustache drooping, scuffed leakproof shoes. It was a relief. I was, at last, anonymous. But what a strange place to be anonymous in! I blended with the foreground. But what a background! Amazing: I belonged on this train.

The boy woke.

'How far to Norquinco?' he asked.

'I don't know,' I said. 'They all look the same to me.'

The man behind me said, 'About two hours.'

He did not gesture out of the window. He looked at his watch. The landscape was no help in determining where we were.

The boy's name was Renaldo. His surname was Davies – he was Welsh. This part of Patagonia was full of Joneses, Williamses, Powells and Pritchards, Welsh families who had migrated across the plateau from Rawson and Trelew and Puerto Madryn with the intention of founding a new Welsh colony. They are tough, independent and undemonstrative people, not the singers and dreamers one associates with Wales, but a different breed altogether, church-goers, sheep farmers, tenaciously Protestant, with a great sentiment for a homeland they have never seen and for a language few speak. (A classic of Welsh literature is called *Dringo'r Andes* – 'Climbing the Andes' – by the Welsh woman Eluned Morgan, who was born in the Bay of Biscay during the great migration.) Renaldo wanted to speak English, but his English was unintelligible to me, and so we spoke Spanish.

'I learned English on a cargo ship,' he said. 'That is not a good place to learn English.'

He had been on a ship for two years, and now he was on his way home.

'If you were on a ship,' I said, 'you must have been to Boston.'

'No,' he said. 'But I was all over America. The whole continent.'

'New York?'

'No.'

'New Orleans?'

'No.' And now he looked puzzled. 'America – not the United States.'

'South America?'

'That's right – all over it. All over America,' he said. 'And Asia – Singapore, Hong Kong. And Bombay. And Africa – Durban, Capetown, Port Elizabeth. I have been everywhere.'

The ship he had sailed in was Peruvian, but the crew was mainly Chinese and Indian – 'the other Indians, different from ours. I liked them, more or less. They talked, we played cards. But the Chinese! I hated them! They look at you – they don't say anything. If they want something, they just – he snatched with his hand. 'Grab, grab, that's all they do.'

I asked him what his impression had been of South Africa. His reply surprised me.

'South Africa is a very bad place,' he said. 'Very pretty, but the society there is cruel. You won't believe me, but they have signs here and there that say "Only for Whites". Taxis, buses, shops – "Only for Whites". The white people go here, the black people go there. Strange, isn't it? And most of the people are black!' He reported this more in wonderment than in outrage, but he added that he did not approve.

Why not? I asked.

'It's no good. "Only for Whites", "Only for Blacks",' he said. 'It's a stupid system. It shows they've got big problems.'

I was encouraged that a Patagonian with no education could show such discernment. I said, 'I agree.'

He said, 'I'd rather spend my life in Barranquilla than Durban. And Barranquilla is really awful.'

'That's true,' I said. 'I was in Barranquilla. I hated it.'

'Isn't it a pig-pen? A really ugly place.'

'They were having an election when I was there.'

'They have elections? Ha!' he said. 'There is nothing there at all!'

He was chortling, thinking of Barranquilla. I looked past him, out of the window at the dune-like hills and the low bushes, the blinding sun, the puffs of dust thrown up by the train. There was a condor – condors didn't flap their wings – circling in the distance. The Patagonian's disgust with Barranquilla was a hatred of slow decay, of mildew and insects. Here nothing rotted. A dead thing was quickly a dry carcass – it shrivelled and was bones. There was no humidity, nothing stagnant. It was desert cleanliness, the rapid destruction by sun and arid air, a dehydrated wilderness, a fossil on the planet's flank. Few live things had survived here, but those that had were practically indestructible.

'So you have seen the world,' I said. 'But why are you going home?'

'Because I have seen the world,' he said. 'There is nowhere like this. I am going to get a job, maybe building houses or fixing engines. In Norquinco or Esquel.'

'I am going to Esquel,' I said.

'It is quicker to take the bus from Bariloche.'

'I wanted to take the Patagonian Express,' I said.

'The old one!'

When we arrived at Norquinco and he pulled his suitcase to the door, he said, 'The Queen of England – you know who I mean?'

'Queen Elizabeth? What about her?'

'She owns a ranch just outside Esquel. Lots of cattle – very nice.'

I spent the afternoon on that train as I had spent afternoons on trains all the way through the Americas. I remembered people who had been cruel to me; I rehearsed cutting remarks that I should have uttered; I recalled embarrassments in my life; I re-ran small victories and large defeats; I imagined being married to someone else, having children, getting divorced; I elected myself president of a banana republic and tried to cope with a noisy Opposition; I went to medical school and set up in practice and carried out tricky operations; I told a long humorous story to a large gathering, but in the end the prize went to someone else. I died, and people talked very loudly about me. It was a fairly typical afternoon of travelling.

I had been using the hamlet of Leleque on my map as a landmark. But Leleque was still hours away. The train toiled, seldom running straight, occasionally stopping – a shout, the bell, the whistle, the bark, and then we were off again. I realized that my trip was ending, but I was not sad when I remembered that, in a few hours, at nightfall perhaps, the train would bring me to my destination and there would be nothing more. My mind raced ahead to the station at Esquel, the plane to Buenos Aires, to my arrival home. Yes, I would take a taxi at the airport – hang the expense. My destination was near; I was impatient.

But this landscape taught patience, caution, tenacity. It needed to be studied to be seen. A glimpse of it told nothing. Down the narrowness of the track beside the desert the labouring engine chugged, always seeming on the verge of spewing its guts out, exploding in a shower of metal and vapour, or else seizing up in a succession of glugs and stopping on a slope, rolling backwards into the dip, and going no more. It seemed a marvel that an old engine like this could keep going, and I came to see the gasps of the locomotive as energetic rather than feeble.

But there was not enough in the engine or the landscape to hold the attention. I concentrated on Boswell and ate grapes and dozed. The sun had dropped; the hills were higher to the west and the sun slid towards them. The wind was colder. I saw that there was no chance of our arriving at Esquel before dark. When darkness fell it did so in that sudden Patagonian way, as swiftly as a dropped curtain, filling the night with chill. In the desert silence was the sound of wind, and the fretting train. The train stopped at the smaller stations near Esquel; the locomotive trembled in the darkness, and beyond it the sky was an immense sieve of blue stars.

It was after eight o'clock when I saw the lights. I looked for more. There were no more. There was nothing to these places, I thought, until you were on top of them. I did not know at that moment that we were on top of Esquel. I had expected more – an oasis, perhaps taller poplars, the sight of a few friendly bars, a crowded restaurant, a flood-lit church, anything to signify my arrival. Or less: like one of the tiny stations along the line; like Jacobacci, a few sheds, a few dogs, a bell. The train emptied quickly.

I found a man with an official-looking cap, and a railway badge pinned to his shirt. Was there a hotel near by?

'Esquel is full of hotels,' he said. 'Some of them are good, too.'

I asked him to name one. He did. I took myself to it and had – but not out of choice – a cold bath. And then to the restaurant.

'What will you drink? Red wine?'

'Yes,' I said.

'And what will you eat? Steak?'

'Yes.'

The usual. But the atmosphere was different here, a kind of Wild West saloon feeling, people in town for the weekend, leathery faces, wearing their leather jackets indoors here, one man with his book propped on a chair-seat. Waiters hurried by with trays. I saw a clock, a calendar, a photograph of what was probably a local football team, a saint's portrait.

I had been planning to go for a walk, to look for a bar. My muscles ached from the ride and I wanted to stretch. But there, in that chair, I started to doze. I shook myself awake and called for the bill.

The sand and grit between the pages of Boswell tumbled onto my chest as I lay in bed. I read a sentence, watched the sand slide out and in the act of brushing it away fell asleep.

It had been my intention to arrive in Esquel on Holy Saturday and to wake on Easter Sunday and watch the sunrise. But Easter had passed. This was no special date, and I had overslept. I got up and went outside. It was a sunny breezy day – the sort of weather that occurs every day of the year in that part of Patagonia.

I walked to the station. The engine that had taken me to Esquel looked derelict on the siding, as if it would never run again. But it had a hundred more years in it, I was sure. I walked beyond it, past the one-storey houses to the one-roomed huts, to where the road turned into a dusty track. There was a rocky slope, some sheep, the rest bushes and weeds. If you looked closely you could see small pink and yellow flowers on these bushes. The wind stirred them. I went closer. They shook. But they were pretty. Behind my head was a great desert.

The Patagonian paradox was this: to be here, it helped to be a miniaturist, or else interested in enormous empty spaces. There was no intermediate zone of study. Either the enormity of the desert space, or the sight of a tiny flower. You had to choose between the tiny or the vast.

The paradox diverted me. My arrival did not matter. It was the journey that counted. And I would follow Johnson's advice. Early in his career he had translated the book of a Portuguese traveller in Abyssinia. In his preface, Johnson wrote, 'He has amused the reader with no romantick absurdity, or incredible fictions; whatever he relates, whether true or not, is at least probable, and he who tells nothing exceeding the bounds of probability, has a right to demand that they should believe him who cannot contradict him.'

The sheep saw me. The younger ones kicked their heels. When I looked again, they were gone, and I was an ant on a foreign ant-hill. It was impossible to verify the size of anything in this space. There was no path through the bushes, but I could look over them, over this ocean of thorns which looked so mild at a distance, so cruel near by, so like misshapen nosegays close-up. It was perfectly quiet and odourless.

I knew I was nowhere, but the most surprising thing of all was that I was still in the world after all this time, on a dot at the lower part of the map. The landscape had a gaunt expression, but I could not deny that it had readable features and that I existed in it. This was a discovery – the look of it. I thought: Nowhere is a place.

Down there the Patagonian valley deepened to grey rock, wearing its eons' stripes and split by floods. Ahead, there was a succession of hills, whittled and fissured by the wind, which now sang in the bushes. The bushes shook with this song. They stiffened again and were silent. The sky was clear blue. A puff of cloud, white as a quinceflower, carried a small shadow from town, or from the South Pole. I saw it approach. It rippled across the bushes and passed over me, a brief chill, and then went rucking east. There were no voices here. There was this, what I saw; and, though beyond it were mountains and glaciers and albatrosses and Indians, there was nothing here to speak of, nothing to delay me further. Only the Patagonian paradox: the vast space, the very tiny blossoms of the sage-brush's cousin. The nothingness itself, a beginning for some intrepid traveller, was an ending for me. I had arrived in Patagonia, and I laughed when I remembered I had come here from Boston, on the subway train that people took to work.

refresh yourself at penguin.co.uk

Visit penguin.co.uk for exclusive information and interviews with
bestselling authors, fantastic give-aways and the
inside track on all our books, from the Penguin Classics
to the latest bestsellers.

BE FIRST ▼

first chapters, first editions, first novels

EXCLUSIVES ▼

author chats, video interviews, biographies, special
features

EVERYONE'S A WINNER ▼

give-aways, competitions, quizzes, ecards

READERS GROUPS ▼

exciting features to support existing groups and
create new ones

NEWS ▼

author events, bestsellers, awards, what's new

EBOOKS ▼

books that click – download an ePenguin today

BROWSE AND BUY ▼

thousands of books to investigate – search, try
and buy the perfect gift online – or treat yourself!

ABOUT US ▼

job vacancies, advice for writers and company
history

Get Closer To Penguin . . . www.penguin.co.uk